UPI-B5

PELICAN BOOK
A958

Pelican Library of Busine...
Advisory Editor

INDUST...

Date	Issued to

INDUSTRIAL SOCIETY

Social Sciences in Management

EDITED BY DENIS PYM

PENGUIN BOOKS

Penguin Books Ltd, Harmondsworth, Middlesex, England
Penguin Books Inc., 7110 Ambassador Road, Baltimore, Maryland 21207, U.S.A.
Penguin Books Australia Ltd, Ringwood, Victoria, Australia

—

First published 1968

—

Copyright © Penguin Books Ltd, 1968

—

Made and printed in Great Britain by
Cox & Wyman Ltd, London, Reading and Fakenham
Set in Monotype Times

Contents

CONTENTS

List of Text Figures

List of Tables

Preface

When the original brief for this book was sent out to the contributors, we pointed out that its aim was to set down for the Pelican audience some of the important and interesting growing points of the industrial social sciences and to show their relevance to a range of management questions. The book was to represent a British contribution to a subject of wider significance. Authors were asked to incorporate, where possible, ideas, approaches, and solutions to problems which reflect a 'British flavour', though obviously we expected them to be also influenced by work elsewhere. This is the course we have tried to hold, though whether or not we have succeeded is for the reader to judge.

We hope too that the text proves useful to those people to whom the industrial social sciences mean very little but who are curious to find out more. The introductory chapter is designed to provide them with a general framework for the remainder of the book and can be ignored by those already familiar with the scope of industrial social research.

I would like to thank all the contributors for their ready response, Noel Pearson for his assistance with the references and Penguin Books for help and advice.

Birkbeck College, London   DENIS PYM

CHAPTER 1

Introduction: The Industrial Social Sciences

DENIS PYM

IN popular usage the term 'social sciences' embraces most subjects devoted to the study of people. This book is about two core subjects of social science – sociology and psychology – and their relevance to industrial behaviour and the organization of work. By tradition the psychologist is concerned with the study of individual behaviour and the sociologist with man's existence in groups and his social organization. However, as these subjects have developed it has become increasingly difficult to delineate their spheres of interest with any precision.

The majority of social scientists in industry are engaged in research and/or practice and work both as scientists and as technologists. As scientists, they seek to further our understanding of social behaviour, whether through the study of individual, group, organization, or community, and are involved in the description, explanation, and prediction of behaviour at work. They may also be occupied with the impact of industrialism upon society. As technologists, in the role of personnel and training officers for example, they apply their knowledge to coordinating man's own efforts in the achievement of organizational and social goals.

Psychologists working in government and industry are generally known as *occupational psychologists*. We are likely to find them tackling questions of personnel selection, training, the design and layout of equipment, morale, working conditions and rewards, and marketing. A detailed explanation of these areas of the psychologist's influence is to be found in a *Chambers' Encyclopaedia* article by Alec Rodger (1961). This general classification will probably embrace aspects of three other specialisms – experimental, social, and clinical psychology.

Experimental psychologists might best be described as biosocial scientists, since many prefer a biological orientation in their inquiries. They study those aspects of the subject open to controlled investigation in the laboratory, notably training techniques and methods and the relationship between man and his physical working environment – the machines he operates and the technical systems, such as computers, which provide him with information. Scientists engaged on these problems may also describe themselves as ergonomists (see Part Three). *Social psychologists* study the behaviour of individuals and groups within the social setting, and their material is obtained largely through measuring and analysing attitudes and opinions. They are also engaged in laboratory experiments with small groups, where the effects of cooperation, competition, and leadership on performance can be studied. Many of the results of their experiments have important implications for questions of the motivation, morale, and organization of people at work. *Clinical psychologists* are mostly concerned with maladaptive behaviour, but their interest in motivation and, if they are psycho-analytically orientated, in the unconscious determinants of behaviour, enables them to make considerable contributions to the study of man at work and also to consumer research. Psychologists engaged in consumer research, that is in the testing out of the attitudes and opinions of people to new products and advertisements, are most likely to be clinically or socially oriented.

Industrial sociologists are chiefly concerned with the interlocking of social roles at work and with social organization. Tom Burns (1961) describes the three main stages of the development of industrial sociology as studies of working groups, studies of the structure of organizations, and studies of the occupational institution as a working community. In their research methods industrial sociologists have drawn heavily on the social anthropologists' techniques of observation, which have undoubtedly influenced the growth of the subject. One result was their early interest in differences between the way management proclaims that work is done and the way it is actually carried out. These differences are characterized in the *formal* and *informal* organization. The interest in the informal system has been extended to the wider field of industrial relations which includes aspects of collective bargaining, strikes, and wages.

Sociologists generally take a broader approach than psychologists. They are more concerned with social policy and have shown greater interest in reforming government and industrial policies. However, on more specific industrial questions psychologists have been applying their techniques for some time, while sociologists have been rather more cautious in offering their services to management. They have preferred to observe and to criticize in order to raise doubts about the methods and techniques of industry. Joan Woodward, for example, has been engaged in a continuous effort over many years to persuade managers that the 'principles of management' advanced by the early theorists such as Taylor, Follett and Fayol are not tenable as universal laws. Another distinction is that while psychology, with its longer history, has been divided into a number of seemingly unrelated specialisms, sociology acts as a unifying subject. Though sociology has no substantive field of its own, the sociologist may be interested in the social processes linked with historical, legal, political, economic or technical issues, so pulling together, as it were, many separated disciplines. In this respect sociology is very much a science of our time.

METHODS OF RESEARCH

There are three main classes of research method: observation, empirical investigation, and experiment. In each of these the researcher can claim to be scientific only in so far as his findings are themselves open to testing and repeating.

Observational methods, used widely by sociologists, derive from anthropological studies of primitive people and have similarities with those of psycho-analysis. Either as an outsider or as a participant in the work situation, the researcher observes and records social interactions within the group or the larger organization. By this method he hopes to obtain a dynamic picture of social behaviour in the work-place. One of his main findings is that occupational behaviour, whether in the boardroom or on the shop floor, is not a rational process but needs to be understood in terms of beliefs, values, and customs. These facts reaffirm the contention that social behaviour is rooted in our emotions. The weakness of observation techniques rests with the difficulty of quantifying information (though some social scientists do not think this important), and the influence of the observer on events. This last problem pertains to all field work and even to laboratory inquiries. Nevertheless, observational techniques are being used more and more, particularly in the study of industrial ferment.

The social scientist who wishes to quantify his data may make use of interviews, questionnaires, the firm's records, government statistics or psychological tests in his inquiries. We have given the umbrella term *empirical investigations* to such approaches.

The interview remains the most essential of the social scientist's tools. It ranges from an unstructured, almost observational, exercise to a host of carefully prepared questions. Its amenability to quantification is increased the more structured it becomes. In some research, use is made of discussions between four or five people. The principal advantages of these group discussions is that they preserve some of the dynamics of the work-place, particularly if the members of the group have conflicting interests.

Questionnaire methods, in their more common biographical form, are familiar to everybody. They are also used in the measurement of work interests, aspirations, performance, morale, and various aspects of man's disposition. More sophisticated measures of such attitudes are called scales. An attitude scale is composed of a set of statistically related items which give a single score. In all this work, problems of sampling and design loom large, and people who undertake empirical investigations need to be familiar with a wide range of statistical techniques. The questionnaire has certain defects inherent in its static nature. Some doubts must always exist over the relationship between data gained from interviews and questionnaires and what takes place in reality.

Often the social scientist will want to make use of the firm's statistical records on, for example, accidents, labour turnover, output or operating costs. This information may be used to explore the validity of an idea or observation, or even to strengthen an argument. When he has completed his field work he may have accumulated a lot of statistical material requiring detailed analyses. Until recently this was a laborious business, but the computer has eradicated many problems of analysis and few calculations now need be done by hand. The bottleneck has moved to another stage of the research cycle, report-writing.

Psychological testing, particularly of people's abilities and aptitudes, is a highly refined method of measurement and is fairly widely used in personnel selection and allocation to work. It gives an indication of the individual's potential based on his performance of standardized tasks, allows easy comparison between people, and it is often predictive of job performance.

The methods of *experimentation* are applied in field studies, but the difficulty of achieving the necessary controls often limits their use to the laboratory. Here experimental and social psychologists are able to take isolated variables and study their effects on individual and group performance in controlled conditions. For example, to ascertain whether or not knowledge or performance was important in general achievement and, if so, whether the amount of knowledge was significant. We might take three groups of subjects, identical with respect to a number of important variables such as age, sex, occupation and intelligence, and give them a defined task. One, the control group, would get no information about their performance, while the other two would get varying amounts. All other conditions would be the same. This is a simple experiment, but experiments of this kind can involve very sophisticated designs and elaborate statistical procedures in the analysis of the results. The methods of experimentation are closely derived from the biological and physical sciences and involve the study of only limited aspects of human behaviour. It is sometimes argued that, in this respect, experimentation is unrealistic. It is extremely difficult to simulate conditions in the laboratory in which people have to adjust to stimuli which affect the whole complex of their customs and habits.

Nevertheless, laboratory experiments enable us to identify with precision the determinants of behaviour, and as new research techniques are evolved so the range of human activity amenable to controlled research will broaden. Experimentalists themselves feel strongly that it is by controlled investigations that the most notable advances in the social sciences will come.

Though each of these methods has been developed and used by one or other branch of the social sciences, no particular method is the exclusive property of any one. Indeed, since each approach has its defects, it is necessary to combine a range of these methods, wherever possible, to overcome the defects. Today more and more research projects are being launched on a multi-disciplinary basis using a variety of methods, all within the same research design.

For example, the University of Aston has a team of psychologists, sociologists and economists in the Industrial Administration Research Unit engaged on a comparative study of organizations (see Chapter 18). The design of the project involves the development of measures of organization, group, and individual variables and the study of their relations to the economic performance of industrial concerns. Although the inquiry has a strong empirical bias it will make use of all the methods outlined above. At the Tavistock Institute for Human Relations the need to undertake the study of complex social systems has led in some inquiries to the combination of social science resources with those of operational research. A recent investigation of communications in the building industry, carried out by the Institute, united the operational researchers' investigations of the decision-making processes in construction with the social scientists' search into client needs using observational and empirical techniques.

The most fundamental problems of industrial research are not to be found in its internal design but in the external conditions of the work-place. No matter how sophisticated the research design, we cannot ignore the simple fact that every industrial investigation is wholly at the mercy of those who sanction the project and those who participate in it. It can be argued that sociologists and psychologists spend too much of their time on questions of design and not enough on preparing their subjects and the organization where the research is to be undertaken. In this respect the social scientist's strategy is often weak. It sometimes reveals a serious lack of insight into the effects he can have upon people, a defect noticeable among those who are vocal about the lack of sympathy from managers. The Americans have coined the apt phrase 'change-agent' to describe the social scientist's role in industry. As soon as people in the boardroom, in the office, or on the shop floor are aware of his presence, doubts and uncertainty may arise. Obviously the researcher can represent some kind of threat to the existing order, even by merely describing what goes on. This may occur whether he is conducting research or whether he is acting as a technologist and is likely to have a more permanent effect upon proceedings. Inevitably, he is going to take up people's time. He may interfere with the work processes. People who find his presence threatening or disruptive are also going to search out feasible excuses why the project must be limited or not carried out at all:

'I am a bit worried how the unions will respond to this.'

'I don't think my managers can spare the time.'

'Could we put it off until the present economic crisis is over?' (which in Britain is never!).

'We've got consultants in and more people would confuse things.'

The social scientist knows that most employees welcome the opportunity to talk about themselves and their work, and after the initial contact managers and workers do not mind being observed. He finds also that the unions seldom object and that after a while people won't even know he is on the premises. In order to prove this he has to demonstrate, as Alec Rodger argues, that his methods are 'politically defensible and administratively convenient, as well as being technically sound'.

DEVELOPMENT OF RESEARCH

The recent history of industrial social research has three overlapping phases characterized by different approaches to the study of industrial behaviour. It began with investigations of the physiological and psychological aspects of behaviour and of the physical factors impinging upon the worker's performance. This *psychophysiological* phase gained its impetus principally from the two world wars. Beginning in the 1930s psychologists, and then sociologists, drew management's attention to social factors, particularly the work group and the boss, and their bearing on industrial performance. Thus began a period of intense interest in *human relations* which led, in its extreme form, to a compartmentalized view of the determinants of behaviour and work performance. The early 1950s marked the beginning of a period of consolidation – of attempts to unite the earlier phases and to consider human resources in the broadest sense. Interest shifted from the group to the organization and the link between its social, economic, and technical systems. The growing recognition among social scientists of the correlations between these independent variables and their interest in the interrelationships between them gave rise to another approach to industrial behaviour, the *systems approach*.

Systematic investigations of man at work followed the growth of large-scale organizations in the latter half of the nineteenth century. This growth coincided with the increasingly severe trade cycles of boom and depression which revealed the need for improvements in the coordination of industrial society. The structure of these great concerns was increasingly bureaucratic (hierarchical and impersonal) and an ideal type for Weber, the scholar of social organization, and the early management theorists, since it involved the application of rational processes to the social environment. While industrial concerns were being modelled on the church and the army, attention was first drawn to the individual's role, not by social scientists, but by engineers. The fathers of time-and-motion study, F. W. Taylor and F. Gilbreth, used the slide rule and the stopwatch to ascertain the 'one best way' for doing a variety of manual jobs. Their solution to the problems of coordinating human effort, such as those inherent in the bureaucratic system of organization, was to get man to simulate the working movements of the machine.

The social scientist's interest in psycho-physiological factors of work began around the turn of the century with psychologists dabbling in questions of employee selection and in the effects of physical working conditions upon worker performance. The two world wars underlined the problems of coordination, the allocation of manpower resources, and industrial efficiency. They offered to psychologists serious opportunities to apply their knowledge of human capacities and limitations. In 1915 the government set up the Health of Munition Workers' Committee under whose auspices physiologists and psychologists investigated accidents, fatigue, and absenteeism among factory workers with particular reference to their physical conditions of employment. In the Second World War new opportunities presented themselves and on a wider front than in 1914–18. Substantial improvements were realized in the procedures for allocating recruits to the various aspects of the war effort. Standards were raised through more precise descriptions of job and trade requirements, by the application of tests of ability, aptitude, and achievement, and as a result of systematizing recruiting procedures. One consequence was the improved performance by recruits in training, where psychologists also participated in developing methods of instruction and techniques for evaluating performance. Between the wars the centre of industrial research was undoubtedly the National Institute of Industrial Psychology, founded by C. S. Myers as a research and consultative service to industry and commerce on personnel matters. Its policy of tackling the practical problems set by industry helped to establish a link between the new academic subject of psychology and industry.

During the Second World War there were two important departures from the more physical approach of fitting the man to the job and changing his working environment. At the War Office a group of clinical psychologists and psychiatrists were applying psychiatric methods in the treatment of mental and emotional war casualties. (Some of these social scientists were later to form the Tavistock Institute.) Meanwhile experimental psychologists were busy investigating the relationship between man and the weapons and the machines he operated. They were particularly interested in the problems of mental fatigue in flying and in vigilance tasks like those of radar-operating. The Applied Psychology Research Unit was set up at Cambridge under Sir Frederic Bartlett to carry on this research.

The Hawthorne investigations conducted at the Western Electric Company in Chicago during the 1920s and 1930s are widely reported in the literature. They introduced a new influence in industrial research often described as the 'human relations movement'. These studies included the observation of human interactions in work-groups under experimental and natural conditions and the first large-scale morale survey. They also mark the beginning of industrial sociology and industrial social psychology. The Hawthorne investigations are important because they triggered a spate of laboratory and field studies in interpersonal relations, small groups, employee attitudes, and leadership behaviour. Sociologists became particularly interested in the informal organization, the intricate set of relations built upon sentiments common to work groups which sometimes conflict with the firm's interests and objectives. Many of the findings of the research which followed Hawthorne questioned the rational economic assumptions about man's behaviour at work, though other features of this limiting conception remained. The working of the informal organization was considered to be pathological and the consequence of irrational motives which, once rectified, would lead to improved interpersonal and industrial relations. There was also a general assumption that interpersonal relations and their bearing on group performance could be considered separately from other aspects of the environment.

It is difficult to indicate precisely what industry gained from the emphasis on human relations, because other factors, such as the improvement of economic conditions, government legislation, and trade-union action, also contributed. However, it could be argued that the broadening of the concept of employee welfare to include social factors and matters outside the work-place is attributable, in part, to the focusing of research in these areas. The development of management and supervisory training, as a force for change, bears the unmistakable stamp of the social sciences. Psychologists and sociologists now acknowledge, however, that management training is likely to be of limited consequence if unaccompanied by changes in the structure of the organization and the beliefs held by its members. This need was recognized, for example, in the Glacier Metal Company project led by Elliott Jaques (1951), which involved the participation of employees in an attempt to first identify and then change the social and psychological forces affecting the life of the firm.

Social scientists themselves benefited most from the human relations movement. They learned a good deal about the realities of industrial life, for inevitably many of the changes they suggested were unacceptable because they threatened the political-power balance in the concern. As a result, some of the most worthwhile advances of this phase – information about group sizes and structures, the value of employee participation in the making of decisions and, more recently, findings on the effects of features of organizational structure and control on performance – have not received fair treatment. True, the economic and technical contexts in which these findings were advanced were widely ignored up to the mid-1950s, but this argument is less tenable now. From these experiences social scientists came to realize the enormous difficulty involved in bringing about significant changes in the internal workings of industry. The lesson was undoubtedly one factor in the shift away from the traditional 'maintenance and repair' role of the social scientist to an interest in the design and development of organizations and of man–machine systems.

The new *systems approach*, at the level of the enterprise, is typified by a concern with management processes and the view that the basic ingredients of the organization, its people, techniques, information, and materials, though they may vary independently, can be optimumly related to each other. Previously, both social behaviour and the enterprise had been construed as closed systems. Attempts were made to explain social events in terms of other social phenomena and the firm's functioning with reference only to its internal structure. These conceptions proved misleading in the study of growth and change and set limitations on our understanding of the way organizations work. The new form of systems analysis emphasizes the relationships between human and other variables and the influence of the enterprise's environment on them. Its promulgators have also moved from investigating simple cause–effect relationships between events towards a search for their many determinants and outcomes. The systems approach also has practical advantages, for it offers the manager a means of uniting information from the engineer and social scientist through a common framework. The development of automation and of data-processing techniques make sophisticated systems analysis a viable proposition, helping the manager to recognize that information is his working material in setting objectives, and manipulating resources to achieve them.

An approach which emphasizes the interrelatedness of variables must hold to a broad definition of the organization's objectives. The firm naturally has its primary task or mission, its purpose for existing, but, when faced with conditions of rapid change, the achievement of that task becomes increasingly dependent on the firm's capacity to adjust to the market and to maintain a flexible internal order. It is largely to achieve these ends that many new categories of experts have appeared whose work links areas often considered to be unrelated. The *market researcher* provides the intelligence about changing consumer needs which assists the firm not only to decide on an optimum range of products and how to dispose of its goods but also to organize itself. The *manpower planner* explores the means for gaining greater control over the human element in work through the systematic gathering and analysis of material about labour supply and demand and through the scrutiny of various factors which affect both. The *ergonomist*, in his experimental study of the man-machine interface, evolves machine and display panel designs to fit the operator's capacities and limitations.

In the enlarged definition of the company's objectives and in the systems conception of the organization, information is the vital factor. Its meaning and significance to the worker and manager is also a strand linking many essays in this book. Holding, in Chapter 6, underlines the function of information in the development of skill: 'successful training methods are those which supply the right amount of information in the right way and at the right time'. Several contributors explore the advantages to be had by increasing employee influence over the firm's operations. Fox argues in Chapter 2 that restrictive practices in the work-place are often the result of management indifference and he goes on to point out that management can only regain control over performance by sharing that control with the worker. Lupton, too, thinks that one condition for an effective payment is that the worker should share in its drafting and operation (see Chapter 14). The employee's constructive influence, whether he is on the board or the shop floor, is a function of how much he knows. His effective control is limited by the amount of information he has about his own job and the plans and policies of the concern.

In elaborating still further upon the systems approach let us take the opportunity of referring to some of the main centres of industrial social research in Britain since the last war.

The best-known internationally is probably the Tavistock Institute of Human Relations. Though its name reflects the Institute's identification, at least in origin, with the human relations phase, it is one of the pioneers of the systems approach. Among its chief researchers are, or have been, men like Trist, Jaques, Herbst, Rice, and Emery. Some of the Institute's best-known work was conducted in coal mines by Trist and his colleagues (1963), where it was found that only by treating the social organization and the methods of coal-getting as socio-technical systems was it possible to carry out a meaningful analysis of organization behaviour. Designing the work-place then became a matter of determining the social system which best fitted the technology. Another Tavistock researcher, Rice (1963), who has conducted inquiries in the Indian textile industry, outlines a model which relates individuals, groups and institutions together and presents organizations as *open systems*. Not only do industrial units import their essential components from the environment before converting them into goods and services, but they must also export them back into the market in order to survive. Rice emphasizes the importance for industrial behaviour of the link between the firm and its market and the part played by information in this process.

At Cambridge, with the Applied Psychological Research Unit at its centre, experimental psychologists like F. C. Bartlett, Broadbent, Mackworth, Conrad, and Welford have been interested in *man–machine* systems. They take the view that man is part of a communication system receiving information from his surroundings through his sense organs, storing it, and using it in his actions. They have studied, for example, how this process is affected by human skill, the effects of ageing, and the design and layout of equipment. Some work in this field is covered in the sections 'Training for Skill' and 'Ergonomics'.

Another important centre has been the Department of Social Science at Liverpool University under Professor Simey. Here a group of sociologists has followed in the traditions of Marx, Weber, and Veblen in assuming a link between technical change and industrial relations. In this department people like W. H. Scott, Joan Woodward, Halsey, and Lupton have taken part in studies of dock workers, clerks, computer technologists, and steel workers.

Yet another group has its base at Nuffield College, Oxford University. From here Clegg and Flanders have undertaken searching analyses of union–management relations and explored their scope in improving industrial efficiency. In particular they have thrown light on the problems of overtime, demarcation disputes, and overmanning and the parts played in them by manager and worker. The publicity gained from Flanders's analysis of the Productivity Agreements at Esso's Fawley Refinery sparked off keen interest throughout the country in union–management bargaining as a basis for improving the effective utilization of manpower.

The late 1960s are proving to be a period of rapid growth for all branches of social science. More and more universities and technical colleges are teaching sociology, psychology, social anthropology, and social economics and their applications in personnel management, social administration, industrial relations, and manpower and management studies, though a serious limitation to the development of the industrial social sciences, until very recently, has been the dearth of postgraduate teaching. The mushrooming of the social sciences in education has led to some serious shortages in other sectors of employment. The government continues to be a major supporter through its employment of social scientists, its financial backing of research projects and its grants to postgraduate research students. Though industry employs the smallest number of psychologists and sociologists directly, in recent years private concerns have begun to make greater use of academics as consultants, and several firms are currently supporting research projects in educational institutions.

THE THEME OF CHANGE

The development of the industrial social sciences is rooted in economic, technical, and social changes which transform the function of man in work and increase the opportunities and influence of the social scientist and technologist. It is to these aspects of the industrial scene that we now turn. Change is no new phenomenon, but in its material and scientific basis, its qualities of speed, acceleration and unevenness, and in the evolution of new electronic technologies which strengthen or replace the mechanical technologies of the past, transformation in the modern world is unique.

Each year feats of a material kind are witnessed which surpass the expectations of even the wildest prophets of a few decades earlier. Change in the status and influence of science has played a central role in this situation. It is just over 350 years since Giordano Bruno was burnt at the stake for defending the heliocentric theory. In the seventeenth century discoveries took an average of a hundred years to be translated into technologies, though the ideas of the eighteenth-century Frenchman, Vaucauson, for the mass-sorting of data took a good deal longer to become a practical proposition. By the nineteenth century the average gap between discovery and exploitation had narrowed to thirty years. Today, the transistor, invented in 1948, is the foundation of an international industry, and the laser beam, first demonstrated in 1960, is already being accepted as the basis for new technologies in industry. This acceleration shows no sign of abatement.

The unevenness of change may be its most important characteristic and is certainly one reason for us becoming more aware of it in recent times. Important, because the adaptation of man and his social institutions has not kept pace with material progress and to this imbalance have been attributed the crises, wars and depressions, the revolutions and counter-revolutions of our time. The effects of technical change upon society have become a central interest of the social scientist. Marx, for example, based his theory of industrial society on man's alienation from his work by technology, though he foresaw a better future for us than did the anti-Utopian novelists Huxley and Orwell. Our consciousness of change can also be linked with its unevenness; if everything moved at the same speed and acceleration there would be no change, relatively speaking. Yet a distinct difference exists between the amount of attention we give to the need for change in normal discourse and our disregard for it in our decisions and actions. Long after the industrial revolution had devastated medieval society man refused to accept that life was any different, and when he could no longer deny it he persisted in believing this 'disorder' to be only temporary. Recent studies of company directors who are permanently overworked have shown that they continue to believe that this problem will not last, as though departure from the golden mean could not be true. Such attitudes are based on the experience of a more orderly past and have also been moulded and reinforced by the limitations of the early machine and of the mechanical technologies on which industrial society expanded. In the simple one-way-only mechanism of the early machine the feedback and control mechanisms are relatively crude and events can only occur in sequence: the keystone of these technologies is fragmentation. Work began with the division of labour, and with each succeeding division the problems of coordination grew apace. The bureaucratic organization structure, Henry Ford's assembly line and F. W. Taylor's 'one best way' were among the solutions and in each, man was to obey the rules of the machine. It is interesting to reflect that nearly all the crises in Western society, whether in matters of production, communication, government, education, or international affairs, continue to be met with the 'solutions' of the mechanical technologies – more specialization and more social regulation. However there is one very important failing in these attempted remedies: though they allow enlargement and extension, they preclude the possibility of real change.

Many of our attempts at social and economic planning also fail because of an inability to discriminate between enlargement and change. This is illustrated in our repeated attempts to predict the future by simply extrapolating past trends. One important reason for the collapse of Britain's first National Plan derives from the failure of its drafters to foresee that our planned rate of economic recovery would coincide with a tightening-up in world trade markets. The Buchanan Committee looked into the future of our urban traffic arrangements and yet could not see beyond the car, which, even before the end of the century, may be as much an anachronism as the horse and buggy are today. If our formal social systems and man's own beliefs omit the possibility of change, one may ask how then it occurs. The answer, of course, is simply that what should be and what is are very different things, and the extent of the discrepancy between a formal organization enforced on social intercourse, whether real or imaginary, and the informal or spontaneous organization is a measure of the chaos and conflict we now endure.

However, the informal organization has a powerful ally in the electronic technologies, which reinforce and replace the mechanical technologies of past centuries. As McLuhan (1964), the expert in media analysis, observes, the electric current makes possible more sophisticated forms of feedback and self-regulation in the machine. It answers too the sequential problems of the early machine by enabling a diversity of action to take place instantly and simultaneously so that we can integrate them into a total picture. These self-regulating and unifying features of the electronic technologies are also those of growth itself, and they open the way for social systems which permit change.

IMPLICATIONS OF CHANGE

It is now widely recognized that the traditional bureaucratic structure which underlies our occupational institutions is inappropriate as a system of organization. Researches indicate that personnel in more successful firms, among those confronted by a range of transformations in their markets and methods of work, have less-specified work roles, enjoy greater participation in decision-making and are more aware of their own and the company's objectives. In industries using advanced technical processes, complex patterns of organization and specialized jobs are being replaced by more simple structures and more complex work roles. For example, we find the process industry, leading efforts to achieve greater flexibility in the deployment of labour and to remove old demarcation lines between jobs. Their problem is that they seek to reverse the trends of hundreds of years of mechanization on which their own organizations and those of the unions and crafts are built. Adaptability is also a function of size, and inquiries in hospitals, coal mines, and military stations have shown that the size of these establishments correlates with absenteeism, accidents, and turnover and is inversely related to efficiency. Taken together these and other similar findings point to the evolution of a number of different ways of organizing our industrial concerns.

As technologies develop we find more and more that the distinctions between the formal and informal organization parallel those between machine and man and their respective roles in the decision-making process. In this context, the emphasis on rational decisions as an objective in much management education strikes one as being out of date, as though it were but another form of the early management theorists' 'rules of thumb'. The purpose of industrial management is to make the best decisions, and any rational processes which precede those decisions may be best carried out by the computer, fed with all the information which is known to be relevant, including that about man himself. The manager's function is to integrate his own intuitive and intellectual processes with his information system. In this activity he cannot hope to be familiar with all his information sources and he will be aware that forces outside his control bear upon the outcome of most important decisions. Thus, characteristics of emotional openness, tolerance of ambiguity, and preparedness to take risks can delineate differences between effective and less effective managers and are themselves influenced by the whole range of cultural, technical, and economic considerations. However, the emphasis on versatility extends beyond those enterprises using the most advanced industrial processes even to those whose technologies derive from an earlier stage of industrial development. The influence of fluctuating markets cannot be neglected, as anybody in the car industry will confirm. In the conflicting requirements of technology, market, and man's own needs, it is man himself who has had to make the adjustments.

The differing influences of technology upon behaviour can be seen in the changing definitions of effectiveness in the worker's job. The man on the assembly line performs simple, repetitive actions and his competence is gauged largely in terms of his propensity to work like a machine. In much the same way the clerk's effectiveness increases the more closely he resembles the computer. The new technologies reverse these developments. They bring responsibility for decisions of importance right to the man on the job. The operator in the semi-automated plant no longer performs an operation but supervises it. His effectiveness is gauged in terms of his capacity to take on responsibility for decisions and his skill in receiving and passing on information about the operation. The competent operator, Crossman (1960) has observed, feels his way into the process, becoming intuitively aware of what is going on. He may also use a logical approach and come to a rational decision, but if he uses methods based on what worked last time he is unlikely to be very successful

By studying the role of the worker in the semi-automated plant or the 'growth' firm we learn that changes are coming about in the concepts of work satisfaction, adjustment, and alienation. In the past, 'satisfaction' was commonly viewed as a function of loyalty – unquestioning regard for one's boss, job, and company. 'Adjustment' was attributed to those individuals or groups who were never absent, had no accidents, and did not change their jobs. Such attitudes and behaviour often demonstrated a perception of reality almost equally inferior to their opposites. New concepts of satisfaction and adjustment need to be evolved based upon a superior perception of reality. These may encompass man's capacity to differentiate between aspects of organizational policy which overlap with his own interests and those which do not. Criticism and suggestions for new courses of action based upon greater understanding of a situation should not be taken as a sign of disloyalty but of commitment to the concern. The definition of alienation is also changing and will come increasingly to signify the degree of control available to the worker in his job.

One of the fascinating consequences of automation, the effects of which we are only now beginning to feel, is the way, as McLuhan observes, it unites production, consumption, and learning. The comment 'in this job you are always learning' is so often heard in the electronics industry that it has become a cliché. For personnel engaged in the marketing of data-processing equipment, it is not easy to differentiate between work and learning. New recruits may devote the best part of two years to professional training, during which they learn by doing, and experienced professionals can expect to spend as much as 20 per cent of their time in the training school. Electronics not only pervades all corners of industry but through television brings the world to our homes. The same processes of fusion are evident between work and leisure. At Birkbeck we are finding in studies of professional employees that those who are paid the most by their firms (and are presumably the most effective, since we equate for age and jobs) demonstrate certain behaviour not found among their less successful counterparts. They report working longer hours, thinking more about work at home, and having more diverse leisure interests. Although we have no evidence we suspect that they probably pursue some of their leisure interests at work. For them there are no demarcation lines between work and leisure.

A NEW ROLE FOR THE SOCIAL SCIENTIST

The dichotomy between technical advancement and social well-being provided the starting point for the social sciences and also presented serious ethical questions to the psychologist and sociologist in industry. As technologists they applied their knowledge of behaviour to the achievement of the firm's objectives, hoping and yet doubting that what was good for the firm was also good for the employee, although a host of studies have failed to show that the worker's performance and his satisfactions are closely related. It can be argued that this discrepancy both raised the social technician's doubts about his own mission and confined his contribution to welfare matters and to maintaining the social machine.

New transformations in society indicate that long-term industrial success must now come through technology and culture, marching forward in harness. The new concepts of organization, human effectiveness, and satisfaction already advertise the demise of the mechanical epoch and the ethical barriers which confounded the social scientist. Together they herald the shifting role of man in work from the simulator of the machine to the innovator and creator of ideas and the growing importance of the human component in industrial management. If the social scientist is to make use of these new opportunities and to make his full contribution to management, it will be as a diagnostician of manpower problems and as an adviser at the point of decision-making on industrial legislation, on the development of organizations and their structure and controls, on the structure and size of work groups, on the design and development of machines, on methods for coordinating man's effort, on selection and training requirements, and on the problems of marketing the concern's output. There is no reason why these functions should detract from his traditional interest in welfare and in man's deficiencies, though success at the planning stage may eventually reduce the importance of this historical role.

But just as the second stage of the industrial revolution helps to resolve old questions, so it creates new ones. Some are ethical and concern the psychologist and sociologist: in *The Organization Man*, W. H. Whyte asks if some social science is any more than a sanctioned form of manipulation. Other problems are more general: we are faced with the enormous task of retraining and reorienting those whose traditional means of livelihood are threatened and superseded by new techniques. We are faced too with the growing problem of stress associated with ambiguous and conflicting work roles and man's fear of new responsibilities which follows generations of dependence and submission.

In spite of the contribution that the social technician is able to make, in some circles the differences between pure and applied research continue to have a social significance of their own. Here the pursuit of industrial success is considered a doubtful realm of science. A few people of a particular political persuasion will also make disparaging comments. The familiar argument that industrial success profits only a small sector of society is becoming less and less tenable. Of all the objectives any country pursues, those with which there is widest agreement relate to economic prosperity. The provision of more and better homes, schools, recreational facilities, roads, and social services remains interwoven with industrial success. Who knows, by resolving the material questions of our time we may help ourselves to more enlightened definitions of the moral purposes of life.

*

The purpose of this book is to highlight some recent thinking and research by social scientists on a number of management topics. Two ways of doing this were considered. We could either attempt to trace the wide range of activities engaging the industrial social scientist or concentrate upon a limited number of topics in more depth. We have chosen the second course and inevitably missed out a variety of subjects the reader might expect to find represented. For example, there is little or nothing on selection, operational research, management appraisal, the mathematical aspects of social research, or matters of industrial pathology such as conflict, accidents, absenteeism, and labour turnover. There is no specific chapter on small groups, though their relevance to the problems of industry, like that of technical change, is a recurring theme of many chapters.

The choice of topics is, as far as possible, in keeping with the *systems* point of view described earlier, though obviously not all the contributors take this stance. In our system the organization is the focal point and each section of this book can be perceived as part of that system. The internal structure and functioning of the concern and the behaviour of individuals and groups within it are dealt with in Parts Two, Three, and Four. There are also forces in the environment which, whether or not they cross the firm's boundaries, interact with its operations. Among these influences are the consumers of the firm's goods and services, trade unions, the government, and educational institutions (Parts One and Five).

In Part One, 'Manpower Utilization and Industrial Relations', the demand feature of manpower planning is emphasized. This subject is highly relevant to the British industrial scene, and in fact to every economy where continuing full employment and a slow rate of industrial growth magnify the need to make better use of available human resources. An examination is made of some internal and external determinants of manpower availability and utilization, such as union–management relations, government legislation, and aspects of social opinion and organization.

Shortage of skilled manpower and rapid technical change inevitably impose a heavy load on the firm's training resources. In Part Two, 'Training for Skill', the social scientists outline training strategies and recent findings on methods for inculcating skill. Education must be viewed as an ongoing process if we are to maintain a flexible labour force; yet such a view conflicts with our preconceptions about the limited trainability of the older worker. Effective training should be preceded by a careful study of jobs, and this can be the starting point for the human engineer as well. Balancing our policies on training is the engineer's and ergonomist's interest in redefining jobs. In Part Three 'Ergonomics', the working models and analytical techniques which the ergonomist brings to his work are described. There are detailed accounts of the subject as a management technology, of optimum environmental conditions in production work, and of the effects of automation on skill. Although the study of man–machine systems has only begun to attract the attention of social psychologists and sociologists, it will not be long before new developments are upon us. Those organization theorists for whom technology is the most important non-human variable in industrial behaviour will undoubtedly be working more closely with the ergonomist than they have in the past. The latter's analysis of man–machine interactions can also provide valuable information in devising better ways of structuring social aspects of organization. Moreover, it could be argued that the study of man's behaviour in the semi-automated plant and the controls they exert on each other will provide us with early insight into the shape and form of society in the future.

Manpower utilization, training, and ergonomics all deal with aspects of the concern's structure and functioning. The organization theorist's interests extend beyond these to include the whole range of methods by which the concern both adjusts to its environment and coordinates the efforts of its members. In Part Four, 'Organization Behaviour', no attempt has been made to integrate the various chapters. Several approaches are represented. The people who manage the enterprise make up one vital component in its functioning and Chapters 11 to 13 cover the social and educational background of industrial managers, effective styles of leadership, and management training. Chapter 13 describes how the more limited notions of changing the individual manager's attitudes and behaviour through training are being extended to transforming the whole climate or culture of the firm. Chapters 14 and 15 look at the impact of some management controls on behaviour. The former investigates the suitability of a variety of approaches to rewarding employee effort and the latter advocates strategies based on trust. Recent work by Joan Woodward and her associates on the links between technology and industrial behaviour is also described (Chapter 16). Objectives, strategies, technology, and structure all go to shape the firm's cultural *milieu* of which morale is also a vital component. In Chapter 17 the influence of some of these variables provides an explanation for the many definitions of morale. Accurate instruments of measurement are needed to provide a basis for the comparative study of organization structure and behaviour. In

Chapter 18 there is an account of efforts by researchers at Aston University to describe more precisely concepts like 'specialization' and 'centralization' which have long been part and parcel of the management theorist's language.

The survival of the concern ultimately depends on its ability to sell its goods and services. In Part Five, 'Market Research', the relationship between the firm and its environment is analysed, but now the emphasis is on the product and its consumer. Like the manpower planner and the organization theorist, the market researcher is eclectic: he is involved in work which takes him across many traditional boundaries. Chapter 19 describes the empirical techniques used to identify important psychological concepts, which, together with the traditional demographic variables of sex, age, and social class, help in classifying and explaining the consumer's purchasing behaviour. A variety of methods, ranging from 'brain-storming' to empirical analysis, are also used in the processes of search and evaluation which go into developing and testing new products (Chapter 20).

The social scientist labours in an area where every man is his own expert and he is constantly faced with the comment 'But it's all just common sense.' It is not necessary to be 'scientific' to have ideas about behaviour – indeed, most novel conceptions originate from people who make no such claims. It is the limits of common sense which interest the social researcher, and in the coordination of man's efforts these limits are nearly always neglected. The dearth of progress in our understanding of industrial behaviour is illustrated by the way many managers today invest unquestioning faith in programmed instructions, productivity agreements, and management development just as their fathers believed in psychological testing, wage incentives, and 'the principles of management'. Many new techniques have begun with a rush of enthusiasm, few have left behind solid achievements, and this will continue until we become interested in exploring their values and limitations. The reader will find that in this volume the contributors at least attempt this considerable task.

PART ONE

Manpower Utilization and Industrial Relations

THE emergence of manpower planning as a subject of national import-ance has several origins. Industrial development increases the need for more complex human skills, a process which is accompanied by a growing realization that a country's prosperity depends heavily on the knowledge, skills, and creative talents of its people. Already the need to exercise control over the human element in work is leading to the scrutiny of labour utilization and availability, the output and perform-ance of educational institutions, training facilities, and in fact of every aspect of labour supply and demand. Manpower planning itself signi-fies a recognition that industry's internal order is interwoven with the total functioning of society, for inevitably the development of a co-herent manpower policy must involve government, trade unions, and educational institutions as well as industry.

The apparent acute shortage of labour in Britain leads us to focus attention on questions of utilization. International comparisons of labour costs and of manning ratios per unit of production cast 'over-manning' in the role of a bedeviller of British industry. In this first section of the book we read something of what the social scientist has to say about the determinants of this problem and his evaluation of corrective actions.

CHAPTER 2

Labour Utilization and Industrial Relations

ALAN FOX

LABOUR UTILIZATION AND WORK-GROUP INTERESTS

E. A. PRATT, declaiming in 1904 against 'the more militant and unreasonable phases of trade union rules or practices' which were 'eating the very heart out of British industry', was at pains to point out that he had nothing against unions of the 'legitimate' type, whose 'chief function' was simply to regulate wages and administer friendly benefits. Unions of the other type, however, with 'their coercive policy, their restriction of output, and their systematic interference with the . . . rights . . . of masters', must be denounced. The distinction which Pratt imagined himself to be drawing was between unions which deliberately confined themselves to efforts at influencing the terms on which labour was hired, leaving the employer a completely free hand as to how he utilized and deployed his labour in day-to-day operations, and unions which encroached upon employer prerogatives by attempting to influence or control these processes.

The difference was largely an imaginary creation designed to serve Pratt's polemical purpose, yet it still raises a point of major importance in public attitudes towards union activities. Popular opinion outside the unions has no difficulty in understanding the role of organized workers in seeking to increase the material rewards of their labour. But there is much less comprehension, and still less approval, of their interest in the way their labour is utilized and deployed.

Yet the interest is as old as wage-earning labour itself, for when men enter into a contract of employment which inevitably leaves undefined the details of how their labour is to be used, they are placing themselves under a discipline whose ends and means they can only partially predict. Their interest in having a hand in their own destiny has usually led them, wherever they could, to try to exercise some collective influence over their work experience. In many cases, trade unions as institutions did not so much create as grow out of these attempts at job regulation. Whether or not the unions formally endorsed particular work-group rules or practices as official union policy, the practices might nevertheless persist. The point is crucial, for it reminds us that although for convenience we often talk of 'union' rules and 'union' practices, the springs of action which sustain many of these efforts at 'job control' lie with the work-group in factory, mill, pit, and workshop.

The nature and degree of this concern, and the extent to which it can be made effective, vary considerably between one work situation and another. The total range of issues, however, which workpeople may seek to influence and if possible control is wide, covering every phase of the employment sequence. Recruitment and training, the pace and methods of work, the allocation of men and tasks, promotion and seniority, discipline and dismissal: all are of potential interest to any work-group with the ability to influence its own fate. When these general categories are reduced to specific and concrete examples, the place of labour utilization in the industrial relations setting can even more readily be seen. There may be controls over recruitment through apprenticeship regulations, and over promotion through seniority provisions governing those already employed. Craftsmen traditionally have mates. 'As much a symbol of the craftsman's prestige as an adjunct to his skill, they wait, perhaps for hours at a time, until the crafts-man has something for them to do.' (Clegg, 1964). Demarcation rules seek to insure that non-craftsmen do not perform work claimed by craftsmen, and that men of one craft do not encroach upon the work of another. Thus non-craftsmen may have to wait upon the time and convenience of craftsmen, while craftsmen themselves may stand idle waiting for a member of another craft to do a job which they could easily do themselves, or soon be trained to do. Mechanization may be resisted if it threatens jobs, earnings, or status. Skilled men may resist the breaking-up of skilled functions into simpler operations which can be carried out by semi-skilled labour – or may try to insist that only men of their own craft are employed on them and at the full skilled rates. The question of the number of men to be employed upon a given machine or process is a frequent subject of work-group concern. Practices of 'going slow' or restricting output have many diverse origins. Men may wish to demonstrate that they are not prepared to give a fair day's work for a wage which they do not regard as fair, or may go slow in order to prolong employment or to protect their slower fellows. They may withhold effort in order to ensure that work remains for overtime at enhanced rates of pay.

Work-groups may also resist attempts to measure work; may refuse to work with non-unionists; may try to insist that work must be shared rather than a minority of men be declared redundant; may make it difficult for an employer to dismiss a worker even for incompetence.

All these are examples of the impact upon labour utilization and deployment of the work-group's concern with its work experience. It would be a rare and fortunate group which enjoyed influence or control over the whole spectrum, but equally rare for a group to have influence over no part of it. The references to craftsmen must not obscure the fact that many groups of non-craftsmen are active and successful in regulating their own working lives. Drivers have their mates, dockers their manning rules, steel workers their promotion system. Even in the most unpromising circumstances it is a poor shop steward who cannot find some aspect of the job to take hold of.

WORK PRACTICES AND MANAGERIAL PREROGATIVES

One can still discern the Victorian notion that this constitutes an illegitimate invasion of managerial rights, though the context within which the argument is presented has changed. In earlier days stress was laid on the freedoms conferred by property rights; nowadays the context is that of the national interest. The employer's obligation is to maximize efficiency, and anything which obstructs him in this task handicaps the national effort. Those efforts by work-groups to regulate their work experience which run counter to what managers would choose if left perfectly free must therefore by definition be 'restrictive' and therefore condemned.

In circumstances like the present the argument may seem persuasive; nevertheless it fails. The key to its failure lies ultimately in the assumption that the employer can meaningfully be said to be pursuing 'maximum efficiency'. This is to commit the fallacy of translating a theoretical postulate of text-book economics into an operating principle. The problems of the manager revolve not around the word 'maximization', but around the word 'optimization'. H. A. Simon, the American theorist of administration, reminds us that 'to consider the administrative activity itself as valuationally neutral is an abstraction from reality which . . . if carried to extremes, ignores very important human values. These values may comprehend the remuneration and working conditions (using these terms broadly) of the members of the group which carries out the activity.' Wages; work pace; 'social aspects of the work-situation'; the 'social and psychological consequences of substituting one type of work-situation for another'; the claims of 'distributive justice'; all are 'value elements' to which ethical as well as efficiency criteria must be applied. In short: 'in the factual aspects of decision-making, the administrator must be guided by the criterion of efficiency', but in relation to value elements 'criteria of correctness have no meaning' (Simon, 1964). In balancing factual (efficiency) elements against value (ethical) elements, the manager has to seek optimum solutions.

What are the implications of this for labour utilization? The first is that, given wide diversity of circumstances, optimum solutions will differ sharply. But this will be explored later. Of more immediate concern is the fact that as soon as we recognize that where human and social values are involved there is no one scientifically discoverable 'correct' solution, we are knee-deep in claims for democratic representation of those who will be directly affected by whatever solution is chosen. The administrator must obviously exercise discretion and those affected have a personal interest in trying to influence it.

Any society, such as ours, which makes 'representation of interests' a basic value would therefore be on very shaky moral ground if it denied representation of the interests of work-groups. As an earlier inquiry into restrictive practices was forced to recognize: 'To assume that whenever and wherever a trade union refuses to allow an employer to do something which he says is essential, the employer is in every case right and the trade union wrong is merely foolish.' (Hilton, 1935.) Thus to argue that it is illegitimate *in principle* for work-groups to assert their will against management in matters of labour utilization embodies a misunderstanding about the nature of industrial enterprise and its place in our society.

This can be made further evident by noting the many other ways in which management is hedged about with restrictions. Not only does all collective bargaining restrict the employer's freedom, but so also do Factory Acts, insurance regulations, public opinion, and welfare enactments of a wide variety of kinds. The modern manager makes his decisions within a complex pattern of limiting conditions, of which work-group pressure is only one. To object to the latter in the interest of 'managerial freedom' is therefore to appeal to a myth.

THE ORIGINS OF WORK RULES AND PRACTICES

This is but one, however, of many confusions in the popular view of restrictive practices. Another common response is to condemn them out of hand as stupid, irrational, and misguided. One of the assumptions encouraging this judgement is that restrictive practices stem largely from fear of working oneself out of a job. Such negative tactics at a time when governments are committed to high-employment policies are evidence, so it is argued, of an inability to grasp that times have changed. A rational appraisal would show that cooperation with management towards higher productivity is the only intelligent course.

The weakness of this line of argument is that fear of unemployment is only one source of restrictive practices. Even if it were the sole source there would still be more to say about their rationality than most critics recognize. Who enjoys being forced out of his job even when there is another available? To protect oneself against imposed and unwanted change is a rational enough response and if increases in output, more apprentices, abandonment of demarcation rules, or reductions in 'manning ratios' seem likely to cause redundancy then restrictions will have their appeal even when new jobs lie to hand. Yet work-groups may retain restrictions even in the face of the most solemn guarantees by the employer that no redundancy will take place. It is from such situations as this that charges of irrationality draw their apparent strength, especially when the workers concerned are inarticulate, as they so often are, about their own case. Their behaviour is readily comprehensible, however, in the light of the fact that there are many values which lead work-groups to seek to control their environment and a given rule or practice may serve any one or several of them.

Under systems of payment by results, work-groups may limit their output for fear that too high a level of earnings will 'spoil the job' – that is convince management that piece-work rates or allowed times are too generous (Lupton, 1963). Apprenticeship and demarcation rules serve other objects besides the assertion of job rights including maintenance of the identity and status of a craft, preservation of bargaining power, and protection of the institutional interest of a union as such. Manning rules may also be linked with maintaining the size and identity of a particular occupational group within an establishment. 'Seniority rules are directed primarily against favouritism on the side of management, but they are also meant to protect skills, the labour market, wages' (Zweig, 1951). Among dockers, rules exist which aim at a fair division of desirable and less desirable jobs, and which seek to maintain a fair distribution of earning opportunities (Devlin, 1965).

A variation on the theme that work-group restrictions are mis-guided and irrational is the argument that by 'obstructing' employers in this manner workers are foolishly ignoring the common interests which unite the members of an enterprise. By impeding the maximum production of wealth, workers are harm-ing their own best interests. Certain of our previous considerations are again relevant here. 'We do not always expect people to do the *possible* since the desirable is also an important consideration. We strike a compromise between what we can possibly do and what we desire to do' (Berg and Kuhn, 1965). We have already noted a wide range of values which enter into the compromises effected by work-groups.

The emphasis being placed here on the rational content of work rules and practices has a positive end in view, for much popular discussion and much of the handling of the subject by economists, managers, and employers has been rendered useless by the absence of any will to understand them. The first prerequisite to changing a social situation is to understand it, and this employers have, with a few notable exceptions, conspicuously failed to do. They have tended not only to assume that right was unquestionably on their side, but also to disparage and deride work-group rules and practices without making any effort towards an imaginative understanding of their origins.

The stress on rationality must not lead us, however, to view all such rules as being cast in this mould. F. Zweig's study (1951), an honest struggle for insight into this difficult field, noted that some employers complained less of restrictive practices as such than of the restrictive spirit – the dead-weight of traditional custom and habit which is jealously preserved despite having outlived its functional usefulness for the workers concerned, and which deters many employers from even minor but nevertheless valuable change. The Devlin Report on the docks drew a distinction between 'practices deliberately created as protective and bad habits which firmer discipline might still cure'. The misfortune so far has been that the tendency to view *all* restrictions as foolish obstructionism has led to a widespread failure to develop creative methods for dealing with them.

Social science has a notable contribution to make in this sphere by unravelling the complexities and subtleties of work rules and analysing their functions and dysfunctions. The beginning has already been made. Zweig's broad survey (1951); Lupton's comparison of two companies in *On the Shop Floor* (1963); the Devlin Report on the docks (1965); and Flanders' detailed case-study in *The Fawley Productivity Agreements* (1964) will take anyone with the will to understand quite a long way, and documentation of the American scene is exemplified in Weinstein's editing of *Featherbedding and Technological Change* (1965), which has many useful references.

THE EMPLOYERS' RESPONSE

There remains much more to be said about the employers' response to the efforts of work-groups to regulate their work environment.

In a considerable number of cases they have acquiesced completely, either by concluding written or verbal agreements or by extending tacit acceptance. National agreements in some major industries such as building, printing, and the docks embody rules on labour utilization and deployment which are the result of union and work-group pressure, and at work-place level written or verbal agreements and tacit acquiescences are widespread. Some of these instances are not seen by employers as restrictive, but would certainly be defined as such by some external observers. Conversely, the inclusion of a practice in an agreement does not necessarily preclude employers from complaining bitterly about it. Of 'the three things which were chiefly complained of as restrictive' by the dock employers, one – the so-called continuity rule – was in an agreement (Devlin, 1965).

Sometimes employers have felt so strongly about a given practice that they have been prepared to fight a long and bitter struggle in the hope of crushing it. Engineering employers imposed prolonged lock-outs in 1852 and 1897 to deter their craft workers from obstructing the introduction of new simplified types of machinery and the employment on them of non-apprenticed labour at lower rates of pay. The boot and shoe manufacturers fought a similar campaign in 1895, and the building contractors tried to rally their forces against craft restrictions in 1899. Engineering saw another three-month lock-out on the issue of managerial prerogatives in 1922.

Explosions of this sort have been comparatively rare, however, and the more common response of employers has been to accommodate to the situation and confess helplessness in the face of union power. Of recent years there has been a tendency to ascribe this stance to the employer's weakness in the face of extreme labour shortage. Some critics have urged that governments should deliberately create unemployment in order to strengthen managerial authority. However, since most restrictions arose when regular cycles of heavy unemployment were regarded as inevitable the argument is not impressive for its logic. Employers have always tended to confess helplessness in the face of work-group or union pressures. Exactly a century ago, the president of the Glasgow Master Brickbuilders was telling another Royal Commission on

Trade Unions that 'unions restrict the enterprise of the employer by their captious and arbitrary action, and in many if not in most cases the employer has no alternative but to submit'.

Nevertheless it is almost certainly true that restrictionism has grown since the war. Labour shortage has indeed caused a shift of power from management to the shop floor, and work-groups have understandably not been slow to turn the situation to their advantage. Unable to mount a frontal assault, employers have had no other ideas, apart from moral denunciation, as to how to cope with the situation.

On the whole, therefore, accommodation has greatly predominated over open conflict. In public, or across the dinner table, employers have denounced trade-union infamy and inveighed against the laziness of the British workman, but in the privacy of their own establishments have made their agreements or simply turned a blind eye. Whenever a serious inquiry was afoot, the nervousness of many lest they be called upon to act has been almost palpable. The results of an investigation in the thirties directed at practices alleged to be 'acting powerfully against the present recovery and future prosperity' of British industry showed employers' associations and representative employers in several major sectors playing down the importance of restrictions (Hilton, 1935). A White Paper of 1959, *Practices Impeding the Full and Efficient Use of Manpower*, also revealed a reluctance on the part of many employers' associations to see their dirty linen publicly displayed lest they be called upon to wash it. Of 112 industries cooperating in the inquiry, 64 (57 per cent) declared that they had no problems.

Thus the characteristic response of employers has been one of grumbling accommodation. Both individually and through their associations, they have tended to play up work-group practices whenever they wished to excuse their own failures, but play them down whenever there was a prospect of being asked sharply what they proposed doing about them.

In such circumstances employers cannot evade sharing the responsibility for their existence. When restrictions are embodied in a collective agreement the responsibility is of course clear and unequivocal, but employers must also share the blame for the many other practices in which they have acquiesced for so many years.

EMPLOYER ATTITUDES – THE HERITAGE OF LABOUR ABUNDANCE

How is this long-standing mood of accommodation to be explained? Part of the explanation may lie in the situation of labour abundance which has been a feature of the British industrial scene for much of its history. An abundance of any factor of production may lead to it being used lavishly and indeed wasted. The economic historian Professor H. J. Habbakuk wrote in 1962 that 'between the boom of 1869–73 and the height of the 1914–18 War there was never a general shortage of labour'. Comparing this with the scarcity and dearness of labour in the United States, he observed that 'American manufacturers were still under a more compelling need than the English to raise the productivity of their labour'; in England 'both employers and workers were . . . conditioned by attitudes engendered by abundant labour. . . .' If this was true up to 1914–18, it was even more so between the wars, when even in the best years after 1920 the irreducible minimum of unemployment among insured workers was 10 per cent and in the worst years rose to 20 per cent. It seems highly plausible that this situation moulded employers' attitudes on the whole subject of labour utilization, leading them to be less watchful and rigorous than their American counterparts towards wasteful practices, bad habits, and a generally loose pattern of labour deployment. It cannot of course account for everything. The question of whether or not an industry is sheltered from foreign competition has always been relevant.

WASTED LABOUR – THE NEED FOR A WIDER PERSPECTIVE

Recognition of the likely effects of labour abundance upon employer attitudes towards manpower utilization requires us at this stage to widen the scope of our considerations. So far the emphasis has been upon the impact of union and work-group pressures. This has taken the varied forms of (a) protective rules rationally designed to serve rational purposes, (b) a restrictive spirit expressing itself in diverse ways which may not lend themselves easily to precise definition but which can nevertheless exert a potent effect, and (c) bad habits which may be curable by firmer discipline or which have been allowed to become so widespread that, in the words of the Devlin Report, they can be 'no longer dealt with by the ordinary processes of industrial discipline against the individual'.

We now have to locate firmly in the industrial relations setting all those forms of work organization which are wasteful of labour but which have their origins not in union or work-group initiative but in the organizational slackness of work design on the part of employers. The significance of this category is testified by the fact that students of this field are increasingly of the opinion that the maintenance of formal restrictive practices is not the major cause of under-employment in industry. The growing view – shared by many progressive managers – is that restrictive practices as commonly interpreted account for no more than perhaps a quarter of it. The remainder arises from tacit and often unconscious acceptance by management and workers alike of traditional job structures and methods of labour deployment. Why should these be relevant to industrial relations if unions and work-groups have played little or no part in creating or maintaining them? The answer becomes clear when we consider trying to change them. It has been argued that workers can be said to develop property rights in work arrangements which employers create for them (Weinstein, 1965). Certainly from a practical point of view employers have to be as careful when they seek to change these as when they lay hands upon the rules of the union or work-group itself.

For example, it is believed that one field in which under-employment is particularly rife is maintenance work. Many traditional ideas here are ripe for review – maintenance standards may be too high and the notion persists that staff must necessarily have periods of idleness waiting for problems to arise. The alternatives are several. Planned or preventive maintenance can save labour; some maintenance might be put out to specialist contractors who serve the needs of many firms; there may be scope for training process workers to do their own simpler maintenance tasks. The implications of these alternatives for the skills, status, security of employment, and inter-union relations of maintenance and process workers are obvious.

Such implications have to be faced, however, for it is beyond question that worker restrictions and employer indifference have between them created a pattern of wasteful labour utilization which is a serious drag on our national welfare (Ministry of Labour, 1966). Management consultants believe that industry as a whole may be employing perhaps 10–15 per cent more manpower than is really needed even with existing production processes, and report that it is by no means uncommon to find firms where a 40 per cent saving in manpower is feasible. Management representatives in several major industries have estimated that the slack in their own fields ranges from 10 to 30 per cent. Industrial case studies confirm the picture. A Special Report of the Iron and Steel Board concluded that 'the output required from British steel works could be achieved by a considerably smaller labour force than at present', and the Royal Commission on the Press in 1962 found that four national newspapers were on average 53 per cent overmanned in their production and distribution departments. Evidence of this sort is increasingly abundant. It stands witness to a loss of managerial control which has persisted and of recent years gathered pace despite all the protestations of maintaining 'management prerogative'.

REFORM AND PROBLEMS OF DEFINITIONS AND METHODS

Given Britain's economic difficulties, it is not surprising that such evidence has prompted demands for sweeping condemnation and wholesale reform. Productivity campaigns based merely on exhortation appear to have had little effect. Why should we not identify and define these wasteful practices and inefficiencies of labour utilization and then contrive some legislative fiat to be exerted against them (Hutton, 1966)? Unfortunately this would be a grotesquely clumsy remedy for such a pervasive disease. Precisely what is to be condemned is extremely difficult to define. The suggestions of most reformers of this and similar schools are over-simple. A group of Conservative lawyers (1958) referred to practices which hindered 'the most effective use of labour, technical skill or resources', or diminished 'the incentive to such use'. Such a formulation assumes an aim of maximizing economic efficiency which employers and managers should and can pursue. But, as we have already noted, we take for granted that all collective agreements, numerous legislative enactments, insurance regulations, social values, and public opinion should set limits to this aim; why should members of the group which carries out the activity be deprived of all influence?

Some observers have sought a way out by drawing a distinction between what is 'reasonable' and what is not. This was the method chosen by the National Joint Advisory Council to the Ministry of Labour, under whose auspices the White Paper of 1959 was published. The Council, focusing only upon 'what are popularly called "restrictive labour practices"', referred to 'those . . . which go beyond what is necessary for the reasonable protection of workers'. But who is to define what is reasonable? As soon as we see the employers not as maximizers but as optimizers the single yardstick has gone, and if there is no one correct answer then the definition of 'reasonable' becomes much more complex than some would-be reformers seem to suppose.

But perhaps at least all *employers* could agree on a definition which would get us somewhere? Alas, there is not even this degree of consensus. It is a further illustration of the trickiness of definitions in this field that not even employers in the same industry are necessarily agreed about restrictive labour practices, never mind about inefficiencies in the overall pattern of labour utilization, which we have seen is the real crux. This fact has dogged every honest attempt at inquiry. The Hilton investigation (1935) complained that 'the employers . . . had widely differing views as to what constituted a "trade-union restriction"', and Zweig (1951) reported that rarely could he find 'a practice which all employers would agree to call restrictive'.

One reason for this is the wide diversity of situations in which the various practices are applied. 'One and the same practice is in purely objective terms restrictive in one situation, and non-restrictive in another' (Zweig, 1951). Some firms may have adapted to a given practice so completely that they are hardly aware of its existence; others, because of their differing circumstances, find the same practice highly irksome. Sometimes an arrangement which an outsider – or another firm – would see as restrictive is advantageous because it is part of a tacit – or even explicit – deal from which the firm derives a net benefit. If employers cannot agree about the iniquities of the work-group, they are still less likely to agree about those inefficiencies of work organization for which they are even more obviously responsible.

This means, not that the task of identifying inefficiencies and restrictions is impossible, but that no blanket definitions will help us. The individual situation has to be examined on its merits. The study by Allan Flanders (1964) of the Fawley situation illustrates how social science can help here by analysing the technological and social structures, the personal and group forces at work, the environmental and cultural factors, and how they interrelate. Any precise attempt at pinpointing those elements that can and should be changed needs some analysis of this sort, whether by outside consultants, by personnel managers versed in the behavioural sciences, or by the rare general manager with time as well as insight.

Some reformers have proposed that the task of identifying restrictions in particular situations should fall to an independent tribunal conducting public examinations into specific cases. The Engineering Employers' Federation has suggested that such a tribunal should 'have power to issue an order requiring those insisting on or supporting a restrictive practice to desist therefrom'. The method would be used not only against unions or work-groups applying restrictions as conventionally understood, but also against employers where they are 'guilty of practices and methods which are in themselves inefficient'.

The merit of this proposal is that by its reference to employer inefficiency it gives at least nominal recognition to the fact that the problem extends far beyond restrictions by work-groups. There, however, its value probably ends. The whole concept of modifying patterns of work within industry by means of authoritative decrees from outside must be considered suspect. Unless the employer himself sees a given feature of work organization as undesirable for *him*, external denunciation gets us nowhere. It is he who administers the situation, and if he chooses to acquiesce in inefficiency then it will remain. No secret police exists or is likely to be created which can sniff out infractions of tribunal decisions on the shop floor. The elimination of restrictions in the field of price-fixing is difficult enough, and prices are far more public than shop-floor practices.

But let us suppose, it might be said, that an employer does identify certain features of which he would dearly love to be rid; would not an independent, external tribunal strengthen his authority in dealing with them? Such a view fails to grasp precisely where the difficulty lies when managements seek to exercise their prerogative against established union or work-group practices. The difficulty lies not in mounting the initial attack, but in coping with its consequences. It is open to any employer to apply coercive sanctions, such as suspensions or dismissals, in an attempt to introduce changes in the pattern of work. A tribunal could impose fines. Such acts are not intrinsically difficult. The real problems come with the subsequent struggle to maintain enforcement. Strikes, overtime bans, and go-slows may be the least of it. As any manager knows, there are a hundred small ways in which his workers can make his life a misery if they set their minds to it. The tribunal cannot help him here. The methods of work-group obstructionism are too easily disguised to be susceptible to policing by an external body. In the most taxing part of the exercise, therefore, the employer is always on his own, and history shows that he does not relish it. This is why, for example, despite their loud denunciations of unofficial strikes, employers almost never take advantage of the law under which they can prosecute workers who strike without giving due notice. The law can impose its sanctions, but it is the employer who has to grapple with the bitterness, the hostility, and the complete withdrawal of goodwill. It is doubtful, therefore, if authoritative decrees by some external body can improve the pattern of labour utilization, whether they are aimed at work-groups or at the employer himself.

The whole method of frontal onslaught does not have an inspiring history in terms of results. As already noted, the engineering employers fought three prolonged and expensive battles in 1852, 1897, and 1922 over the issue of managerial prerogatives. Yet their *Evidence to the Royal Commission on Trade Unions and Employers' Associations* contains case-histories of current union restrictionism which, given a few transpositions of technical terms, could have been written at any time during the last hundred years. Authoritarian gestures may, like many patent medicines, give temporary relief, but they are not a reliable method for achieving permanent and accepted changes in labour utilization. The very nature of the method, moreover, is so prejudicial to industrial co-operation that a very heavy price is paid for what little is achieved. It can hardly be seen as a viable technique for the post-war world in which labour shortage has shifted the balance of power in favour of the work-people.

REFORM THROUGH PRODUCTIVITY BARGAINING?

The argument thus far may seem to have led us into a depressing *impasse*. Only the individual employer can identify what is inefficient labour utilization for him. Upon him, and not upon any external authority, rests the responsibility and the burden of introducing change and handling the consequences. We know that, historically, British employers have been content with slack standards in this respect. When they have chanced their arm and tried to enforce their managerial prerogative, the results have not been impressive. Maximum ill-will has been created and work-group restrictions have tended to reassert themselves.

Fortunately a way out of the *impasse* has now begun to be manifested in action. As the sequence of the argument suggests, however, it has to begin with the employer recognizing that constructive change is both necessary and possible. It has to begin with the employer willing himself not only to end those accommodations to which he has given tacit acceptance for so long, but also to see, perhaps for the first time, inefficiencies which he has long taken for granted as part of the natural order.

Such beginnings are now visible. It has been clear for two or three years that an important shift of attitude has indeed begun to make its way among a few of the more vigorous and progressive

British managements. This recognizes that the days of labour abundance have gone for ever; that it must be treated as a highly scarce resource and used with the utmost parsimony. Under-utilized labour must be combed out and re-deployed; tasks must be re-defined to minimize labour requirements; work patterns must be recast to get more done with a given labour force. We are watching business attitudes beginning their slow, painful adjustment to the Labour Scarcity Revolution. In terms of the shift in mental attitudes that this requires, it could prove, if it became widespread, to be among the most important general changes to visit British industry since the steam engine.

But a shift in attitudes is only the first step. By what methods are the requisite changes to be carried out? What is their significance for the techniques – and the temper – of industrial relations? One thing is clear. If change by coercion or by external authoritative decree is ruled out, only change by consent is left. But this in itself helps us little, for there are diverse ways of pursuing it. Some employers down the years have hoped that if they extended a paternalistic generosity to their workers they would be rewarded with a free hand to rule as they wished. This view of the workers as children, dominated however kindly by paterfamilias, commands less and less respect among those to whom it is directed. Others have hoped that the workers could simply be persuaded, exhorted, cajoled, or shamed into accepting change. This view ignores the fact that workers have acquired rights and legitimate expectations in the existing pattern of work organization which employers have created for them, and to expect them to sacrifice these without any *quid pro quo* is to deceive oneself about the essentially contractual and utilitarian nature of the modern employment relationship. To attempt to counter this by asserting that a larger total product would mean bigger shares all round is to offer too hypothetical a compensation. Unions 'cannot take on trust how the benefits of rising productivity will be shared out' (Flanders, 1964). The way out of these difficulties lies through the process of collective bargaining. Only through *negotiation*, in which management specifies and guarantees the workers' share of the benefits accruing from their surrender of their interest in the *status quo*, can the unions play what for them is a meaningful role in this kind of exercise.

Through negotiation the right of work-groups to a voice in the determination of their own work experience can be respected during the very process of changing that experience.

The idea of negotiating the detailed deployment and utilization of labour is not one to which many managers take kindly, for they see it as threatening the concept of the manager's prerogative to rule unchallenged in his own house. That this concept is highly suspect has been argued elsewhere (Fox, 1966). Suffice it here to say that, throughout all the verbal insistence on the sanctity of managerial authority, authority has undergone increasing erosion by the unilateral action of work-groups and the drift of events out of management control. This loss of control has been a direct outcome of management's failure to adapt to the post-war shift in power relations at the work-place. They can only regain control by recognizing the reality of work-group power, by coming to terms with it, and by containing it within the limits of negotiated regulation. To pretend that it does not exist, or to suppose that coming to terms with it is somehow immoral, is to allow it to grow unchecked.

PRODUCTIVITY BARGAINING: ITS PROMISE AND ITS PROBLEMS

We thus come to what has become popularly known as 'productivity bargaining', which brings issues of labour utilization and deployment into the field of negotiation, where they belong. A considerable creative element lies here in so modifying work rules and organization that the divergent interests of the various groups involved, including management, are reconciled at a higher level of practical cooperation than before.

The concept is in some danger of becoming blurred. Often, for the sake of brevity, it is described simply as a process by which large monetary inducements are offered to workers in exchange for the surrender of restrictive practices. This definition is inadequate, however, on four counts. First, financial inducements are a necessary but far from sufficient condition. They cannot relieve management of the hard preliminary analysis of work systems which identifies the elements to be changed, nor of the gruelling negotiations required to modify deep-rooted beliefs and norms of behaviour, to provide re-assurance about the future, to minimize inter-group jealousies and to make the many contingent adjustments that are invariably necessary. Secondly, such a definition does not even hint at the problems for management in administering the new and different pattern of work. Thirdly, an over-simplification lies in limiting the focus to restrictive practices, for as we have seen the object of attention may be any aspect of the methods or organization of work which are wasteful of labour, whether these were initiated by the work-people or not. Finally, productivity bargaining must not be confused with situations in which wage concessions are exchanged for vague general arrangements for future cooperation in pursuing greater efficiency. The changes to be made in work practices, methods or organization must be specific, precisely defined in the agreement, and actively administered by management.

Only the first major example of productivity bargaining has received close, detailed examination, in Allan Flanders' study (1964) of the Fawley agreements. Some aspects of that study have been under-stressed. Commentators have been rightly quick to play up the solid achievements of the exercise – the substantial reduction in wasteful and unnecessary overtime, the abolition of craftsmen's mates and their redeployment on other tasks, the re-allocation of jobs on a simpler basis, with the re-grouping of some semi-skilled and unskilled workers into one grade able to perform a variety of labouring jobs, and the elimination of time allowances for travel and washing in return for a forty-hour week. But other features of Flanders' analysis have received much less stress – the rigorous preliminary analysis; the efforts needed to convince the whole management team of the validity of the exercise; the care and sensitive diplomacy required for the approach to unions, shop stewards, and work-groups; the long wearisome negotiations. And not least, of course, those characteristics of the new situation which managers may find less pleasing – the greater formality of labour relations, the increase in shop-steward influence on union negotiations, and the heightened rivalry between the main union groups, all giving rise to new stresses and strains in management–union relationships.

What we know of the productivity agreements which followed Fawley confirms this overall picture. Many of them can show negotiated changes which in the context of British industrial relations must be considered impressive, and not a few improve on Fawley either in method or content or both. Besides many other agreements in oil-refining, the movement has spread to the electricity supply industry, civil aviation, shipbuilding, municipal buses, Imperial Chemical Industries, Alcan, the Steel Company of Wales, and British Oxygen. These are only some of the better-known examples and there are numerous others.

Productivity bargaining has unquestionably become fashionable, though the exuberance with which it was first hailed has very properly become somewhat muted. An interim report produced in December 1966 by the National Board for Prices and Incomes (*Productivity and Pay during the Period of Severe Restraint*) turned upon it a sober and stringent eye – 'Most managements are far from ready to consider undertaking the tasks of preparation, negotiation and control which are required. . . .'

The managerial problem of *maintaining* the agreement, for example, must not be underestimated. Where, for instance, overtime has been drastically cut or where craft and process workers have agreed to interchangeability of functions at the margins of their work, one may find permanent pressures operating which make for a reversion to the original pattern. For managers under pressure, overtime is often the easiest way out, and workers seeking to maximize earnings may not be slow to grasp the fact. The result may be a gradual tendency for overtime to climb back to its former level. Similarly with regard to interchangeability of work. However precisely the agreement seeks to define it, day-to-day decisions by operating management will be required to give it effect. Where work-groups are nervous of its possible effects on job rights, status, or security, a harassed manager may revert to traditional demarcations rather than lose goodwill. Once we recognize that at least some of the practices and job patterns which we wish to change have deep roots in characteristic responses, we can see that a continuing struggle may be necessary to prevent them reasserting themselves.

Where such difficulties arise, they usually indicate no more than that the right pattern of control has not yet been found. The over-time problem may be solved by abolishing premium payments altogether and substituting time off instead. The examples are quoted simply to demonstrate that work rules and practices must be re-structured in ways which provide management with the necessary kind and degree of control. A further report by the National Board for Prices and Incomes on productivity agree-ments (1967) revealed 'little evidence that the gains of productivity agreements will slip away through failures of managerial control or through workers slipping back into old habits or inventing new restrictions'. But the link between improved utilization of labour and improved managerial structure and organization is crucial, and unsophisticated ventures which fail to take the point could hardly get off the ground. This reinforces the earlier argument as to the weakness of definitions which refer simply to 'buying out restrictive practices'. Successful productivity bargaining on any comprehensive scale proves to be nothing less than a major recon-struction of work rules and relationships in which management's own role is scrutinized no less rigorously than that of the workers.

Other cautionary notes have been struck. Suspicions have been expressed that restriction is sometimes being bought off at too high a price. Mr Norman Sloan, speaking about shipbuilding to the Royal Commission on Trade Unions and Employers' Associa-tions, confessed that 'we are finding it a very expensive way of dealing with it, desperately expensive'. There have also been speculations that some companies and unions might seek to use productivity bargaining as a respectable façade behind which to subvert all attempts at restraining the rise in money incomes. Besides being good for public relations, it enables high wage claims to be indulged without incurring the disfavour of public opinion. The National Board for Prices and Incomes, however, has shown itself very alive not only to these dangers but also to the undesirability of assuming that workers and companies should reap the whole benefit of productivity agreements. 'The under-taking should be ready to show clear benefits to the consumer through a contribution to stable prices' (N.B.P.I., 1967).

Employers' associations have contributed their own doubts. The award of large wage increases triggers off claims elsewhere, they argue, which employers may be forced to concede but which are not accompanied by productivity improvements, thus aggravating inflationary earnings drift. The National Board for Prices and Incomes, however, found 'little evidence so far that a *bona fide* productivity agreement in one undertaking tends to push up wages regardless of productivity in other undertakings' (1967). Employers' associations have also argued that productivity bargaining plant by plant is a painfully slow method of improving labour utilization. The view of the Confederation of British Industry is that while a primary objective of collective bargaining in the future must indeed be 'the efficient use of manpower', ways should be explored whereby this can be pursued at the national or industry-wide level of negotiation, with new joint machinery to ensure that the intentions of the national agreement are observed at the plant level. National productivity agreements would thus constitute a regulatory framework within which plant agreements could be pursued.

This view of the C.B.I. is but one contribution to a debate about the whole place of national or industry-wide bargaining in our system of industrial relations; a debate in which considerations of labour utilization have an important part. It has been argued that since employers' associations have to insure that the wage rates which they negotiate with the unions at national level are within the means of their least efficient, least profitable employer-members, those rates are too low for the more profitable firms which are able and willing to pay more in order to attract and retain labour. Such firms therefore supplement the pay-packets of their workers by a variety of means, such as unnecessary overtime and loose incentive schemes, which prejudice the efficient use of labour and foster inflationary earnings-drift. On this argument, therefore, the interests of labour utilization and incomes policy would be better served by a system of plant bargaining freed from the constraints and conventions of national negotiation. Productivity bargaining at this level could evolve more efficient work practices, tighten up managerial structures and attitudes, and reform chaotic pay systems. The plausibility of this line of approach explains the anxiety of the C.B.I. to find a fruitful, mutual accommodation between national and plant negotiation.

Whether national agreements would really extend the coverage of productivity bargaining remains to be proved. Their translation into meaningful and effective agreements at plant level would rest entirely on the vigour and ability of individual managements, for employers' associations have no powers of compulsion. Their efforts of recent years to spread the gospel of work study have not produced impressive results, and manpower utilization is an even trickier field. The experience of electricity supply shows that even within a unified nationalized industry the success of a productivity agreement nationally negotiated is likely to be very patchy (National Board for Prices and Incomes, 1967). In a private industry composed of many employers it is likely to be even more so. Nevertheless, employers' associations could certainly contribute by issuing guide lines, suitably adapted to the industry's circumstances, which members would be expected to observe in their productivity agreements. Agreements might be registered and information about them disseminated to other employers and unions.

None of these cautionary notes about productivity bargaining refutes its claim to be the most fruitful approach yet devised for improving manpower utilization.* The report by the National Board for Prices and Incomes (1967) on seven agreements found that they had 'in general led to overall savings in costs, in the sense that the costs are less than they would have been without the agreements, and in some there are prospects of further savings which could not have been expected in the absence of the agreements.' There was 'a strong case for encouraging the spread of productivity agreements which conform with the requirements of a prices and incomes policy.' The Board's current guidelines in this field are that:

(i) It should be shown that the workers are making a direct contribution towards increasing productivity by accepting more exacting work or a major change in working practices.

(ii) Forecasts of increased productivity should be derived by the application of proper work-standards.

* Although this chapter is concerned with the utilization of *labour*, it must be remembered that productivity bargaining may also concern itself with changes in the utilization of *capital*.

(iii) An accurate calculation of the gains and the costs should normally show that the total cost per unit of output, taking into account the effect on capital, will be reduced.

(iv) The scheme should contain effective controls to ensure that the projected increase in productivity is achieved, and that payment is made only as productivity increases or as changes in working practices take place.

(v) The undertaking should be ready to show clear benefits to the consumer through a contribution to stable prices.

(vi) An agreement covering part of an undertaking should bear the cost of consequential increases elsewhere in the same undertaking, if any have to be granted.

(vii) In all cases negotiators should beware of setting extravagant levels of pay which would provoke resentment outside.

It remains to be seen how fast British management can develop the will and the skills necessary for this creative approach to the problems of labour utilization. Meanwhile, criticisms of the method need themselves to be scrutinized with caution. Some are inspired by social attitudes which have little to contribute to labour relations in the second half of the twentieth century. Feelings that workers should simply submit to management authority in these matters; that no vested interest of work-groups in the *status quo* should be recognized; that 'compensation' is therefore nothing but an immoral bribe; these and similar emotional responses fail by the very criterion to which they purport to attach such importance – that of practical success.

These have been the attitudes which have so far predominated in our industrial history and they point to the changes needed in the training and ideology of management if a more creative approach to labour utilization is to spread throughout British industry. The paradox which managements find such difficulty in accepting is that they can only regain control by sharing it (Fox, 1966: Flanders, 1967). It cannot be said that the appropriate mental stance is sufficiently widespread to give hope of quick progress. 'A productivity agreement entails . . . a radically different approach to the problems of personnel management from that general in British industry' (National Board for Prices and Incomes, 1966). The social sciences and the institutions of management education face a long haul.

CHAPTER 3

Redundancy

DOROTHY WEDDERBURN

THE use of the word 'redundancy' to describe a situation where the labour force of an enterprise is being reduced by dismissals is unique to Britain. The word does not exist in this sense in France or Germany. Even in the United States there are 'lay-offs' and 'dismissals' but not 'redundancies'. Some sympathy can be felt, therefore, for those workers in Britain who say that redundancy is only a euphemistic word for the 'sack'. But in Britain in recent years much attention has been devoted to the development of techniques to minimize the hardships arising for workers involved in dismissals, and the point of departure for the development of this policy has been the phenomenon of redundancy itself. One result is that this country is unique in having legislation (the Redundancy Payments Act, 1965) which provides financial compensation for the great majority of workers who lose their job as a result of redundancy.

In this chapter we shall review the growth and development of such policies in Britain, and attempt to assess their significance for the functioning of the labour market. In addition we hope to show that the results of research which has been carried out in this area point overwhelmingly to the need for a more integrated approach to the problems. At the level both of the individual firm and of government, and from the viewpoint of both economic efficiency and the well-being of individual workers, the utilization and distribution of labour needs to be studied, not only at the point when dismissals take place, but in the total setting of the labour market, where many complex social and economic forces operate.

THE DEVELOPMENT OF REDUNDANCY POLICIES
IN BRITAIN

As the usage of the word 'redundancy' grew more common in Britain in the fifties, it carried with it the connotation of large-scale dismissals. As defined in the 1965 Act, however, a single worker can be dismissed by reason of 'redundancy'. The Act defines such a dismissal as one that:

is attributable wholly or mainly to –

(*a*) the fact that his employer has ceased, or intends to cease, to carry on the business for the purposes for which the employee was employed by him, or has ceased, or intends to cease, to carry on that business in the place where the employee was so employed, or

(*b*) the fact that the requirements of that business for employees to carry out work of a particular kind in the place where he was so employed, have ceased or diminished or are expected to cease or diminish.

This is a very broad definition, embracing most cases of dismissal which do not arise from the incompetence, unsuitability, or misdemeanour of the individual worker. We may note, however, that even this broad definition gives ample scope for legalistic argument; and already a case has been brought to the High Court to determine whether an old employee asked to take on new duties which he could not perform was dismissed for 'incompetence' or by reason of redundancy.

The causes of redundancy will be varied. This is well illustrated by some of the recently published case-studies of particular redundancy situations. It may result from a relatively temporary recession in demand, as in the motor-car industry in 1956 (Kahn, 1964), or again the large-scale dismissals in the Midlands car industry in 1966. It may result from the cancellation of a government contract (Wedderburn, 1964). Or it may be the result of permanent long-term decline in an industry, itself the product of shifts in demand to other products or services, combined with technological change within the industry itself. These were the forces which led to the closure of some of the railway workshops (Wedderburn, 1965). Redundancy is in fact linked with all aspects of the process of industrial change. But we must not conclude that change necessarily means redundancy. It is an important part of our argument that too much emphasis upon the techniques for handling redundancy may obscure the importance of other techniques for avoiding redundancy altogether.

Only a few years ago it was being suggested that Britain was backward in its standards for the protection and compensation of dismissed workers, and had been slow to develop, either by agreement between trade unions and employers, or through legislation, procedures for deciding on the selection of workers for dismissal or for handling the reinstatement of workers (Goodman, 1962). Apart from flat-rate unemployment benefit available to insured workers who found themselves without a job, and the service of the Ministry of Labour Employment Exchanges to help in finding new work, there was no general provision for redundancy. In 1956 for instance it was possible for B.M.C. to dismiss 6,000 workers with only three days' notice, and only after a strike did the management agree to make payments 'in lieu of longer notice', of one week's wages for men with between three and ten years' service and two weeks' for those with ten or more (Kahn, 1964). In the late fifties and early sixties there was an extension of private arrangements covering various aspects of the redundancy situation. The nationalized industries led the way in this. Perhaps the most elaborate and generous, in terms both of length of notice and financial assistance, was the Redundancy Agreement signed between the Railways Board and the Trade Unions in 1962. In the private sector the adoption of policies appears, usually, to have been the result of management initiative. By 1964 it is estimated that altogether 23 per cent of the employed population was covered by some arrangement for severance pay for redundancy, although the terms of the coverage varied widely.

This was the background to three major pieces of legislation within three years. First, in 1963, came the Contracts of Employment Act laying down minimum periods of notice of dismissal, which vary according to length of service. The maximum is four weeks' notice for employees with five years' or more service. Then in 1965 came the Redundancy Payments Act. Workers with a minimum of two years' service who are over the age of 18 and below the age of 65 are entitled to redundancy payments when dismissed. These are calculated on the basis of one and a half weeks' pay for each year of employment in which the employee was not below the age of 41; one week's pay for each year in which the employee was between the age of 22 and 41; and one half a week's pay for each year in which the employee was below the age of 22. The maximum total period of service to be taken into account for these calculations is twenty years and the maximum amount of a week's pay is £40. The maximum possible payment, therefore, is £1,200. Employers are able to claim rebates for any redundancy payments they may make, from a Redundancy Fund set up by the Act and financed by a levy on employers. These rebates also vary according to the age of the worker, with the general effect that the employer gets back two thirds of any payment he makes in rebate. Finally, in 1966 the third piece of legislation introduced wage-related unemployment benefits. These are payable as supplements equal to approximately one third of the amount of that portion of a worker's average weekly earnings which lie between £9 and £30. They are payable for up to six months of unemployment, in addition to flat-rate benefits including increases for dependents. The total payment is subject to a maximum of 85 per cent of average earnings.

It is interesting to note that on the issue of redundancy pay the pace was certainly set in Britain by the government itself. It acted, at the time, in the face of a marked lack of enthusiasm from both the trade unions and employers' organizations, who were agreed that priority should be given to wage-related unemployment benefits. When the legislation was first drafted, however, the trade-union opposition not unnaturally disappeared, since it offered substantial financial advantage to many workers. But on both sides there was also some apprehension about the consequences of departure from the traditional position of no legal interference with the terms of the employment contract.

The gap between the British and European position in the general area of dismissal is now considerably narrowed. It is, however, still more common, on the continent, for there to be some control over the principles by which workers are to be selected for dismissal. It is also more likely that there will be established principles requiring consultation with workers' representatives in the case of large-scale dismissals. These principles may be established by statute or by collective agreement between employers' associations and trade unions. But the only country which has, so far, even approached British practice on redundancy payments is Sweden, where in 1964 the employers and trade unions agreed to establish a fund out of which severance payments should be made. In the United States there is very little legislation, but provisions concerning length of notice, the selection of workers to be dismissed or retired, and entitlement to severance pay have increasingly figured in collective agreements over the last few years (Shultz and Weber, 1966). These agreements still cover a minority of the working population, however.

THE PHILOSOPHY BEHIND THE LEGISLATION AND ITS EFFECT

A number of factors have contributed to the change of scene in Britain. First, against a background of generally full employment, large-scale dismissals appeared all the more shocking when they did occur, and the need for measures to protect the workers appeared all the more urgent. Second, the discussions about British entry into the Common Market made many people aware, for the first time, of European practice. But the main emphasis in the discussions was placed upon the fact that in a dynamic economy in which there was a high rate of technical advance, job-changing was also inevitable. Policy must therefore aim at reducing the opposition to such change, indeed at facilitating it, at the same time as minimizing hardship for the individual. What evidence, then, is there that present policies succeed in doing this, and indeed are directed to the right areas?

First there is the question of notice. All the studies of redundancy that have been made in Britain, and elsewhere, point to the value of prior notice of dismissal and warning of impending change. Given the availability of other jobs a reasonable period of notice enables the worker to look around for alternative employment and frequently to find another job which he can move to immediately. There is then no waste of resources through idle labour and the worker does not suffer a loss of income through unemployment. The provisions of the Contracts of Employment Act in respect of length of notice are not particularly generous. The Railway Redundancy Agreement in 1962 had already laid down a minimum period of six weeks' personal notice for men with four years' service or more. More important, every effort was made to give much longer warning of the impending closure of a workshop, and a minimum of six months' general notice of intention to close was written into the agreement. In a period of two years the labour force in the workshops was reduced by 18,000. Nearly half of these men left to go to other employment, before their personal notice was received or expired, because they had plenty of time to look around.

It is sometimes argued by management that the necessity to give long notice is embarrassing. Not only does it reveal information to competitors, but, by encouraging voluntary leaving, the best workers go first, or production is disrupted because certain key personnel leave. Such difficulties can be exaggerated. One company in Britain has recently relied entirely upon voluntary leaving, induced by an offer of financial compensation, to achieve a fairly substantial reduction in the labour force. Where difficulties do arise they can be minimized, as we shall see later, by long-term planning within the enterprise.

One interesting problem arises when compensation for dismissal is to be paid. If entitlement to such money is tied strictly to formal notice this may discourage workers from taking advantage of any early warning of impending closure or dismissal to leave for other work. Some employers are already claiming that this is one of the disadvantages of the Redundancy Payments Act. Employees, they say, are encouraged to 'wait around' until formal dismissal. Certainly to qualify for redundancy payment under the 1965 Act the employee has to be 'dismissed' within the meaning of the Act. A worker who receives informal warning that notice will be given to him some time in the future may well choose to leave at an earlier date if a good job comes along; and then he will not be 'dismissed' at all and the impending redundancy will not qualify him for a payment under the Act.

Appeals under the Act are referred in the first place to the

Industrial Tribunals, but appeals on points of law go to the High Court. There have already been at least two almost conflicting approaches to the problem of early leaving. In one case a worker who was told that the works would move by a specific date found himself another job and left with the agreement of the firm before he received his formal notice. The Tribunal decided that he was entitled to a redundancy payment (Overhill v. Alfred Cox (Production)). In another case a foreman was told that his services would not be needed in the future because of reorganization of the works involving the closure of his department at some unspecified date in the future. He also left and found another job, and the Industrial Tribunal awarded him a payment. But on appeal to the High Court this was reversed as being wrong in law; he had not been 'dismissed' (Morton Sundour Fabrics v. Shaw). From management's point of view, linking the right to redundancy pay strictly to the giving of a dismissal notice can be a means of controlling more precisely which workers leave and when. From the long-service employee's point of view, however, the advantages of long warning are seriously diminished if the legalistic approach of the High Court is maintained.

The evidence from the case-studies of redundancy suggests that, given notice of at least four or six weeks and given a low general level of unemployment of one to one and a half per cent, then about 80 per cent of dismissed workers are likely to find their way immediately to new jobs. With the general level of unemployment above 2 per cent the picture changes considerably (Wedderburn, 1965). It changes, too, if the labour force affected is above average age. The major employment problem which emerged from the railway workshop study was that of the older men. Their difficulties, too, are reflected in the fact that, when unemployment is 2 per cent or below, between a quarter and a third of all the wholly unemployed persons on the registers of the employment exchanges in this country are aged 55 and over. In a special inquiry into the characteristics of the unemployed, undertaken in October 1964, the Ministry of Labour estimated that 61 per cent of the unemployed aged 55 and over were difficult to place because of their age (Ministry of Labour, 1966). The difficulties of re-employing the older worker are not confined to Britain, and almost certainly require the development of special policies to deal with the problem (Sobel and Wilcock, 1966). Retraining programmes for older workers are discussed later in this volume. Other measures to be considered are the adaptation of industrial tasks to fit the capabilities of the older worker and the development of special employment services. Apart from special groups of this kind, however, we can conclude that legislation to impose minimum periods of notice goes some way to protect workers and to facilitate their shift from one job to another with the minimum of economic loss.

It was principally in relation to financial compensation as embodied in the Redundancy Payments Act, however, that the philosophy of encouraging mobility and of reducing resistance to change was most fully developed: 'A major impediment to industrial mobility is the natural resistance of workers to change, especially change involving redundancy. To reduce the fear of redundancy and mitigate the financial hardship it can bring, the Government has introduced statutory redundancy payments and earnings related supplements to unemployment benefit'. (Ministry of Labour, 1966). There are three distinct strands in the argument.

First, that compensation for loss of job will minimize financial hardship; second, that it will reduce workers' opposition to change; third, that it is 'required' to compensate a worker for the 'property rights' which he develops in a job.

Let us examine these in turn. Take the first point – the minimization of hardship. Any extra money made available to a man who is about to be unemployed is likely to 'minimize hardship'. Redundancy payments, however, are available not only to men who will be unemployed, but also to those who move straight to another job. It is, therefore, an indiscriminate way of minimizing hardship. It was interesting to find that the Railways Board approach, of splitting financial compensation into two parts, a lump-sum compensation for all who qualified, and an additional continuing supplement to unemployment benefit for those who remained unemployed after they left the workshops, was much appreciated by the men. They recognized that unemployment was the real burden. The lump sum was important psychologically for softening the blow of dismissal. But fears were expressed about the temptations of 'blueing' a lump sum, especially when people had to assess, for themselves, the probabilities of remaining unemployed. On these grounds, of minimizing hardship, alone, therefore, using available resources to maximize unemployment benefit would be the most effective method, with one possible exception. A lump sum may assist the man who, even though he goes immediately to another job, has to move house and incurs expenses in this way.

On the second point, there is little evidence that lump-sum compensation for the loss of job reduces worker opposition in general to dismissal. Workers' attitudes to change, and in particular to change which involves a reduction in the labour force, are shaped by many complex factors. Important among them are the general state of employment, the prospects for the industry as a whole, the traditions of worker militancy, etc. (Touraine *et al.*, 1965). If, for instance, there does exist, within the industry affected by redundancy, a strong fear that new jobs will not be available, and a tradition of trade-union action, it is most unlikely that the existence of redundancy payments will prevent, say, a strike against the decision to dismiss workers. The motor-car industry contraction in the autumn of 1966, after the Redundancy Payments Act came into force, produced a great deal of worker opposition. As for positively encouraging the mobility of labour, this can scarcely operate by influencing the workers' behaviour, through his entitlement to payment, since, as we have seen, a redundancy payment is only due when the worker is quitting his job involuntarily, that is when he has already been dismissed. It might, of course, induce management to dismiss workers more easily and there has been some indication that this is so. But, for those workers not threatened with dismissal, the linking of redundancy payments to length of service and to a narrow legalistic concept of 'dismissal' may positively work in the opposite direction. Voluntary moves may well be discouraged for fear of losing entitlement to redundancy pay.

The third strand in the case for redundancy payments is the notion of compensating a worker for the loss of the property rights which he has acquired in his job. As the Minister of Labour said in the debate on the Redundancy Payments Bill '. . . *The Times* said in a recent leader commenting on the Bill, "a man has some rights in his job just as an employer holds rights in his property, and his rights gain in value with the years". I would say to the House that if a man is deprived of those rights by economic circumstances outside his control he ought to be compensated. . . .' (*Hansard*, 26 April 1965). He then went on to speak of the need to compensate for loss of security, possible loss of earnings, fringe benefits, and for anxiety. The division between these aspects of job change and 'hardship' is not a hard and fast one. Loss of earnings and fringe benefits are an aspect of 'hardship'. But – more important – it seems possible that the recognition of such property rights may actually increase inflexibility of labour, and strengthen opposition to change of a less dramatic kind than that involved in the loss of a job.

If a man is to be compensated for the loss of a job arising from dismissal it is but a small extension of this principle to include the notion that he should also be compensated for a change of job with the same employer, should that change bring loss of earnings or status. Indeed that is almost the present implication of the Redundancy Payments Act. As the legislation stands, if the change of job is such that the employer terminates one contract of employment by notice of dismissal and offers a contract for another job, which is refused, the worker is not then entitled to a redundancy payment provided that the offer constitutes an offer of employment 'suitable to the employee' which the employee has 'unreasonably' refused. As might be expected, however, the interpretation of 'suitable' has given rise to many cases before the Industrial Tribunals. Some of the decisions which have emerged appear almost conflicting. Thus, in some cases, loss of opportunity for overtime has been deemed to make a job unsuitable, in others it was not considered a material factor. In some cases extra travelling time has been deemed to make the job unsuitable, in others not, although in these cases the tribunals have frequently, in reaching their decision, given a lot of weight to the domestic circumstances of the individual (especially to the opposition to change by the wife, or adverse effect on children's schooling, etc.). In yet other cases a marked change of status for the employee has been deemed to make the offer unsuitable. It is rather early to judge the total effect of such decisions, particularly since very few appeals have been heard in the High Court. But it seems every bit as likely that they will contribute to strengthening a tendency towards immobility – that is an unwillingness for workers to move both geographically and occupationally – as that they will contribute to increased mobility.

THE WORKINGS OF THE LABOUR MARKET

The redundancy policy we have discussed so far, therefore, despite claims made for it, has been more successfully directed to dealing with hardship than to encouraging desirable mobility. But here it must be stressed that even from the viewpoint of economic efficiency labour mobility is not an end in itself. Indeed, as many employers concerned with problems of labour turnover know only too well, it has many disadvantages. 'Desirable mobility' therefore must be defined as that mobility which achieves the economic objective of redistributing labour forces to more valuable economic activities. At this point it is important to examine the redundancy problems against the background of the functioning of the labour market. First of all the case studies referred to above have shown that, when labour is dismissed, the process by which it is reallocated to new jobs and industries is an extremely random one. There is no mechanism which can guarantee that labour from a contracting industry moves into those sectors of the economy where, on grounds of economic efficiency, more labour is needed.

Although a half to three quarters of dismissed workers in these case studies turned to the Ministry of Labour Employment Exchanges for help in finding new jobs, only about one in ten was successfully re-employed through this channel. The vast majority relied upon their own efforts, or upon a network of family and friends. For manual workers in particular, the area in which they sought jobs and their conception of job possibilities has been shown to be extremely limited. Partly as a result of the position revealed by this research the Ministry has recently been taking some steps to improve the functioning of the employment exchanges. There have been steps to improve staffing in order to increase the information available in the exchanges about local industries and occupations, and to improve contact with the medium and small firms which frequently had no contact at all with the local office; and an occupational guidance scheme for adults has been introduced on an experimental basis. But in the first place, these steps are limited; in the second place, they do not put the exchanges in a strong position to help in the purposive redistribution of labour as we have defined it above, when they are faced with an unemployed worker. Again the case studies have shown that, whether looking for jobs by their own methods or through the labour exchanges, men made redundant want work; first and foremostly they want 'a job'. If they can exercise any choice they will be concerned with earnings; and not so much in the sense of looking around for the highest-paying firm, for, as many railway workshop men said, 'money isn't everything', but rather with a notion of a minimum acceptable level of pay below which they will be reluctant to fall (Wedderburn, 1965). Secondly they will look for work similar to the work they have been used to doing, consistent with their skill and experience and judged to be interesting. Thirdly they will look for security and good working conditions. But having found a job which satisfies even some of these requirements it will not matter to them whether, for instance, it is in a manufacturing or a service industry, and certainly not whether the industry exports or not.

Indeed, by concentrating on redundancy as a mechanism for reallocating labour, there may be a danger of concentrating on a relatively small and unimportant part of the total mechanism of change in the labour market. This is still an area where more research, particularly by social scientists, is badly needed. But we do know that voluntary job-changing far outweighs involuntary job-changing. Moreover voluntary job-changing is directly related to the general level of employment. The higher it is and the more secure people feel generally about their prospects of having some sort of a job, the more they will be influenced by other aspects of job satisfaction (such as the level of pay, the kind of work, etc.) to seek out the best that they can do for themselves (O.E.C.D., 1965).

Even less is known, however, about how workers come to

change their occupation or industry, because many job changes will simply represent a change of employer, not necessarily a change of occupation or industry. How can the expanding and economically important industries attract labour? There is still a good deal of disagreement about the precise role of earnings differentials between industries and occupations in achieving movements of labour. It has been suggested, for instance, that the earnings structure is more important in terms of retaining labour, or in impelling it to move, than in attracting it to specific activities (O.E.C.D., 1965). Certainly the evidence we have at the moment suggests that the intake of new entrants to the labour force from among school leavers, or from women re-entering the labour force, is likely to be a more important mechanism for achieving shifts in the distribution of the total labour force than any reallocation through redundancy.

In such studies as have been made of the labour market we are still the victims of the fact that the available statistics measure only shifts of labour between very broad industry and occupational groups (O.E.C.D., 1965). Moreover, important redistribution of labour can take place without any change of employer. Diversification of the activities of the individual firm, and shifts in the allocation and usage of labour within it, can be economically of great significance. In the present state of statistical knowledge, however, such changes are much more difficult to document. But the fact that they occur re-emphasizes the importance of seeing redundancy policy as only one aspect of the total manpower policy both of the individual enterprise and of government.

GENERAL MANPOWER PLANNING

Some of the most far-reaching examples of industrial change occur within a given enterprise and without redundancy. A recent study of twenty-nine examples of major change at the enterprise level, occurring over the last ten years in eight different countries, showed that although in twenty cases there were overall reductions in the labour force, in only eight of them did dismissals take place. This was to a large extent due to the fact that some kind of manpower planning methods, however elementary, were used, which enabled the firm to forecast labour requirements and to take steps to meet them (Wedderburn, 1968).

Early identification of change and of the need for a cutback in labour means that a firm or organization may be able to use natural wastage to reduce its labour force. This is particularly true if the labour force contains a relatively high proportion of older workers approaching retirement age, or of women workers, whose labour turnover is high.

The introduction of automation into offices has resulted, for instance, in a relatively small amount of dislocation of the existing labour force, both because clerical workers affected are often women, and because the changeover has taken some time. Thus, by ceasing to recruit labour, the necessary total reduction in manpower has been achieved (Ministry of Labour, 1965). The rundown in the labour force in the coal industry in Britain over recent years has also been facilitated by a relatively high wastage rate (O.E.C.D., 1967).

Another way in which change can take place, and manpower can be reallocated, is by transfer within an organization. Such transfer has two aspects, the first geographical, the second occupational. Geographical transfer is the most difficult to achieve, particularly among manual workers. Even where housing is made available and some financial assistance is offered, only a minority of workers are likely to move (Fox, 1965). Occupational transfer is likely to be more successful. Large organizations have a particular advantage here. It is more likely in such an enterprise that there will be a diversity of interests not all of which will be contracting at the same time. The successful use of transfer programmes demands a full knowledge of the trends in labour requirements of the total organization, as well as information about the skills of the workers being released and the nature of the jobs becoming available. It requires manpower budgets of a detailed kind. But even in such cases transfer may rely, to a very large extent, for success upon the willingness of firms to develop retraining and training programmes.

Training and retraining become, in fact, a major part of any manpower planning policy both inside and outside the individual enterprise. The Government has stressed its own responsibilities in this direction recently. An expansion of the number and capacity of government training centres for skilled crafts has been announced. As a result of these proposals the number of places in government training centres will be approaching 10,000 by the end of 1968. With six-month courses this will represent an annual output of 20,000. This is still a small number of places in relation both to the known numbers of long-term unemployed and to the known number of individuals affected by redundancy (48,259 payments were made in the first six months of operation of the Redundancy Payments Act). It would be foolish to imagine that all workers who become redundant require retraining, but the number of places is also small in relation to estimates of the likely future requirements of skilled manpower (Leicester, 1963). With the passage of the Industrial Training Act 1964 the government has sought to encourage the development of training programmes within industry. This Act establishes training boards with powers to impose a financial levy upon all employers within an industry. From the fund so established grants will be made to those employers undertaking approved training schemes. The Government itself has also recently announced its willingness to make grants towards the capital cost of setting up additional places in training centres or bays run by employers and other assistance to firms in development areas. Training within industry is important not only for handling situations of change and the transfer of labour, but also for dealing with new recruits to the industry.

All of this activity is to be welcomed. At the same time social science research suggests that for the success of such programmes careful attention must be paid to practical matters, such as the remuneration of the worker while undergoing training, and to the development of positive attitudes towards training and retraining (Wedderburn, 1965; Belbin, 1965). Ironically, once a man is made redundant it may be more difficult to interest him in retraining than if he can retrain with his existing employer. As the government training centres are placed at the moment there can be no guarantee of another job for a trainee once he has completed his course and he may well feel he will be letting the best jobs go while he is retraining. But when retraining with the same employer, a worker will feel much more secure, arguing that his employer would not invest in him if he was going to be dismissed in a short time. There is also the problem of the level of the weekly payments received during retraining at such centres. The position is much improved now that earnings-related supplements are payable on the same basis as unemployment benefits. Once again, however, when retraining with the same employer a drop in pay may be avoided because of the operation of a guarantee of earnings. Finally, morale tends to be lower after a man has been dismissed and the loss of his job may make him doubt his own abilities.

Redundancy then, and the policies developed for the handling of redundancy, are but one aspect of a total manpower policy. At national level we require first more information about what labour is needed and where; and second, to know what are the influences at present operating on the allocation of labour. But in order to obtain some, at least, of this information, more information is required from the individual enterprise, some of which is not obviously and readily available. This could be made available as a by-product of manpower planning.

Sometimes manpower planning at the level of the firm is regarded with scepticism because future estimates of manpower requirements will always be subject to a margin of error and are likely to be upset radically by major changes in the market situation. But an important first step on the road to manpower planning for many firms is still an inventory of the use of existing manpower both in terms of quantity and quality. Not knowing what is happening at the moment makes it that much more difficult to assess the implications of a given technical or administrative change in terms of manpower requirements for the future. Such assessments, moreover, need to be a continuing operation even when no major change is contemplated. Failure to prepare and to plan ahead is an important element contributing, in many cases, to the creation of redundancy situations. Time is of the essence of some of the techniques, like wastage, transfer, and retraining, which are alternatives to dismissals.

Ideally the net needs to be cast wider than this. Assessments of future labour requirements are subject to margins of error because, for instance, of the difficulties of predicting future demand. But we still find situations where certain kinds of technical or organizational change, the scope of which it is possible to know, are decided upon by management without any consideration of their manpower implications. The notion that these implications must be taken into account at the stage when the technical decisions are made is a simple one, but one which should pay many dividends.

This raises a final question. What should be the role played by worker consultation in the handling of manpower changes? As we pointed out earlier, some European countries have statutory or collectively agreed duties, laid upon employers, to consult with workers' representatives when mass dismissals are envisaged. In Sweden the duty is broader than this, and where a works council exists, the employer has to inform it of important changes in production or new methods of work. In this country there is no such general provision, but some trade unions have recently pressed for more consultation (for instance, the Amalgamated Engineering Union in their evidence to the Royal Commission on Trade Unions and Employers' Association). Such consultation is not a panacea. It will not remove all opposition to proposed changes on the part of workers, particularly if these changes do include dismissals. But it is an important element in creating a positive attitude to change and certainly important in minimizing hardships for the workers affected. If this is the case there can be little doubt that the establishment of continuous manpower planning, as suggested above, facilitates consultation with workers' representatives, because it is then possible to communicate the firm results of this budgeting to workers' representatives at an early stage (Wedderburn, 1968). What social science research suggests is needed is not novelty in euphemism – 'redundancy', 'redeployment' or 'shake-out' – but more manpower planning and worker consultation.

CHAPTER 4

The Misuse of Professional Manpower

DENIS PYM

ONE of the more widely recommended solutions to Britain's economic problems is that we should follow the example of industrially successful countries like the U.S.A., Russia, and Canada and increase the flow of highly qualified personnel into the economy. It is taken for granted that employers for their part will be ready to make the fullest possible use of these additional skills, but is this in fact true? Although the numbers of scientific and technical manpower have been increasing by an average of 7 per cent *per annum* for the past decade, there has been no corresponding increase in industrial production. There are today approximately one and a quarter million people who have qualifications in higher education at work in the United Kingdom, probably one half of them employed in industry. How well do we use their talents and, if the answers are not favourable, why are they not? These are the questions which interest us here.

Our point of departure is to dispute the widely held assumption among manpower planners that their function is to manipulate supply variables like education and vocational training to meet given labour requirements. The neglect of the demand feature is explained, but not excused, by the difficulty of obtaining information about utilization and the effects of innovation on industry's estimated requirements. Nevertheless, the dangers of such a course, as William Allen (1966) tells us, must be underlined. If we manipulate the supply variables without adequately controlling demand, all we do is perpetuate our misuse of manpower. The weaknesses of current thinking in this field are well illustrated in two recent reports of the Committee on Manpower Resources for Science and Technology (1966). These reports make much of two things, the reluctance of scientists and technologists to take jobs in industry and the seriousness of the gap between forecasts for future demand and the likely supply. Most of the remedies proposed involve changing the attitudes of students and teachers to industry. There has been no suggestion that professional people might have sound reasons for not seeking employment in industry. Moreover, though reference to the question of utilization was made in both the reports outlined above, it was not considered sufficiently important to warrant investigation.

We will begin this chapter with an analysis of attitudes to science and technology before turning to the major purposes, which are to draw attention to the misuse of professional personnel in industry and to explore some internal features of industrial organization related to this problem. We will be considering the question of misuse in conjunction with that of technical change, for their interdependence cannot be ignored. Technical change provides a basis for uncertainty in the formulation of manning requirements and in this context social factors, in which we are interested in this chapter, can assume considerable significance. Utilization and innovation are two key variables in the demand for skill and we are interested in them both.

HISTORICAL AND SOCIAL PERSPECTIVE

It is reasonable to assume that the predicament of the professional employee in industry will be linked with his status in society. The evidence, which we have only limited space to present, suggests that attitudes to science and technology in our cultural milieu savour at best of indifference and at worst of hostility.

To develop this argument let us begin with the technical expansion of the eighteenth century, when we find religious factors interwoven with the development of both science and capitalism. The importance of these bonds are shown by Goldsmith (1963), who reports evidence that 'between 1750 and 1900 a Quaker, or a person of Quaker descent, had thirty times more chance of being elected a Fellow of the Royal Society than a non-Quaker'. During the early part of this period no dissenters were permitted to enter English universities. Science, in one sense, was condemned by association. This condition carried into the nineteenth century when, as Cardwell (1962) observes, the roles of scholarship and science were hardly considered at all. Though science forced its way into all the major educational institutions during the course of the nineteenth century, Goldsmith relates, 'technology like an errant child was left in the care of the "lower classes" – the labourers, the craftsmen and the technicians'. Even as late as 1931, Miall could lament the neglect of science: 'What minister in Great Britain ever attempted to cherish the sciences or to reward those who cultivate them with success? If we except Mr Montague, who procured the place of Master of the Mint for Isaac Newton, I know of no one.'

Recently, Ben-David (1962) has conducted a searching analysis of the factors contributing to the rate of development of science in the major western powers between 1800 and 1929. The growing supremacy of first German and then American science he attributes to a higher regard for educational institutions than was shown in France and Britain. Whereas Germany favoured professionalism and awarded research chairs to outstanding scientists during the nineteenth century, Britain and France encouraged the dominance of the amateur and awarded university chairs to older people who were frequently aided by substantial private means. Ben-David notes that the effects of a non-competitive and centralized system of education were achieved in Britain 'through the more subtle functions of a class system in which academic people were kept in their place through internalized traditions and a network of semi-formalized bonds among persons, groups and independent organizations'. Goldsmith (1963) puts it more bluntly: 'The Establishment demonstrated how it could meet challenges to its rules by enclosing the scientist within university ivory towers, there to procreate the specialist, a snob unsullied by the materialistic world.' This comment leads us to ponder the role of education in the misuse of talent. We recognize the importance of education in increasing the supply of professional manpower but we should not discount its influence on demand. If, as industrialists are apt to claim, professionals are frequently unable to adapt themselves to problems outside the narrow limits of their specialization then the more heterogeneous or interdisciplinary in nature the questions set the professional the more likely he will be misused. One of the culprits in this case would be an educational system which does not develop adaptability. More of this towards the end of the chapter.

Returning to the contemporary scene, in broad perspective, we observe again the neglect of science in spite of the fact that British scientific and engineering successes are second to none. Since the last war, for example, our scientists have been awarded significantly more Nobel prizes per head of the population than the scientists of any other leading nation. In patents of invention, the first step towards the commercialization of new developments, our performance, on a *per capita* basis, is less distinguished. We fall well behind Germany. The downward trend through the manufacturing cycle of development, production, and marketing is well known to us all. Along with the basic deficiencies of our industrial machine runs a continuing underestimation of what scientists and professionals can do. It has cost Britain dearly, as the following examples show.

In 1920 Fleming discovered penicillin and, after its development by Florey and Chain, British companies went into production of the drug, unsure of its commercial value, using relatively primitive means. At the same time American firms sought more effective ways of producing penicillin and evolved the deep-freeze fermentation process. Subsequently British concerns found themselves having to buy licensing rights from the Americans to produce the drug.

Again in the early 1950s Britain was abreast of the U.S.A. in the development of data-processing techniques, largely through the efforts of the Cambridge University Mathematics Departments and the researches of F. C. Williams at Manchester University. Many firms began by dabbling in the new field; few saw its real potential. Until almost too late, the government did not think to help the electronics industry rationalize itself or find a market for its products.

The aircraft industry provides yet another example of wasted inventions and opportunities. The successes of British aircraft designers and engineers include an impressive list – the jet engine, short-run and vertical take-off aircraft, variable-geometry aircraft and the hovercraft. Yet today the industry faces a decline which, according to speeches reported in the Parliamentary

Debates of the 9 February 1965, is due to a combination of disasters, poor administration, uncompetitive prices, and inferior selling methods.

It could be argued that the Second World War was the first occasion in the country's history in which scientists were able to play a part in decisions of consequence. Industry was to benefit afterwards. The success of Mountbatten's 'freakish sideline' Combined Operations with scientists Bernal and Zuckerman, and the success of the 'Sunday Soviets', which brought the scientists of Telecommunications Research and senior Royal Air Force officers together, were the kinds of exceptions which prove the rule. Only at a time when the nation's survival was in the balance was society prepared to allow scientists the freedom of action and access to the decision-makers which are necessary for them to make their full contribution.

In summary, we have noted several recurring features within the social *milieu* which appear to have set limits on the development of science in Britain. Since its beginnings, it has endured limited support from the state and some degree of antipathy from the ruling classes. As a consequence, scientists and their ideas have been relatively undervalued by society.

DIFFICULTIES AND DISTASTES OF WORK

If the unfavourable attitudes to science observed in society carry into the internal order of industry, as we might expect them to do, then we would predict that industrial organization sets severe constraints on its scientific and professional manpower. These we expect to take the form of limiting the scientist's and engineer's responsibility and authority and preventing them exploring and using their talents and skills to the full.

To test this argument a postal survey was conducted among members of the Royal Institute of Chemistry and the Chemical Society engaged in research and development (Pym, 1964). One of the questions invited respondents to list the difficulties and distastes of their jobs, if they had any, which they felt hindered their effective performance. The results are summarized in Figure 1.

There are marked differences between chemists employed in industry and those in education. Furthermore, the results of the inquiry showed chemists in industry to be less satisfied with their conditions of employment than their counterparts in education and government. Features of organization and control are further broken down into such things as: insufficient responsibility, lack

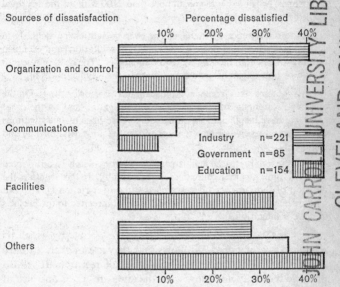

Figure 1. Dissatisfactions among chemists in research and development by employer (n = 460)

of long-term research policy and aims, interference by non-technical personnel, 'politics', too much pressure for results, and inadequacies in the structure of the organization. The extent of these constraints on work performance can be gauged by the fact that they average one for every chemist in the industrial sample.

Let us enlarge on two of the most frequent dissatisfactions with a few quotations from chemists in this study.

Many people consider a scientist to be vague, living in an ivory tower and therefore not fit to be entrusted with practical matters ... supply of equipment, staff recruiting, finance, organization etc. I find frequently that I get a response which implies yes, you may be the Laboratory Manager, but you are still a scientist and so we will do this for you as you are not really capable of such practical matters.

... Although our research manager is responsible for a total staff of 250 people, he is unable to spend more than £100 without the approval of the board. ...

... the interference by management over trivialities, particularly in small things such as interdepartmental consultation and detailed ordering of essential day-to-day requirements. ... The head of research should be able to run his own department in the way he thinks fit.

My problems stem from a combination of two shortcomings. On the one hand we pursue too many lines of investigation and on the other hand, we have insufficient say in deciding those lines of investigations which should receive prior attention and in the allocation of time and resources.

In commercial research departments, a scheme is likely to be adopted only if it fulfils a basic requirement of profitability. In these matters the decision of the Director of Research is often over-ridden by a Board whose scientific knowledge is extremely low or unrelated to the projects under consideration.

Now if the research laboratory lacks the autonomy which its scientists say they need, it follows that they are unlikely to have much say in determining the objectives of research. It is also possible they may not know what the aims are. Over one fifth of this sample claims that their company appears to have no long-term research policy.

My effective performance is severely limited by the lack of a sound research policy in the Company for which I work. ...

... an attempt is required to define the major problems which our institute might attempt to solve. We don't really know what the practical problems of the industry are.

I am not fully occupied. As I am not informed about the Company's plans I find it difficult to choose problems on which to work. None of my colleagues are fully occupied and a general feeling of dissatisfaction exists in the research department.

The Company is looking for quick returns on its research expenditure and this attitude tends towards short-term, poor-quality development work. Research programmes are revised, discontinued, revived far too haphazardly and too frequently for systematic well-planned research to thrive.

From this study we are able to gain some insight into the problems facing professional employees and into their relevance to misuse. For example, it is evident that the organizational structures imposed upon research and development units are frequently inappropriate, at least from the scientist's point of view. Complaints about 'lack of responsibility' and 'interference by outsiders' also suggest that executive managers in charge of research ventures may lack confidence in themselves and their scientists; a point we will return to later. The evidence also indicates a good deal of underemployment, but it would be difficult to estimate the numbers and the extent of the problem. In all this we face difficulty in interpreting the information. It is widely recognized that the values scientists bring to their work can conflict with those of industrial management, so exaggerating the problems.

In order to obtain more precise information about the 'misuse of skills', the author, in conjunction with Hilary Graham at Birkbeck College, conducted another inquiry. On this occasion a sample of 1,000 members of the Institute of Mechanical Engineers was sent a postal questionnaire. As a body mechanical engineers are rather different from chemists, particularly in experience. Most are employed in industry, and only a minority has been to university. They have a stronger grounding in industrial life. One of the questions in the form invited them to check off from a list of items those that they felt caused them greatest dissatisfaction. The relevant answers are shown below, and support our earlier observations.

There is some degree of overlap between the three items in Figure 2 (correlations ranging from ·21 to ·41) which justifies labelling them as indicators of misuse. Although we hear regularly about the shortage of mechanical engineers in the United Kingdom, 52 per cent of this sample complain that their skills are not fully utilized. Before progressing with our explorations and explanations there are two important questions to answer: how accurate are these figures, and do they matter?

In the Mechanical Engineers project we interviewed on the job more than seventy men in fourteen firms, and the results fit with the findings in Figure 2. Although the sample represents a response rate of only 55 per cent – the dissatisfied engineers could be over-represented – the fact remains that 72 per cent of the respondents checked at least one of the three distastes. A series of case studies conducted among professional personnel in firms in the chemical, electronics, and petroleum industries provide corroborating

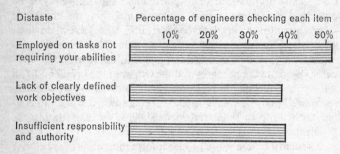

Figure 2. The misuse of mechanical engineers (n = 550)

evidence. In these investigations, with high questionnaire return rates, between 27 and 76 per cent of professional personnel claim to be 'employed on tasks not requiring their skills and abilities'. The most favourable results come from a subsidiary of an American Company. The mean for all inquiries is just below 50 per cent complaining that their talents are not fully used.

Work dissatisfactions are important to the individual reporting them, but they assume more significant proportions if they are associated with poor work performance. Let us assume that effectiveness has two facets, the respondent's desire to remain with his present employer and his desire to work differentially on the job. Taking the former first, we find that the three items of misuse in Figure 2 are closely related to professional employees' intentions 'to leave their present employer'; the first two items are nearly always more important than any other dissatisfactions, including poor remuneration. With respect to performance on the job, numerous studies here and in the United States (e.g. Pelz, 1957; Herzberg, 1966; and Pym, 1966) show that employees who aspire most strongly for the opportunity to explore fully their skills and abilities and to exercise control over their jobs are numbered among the most competent. Jobs which deny employees these opportunities may be said to be limiting their effective performance. From our studies we conclude that the under-utilization of professional skills reaches considerable proportions and has serious consequences.

UTILIZATION AND INNOVATION

Before moving to a detailed consideration of the problem and ways of dealing with it, let us make quite clear what we mean by utilization and innovation and how they are interdependent.

We will take the word 'utilization' to refer to the adequacy of the fit between the demands of the job and the skills of the incumbent, assuming that the job is necessary in the first place. Skills and their differences can be calculated with respect to their levels and types. For example, a scientist may be *underemployed* on work below his skills and experience if he has to devote a high proportion of his time to routine laboratory testing or clerical work which therefore interferes with his effective performance. Linked with the level of skill is the amount of choice or discretion the individual can exercise over his work. A scientist will be under-utilized if he has little or no discretion over what he does and how he does it. In many ways this question of influence is more closely related to what we want or don't want in a job rather than our capacity to do it, but, for the sake of simplicity, we will take the term skill to cover both. Now a professional man can also be *misemployed* if he is engaged on tasks which require professional expertise other than his own particular type. These are then two quite different problems in the study of misuse. *Under*employment is obviously industry's responsibility, while *mis*employment is partly industry's problem though, as we have already noted, it may also reflect deficiencies in an educational system which has failed to develop versatility in highly educated people. The misuse of manpower therefore has two facets in the context in which we are considering it, underemployment and misemployment. Our interests are primarily in the former.

The term innovation is used in the broadest sense. It includes industrial changes which vary from the 'single event' such as the installation of a new piece of machinery to the continual and rapid evolution of new technical systems and consequent social reorganizations. The role of the professional employee in these situations varies from the originator of the change to the operator of the new work-process. Many new ventures appear to call for the recruitment of professional manpower and it is widely recognized by students of manpower that technical change increases the demand for higher-order skills, while decreasing the opportunities for the unskilled. The weakness in our thinking about the increasing need for higher-level skills is to assume that this effect is due entirely to the technical aspects of innovations. Technical changes do not take place in a vacuum. Yet as far as we know, no serious attempt has been made to estimate the extent to which associated social and human factors interact with the technical requirements to exaggerate and shift demand. One such variable is our concern for *prestige*.

There are interesting similarities between innovations and the projective techniques some psychologists use to study personality. The essence of both is a lack of structure. Their ambiguity is an ideal situation into which we can project our hopes and fears. In this context, the concern for prestige often influences our calculations in staffing. By prestige we mean the desire to impress colleagues or competitors for the purpose of enhancing our reputations. Its influence on recruiting is double-edged; it can lead to a gathering together of talented people which could pave the way to industrial successes, or, and more probably in view of the present predicament of the professional, it can lead to great waste. Though we have no documented evidence to substantiate the claim that the concern for prestige is a factor in misuse we cannot ignore the abundance of anecdotal evidence. How else can we explain the decision of Company X to recruit five doctoral scientists to investigate the corrosive properties of selected materials, work which in the event turned out to be mostly routine testing? How else can we explain the almost inevitable raising of entry standards which follows the setting up of a new training establishment, when logically we might expect standards to be dropped? How else can we explain this curious annual ritual in which personnel men, academics, and graduates take part in a kind of primitive courtship dance which goes under the misnomer of graduate recruitment? The resulting process is a familiar one. A fashionable laboratory, for example, needs people with prestige, so advertisements go out for the 'best men' that can be found, 'best' being defined as doctoral scientists, graduates with first-class or second-class degrees and preferably from Oxbridge. This may lead to the accumulation of considerable talent, but unfortunately the story does not end there. The researchers in the laboratory are unlikely to be told that they are involved in an exercise in reputation-enhancing. Uncertainty develops as to what they are supposed to be doing. Frustration and ineffectiveness follow close behind. There is no easy solution to this question of prestige, but it will help if we draw people's attention to it at every opportunity.

There are other social influences which can exaggerate manpower 'requirements'. Management tends to impose upon the new venture the social structure with which they are most familiar, whether it applies or not. The incoming professionals bring with them attitudes, built upon allegiance to their 'science', to their 'profession' and to comparable value systems which may conflict with the company's modes of operation. More of this later, first let us return to the problem.

DEALING WITH THE PROBLEM

Three courses of action are available to employers faced with under-utilization. First, they can begin recruiting fewer professionals but more supporting personnel (pass-degree graduates, technicians, clerks, etc.). This solution has the drawback that it severely limits any plans the concern may have for growth, though against this must be balanced the inevitably high wastage rate among dissatisfied professionals who are looking for better opportunities. Second, they can reduce numbers while holding the work-level fairly constant. Argyris (1964) reports how understaffing, within limits, leads to greater effort and increases the employee's experience of difficult and challenging tasks. One well-known international company in the electronics industry pursues a policy of 'extending employees' by slight under-manning which is known to the author to work well. However, the consequences of excessive under-manning can be very serious, resulting in work stress among employees and deteriorating performances. The third course of action open to management is to change the social organization, so improving the utilization of skills and increasing employee commitment. The second policy requires no expansion and in many ways the first can best be achieved in conjunction with the third, which we will explore in two parts: changing the basis for the division of labour in work-groups and organizations, and improving the social systems of management.

CHANGING THE DIVISION OF LABOUR

It is recognized in enlightened sectors of industry that 'one of the most important tasks facing industrial management in the coming years is to provide the right kinds of organization and environment for getting the best possible results from research and development' (Brookman, 1963). Our surveys among professional manpower suggest that most administrators have little insight into what these appropriate kinds of organization might be.

We begin our search for some of the determinants of misuse by investigating the formal structure of the group or organization, the division of labour. We observed earlier that employees can be misused by being employed on tasks below their level of skill or on jobs which require skills other than those they possess. A hypothetical division of skills by Level and Type, avoiding reference to educational achievement, is shown in Figure 3. The level of skill also refers to the difficulty of jobs, for the degree of discretion exercised by employees increases as we move up the hierarchy. Two ways of looking at 'type of skill' are shown. One, a general classification, is typical of the way various departments are described in the traditional structure of the firm. The second, more specific classification, is relevant to discussions about professional work-groups.

TABLE 1: *Hypothetical division of skills by level and type*

Level of Skill		Type of Skill
Managerial	A	(*General*): Technical; Production; Sales;
Professional	B	Finance; Administration; Personnel
Technical/Clerical	C	(*Specific*): B(i) Chemists; B(ii) Physicists;
Craft	D	B(iii) Chemical Engineers
Operative	E	
Unskilled	F	

There are a number of ways for deploying people, whether in work-groups or in larger organizations. Four such arrangements are shown in Figure 3, using information from Table 1. On the left-hand side we see that people can be deployed according to their speciality: for example a research section made up *entirely* of chemists. This system of deployment according to function is an important dimension of bureaucracy and presupposes that the tasks coming to the group are relatively uniform. At the other extreme of Figure 3, skills are mixed with respect to both levels and types. Such a work-group, engaged for example on research into biochemical problems, might be composed of chemists, biochemists, biologists, technicians, clerks, and craftsmen. This arrangement is based on the assumption that the tasks facing the groups will vary in nature and difficulty. It is variously known as organization by problem, product, or project.

Technical factors are important in deciding the optimum arrangement of skills. Deployment according to specialism seems to go along with batch production methods and office work. Where more advanced technical systems are to be found (for example the process technology, marketing complex equipment, R. and D. establishments) a mixing of skills may be needed. Indeed when technical change takes place we can expect many tasks to become more heterogeneous, so calling for mixed-skill groups. 'Organization by function or machine grouping is often no longer practicable. The department if subdivided at all should be organized by product line or part line, with all functions related to a particular product coming within one group' (Diebold, 1958).

This may be so but, judging by the comments obtained from professionals about their own organizations, a very large number of new ventures have the traditional methods of the division of labour imposed upon them. According to our own reckoning, this will lead to the misuse of talents and ineffective individual and organizational performance. Let us pursue this argument with reference to two studies.

The first concerned the marketing branch of a company engaged in manufacturing electronic equipment. This firm deployed its manpower along traditional lines. We will attempt to demonstrate

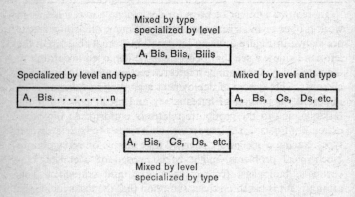

Figure 3. Some methods of deploying skills in work-groups. (The letters are coded for skills described in Table 1)

that a relationship exists between this fact and the poor sales performance of the concern over recent years. At the time of the inquiry the firm recruited professional personnel, mostly with technical and scientific qualifications, to do the work. The training given to these men and women by the concern was almost entirely technical (the reader will already have noted that the manning and training programmes both reflected a familiar British bias against selling and salesmen). The broad objectives of the marketing concern were seen by the author to be two: to persuade existing customers to purchase or lease new lines of equipment and to find new customers. The firm's emphasis on technical expertise favoured the holding part of its marketing policy at the expense of expansion, and this in an extremely competitive market.

Over recent years the equipment became increasingly complex, but the company persisted with the belief that the same person could carry out both selling and technical aspects of the job. The men were deployed in small specialist teams. Of these men, 140 were asked for information about the way they spent their time, to estimate the percentage of time devoted to various activities. The results in Figure 4 indicate that they were spending less than half their working time on their two principal activities.

When asked about the difficulties of the job many listed 'customer relations', and, more specifically, 'making cold calls'. They were not salesmen and they did not like selling. Additional material showed that they spent a third of their working time in their own

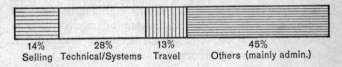

| 14% | 28% | 13% | 45% |
| Selling | Technical/Systems | Travel | Others (mainly admin.) |

Figure 4. Distribution of working time among 140 professional employees in a marketing concern

offices. The dearth of clerical and secretarial assistance is illustrated in their most serious work dissatisfactions, 'lack of support' (39 per cent) and 'excessive paper work' (60 per cent). Not only did they lack selling expertise but they were deployed for a considerable part of their time on menial tasks. The evidence strongly suggests that the objectives of the marketing operation, from the point of view of employees, were not clearly defined and that it was badly balanced with respect to both the levels and types of skills possessed by its personnel, who should have been deployed in groups with mixed rather than specialized skills. Two of the firm's more successful competitors were using sales teams with mixed skills. Now to the second inquiry.

In the study of chemists reported earlier it was possible to test the link between the structure of the work-group and individual effectiveness. We took the fifty chemists who rated themselves as being *most effective* and fifty chemists who rated themselves as being *least effective*, and we compared the composition of their work-groups. The average sizes were similar, but the effective chemists' work-groups contained fewer chemists and substantially higher ratios of non-chemist scientists, technicians, and clerks and typists. Since much chemical research is interdisciplinary, the importance of having scientists from other disciplines needs emphasizing. In America, Pelz and his associates (1953) have found that highly rated scientists spend more of their time with scientists from other disciplines than with those of their own. On the question of technical support, the Triennial Manpower Survey (1966) shows the ratio of technical assistants to be three to every scientist or technologist. This figure is likely to give the impression that professional personnel in industry are well supported. This depends, as we have seen, on how they are deployed. In fact many researchers in industry have little direct technical support. In the author's studies the ratio of scientists to technicians working in the same groups has never exceeded 1:1. Carter and Williams (1959) report similar findings.

The picture we have so far described in marketing and research can also apply to production. The need for more integrated systems for deploying labour has been strongly underlined in the chemical and petroleum industries at the operator and craft levels, but it applies equally to all levels of organization. Efficiency in these industries is very much a function of uninterrupted production, the very condition in which maintenance operations are elevated to a production function. Yet, in the traditional structure not only are both production and maintenance divorced from each other but they frequently have conflicting objectives.

Let us summarize the advantages of mixing skills or more correctly of dividing labour by project or product. This arrangement:

(1) is most effective when the nature of the work is varied,

(2) requires *fewer* professionals and is therefore cheaper to staff.

(3) involves all personnel in 'larger jobs', so increasing commitment, and

(4) is more adaptable to changing conditions.

This last point is particularly important. We know that the

precise aims and objectives of a new venture may take some time to emerge and in this context the group with mixed skills is at a decided advantage over the specialized section.

However this 'new' division of labour also has its weaknesses. Equipment and apparatus costs may be higher, and, as a result of greater autonomy, groups ordered in this way often tend to be very self-sufficient. They cut themselves off from the outside influence which is essential if professional standards are to be maintained. One method for insuring that this does not happen is to disband the team at the end of the project or to change its membership at convenient times. In fact, research findings (Ziller *et al.*, 1962) suggest that greater creativity and production can be achieved by maintaining work-groups as open systems. In our experience work-groups become increasingly unstable, in the sense that they are constantly changing, as more sophisticated technical processes are introduced, so that this question of becoming isolated is less important than appears at first sight.

IMPROVING THE SOCIAL SYSTEMS OF MANAGEMENT

Traditional methods for deploying manpower are linked with a system of values which conflict with the values professionals bring to their employment. These differences have been described by Shepard (1957). Traditional organization is characterized by the following:

(1) Senior managers take as many decisions as possible, so reducing the need for decisions by personnel further down the organizational hierarchy;

(2) Communications are mostly vertical through the supervisor or manager and limited largely to what is necessary for the operation of the task;

(3) Job responsibilities, limits, and obligations are closely defined and governed by the instructions and decisions of supervisors;

(4) There is an insistence on loyalty to the firm and obedience to the orders of supervisors as conditions of membership.

In such a system, communications and innovative ideas are

thwarted and distorted and employee dependence and submissiveness encouraged. It cannot effectively assimilate the influx of professional personnel into the organization. The values professionals bring are in direct conflict. These are as follows:

(1) Independence of thought and action is developed;
(2) Communications of the widest kind are encouraged and secrecy is anathema;
(3) Power resides in the weight of scientific opinion;
(4) Superior–subordinate relations emphasize the development of the latter; and
(5) Honesty, objectivity, and respect for fact are all important.

Each of these facets is also to be found in newer theories of management.

As Burns and Stalker (1961) point out 'the interplay between the hierarchical structure of the concern; the requirements of changing conditions for organic procedure; the attempt by professionals to substantiate their claims for higher status and the struggles by powerful groups to establish control over disputed areas of the concern can cumulatively render the situation at any one time extremely complicated.' These problems have to be faced by the managers of professionals and it is to aspects of their role that we now turn.

Let us begin with the distinction we have observed between *institutional* and *professional* values. As a result of accepting a managerial appointment, a professional is expected to adhere to the culture of the institution more closely. This often provides serious conflicts for the manager if, as is customary, he was selected because of his professional competence. Nearly always the outstanding engineer becomes the development manager, the best salesman the sales manager, and the best systems analyst the data-processing manager. Whether these people have the necessary skills to manage is another matter. In our experience they often do not. By taking on administrative responsibilities the professional ceases to be a technical expert. This may prove an unsettling experience when, like the foreman, he finds himself the 'marginal man' between two value systems.

This predicament is neatly illustrated in a piece of work being conducted by J. K. Eastman at Birkbeck College. He has asked members of a research and development establishment to assess the influence over laboratory operations of each hierarchical level in the concern. Some of the results are shown in Figure 5. We

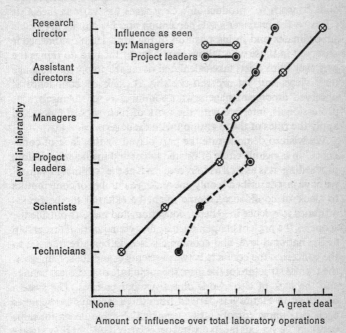

Figure 5. Influence over laboratory operations as seen by two levels of personnel. Respondents are asked to indicate how much influence employees have at each of the levels shown above. The answers of people at two levels are shown in the graph

observe that the Project Leaders, men at the pinnacle of their professional performance, perceive of influence in a way which tends to indicate a belief in the authority of skill (professional values), whereas their bosses, the managers, see influence distributed according to the authority of office (institutional values). Observation of the precarious position of middle management in sophisticated work systems leads us to a management variable which we describe as *confidence*. It is particularly relevant in the management of professionals and may be distinguished from other well-known dimensions of leadership such as 'concern for people' and 'concern for production'. *Confidence* has various facets. It refers to the manager's self-perception and his confidence in his subordinates and in his position in the firm. High confidence is observed in those who: allow people under them to do things the way they think best; take calculated risks; are prepared to change their views and yet *are still decisive*. A lack of confidence is observed among managers who continue to see themselves as professionals, interfere with the work of their subordinates, and apply the rules of the institution with exactness.

We wish to demonstrate the part played by the 'lack of confidence' in a vicious circle of wasted talent and inefficiency. Before proceeding it is as well as to recognize that the 'conflict in values' we have just described is only one among a number of contributors to 'lack of confidence'. Some might be external to the firm – attitudes to science in general, education, and matters outside the scope of the present chapter such as uncertain political leadership at the national level and economic crises. Others are internal to the concern – the conflicts between scientists and their managers, the formal structure of the firm, the rapid rate of technical change and the lack of clear work objectives and policies. The system described in Figure 6 is derived from three separate case studies each providing corroborating evidence. The interrelationships between the various facets are not necessarily high, but they always exist.

Let us take as our starting point the manager's lack of confidence (see Figure 6). In order to assert himself and to gain the authority which his position in the hierarchy makes him feel entitled to, he is likely to do several things. He will withhold information from his subordinates, ask for more information than he needs, and attempt to do his subordinates' jobs for them. In such circumstances many professionals will claim they have only limited influence in their jobs and over the firm's operations. Those scientists who are growth-oriented (desire to use their skills and abilities and to have autonomy), and who are usually the more effective (see Chapter 5), are most likely to leave. The professionals prepared to put up with these conditions will be more likely to be motivated by concern for safety and security, to be submissive and to hold stronger institutional values. Their kind of commitment is largely out of loyalty to the firm. Their work performances will be mediocre, which in turn will reinforce the

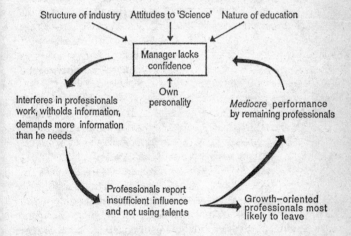

Structure of industry   Attitudes to 'Science'   Nature of education

Manager lacks confidence

Own personality

Interferes in professionals work, witholds information, demands more information than he needs

Mediocre performance by remaining professionals

Professionals report insufficient influence and not using talents

Growth−oriented professionals most likely to leave

Figure 6. A reinforcing system of ineffectiveness

manager's lack of confidence in his men and so the vicious circle goes on. This lack of confidence has other serious consequences. The manager may believe that the problem rests with the absence of talent among his subordinates and so selection standards are raised and new experts come and go.

Where confidence (see Figure 7) is observed among managers of professionals, the unit is frequently said by outsiders to have a 'good atmosphere'. In relations with his subordinates, the confident manager is recognized for delegating control and passing on information about the concern. Employees who are looking for the chance to exercise choice and to use their talents to the full have their aspirations reinforced, while those who wish to be directed find the uncertainty and the ambiguity of the work-place stressful and are more likely to leave the firm. The commitment of those who stay is to the task and to company objectives. Successful group or individual performance can in turn confirm the manager's confidence, so enabling the concern to achieve its objectives.

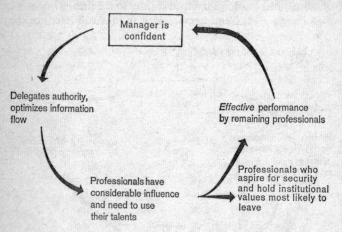

Figure 7. A reinforcing system of effectiveness

Two simple tests are available for discovering which of these two systems is in operation in any unit. We can relate the professional's 'intention to stay or leave' the company to his aspirations for growth. (For measuring this dimension, see p. 327.) If staying is associated with a greater desire for growth, then we have a reinforcing system of effectiveness in operation. Similarly we can relate each person's assessment of his own competence to his desire for growth. If people who are less interested in exercising discretion and using their talents are found to believe that they number among the most competent, then we have a system of values which reinforces 'playing safe' rather than initiative and innovative behaviour. It is almost certain that the managers in such a situation will lack confidence which, of course, can also be tested.

How then can confidence be increased? We have already seen that part of the answer lies in the external environment of the firm, but inside the firm matters can be greatly improved upon by changing the formal structure of work-groups and by clarifying objectives. Within the laboratory, the data processing unit, and the operations research department there is room for improvement in the selection of managers above the first level. In this, more emphasis must be given to managerial expertise. The relationship between the professionals and the rest of the concern can be greatly improved through the methods of organizational development and training outlined in Chapter 13. (The writer has been involved in one such exercise in a refinery which is attempting, with some degree of success, to increase the confidence of managers and release the innovative drives of its employees.)

EDUCATION AND MISUSE

We began this chapter by reviewing the influence of social attitudes on the role of science in industry. Before concluding let us return briefly to consider the role of education in the misuse of professional manpower.

Misemployment, that is the use of professionals on work 'outside' their range of skills, has received scarce attention in this chapter. It is a matter which is as much the responsibility of our educators as it is industry's. The crux of the matter is the lack of fit between our educational processes and the realities of industrial life. While our educators, with few exceptions, continue to press for specialization in study and to give a disproportionate weight in learning to analyse and maximize information, industry and indeed contemporary life call more and more for the ability to synthesize and optimize information, and in particular to be adaptable. Society places great store in formal educational accomplishment and so favours those who invest their time and energy in its processes of specialization. Industry, too, is being led to think that people with the highest and best educational qualifications will also be the most versatile. However, a few people are coming to suspect that the kinds of education we receive do not develop our versatility. In the writer's investigations of man's behaviour in the work-place, attitudes, values, and emotions which reflect an openness to new experiences, rather than skills and abilities, are proving to be the critical prerequisites for versatility. It may not surprise the reader that we have found no clear relationship between adaptability and educational achievement among the populations described in this chapter. If the primary purpose of education is preparation for living then in many of its forms our education may be failing us badly.

No reference has been made in this chapter to the activities of the professional associations *vis-à-vis* their members' conditions of employment. By and large the scientific and engineering institutions have exerted much less political influence in society than has, for example, the British Medical Association. There are signs of a change. The Council of Engineering Institutions, formed to bring together a number of separate bodies, is already showing an active interest in the status, education and training of engineers. Furthermore, recent surveys of members by the C.E.I. and other organizations like the Royal Institute of Chemistry signal their intention to take a more active part in determining the professional man's employment opportunities.

*

We have tried to show in this chapter that the misuse of professional manpower in industry is widespread. Indeed it could be argued that our leading firms are not in need of more professionals but are simply failing to utilize the talents of those they already employ. We have attempted to relate this problem to social attitudes external to the work-place which undervalue scientific and professional endeavour and also to aspects of the internal order of industry itself. In this analysis we have found it necessary to consider the effects of misuse and technical change together. Those features of industrial organization which we have investigated are: (*a*) the application of inappropriate organizational structures to highly technical work processes, (*b*) the 'lack of confidence' among managers of professionals, and (*c*) the influence of prestige in the recruitment of professionals. Finally, we have suggested that educational institutions themselves, through their processes of specialization, are contributing to one important aspect of misuse, the inability of many professionals to apply their skills to a wider range of industrial tasks.

PART TWO

Training for Skill

UNTIL very recently, the expression 'industrial training' was likely to conjure up visions of wasted time and opportunities. Learning a job is often a haphazard affair but it doesn't need to be, and from an economic standpoint training should aim at systematizing the process to improve the speed and extent of learning and eventually performance on the job. From a personal viewpoint we are more likely to see the purpose of training in terms of increasing our opportunities to pursue the work of our choice.

The development of vocational training in Britain is now being aided by two important factors. First, we have had the Industrial Training Act of 1964, which is an indication of support for training at the highest level and in a direct tangible way. One of the purposes of the Act is to secure improvements in the quality and efficiency of industrial training. Second, the industrial training effort is sufficiently new to be independent from the limiting traditions and customs of our educational institutions. Those engaged in vocational training are thus in a position to make maximum use of a wide range of new techniques and practices, some of which are outlined in this section of the book.

Research into training may take place in the laboratory or in the field. The reader will find in the next three chapters that the dialogue between the applied social scientist and the laboratory researcher continues on a high plane.

In the laboratory, the experimental psychologist who looks upon the theory of learning as a theory of behaviour will probably be concentrating his attentions on the processes of learning. He may also be interested in the applications of his findings to optimizing methods of instruction. Programmed instruction is one example of a training principle which originated from learning experiments in the laboratory.

The industrial researcher will probably have a more prescribed brief than the laboratory psychologist. He will be aware of the range of jobs for which employees are needed and, knowing in as much detail as possible their capacities, will develop the subjects and methods of instruction accordingly. He might, as Tilley does in Chapter 5, look upon his own function as the developer of an effective technology of training, a conception which both raises the status of training and can be closely allied with the viewpoint of the organization theorist. Technical change, too, has the effect of making training an important facet of the firm's functioning; no longer a once-and-for-all exercise it is increasingly concerned with the updating of techniques and the teaching of new skills to people whose old ones have been superseded.

The central role of information in instruction, the use of electronic training simulators and of concepts such as feedback, perceptual cueing, and evaluation (each explained in this section) lead the training expert quite naturally to look upon his subject in a manner which complements the systems conception of industrial behaviour.

CHAPTER 5

A Technology of Training

K. TILLEY

THE strength of any organization depends very largely on the knowledge and skill of the men it employs. Making the best use of the talents available to him and wherever possible extending the range and depth of these talents has always been one of the manager's major concerns, but has become even more critical with the increased rate of technological change and development.

Possibly the most striking feature of recent work on training methods is the interest which is being shown in developing an effective technology of training. This chapter examines what is implied by the concept of a technology of training and considers the various steps involved in its achievement.

The idea of a technology of training is closely bound up with the distinction which is made between learning and performance. Learning refers to the internal processes which underlie and accompany changes in performance. Performance is the observed effect of learning on behaviour. Although it may sometimes be an imprecise and even ambiguous indication of the learning that has taken place, performance nevertheless can be more readily studied and controlled than the internal processes themselves.

Learning may and indeed often does occur without formal training, but the aim of a technology of training is to expedite the process by arranging conditions so that students learn more rapidly and effectively. Many factors affect ease of learning and these factors interact in quite complicated ways. The real significance of attempts to develop a technology of training is that analysis of human behaviours, despite its complexity, is beginning to reveal conditions which are relevant and necessary in bringing about specified changes in performance.

What does the development of a technology of training actually involve? Although authors differ in the terms they use to describe the process most agree that it consists of a number of interrelated steps. Figure 8 sets out the various stages of the process.

ANALYSIS OF THE OVERALL SYSTEM

Training is one way of improving work efficiency, but it is not the only way. Before concentrating on ways and means of improving training other possibilities have at least to be considered.

In some circumstances it may be possible to select men to do a particular job who already possess the knowledge and skill demanded or whose intelligence and attainments suggest they will readily acquire them. More often, however, the advantages of such a policy in terms of reduced training costs are likely to be more than offset by difficulty in finding enough men of the right calibre and in providing them with work and careers commensurate with their high ability in order to retain them.

Another approach is to fit the job to the man rather than the man to the job. In many instances it is possible to simplify the job so that it can be performed successfully by men of more ordinary ability. There are several ways in which this may be accomplished.

(1) Specialization

A job can often be made easier by breaking it up into a number of more specialized tasks which greatly reduces the range of skills involved in each job. This can considerably reduce training costs, but these advantages have to be viewed against the increased manning costs which are likely to come with increased specialization.

(2) Job aids

Jobs can be greatly simplified by providing men with suitably designed procedural guides. Several studies have shown that instructions and regulations are often made unnecessarily difficult to understand by the language and grammatical structure used in them. The use of negative statements, qualified statements and sentences with a number of disjunctive clauses have all been shown to reduce comprehension significantly.

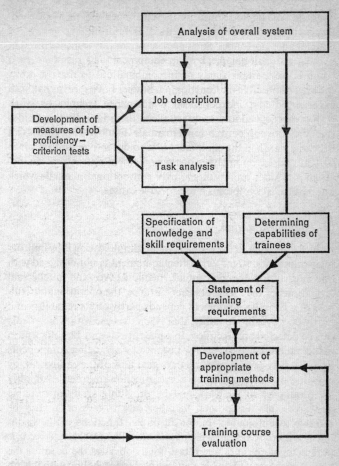

Figure 8. Steps in developing a technology of training

Jones (1964) has shown that the use of logical decision trees reduces confusion and errors in following printed instructions. A decision tree breaks down a complex set of instructions into a series of questions each of which requires a simple yes/no answer. The answer given to the first question determines what the second question will be and so on until a clear-cut decision is reached. Decision trees have also been used as fault-finding guides for maintenance personnel. Such guides list various steps involved in making a functional check of an equipment. The results of each test are used, either singly or in combination, to narrow down the area of possible malfunctioning. Studies have shown that both experienced and inexperienced maintenance technicians work with greater speed and accuracy using these fault-finding guides than they do with conventional manuals. Fault-finding guides can be available when the equipment first comes into operation, since they are based on analyses of the equipment's structural characteristics. This is an advantage over conventional manuals which attempt to list symptoms and probable causes.

(3) Equipment design

A third approach to the problem of job simplification is by improving equipment design. Very often equipment is not designed with due regard for the perceptual, manipulative, and intellectual limitations of the operators. For instance, the operational usefulness of a complex equipment depends partly on its reliability and partly on its maintainability, that is, on the ease with which faults can be detected and rectified. In some cases it may be sufficient to make maintenance easier, for instance by arranging components in such a way as to emphasize the signal flow of the equipment, by ensuring modules perform a single function in order to simplify symptom-pattern analysis, and by providing easily identifiable and accessible test points. In other cases, however, it may be sensible to automate some or all of the functions of the maintenance man. A system which automatically samples and records parameter states at different test points obviates the need for the maintenance man to do his own testing, but leaves him with the job of analysing the data to locate the fault and carrying out the necessary rectification. More complex automatic check-out devices are capable not only of sampling parameter states, but of comparing this data with normal state values, storing the comparisons and printing out diagnoses of likely faulty components. Such devices deal with both fault detection and fault localization, leaving the maintenance man to deal simply with rectification.

Analysis of the overall system insures that all these possible ways of improving operational efficiency are considered in any given set of circumstances.

JOB DESCRIPTION

The first step in designing a training course is to obtain information about the job for which the training is thought necessary. Job descriptions attempt to answer two questions. What does the man have to do and what are acceptable criteria of his success in doing it?

A job will usually consist of a number of different duties. The duties of a motor mechanic, for instance, include engine-tuning, wheel-changing, checking wheel alignment and balance, etc. Each of these duties can be further broken down into a sequence of operations. Engine-tuning for example involves checking ignition, timing, and carburation. These various operations can again be subdivided into a number of sub-tasks. In checking the ignition the mechanic has to test the coil, distributor, and sparking plugs. One part of an adequate job description is to identify the elements which go to make up the job, and another is specifying their frequency of occurrence.

The other important function of a job description is to indicate what standard of performance is required. What is acceptable proof that a man can do what is required of him? Answering this question satisfactorily is sometimes more difficult than it seems. Reading, for example, has been defined as any behaviour which is made in response to a written or printed text, but the range of possible responses is quite wide. Naming the letters or speaking the words are possibly the simplest responses. Other possible responses include following printed instructions, summarizing the text, restating it in other words, or answering questions about it. Any or all of these responses could be taken as evidence of an ability to read the text, and it is important to specify which are acceptable in any given circumstances. Unless a precise behavioural objective is specified the training requirements must remain ambiguous. Training objectives are still frequently stated in such terms as 'must know how a radio receiver works'. Such a statement is not precise enough because it does not indicate what the trainee must do to demonstrate his knowledge. For example, is he required to describe the function of various components, diagnose faults on the equipment, or even build a receiver from an assembly of components?

Considerable progress has been made in developing methods for arriving at adequate job descriptions. Such descriptions achieve two things. Firstly, they reduce the time spent on training men to do things which they will do only rarely in the job and they ensure that important features of the job are not overlooked. Secondly, by specifying objectives in terms of observable behaviour they go some way towards meeting the requirements for measurement, since objectives must be describable if they are to be measurable. These are very real virtues, but they do not in themselves provide sufficient basis for designing a training course. Whilst a job description states what men are required to do, it says little about how they actually do it and little also about the sort of training needed to enable them to do it. There is one other reason why a job description alone cannot provide all the information needed to design a training course. In certain skills, such as copytyping, the elements of the job are relatively few in number, but a job description will usually include a large number of specific behavioural objectives. Because of their number and because each is quite specific it is difficult to devise an economically and administratively feasible criterion test which adequately covers them all. A method of isolating different classes of behaviour which have a formal identity irrespective of their particular contents is needed.

TASK ANALYSIS

Once the performance expected at the end of the training has been specified objectively, it is necessary to identify different classes of terminal behaviour which require different types of training for their accomplishment irrespective of content. Task analysis is the term which is used to describe this process. A number of suggestions have been made about how it can best be done. These differ in the number of categories of behaviour which they postulate and in their emphasis on the various categories. But they are all primarily concerned, not with the work to be done, but with the learner's behaviour and the stimulus–response characteristics of the tasks he has to do. In performing any task an individual must recognize cues which serve as signals that some form of action is called for. Task analysis attempts to classify stimulus and response characteristics and the relationships between the two that can indicate the sort of training procedures which will be needed to achieve effective learning.

A good example of some of the recent thinking on the problem of task taxonomy is the work of Gagné (1965). He takes as his starting point the fundamental fact that stimulus–response relationships do get learned. Without entering into the argument about the conditions which are necessary for this to occur, he describes the categories of learned behaviour which can be built out of simple conditioned response units. He also attempts to arrive at a set of categories which are hierarchical in the sense that competence in the higher-order categories presupposes competence in the categories of lower order. The six categories will be dealt with one by one.

(1) Response differentiation

A basic form of learning is that involved in response differentiation. Learning to speak by copying the sound given as a stimulus is a simple example of this sort of learning. Response differentiation learning plays an important part in the acquisition of skills such as shorthand writing and handwriting. Although response differentiation is only occasionally a major training objective in itself, it is often a prerequisite for more complex types of behaviour. Most modern methods of teaching foreign languages stress that learning to differentiate the sounds of the unfamiliar language is the essential first step in both speaking and comprehending it.

(2) Associations

In many situations the learner is required, not simply to reproduce the stimulus he is given, but to make some qualitatively different response, for example to use a new technical term to name a component or to press a button on the appearance of a light. Three things are involved in building up associations of this kind, each of which has its own implications with regard to training:

(1) The ability to distinguish the relevant stimulus from the irrelevant stimuli.

(2) The availability of an appropriate response. Being unable to pronounce a foreign word will affect the learner's ability to associate it with a word in his own language.

(3) A coding process which links stimulus and response. It may be helpful in certain cases to use some previously learned response as a mediator rather than try to link the stimulus and response directly.

(3) Multiple discriminations

Usually the learner is required not merely to associate a single response with a particular stimulus, but a number of responses with their appropriate stimuli. Multiple discriminations of this kind are typical of such activities as learning the Morse code or the vocabulary of a foreign language.

The main difficulty in dealing with multiple discriminations, apart from the fact that more than a single association is involved, is that stimuli and their associated responses are likely to be con-fused. Acquiring one association interferes with the acquisition of others. This possibility is minimized if both the stimuli and the required responses are made as distinctive as possible. Adding artificial cues which can subsequently be withdrawn or 'vanished' as learning proceeds is one way of making it easier to discriminate between stimuli. Responses can also be made more readily avail-able. Preliminary practice in pronouncing foreign words makes it easier for the learner to deal with the problem of associating these words with others in his own tongue.

(4) Behaviour chains

A single association consists of a stimulus, a response, and some linkage between the two. Many procedural tasks, such as certain arithmetical computations, cockpit checks etc., consist of a number of such elements which have to be performed in a definite sequence. Before an individual can master these behavioural chains he must have learned the individual associations which make up the chain and must also have learned any multiple discriminations which represent a possible source of confusion.

Several writers have suggested that the 'part-progressive' method is an effective way of dealing with procedural tasks. If a task consists of three activities A, B, and C, A is practised first. When this has been mastered A and B are practised together, then C is brought in and all three activities are practised. Recently Gilbert (1962) demonstrated that there are advantages in dealing with procedural tasks retrogressively. In this, the final act is practised first, then the last but one act, and so on until the first act, which begins the sequence, is included.

(5) Concepts

Objects and events which serve as stimuli will vary on different occasions according to the circumstances. For example, chance factors will affect the sonar echoes received from the same target on two different occasions. Men must be able to deal with this sort of variation in the signals to perform effectively. Concepts are classifications of objects and events which can be treated as identical for some specified purpose. Establishing a concept involves setting limits to the variability which can be tolerated before the object or event ceases to be an acceptable member of a given class. Acquiring the concept of an act of leadership, for example, might first involve distinguishing acts producing changes in the behaviour of other people from those which did not have this effect. This would be followed by teaching the individual to discriminate acts within this class which involved no element of physical coercion. Again, within the class of acts not involving physical coercion, it would be necessary for individuals to distinguish those in which there was an element of willing compliance on the part of followers from those where there was not. When this concept is established it is possible to identify cases correctly over a range of situations although they have not been seen in exactly the same form before.

(6) *Principles*

Teaching principles or general rules is an objective of most forms of instruction. At its simplest a principle deals with the relationship between two concepts, A and B, and can be stated in the form 'If A, then B'. Principles can certainly be more complex than this and may include two or more simpler rules. It has been suggested that complex principles embracing a number of simpler elements should be regarded as a separate category and referred to as 'strategies'. Whilst it is at present uncertain if this is a necessary distinction to make, it is accepted that principles, whether simple or complex, can be learned only when the concepts with which they deal have already been acquired.

This categorization of behaviour irrespective of its content has important implications. First, it suggests that slowness and difficulty in learning are largely attributable to insufficient or inappropriate pre-conditioning of the learner, resulting in more than one kind of behaviour having to be acquired at the same time. As the various categories of behaviour demand different training conditions for their acquisition there is an inevitable loss of efficiency. An effective sequence of instruction must proceed from the lower-order to the higher-order categories, that is from associations to multiple discriminations to concepts to principles and not the other way round.

A second important implication is that a sequence of instruction is only likely to be effective if it takes due account of the capabilities that students already possess when they enter training.

DETERMINING THE CAPABILITIES OF TRAINEES

Training will be ineffective if it fails to focus on the critical elements of the tasks to be learned. It will also lose in effectiveness if it fails to take account of the knowledge and skills which students possess when they commence training.

Learning the resistor colour code and learning to identify sonar echoes are both examples of multiple discrimination tasks. Apart from the number of associations involved in the two tasks, they differ in another important respect. Sonar operators are highly unlikely to be familiar with the sounds they are required to identify when they enter training. Trainees learning the resistor colour code, on the other hand, will almost certainly be perfectly capable of differentiating between the colours from the very beginning. Time spent on improving response differentiation, whilst essential in the first case, would be quite unnecessary in the second.

Several writers have stressed that more effort must be made to accommodate individual differences in training. Mager (1962) makes the point that 'student-controlled' instruction differs from conventional instruction not only in content, sequence, and emphasis, but also in effectiveness. In one study an attempt was made to restructure an orientation course given to graduate engineers on joining an industrial company. The existing course covered such subjects as machine and instrument operation, manufacturing processes, and company procedures. Each trainee attended a course of lectures lasting six weeks, then spent six weeks circulating through the various departments, and finally served as an assistant to an experienced company engineer for twelve weeks. In the redesigned experimental course students were given a statement of the course objectives but were free to decide for themselves what they needed to be taught, how much time they would devote to different topics, and on the sequence of instruction they would follow. There was a marked reduction in training time (65 per cent) and a consequent reduction in effort on the part of the permanent staff of the company, and the trainees also were considered better equipped to take their place in the organization. Studies of this sort also emphasize that stating course objectives explicitly can help students to help themselves, quite apart from the impact such a statement has on course design.

Despite the growing awareness of the need for improved methods of diagnostic testing, not a great deal of information on this subject is available. Most laboratory studies of learning have tended to regard individual differences as a source of error variance and have done everything possible to eliminate them. Animal studies have been on cheap short-lived species with controlled heredity and experience as subjects. Where human subjects have been used, they are often chosen to be as homogeneous as possible. The information obtained has little immediate relevance for the trainer in attempting to solve urgent practical problems.

Although a lot of information is available about aptitude and attainment tests, most of them have been validated against performance in fixed training courses. They reveal little about the ways in which individual differences in aptitude and attainment interact with various methods of training.

Criterion tests are given at the end of training and are primarily concerned with demonstrating that students can perform the activities associated with their jobs. Diagnostic tests given before or during training are designed not merely to show whether or not students can do certain things, but also to reveal the reasons for failures and what needs to be done about them. Knowing that a student has failed a question involving the use of Ohm's Law, for example, does not indicate whether he has forgotten the formula, is unable to transpose formulae, or has simply made a mistake in his arithmetic, and this sort of information is needed to decide how he can best be taught.

Developments in programme instruction have done a great deal to stimulate interest in the problems of diagnostic testing and the prescription of remedial sequences of instruction. In most early examples of branching programmes the material presented was determined by the student's response to the preceding item and programmes often repeated previously presented material when the student made an incorrect response. Recent studies have underlined the need to base decisions about remedial instruction on a pattern of responses rather than a single answer and the importance of choosing the type of remedial instructions according to the types of error. Instead of simply repeating material which the individual has failed to understand, attempts are made to restate it in different terms, to provide different and more varied examples and to introduce general review passages, etc.

It is not suggested that producing adequate diagnostic tests is easy, although the availability of computers for instructional purposes will help. What is suggested is that attention to this question could bring about substantial improvements in training effectiveness. A precise statement of training requirements can only be achieved by comparing and contrasting the capabilities needed for successful job performance with those already possessed by students at the beginning of their course.

DEVELOPING APPROPRIATE TRAINING METHODS

The next step after defining the objectives of training and establishing the existing capacities of the trainee is to decide what conditions will bring about the required changes in behaviour. These questions mainly concern how to display to the student the material to be learned and how to get him to work with this material. There are several issues involved.

Sequencing the material to be learned

One problem in planning instruction is to determine the sequence in which the material should be presented to the learner. Although the problem is an important one in programmed instruction, the literature has more to say about the specification of terminal objectives than about the component behaviours, which can be gradually modified and combined to produce the required terminal behaviour. Task analysis, which divides complex behaviour into simpler stimulus–response elements, reveals ways in which the elements should be ordered in construction, and probably affords the most explicit guidance currently available to the trainer.

Research findings on the order of presentation of material have shown that it frequently, though not always, has an important effect on ease of learning. Several possible explanations suggest themselves. Order seems to be more important for some subject matters than for others. In learning mathematical material which possesses a structure of its own, sequencing appears to be more important than in more loosely structured material like vocabulary. It is quite possible that in some cases what is the best order for one person is not for another, in which case the programmer cannot produce the best order for everybody. It has been suggested that the best approach is to let the student write the programme – it is certainly true that students will often demand orders of presentation of material which seem inappropriate to the expert in the subject, though they may not in fact be any more appropriate. In any case, individual differences will be taken into account in determining order as well as rate of presentation of material in programmed instruction.

Tailoring instruction to accommodate individual student's needs is becoming feasible with the increased availability of computer-aided systems of instruction. Such systems will be able to base training decisions on more detailed analyses of the capabilities and interests of trainees, and they will be able to provide greater flexibility in the type of remedial instruction which can be contemplated. However, the realization of the full potential of computer-aided instructions is dependent on the trainee's ability to define more precisely the factors which are relevant to various training decisions and to classify the various ways of presenting information to the student.

The interactive capacity of the computer offers other important advantages. It becomes feasible, for instance, to think of simulating various types of experimental work. Computers have already been used successfully to simulate chemical experiments, where the student indicates a test he wishes to make and is provided with the information he would have received in actually carrying it out. Similar work has been done in connexion with the problems of medical diagnosis. Given a statement of symptoms the student asks the computer for further information until he feels himself in a position to make a definite diagnosis.

Concepts concerned with the rate of change in functional relationships can best be taught by giving the student control over a dynamic display, where, by manipulating one variable, he can establish the effects this has on other related variables. This is another example of the potential of the computer which has been successfully exploited. Computers have been used as a means of improving understanding of the symbolic representations of mathematical functions by generating appropriate graphical representations. The student types the coefficients of an equation and the computer displays the corresponding curve on an oscilloscope. This arrangement provides the student with a very powerful tool for exploring and manipulating the concepts he is attempting to learn.

Providing reinforcement

In a number of learning situations the trainee progresses by making responses and subsequently modifying them according to the information he receives about their adequacy. Reinforcement is concerned with ways of strengthening appropriate responses, that is, with increasing their rate, their intensity, or probability of occurrence. The precise effect of reinforcement depends on the schedule according to which it is administered. It may be given after every correct response, only after a number of such responses (ratio schedules), or even after fixed or variable amounts of time have elapsed (interval schedules). It is generally thought that reinforcement of every correct response is the best way of establishing a new response but that intermittent schedules are more effective in controlling the rate and intensity of a response already learned and in maintaining it.

A distinction is made between extinguishing a response and forgetting it. If a response is repeatedly made but is not rewarded or reinforced in any way, the response eventually drops out and is said to be extinguished. If, on the other hand, a response is not made at all over some period of time, its subsequent weakening is said to be a function of forgetting. It has been suggested that much apparent 'forgetting' is not so much due to lack of use of responses as to the subsequent acquisition of competing or incompatible responses or to initial failure to appreciate the full range of occasions on which the response is appropriate. Learning one set of facts, for instance, might compete with a set learned earlier resulting in both sets being confused with each other. In the second case, a student might be perfectly conversant with a particular procedure but be unaware of its relevance in a particular situation.

Reinforcement schedules are effective in maintaining responses when the cause of weakening is extinction, that is there is no reinforcement although the response continues to be made. For example, the 'proper' speech that a child might be taught at home is not reinforced when he is with other children who use slang. A similar situation in industry, where a suitable reinforcement schedule is appropriate occurs when trainees are required to learn safety precautions which conflict with the established practices of seasoned workers in the field.

Reinforcement schedules are also likely to be important in situations where there is no obvious means of conveying to the learner exactly what it is he is required to do. Training animals is an obvious example, but similar situations also occur in human learning – learning a golf swing or learning to serve at tennis, for example. In such cases instructions are only effective as eliciting a response which is a very rough approximation of what is desired. In these circumstances the best that can be done is to wait for a response to be made which is a reasonable approximation to the required response and to reinforce it. The required response is then gradually shaped by reinforcing successively closer approximations.

Providing guidance and prompting

In other situations, unlike the one just mentioned, there are perfectly adequate ways of eliciting the required responses, if necessary by having the learner simply copy the example he is given. The problem is not one of getting the learner to identify the correct response or even of getting the response to occur, but of getting him to make it on the appropriate occasion. This is almost certainly best achieved by prompting the required response and, subsequently, gradually withdrawing or 'vanishing' the prompts. It is necessary to withdraw the prompts to prevent the learner becoming over-dependent on them in providing his answers. For the large class of responses that can be elicited by suitable instructions the question of reinforcement is not one of any great significance. Discussions about the relative importance of prompting and reinforcement could usefully be replaced by attempts to specify more precisely the circumstances in which one or the other is appropriate.

There is some evidence that in learning paired associates prompting procedures are superior to confirmation procedures, but it is not conclusive. What seems more definite is that confirmation decreases in importance as the adequacy of prompting increases. Students working with programmed instruction often ignore the confirmation frames when the programme on which they are working contains adequate prompts.

Various techniques, including such things as sentence structure, relational words, etc., have been used to provide prompts. A long-established practice in teaching children to read is the prompting of the required vocal response to a word by showing a picture of the object the word represents and gradually withdrawing the pictures so that the child responds to the word alone. Similar techniques have been used in teaching children to name colours and numbers.

One interesting approach used to teach students a reading vocabulary in German employs redundancy in language to provide appropriate prompts. Certain words in the English text were replaced by their German equivalents without any loss of understanding of the content, as the words replaced were redundant. After a few key words in German have been mastered the programme began to change the word order of the sentences to conform more closely with the grammatical structure of German sentences. Gradually, the number of German words used was increased and the grammatical structure was made more and more like that of German.

The aim in trying to produce a technology of training is to expedite learning. If more guidance can be given to the learner by prompting and related cueing techniques, it may be possible to reduce the need for much trial-and-error learning and thereby reduce the need of corrective feedback. Before this is likely to be possible a clearer understanding of the ways in which prompts can be introduced and withdrawn for different types of subject matter is needed. Specifically it will be necessary to know:

(1) What factors govern the rate at which prompts should be withdrawn to obtain the best retention and rate of acquisition of information?

(2) The effects on learning of adjusting the strength of the prompts used in a frame from zero up to the point at which each student is able to respond. Almost certainly computers will have to be available to make this possible.

(3) How frequently should previously learned material be re-

introduced into the programme, that is, what form and spacing of review sequences are called for by different types of subject matter. The schedule of reinforcement is probably more relevant to review patterns than to the initial acquisition of behaviour. Here again, the flexibility called for is something which is only likely to be possible with the use of computers.

Providing opportunities for practice

Tasks are rarely mastered after a single or even several presentations of the relevant material. Criticisms of the simple repetition of material method used in early programmed instruction have suggested that it is monotonous and fails to ensure retention. The real need is for the learner to be able to manipulate the material in order to perfect the discriminations and responses he is required to make. Providing an opportunity for such practice is never easy because of the cost of the training time it demands and the difficulty in obtaining the necessary equipment. In circumstances such as these it becomes necessary to consider the possibility of simulating the learning task.

As complete realism of simulation is usually impossibly expensive it is essential to identify the critical elements of the task to be learned. For example, exact reproduction of joystick pressures in constructing an aircraft simulator is unnecessary if it is to be used in teaching cockpit drills and procedures but it would be necessary for teaching the motor skills involved in handling an aircraft. In general, the usefulness of a simulator will depend on the extent to which it preserves the essential dynamics of the real task.

Shriver's work on the problem of training men to diagnose faults on complex equipments (1960) is a good example of improving training by specifying the critical elements of a complex task. Shriver contends that any job can be described in terms of cues and the responses men are required to make to them. He further maintains that cue-response associations is the type of learnt material that has most effect on job performance. In diagnosing faults men have to:

(1) Recognize symptoms of malfunctioning which can be

used to determine a sequence of tests which will isolate the fault.

(2) Actually carry out the necessary tests.

The indications are that men experience more difficulties with the first of these than with the second. They must obviously be able to use test instruments and locate test points, but it is less easy to decide on an appropriate test sequence. This suggests that training should be mainly concerned with teaching men to discriminate correct from incorrect readings at various test points and in training them to discriminate those parts of the system which do affect the readings at a test point from those which do not.

Shriver's approach regards an equipment as a system for processing signals in certain ways to produce various effects. The aim is to make the structure of the equipment, the 'what affects what', as explicit as possible. Circuitry is analysed into blocks, each with its own inputs and outputs. Blocks are so defined that the failure of any component within a block will affect the output of that block, but will not affect the output at test points earlier in the signal flow, that is, in defining blocks, feedback circuits and 'reflected' faults are taken into account. Once blocks have been defined an attempt is made to determine and list the symptoms which would result from the output of the various blocks being out-of-tolerance. Significantly, it is not always possible to do this from first principles. It is often necessary to disconnect components and then record the resulting symptoms. Next, the systems analyst lists the location of each test point together with its normal output (voltage or waveform) and the necessary conditions of testing, for instance the test gear which must be used and any switching or disconnecting operations. This information makes it possible to isolate a fault to within a single block. The final step is to list the voltages and resistances at the end of chains of components within each and every block.

Signal-flow diagrams can also help trainees understand the structure of the equipment. Unlike many circuit diagrams, which are designed to indicate the physical location of components rather than the functional interrelationships between components, signal-flow diagrams are mainly concerned with the linear, divergent, and convergent chains and feedback loops which make up the equipment. Such aids are essential if men are to learn effective ways of searching in structured systems.

Shriver's analysis of fault diagnosis reveals three main elements:

(1) Decisional and interpretative skills, that is the ability to determine an appropriate sequence of tests.

(2) Mechanical and familiarization skills, that is ability to use test gears, confidence in working on high-voltage equipments, etc.

(3) Operational skills, that is being able to locate and get at various test points, etc.

Operational skills need to be taught on the actual equipment, the other two do not. Mechanical and familiarization skills can often be acquired on obsolete equipment and the decisional element may not require the use of equipments at all, and can usually be dealt with by programmed instruction. The trainee is presented with a symptom syndrome and asked what further information he needs in order to isolate the fault. As each test is indicated the trainee is given the information he would have received had he made that test on the actual equipment. This process is continued until the individual can make a definite diagnosis. Programmed instruction provides a useful way of supplementing the fault-diagnosis practice which men can receive on the actual equipment. Not only does it represent an economical use of training time, it has the added advantage of concentrating on the critical decisional element of the task rather than the less-demanding element of actually carrying out physical checks on the equipment.

Adjusting the difficulty of the practice to the trainee's current competence is another problem. Many of the words used to describe skills – smooth, unhurried, effortless, etc. – show that the ease of achieving performance is important as well as the standard of performance. This has been assessed by taking performance on a secondary task as a measure of 'spare capacity', for example doing mental arithmetic while driving a car.

Interest is currently being shown in ways of varying the difficulty of the primary task directly rather than by using a secondary task. In certain control tasks, steering a submarine for instance, this can be done by varying the way in which information is fed back to the operator. Control can be simplified by providing what have been called 'quickened' displays. Instead of receiving information about the magnitude of error the operator is provided with information about the rate of change of error. He is thus in a position to alter the control settings when the rate at which error is accumulating begins to rise rather than wait until the total amount of error is large before he takes the necessary corrective action. By systematically varying the amount of quickening which is provided it is possible to adjust the difficulty of a task to conform with the individual trainee's threshold of skill. This method has been used successfully in training helicopter pilots. Perhaps the best-known example of an adaptive trainer however, is SAKI, a device which has been used in punched-card operator training (Lewis and Pask, 1965). Here a moving spot of light successively picks out the digits to be punched in a practice exercise. The appropriate keys on the keyboard are cued by simultaneous illumination. The individual's errors and speed of reaction are used to determine the symbols which need to be practised and their rate of presentation and the provision of additional cues. As performance improves, the rate of presentation of the test exercise is speeded up and the additional cues gradually withdrawn.

These are some of the factors which enter into decisions about appropriate training methods. As their relative importance in different learning situations is likely to vary, training methods, whether in the form of programmed exercises, audio-visual presentations, or simulation, will have to be developed to cater for specific needs. The stimulus–response characteristics of the material to be learned dictate both the methods to be used in presenting information and the degree and type of control over the material which will need to be provided.

EVALUATING THE TRAINING COURSE

The distinguishing features of a technology of training are the specification of behavioural objectives and the assessment of the ability of training methods to realize these objectives. To accomplish this, instruction must be based on frequent tests of performance. The importance of adequate diagnostic testing has already been mentioned. A number of questions can also be raised about the type of terminal examinations which are required in order to evaluate training courses.

In general education, it is usually impossible to specify with any accuracy just what jobs students will eventually be required to tackle. This leads to a statement of educational objectives which emphasizes the student's ability to transfer or apply what he has learned to novel situations. In training, on the other hand, men will be taught those skills which task analysis has shown to be key elements in the overall job. The emphasis on specificity or generality in training is dictated by the nature of the training objectives themselves. Associations, multiple discriminations, and behavioural chains, for instance, involve the production of specific responses to stimuli having specific physical characteristics. Such objectives are in a sense the antithesis of transfer. This is not the case, however, with concepts and principles. These objectives are necessarily concerned with the generalizability of learning. Concepts and principles can only be said to be adequately elaborated if the stimuli subsumed as members of a class cover all instances which the learner can expect to meet in practice. Whereas the simpler forms of behaviour associations, multiple discriminations, and behaviour chains imply the avoidance of transfer, the more complex forms of behaviour require it.

Differences in the objectives of education and training are reflected in the types of examination needed to assess proficiency in the two situations. Examination scores can serve two purposes. The first is to indicate what the student can or cannot do – for example, whether he can write an acceptable report or diagnose various specified faults on an equipment. The second is simply to order individuals in terms of their performance.

The main difference between the two types of information is the standard which is used as a point of reference. Behaviourally defined objectives describe specific tasks which are associated with a given level of competence. Such a measure is quite independent of the performance of other people. Tests which are essentially normative, on the other hand, say very little about absolute levels of performance but simply indicate how one individual did in relationship to others on that particular test.

Educational examinations are usually of the normative type, being mainly concerned with ordering students in a class rather than assessing their attainment of specified objectives. This is partly due to the very general nature of educational objectives. It can be argued that educational testing should concern itself more with assessing attainment of specified objectives – indeed there are some indications that this is happening. It is true, however, that the achievement of an effective technology of training is dependent on the development of appropriate criterion-based tests of proficiency.

*

The various steps involved in developing a technology of training have been outlined. Three features of this approach are perhaps particularly significant in terms of the potential contribution each offers to the improvement of training:

(1) Emphasis on defining training objectives in behavioural terms and particularly attempts to define complex behaviour in terms of its simpler constituent elements.

(2) The attempt to define appropriate training strategies in terms of interactions between student capabilities and subject matter characteristics.

(3) Assessing the effectiveness of training in terms of the results it actually achieves.

CHAPTER 6

Training for Skill

D. H. HOLDING

A RECENTLY published survey of Post Office training officers, carried out by Martin (1965), was designed to provide a pen-portrait of successful instructors. Analysis of the replies showed that the best type of instructor is: 'a man who benefits greatly from his experience; has a good voice and facility with words; has had sound occupational training and possesses a good knowledge of the work; has a broad experience; makes full use of his intelligence; is acceptable to others and has a good influence on them, and is popular, self-reliant and confident'.

Such a man is clearly valuable in any profession. However the odd thing about this description, admittedly taken out of context, is that it contains no suggestion that the ideal instructor should know anything about training methods. Those of us who are unpopular, dependent, and diffident, having weak, hesitant voices and little influence on other people, will feel that this is unfortunate, since it is often possible to use systematic knowledge to greater effect than a magnetic personality. To the extent that knowledge and techniques are objective and scientific, they are available to all; the building-up of an integrated body of experimental results on human skills and human learning seems therefore to offer a long-term advantage in dealing with problems of industrial training.

The laboratory study of skills has gathered a great deal of momentum since the war in this country largely owing to the work of Sir Frederic Bartlett and his staff at Cambridge. Many kinds of human activity have been measured and analysed, and the central importance in most skills of factors like the timing of movements and the anticipation of later stages of the activity have been demonstrated. In addition, techniques and ideas imported from modern engineering have made for informed comparison of the characteristics of men and machines, so that their functions may be better understood and compatibility established in man–machine combinations.

A major development has been the recognition by psychologists that the human organism resembles in many ways a complex *servomechanism*. A servomechanism, or self-regulating device, is an arrangement like the automatic steering gear of a modern ship, or the prediction and control devices of a guided missile or a moon probe. What these mechanisms have in common is that they all make use of *feedback*; that is, their output is not merely determined by the initial control settings but is modified according to the degree of mismatch between their current state or position and a target value. In the case of the steering gear the target value is a static one, since we are using the device to maintain a steady compass bearing against the perturbation of wind and tide. For the guided missile the target is moving, but the object is still to reduce the discrepancy between the current and the wanted position, so that the size of the discrepancy is arranged to feed back in such a way as to modify the output.

Most of the actions of human beings are also regulated by feedback. A man reaching for a screw head with a screwdriver does not fling out an arm like a pebble from a sling, but initiates a muscular output which is regulated by his perception of the decreasing distance between his hand and the screw head so that there is a controlled deceleration of the movement towards the target position. Using a fretsaw to cut round a pattern, catching a butterfly, or running for a bus are examples of cases whose feedback information is related to a moving target. In many skills the information received by the brain will be predominantly visual, at least during the early stages of learning. Later on, the skilled man comes to rely more upon the 'feel' of an operation for his feedback. He can then 'do it blindfold', although his performance will deteriorate if uncorrected.

When visual or other sensory feedback is related to a goal or target by a human operator, we tend to say that he receives *knowledge of results*. Clearly, the maintenance of efficient performance depends upon a continuous supply of such information. This is true, not merely of separate human movements, but of longer sequences of action. A precision machining operation will require a good deal of fine feedback control during its execution but the crucial piece of knowledge of results, which will determine the next sequence of operations, is obtained when a micrometer is used on the machined part. The more complicated the operation, the more feedback is needed by the operator.

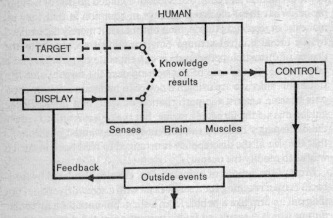

Figure 9. The feedback loop in human performance. The 'control' element may represent human limbs or equipment; similarly, the 'display' may involve perception of one's own body or of equipment changes; the 'target' may be internal or external

KNOWLEDGE OF RESULTS

Since knowledge of results is essential to performing an operation successfully, it has been natural to investigate the part which knowledge of results plays in the learning of any new skill. It has usually turned out to be considerable. If, for instance, a man is learning to fire at a distant target the bullet holes will not be visible to him, so that he will make very little progress unless someone signals back his score. Again, a man learning to send Morse code will sometimes transmit · − · · (L) instead of · · − · (F). Obviously if this goes uncorrected he is likely to repeat the mistake, which will become habitual and difficult to eradicate.

An important concern of the trainer will therefore be to arrange for the best supply and use of knowledge of results. He must help the learner to discriminate, from what may often be a confusing barrage of perceptual information, the important feedback signals; he must help the learner to relate these signals to the appropriate movement in a sequence of actions, and get him to watch for the perceptual cues in the task – visual appearance, noise, feel, and so on – which precede any wrong movements. Sometimes the trainer can help by modifying the equipment so as to give extra knowledge of results during the training period, but this is a technique which will need further discussion a little later on. He can certainly help by giving long-term knowledge of *progress*, day by day or week by week, which will give the learner a standard to aim at and will help to keep up morale.

Experiments on knowledge of results have explored a number of different issues. An early demonstration was devoted to showing the effects of removing feedback altogether. Here the task was one of drawing short lines of 3, 4, 5, or 6 inches, a job which requires repetitive, accurately graded movements, just as do many industrial production-line tasks. The people taking part in the experiment were blindfolded and asked to draw a test set of lines, which were then measured for errors. Half of them then continued to draw the lines blindfold without any information to help them, while the other half were given verbal knowledge of results by the experimenter, who said 'right' or 'wrong'. This second group, under the influence of verbal correction, made steady and considerable improvements in accuracy. As one might expect, the scores of the 'no information' group did not improve, becoming less accurate in terms of average error. However, the lines which they drew did become more consistent in length, which seems to point to the development of some kind of internal standards.

This same simple design of experiment, in which one group gets knowledge of results while another does not, has also been used at the other end of the scale to investigate long-term knowledge of results in an extremely complex task. Here, thirteen-man crews in air-defence radar stations had the job of detecting and following 'enemy' aircraft in their sectors, keeping near-by radar sites informed, and controlling the appropriate interceptor aircraft. Knowledge of results in the form of 'debriefing' sessions, at which crews discussed their operating procedures, problems, and mistakes with an instructor, gave results twice as good as those obtained by uninformed crews.

The knowledge of results obtained at debriefing, despite its effectiveness, was made available a long time after the relevant actions had been carried out. This raises the question whether a time delay in giving knowledge of results is an important factor in learning. Certainly in a task where continuous adjustment is needed, such as steering a simulated car along a filmed roadway, a delay of all feedback for one or two seconds may so disrupt the skill that practice becomes almost impossible. It is not yet clear to what extent continued learning can overcome this difficulty. On the other hand, where single movements are required which are complete in themselves a pure time delay seems to make very little difference.

Several experiments on the adjustment of control levers have shown that what matters most is the time interval allowed between successive movements. This is because the use of an item of knowledge of results in learning lies primarily in helping to amend the *next* movement in the series – the movement which gave rise to the result is already past. Thus, if the interval between movements remains the same, delaying knowledge of results after a first lever-press merely brings it nearer the next, so that any amendment needs to be borne in mind for a shorter period. However, lengthening the interval between successive movements means that the time lapse both before and after the knowledge of results becomes longer, so that learning tends to suffer.

Of course, if the delay of knowledge of results is so long that other movements intervene before the result of the first movement is reported the position is more complicated. Learning then seems to be less easy the more interfering movements are inserted. Even here though, when we measure the amount of learning retained by people some time after knowledge of results has been withdrawn from the training programme, we sometimes find that the delay has had no ill effects. The reason is that human beings, particularly when they use language as a tool, are capable of spanning long periods of time. Thus what really matters most is that a particular item of feedback should be clearly seen in relation to the response which gave rise to it and to its successor, and here the trainer can often help.

When knowledge of results is artificially supplied by the trainer, delaying it at least until the end of an adjusting movement is one way of making sure that the trainee does not come to rely too much on this kind of information. Over-reliance on extraneous signals, or *cue-dependence* as it is sometimes called, is a danger which limits the usefulness of giving extra knowledge of results. The effectiveness of any artificial technique must therefore be judged by the trainee's performance after any extra cues have been withdrawn.

An experiment which shows up this kind of effect was carried out by Annett (1959). Trainees were set to learn how to apply a fixed pressure for a few seconds by pushing a plunger. During training, one group was able to regulate each movement as it was made by watching a small light which moved up and down in step with the plunger, on a scale with a red line at the target pressure. For another group, the scale was hidden each time until an attempt had been made to reach the target pressure. At the end of thirty learning trials, both kinds of feedback were removed and testing continued for seventy more trials in order to see the effects.

What happened was that the first group made rapid progress during the learning trials, since it was easy to make use of the information on the scale. The second group learned slowly, making only a few correct pressures towards the end of the training trials. However, once feedback was removed it was clear that the first group had become 'cue-dependent' – their scores dropped rapidly, and after twenty trials some movements became so wild that the apparatus was damaged. By contrast, the trainees whose knowledge of results had been held back until the end of the movement had been forced to make use of the permanent cues intrinsic to the task, so that their level of performance was far less affected.

The way in which artificial, extra feedback can give an apparent but temporary improvement is also shown in some of the work on gunnery. When trainees are given practice on a simulator, the time during which they manage to keep an aircraft in the gunsight may be accurately recorded and an extra signal may be given at the same time to show when they are on target. The signal might consist of reddening the appearance of the aircraft, or simply of sounding a buzzer on the apparatus. Unfortunately, although introducing the buzzer gives an immediate, dramatic improvement in scoring rate the effects do not last during later trials without the buzzer. This is shown particularly clearly when the buzzer is sounded only on every other trial. The scores then move up and down neatly in step with the appearance and disappearance of the buzzer. The buzzer is clearly being used as a 'crutch' and the trainees are not being encouraged to make use of the inherent properties of the task.

A more encouraging feature of the same experiments, however, is that giving verbal feedback seems to work out comparatively well. Telling trainees their scores has a more lasting effect in many experiments, since it always occurs after the learner has had to cope with the normal version of the task. Verbal methods can also be made more elaborate than most. In the gunnery example the trainees were told what proportion of the time they had been on target, their performance compared at different parts of each aircraft 'attack', and their present score compared with their previous record.

At least one other kind of artificial knowledge of results seems relatively immune from the cue-dependence effect. The form of non-verbal feedback in which graphs of movement or detailed records are made available to the learner, to help him understand tricky sequences of action, usually seem worthwhile. For example, an early study showed that recruits could be efficiently taught to squeeze the trigger of a rifle by the device of hollowing out the butt and inserting a rubber bulb connected to an indicator tube or recorder. Improvements were obtained, by comparing recordings of each squeeze with those made by an expert, which clear verbal directions would not bring about. In another context, it has been shown that force-time graphs of a runner's front-foot movement can be used to speed up sprint starts. In both these cases the learner receives from the records information which ordinarily is just not available to him, with the result that learning is permanently improved.

The trainer's job, then, is to present the right kind of information to the learner and to make sure that he can make efficient use of it. So far we have dealt only with information presented during training in the form of knowledge of results, which has been the main subject of research in the past. At the present time, however, there are signs that a change of emphasis is taking place. Research workers in several related fields are beginning to explore systematically the idea that information may often be better used to *guide* the responses of the learner than to correct him. The trainee may be given a variety of cues to help him acquire a skill, but these need not always take the form of knowledge of results.

PERCEPTUAL CUEING

Insisting that learning is purely a function of knowledge of results commits one to the use of trial-and-error procedures. The learner makes an attempt, sees a discrepancy, makes another attempt in order to amend the discrepancy, and so on until the correct action is achieved. It is clearly tempting to short-circuit this procedure by inserting more information earlier in the sequence. In effect, we can try replacing the sequence *signal for action – attempt – knowledge of results – correct action* by the sequence *signal for action – guidance – correct action*. It is this second kind of technique which now concerns us.

Although its potentialities and limitations are not yet fully explored, the guidance type of training procedure has been shown to work. Nearly a decade ago the author (Holding, 1959) concluded that 'what seems to be necessary for the acquisition of motor skill is the occurrence of the correct response; and knowledge of results is merely an incidental, though common, means of achieving the correct response.' It is now clear that this conclusion holds good in many kinds of training and for tasks quite different from manual skills.

In the field of programmed learning, the issue takes the form of 'prompting' versus 'confirmation'. Teaching machines are devices for presenting programmes of instruction, which are carefully prepared sequences of material designed to guide the learner step by step in easy stages. In these procedures the use of heavy prompting is universal, the whole object being to prevent the learner from floundering among errors into which he has led himself. The form of question put to the learner is therefore so phrased as to 'give the answer away'. This means that he is almost always correct in his answers, with little reliance upon knowledge of results for correction.

The other main area in which prompting or guiding techniques are becoming important is that of *perceptual skills*, like those involved in radar watch-keeping and in many kinds of industrial inspection. Of course all skills have a large perceptual element, even those normally classed as manual or bodily skills. In a task like that of electronic assembly soldering, the brain of the operator is continuously busy, whether consciously or otherwise, calling up both techniques and recent events in the process from memory, making decisions about when and where to act, planning, checking, and controlling the necessary movements and processing the incoming sensory information from visual, touch, and warmth receptors.

So important is this 'input and central processing' side of an industrial skill that the ordinary time-and-motion study records in terms of 'therbligs', or units of movement, do not give anything like an adequate job analysis for the purpose of skills training. Crossman (1956) has put forward an improved 'sensorimotor process chart' which carries analysis much further. Symbols are provided not only for movement units but for perceptual units, or perhaps 'namsorcs', like plan (V), initiate (o), control ($\frac{3}{2}$), and check (Λ), which are recorded under a number of columns representing memory, decision, and the different human senses. In order to understand what trainees have to learn a thorough job analysis is always necessary; this will always involve a careful study of perceptual factors.

However, there is a class of skills in which muscular adjustments are at a bare minimum, where the operator's task is primarily to detect finely discriminated sensory signals and where action is needed only at infrequent intervals. This kind of skill is required in listening to electric motors to detect faults in bearings and brushes, inspecting glass bottles for cracks and bubbles, or in power-station control duties or chemical process monitoring. Maintenance work, too, often demands fault-finding skills which rely more heavily upon decision-making processes than upon bodily activity. The spread of automation has meant a big increase in the proportion of jobs of this kind, at the expense of the traditional manual skills. Industry has yet to recognize many of these new skills and to devise appropriate training methods.

The kind of laboratory work which seems relevant has usually compared knowledge of results with prior prompting or 'cueing'. In one unpublished experiment, again by Annett, the object was to train people to report accurately different numbers of dots scattered over a white background. Up to fifty dots were exposed to view at a time, and accuracy of reporting was measured before and after an hour's training. During training one group was required to guess the number of dots and was then told the actual number – a form of knowledge of results. The alternative, 'cueing' procedure was to tell the trainee how many dots would be shown before each presentation. Both kinds of training, which were compared with a control procedure in which no information was given, gave a roughly equal improvement in accuracy.

On the other hand, cueing proved more effective than knowledge of results in a second perceptual task, which took the form of detecting the position of gaps in incomplete circles. There were patterns like the letter 'C', in which the gaps could face east or west. Groups who were given 'right or wrong' information after each guess, or given summary scores after each set of twenty guesses or else given practice made easier by enlarging the gaps in the circles, were all inferior to the group guided by simultaneous cueing. This was arranged by showing all the right-hand gaps against red backgrounds and all the left-hand gaps against green backgrounds, a technique which left the pattern unchanged but provided extra information without involving cue-dependence.

Similar results were obtained in an experiment which duplicated the task of the 'sonar' operator, who has to listen out for underwater echoes. Training the operator to press a key on hearing a low frequency 'pip' against a background noise, giving a coloured light beforehand as a cue, was better than changing the task by lowering the noise level and better than knowledge of results. When this kind of experiment was repeated more elaborately at Sheffield University, both cueing and knowledge of results improved the trainees' performance, just as was found in the 'number of dots' experiment. This time, however, it was possible to measure an interesting difference in the ways that the two types of procedure brought about their effects. The trainees receiving guidance from the artificial cues made an increased number of correct detections, while decreasing the number of unjustified key-presses or 'false alarms'. The knowledge of results

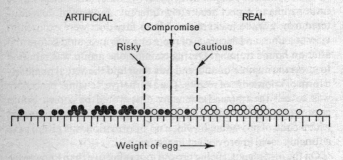

Figure 10. A version of signal detection theory. The 'risky', 'compromise', and 'cautious' lines represent different criteria of judgement

group, on the other hand, did better by increasing their total number of key-presses, thus stepping up both detections and false alarms alike.

Experimental psychologists nowadays deal with this kind of situation in terms of *signal detection theory*. This allows one to separate out two different factors which influence people's decisions when they are asked to judge whether or not a signal is present. Let us assume that a mistake has occurred at an egg-packing station, with the result that a packer is set to pick out a consignment of hen's eggs which have become mixed with a batch of modern lightweight nest eggs. He knows that in the main the real eggs are heavier but there is some overlap, as shown in Figure 10, since some of the hen's eggs are lighter than the heaviest of the artificial eggs. At what weight is he to guess that any egg is a real one? If he puts the dividing line at a large weight some of the ones he wants will be left behind with the artificial eggs, although the ones he picks out will all be real eggs. He may do this if he is cautious, or if he has been told to make sure that he *only* picks out real eggs. If he has been told to be sure he gets *all* the real eggs, or is 'risky' in his judgements, he will use a low dividing line instead. This will give him all the real eggs, but at the expense of including some of the artificial eggs by mistake. The best compromise lies between these two policies, and can be computed mathematically. It is easy to see that one factor affecting his judgements is the dividing line, or *criterion*, which he uses. The other factor is obviously his perception of the difference between the two groups of eggs. If the apparent separation of the two kinds increases because he has learned to discriminate better between them, or if he is presented with ostrich eggs instead, he can easily pick out all the wanted eggs with less risk of mistakes.

We can regard the real eggs as the 'wanted signals' in our sonar experiment. The artificial nest eggs correspond with the background noise and wrongly selecting a nest egg as a real egg constitutes a 'false alarm'. If we now reconsider the results of the different forms of sonar training we can see that what seems to be happening is that the 'cued' group are learning to discriminate better. The effect on the knowledge of results group seems to be different. Since these trainees are increasing both their correct detections and the number of false alarms, it looks as if their criterion is being shifted downwards; the training is making them 'riskier'.

Something similar has been shown in American work, where operators were trained to report on the occasional extra jumps of a clock pointer. In this case, ordinary knowledge of results again made for a shift in criterion level. However, better overall discrimination resulted when they were supplied with what was called 'full knowledge of results', but which actually consisted of giving information about every signal whether or not the trainee responded. Again we can see that what matters is the provision of relevant information, not necessarily that it should occur as a result of the learner's actions.

It is possible that extra information is only helpful at the outset of learning when the characteristics of the signal have to be recognized. A further problem in many perceptual tasks is maintaining vigilance over a long period of watch, and it would be useful to find training aids which improved prolonged performance. Unfortunately a careful, recent study by Colquhoun (1966) showed negative results. After giving preliminary training by both guidance and knowledge of results to six different groups of naval ratings, he gave each group a different training procedure for over a thousand trials and followed this by a test period of a further thousand a week later. All the groups, including one given no extra information, improved progressively in discriminating while exercising greater 'caution' in their decisions.

The explanation of this lack of sensitivity to different training aids may be that the effect of providing information in this context is mainly to make the trainee familiar with the average number of signals being presented. 'Full' knowledge of results or cueing will both do this efficiently, although knowledge of results which genuinely depends upon the learner's actions will not. Knowing the number of signals will change the trainee's criterion during the preliminary training but further information during the main training period will have little effect, although he may become more cautious for other reasons. This kind of explanation is partly speculative, so that it is clear that more work, on a wider range of perceptual skills, will be needed to describe unambiguously the part played by cueing and other artificial sources of information in perceptual training.

AUTOMATIC GUIDANCE

The cueing and prompting techniques reviewed so far have all relied upon guiding the trainee by offering additional sensory signals, without really constraining him to act correctly. It remains to inquire how far we can teach skills by direct physical manipulation, arranging for 'artificial learning' by taking control of the trainee's movements. This is the problem which has recently been tackled by the author and his colleagues in a series of experiments at the University of Leeds. In all of these experiments guidance has taken a physical form, the trainee's movements being regulated by a variety of automatic aids. This same kind of movement information is often available, for instance, to the pilot of an aircraft fitted for automatic landings, and how much he learns from this is of practical interest. There are indications, too, that guidance methods are practicable in training the blind.

The traditional use of the term 'guidance' to cover these physical methods is not particularly apt or explicit, but has always included two main kinds of training technique. In the early work, for example, people were blindfolded and asked to drive a wooden stylus through a model maze; they could be helped to learn this task by having the experimenter drag the stylus along the correct path, or by finding the wrong alleys artificially blocked off. These two methods, which we shall distinguish as the *forced-response* or *restriction* techniques, are alternative ways of ensuring that the learner practises making the correct movements and thus that errors do not become engrained. Both methods may be applied to a range of manual skills.

In fact, the skills which have been studied vary from the relatively simple 'line-drawing' kind of precision movement to the very difficult 'tracking task', where the operator has to match a pointer to the rapid oscillations of a small target spot of light. In between these two extremes lay a 'serial' tracking task, where the job was to move a joystick in such a way as to put out lights which appeared one after the other in different positions. This task could be made more difficult by varying the spatial relationship between the lights and the lever positions which extinguished them.

First of all we compared guidance with different amounts of knowledge of results in learning the 'line-drawing' task. This actually consisted of pushing a small knob along a metal rod, blindfolded, attempting each time to move an exact distance of four inches. For guidance by restriction a stop was placed on the rod at the four-inch mark. Practising with this brought about a sizeable increase in accuracy, greater if anything than did knowledge of results. The forced-response guidance was achieved by attaching to the control knob an ordinary door return spring, modified so as to drag the trainee's hand along an exact four inches. This gave a definite improvement, which is of some theoretical significance, although for practical purposes the amount of learning was relatively small.

There seem to be two reasons for this. One is that trainees whose arms are dragged along tend to resist the spring and thus to practise *pulling*, while they are later tested on *pushing*. We checked this possibility by training a further thirty people by the same two methods, this time for a version of the task which required them to 'let go' of the moving knob when it had been pulled for four inches. This neatly reversed the apparent effectiveness of the restriction and forced-response procedures, so that it seems clear that part of the difficulty about forcing is that in many ordinary tasks it will lead to the learner practising a movement which is not really compatible with the demands to be made upon him. The other possibility is that the trainee has little chance to compare the right distance with the wrong alternatives and so receives less information than he might. We checked this by guiding people at a range of different distances, telling them in advance which was correct. This also worked, suggesting that if the task itself does not offer 'knowledge of alternatives', then the guidance should.

Knowledge of alternatives presents no problem in the 'serial tracking' task, since the trainee is constantly moving the control lever between different positions in order to put out the signal lights. In this task we compared forced-response, provided by an electric motor driving the joystick to the correct positions, with a kind of restriction technique which we call *hinting*. For this, we loosened off the clutch which linked the lever to the motor, so that the guidance mechanism merely opposed the trainee when he tried to move in the wrong direction or overshot a light position. Like restriction in the 'push' version of the line-drawing task, hinting seemed to turn out better than forced-response.

In the comparisons made so far, we have chiefly been concerned with the effectiveness of guidance in acquainting the trainee with movement information, with the 'how' rather than the 'what' of the skill. However, in order to learn he needs a good deal of perceptual information about what it is he has to do, about what to look for among the sensory signals reaching him and the ways in which they are related to his movements. In order to investigate how well guidance shows people what to do we varied the perceptual load on the operator, while keeping the movement require-ments unchanged. This was arranged by comparing ordinary practice with guided training on three forms of the task.

In the 'direct' form, moving the lever to the right extinguished lights to the right and vice versa; in the 'reversed' form, moving to the right extinguished lights to the left; and in the 'random' form, there was no obvious spatial relationship between the lights and lever positions. These three tasks formed a progression in which more and more perceptual translation work was demanded of the trainee, although in each case he made an equivalent series of movements. The outcome of this increase in perceptual load was that the capacity of either kind of guidance to supply additional information became progressively more valuable. Both forcing and 'hinting' increased in effectiveness until, in the most difficult random form of the task, both produced more learning than an equivalent period of normal practice.

There is, of course, a limit to the amount of information which an operator can cope with in a continuous task. In circumstances where this limit is exceeded it appears that guidance may be used partially to off-load the trainee, allowing him to concentrate upon learning the important features of the task. This is presumably what happened in our experiment on the continuous tracking task (Macrae and Holding, 1966), where again we used three levels of difficulty. We taught groups of people to track – match pointers continuously to the movement of – spots of light in simple, inter-mediate, or complex motion. Some were taught by normal prac-tice, some by guidance, although for technical reasons it was only possible to arrange forced-response guidance. In this condition the trainee held on to the knob which controlled the pointer, while the machine tracked itself.

After the learning period we gave them all test trials on the intermediate course. This meant that those who had received training on the simple or complex courses had to *transfer* their learning to the new situation, thus undergoing a fairly stringent test. The simple form of the task did not demand too much during training, and both the guidance and the normal practice groups learned quickly, transferring equally well to the test course. Training on the complex course, however, proved too demanding for the normal practice group and they transferred with poor results. It is significant that the guided group, on the other hand, transferred so well that their results were as good as the scores obtained by the two groups who had trained on the simple task.

The advantage of the guidance procedure in this case is that it adjusts both the amount of information and the type of information which remains to be handled. As the machine tracks automatically the trainee can 'switch off' selectively, ceasing to pay attention to the movement information at the times when he is overloaded. This means that he is free to concentrate on the perceptual aspects of the task, learning to anticipate features of the visual display and the effects of control movements. The trainee practising without automatic guidance cannot do this, since when he stops attending to manipulating the control, he loses the target and the displayed information becomes useless for learning.

*

The key to understanding the guidance experiments is therefore the concept of *information*. What we are doing is adjusting the amount and kind of information which the learner gets. Experimental psychologists use the term 'information' in a wide but precise sense, to cover all the ways in which human uncertainties may be reduced. Any procedure which specifies some out of many alternatives is a way of presenting information. In this sense we can convey information by words, or by signal lights or buzzers, or by automatic movements of a control knob. We can therefore view the trainer as attempting to use his repertoire of training aids in such a way as to optimize the learner's supply of information.

If we look back over the work reviewed earlier we can see that this is true, not only of the automatic guidance methods, but of the work on knowledge of results and of the various aids to perceptual skills. The differences between the guidance and the knowledge of results methods seem less basic when they are viewed as alternative ways of supplying information. In fact, guidance information before one movement will often provide *knowledge of results* for a previous one, while knowledge of results is best used to *guide* the next. In experiments with both kinds of emphasis we have considered the efficiency for training of adding or manipulating information in such a way that it is of maximum use to the learner. We want him to have enough information, so we often supply extra cues in one form or another. At the same time we do not want to overload him, so that we will sometimes find it better to lighten the task during the early stages of learning by automatic methods, or else by splitting the skill into component parts which are practised separately.

All ways of presenting information to the learner are not equally efficient, since the information may be inappropriately coded, or inserted at the wrong point in a sequence of skilled activity. It is obvious that giving an English trainee instructions in Turkish is bad coding but less obvious that, for instance, visual information may be inappropriate to an operation carried out mainly by 'feel'. It is obvious that showing a trainee his machining faults in the middle of cutting a new piece is poor timing, but less obvious that elaborate instructions, given before beginning a manual operation, may overload his memory and slow down the learning process. Finding the most efficient ways of giving information needs care, but can be tackled by systematic research, where possible supplementing the laboratory results by investigations carried out on real industrial tasks.

We know, therefore, that successful training methods are those which supply the right amount of information, in the right way, at the right time. Although the research story is incomplete, so that we do not always know how to implement these recommendations in detail, a great deal has already been discovered. Translating the findings which have emerged from general principles into training practice on the shop floor or apprentice school may often require some effort on the part of the trainer, but the effort will be justified by the returns from informed training for skill.

CHAPTER 7

*Retraining and the Older Worker**

EUNICE AND R. M. BELBIN

TWENTY-FIVE students on a course for industrial training officers were asked the following question at a time of large-scale redundancy in the motor-car industry:

Imagine yourself responsible for the appointment of semi-skilled operators to your organization. Faced with the choice between two men recently made redundant in another industry, which would you choose:
  (a) The man of 45;
  (b) The man of 25;
or (c) Don't you know?

They were further asked to expand on their replies by saying why they decided not to employ the one they rejected, or if they didn't know, how they would proceed to make a choice. If any answer could have been judged 'correct', it would have been 'I don't know – it all depends on . . .' But only five chose this response. The remainder were divided in the ratio of 4:1 in favour of the younger man.

WHY OLDER TRAINEES ARE REJECTED

The preponderant reason for rejecting the older man hinged on some common concept 'less adaptable to change', 'more difficult to train', 'a slower improvement rate', and 'more difficult to retrain again when necessary'. The only other frequent response was that citing 'a shorter working life with the firm', a reason which is not supported by personnel statistics. Whatever the reasons given, the fact remains that firms show great reluctance to

* Some of the work mentioned in this chapter which is being conducted by members of the Industrial Training Research Unit, University College, London, is as yet unpublished. Such work is indicated here by an asterisk.

train workers over the age of 35: there is very little evidence that displaced middle-aged and older workers are being taught new skills in any significant numbers. Some of the problems are economic. Age barriers to recruitment may, for example, reflect problems of late entry into pension schemes. And it is not easy for an older man or woman to accept a learner's rate of pay.

Even if the economic obstacles can be overcome a big barrier still lies in the belief – both of management and of the worker himself – that older people are less likely to make progress in adapting themselves to a completely new job or in acquiring a new skill. The loss of adaptability and trainability with increasing age does seem to present a real problem which is not simply a matter of prejudice. But if means could be found whereby older workers could be more effectively retrained, then the prospect of retaining their employability in a rapidly changing job market might remain bright throughout working life.

UNDERSTANDING THE DIFFICULTIES

Fortunately, the nature of many of the difficulties of mature adults in learning are now reasonably well understood as a result of two or three decades of research work in the psychological branches of gerontology (the study of ageing). Much of our current knowledge springs from the work of the Nuffield Unit for Research into Problems of Ageing, which was attached to the Psychology Department of Cambridge University. From this research came the classic *Ageing and Human Skill* by Welford (1958). A popular presentation of the problems of ageing is *The Psychology of Human Ageing* (Bromley, 1966).

The way in which these problems of ageing may be successfully overcome in the industrial situation of learning a new skill forms another aspect of gerontological research. This is the basis of the work of the Industrial Training Research Unit, attached to Professor Drew's Department of Psychology at University College, London. The British effort to understand the fundamental problems of older workers and to apply this knowledge to industry is therefore quite considerable. A good deal of research is also being carried out in the United States and some very useful information is contained in *Handbook of Ageing and the Individual*, edited by J. E. Birren (1959).

One of the more persistent manifestations of ageing as it affects performance on a new skill is the difficulty experienced in casting off errors once committed. It is often more difficult to eradicate a wrong response made during the acquisition of skill than to learn an entirely new one. Learning that something 'is not so' is a particularly difficult form of learning, to which Kay (1951) has applied the term 'unlearning'. The phenomenon of unlearning was well illustrated by Kay in some experiments in which subjects of various age groups were required to extinguish a series of lights by depressing a row of keys. Inevitably in this trial-and-error situation subjects produced errors which they then had to overcome. The older subjects, however, showed a marked propensity to make the same mistake over and over again.

In manipulative skills the learning of an incorrect sequence leads to the cultivation of a bad style and bad habits – either of which can retard performance. Even comparatively young people will find it difficult to change their 'style' – as those familiar with sports such as tennis, cricket, or swimming will readily recognize. A recognition that difficulties in discarding bad habits increase with age hardly arises in sport – nor for that matter in the playing of musical instruments – because the problems are regarded as so critical that in practice learning is nearly always carried out in youth or childhood.

In the case of manipulative skills performed in industry, small numbers of people try to acquire them in middle age, and some succeed. In the main, however, there is a marked deterioration in learning achievement as age advances for those with no previous relevant experience. Some early American studies, for example, have shown that 'ageing' becomes a significant factor in certain engineering operations in early adulthood. Decline was noted from the age of 25 on punch-press operations and from 19 on a coil-winding job. So it is useful to consider whether in skills such as these some of the difficulties may be due to an unlearning problem creeping into performance at some stage during training.

Perhaps the most common industrial operation on which age makes itself felt in training is that of sewing machining. Age difficulties are nearly always manifest from the mid-twenties. A number of firms with a progressive outlook have endeavoured to offer special facilities for training middle-aged women, but have had to abandon the attempt in spite of the severe shortage of young recruits. The underlying basis for at least some of the difficulties experienced was suggested by Toye*. He observed the performance of an inexperienced 50-year-old trainee machinist who was recently recruited into a training programme in a clothing factory to act as a guinea pig for the study of age difficulties. The trainee had 'failed' after eight weeks on the traditional course and was then passed on to the research worker for training. He sought the nature of the difficulties by 'starting again' on a different operation – making pockets.

The job of making pockets was broken down into its various components or elements, for which a time value appropriate to a skilled worker was available. What transpired was not that the trainee had difficulty in achieving the target time once the correct pattern of movement was established, but that the trainee insisted on using a method that she believed was right, although it was in fact wrong. To fold a piece of cloth and present it under the shoe of the machine in the correct manner may seem a simple task. In fact numerous wrong trials on this and similar operations would tend to take place before the first correct sequence was established. These mistakes would recur later on so that the pattern of progress was long and frustrating.

SLOW-MOTION TRAINING

The solution to the problem of unlearning is practically self-evident. Bad habits must never be allowed to appear. The question is: how can they be avoided?

One possible method is the use of slow-motion training. By this technique the trainee is required to go through the motions very slowly – in the style of the gymnastics which are currently practised by aged Chinese. The technique takes some time to establish, since the trainee invariably goes faster than is intended. But once the idea is grasped it is comparatively easy to achieve the desired sequence of movement. One advantage is that the trainer is given a much better opportunity to observe the trainee's method. At normal speed, deviations from the best method are easily missed or only become apparent on close observation after a large number of trials. Another advantage is that the trainee experiences much less conflict and uncertainty about how the job should be performed and the correct method soon becomes the preferred way of doing the job.

GAINING SPEED

Although the establishment of the correct method provides the essential condition for achieving the target time, it does not follow that this will by itself enable the target time to be reached. The trainee may place such emphasis on care and accuracy as to preclude the achievement of a reasonable speed. For this reason 'forcing the pace' can become the complement of slow-motion training. Forcing the pace is the term used to indicate that the trainee is given a count-down for the completion of the element. The correct movement to introduce the technique depends on the discretion of the trainer, for if the pace were forced too early the result would be disastrous. Experience suggests that forcing the pace acts as a particularly strong stimulus. As some psychologists would put it, it has high 'arousal value'. It also has reinforcement value. It is very rewarding for a trainee to learn after only a brief period of coaching that she is achieving the time of a skilled worker for some component of the task.

The method is particularly useful in the clothing industry, where a cycle of work may take as long as two to three minutes. Once all the work elements are put together in a cycle, a trainee is apt to find that the target, as measured by an industrial timer, has not been achieved. Exactly where the trainee has fallen behind is not apparent and she is inclined to become depressed. But when she is paced in her progress throughout the cycle it is easy to recognize the elements in which her performance has fallen behind and to provide revision in the appropriate place.

Pacing, however, is rather expensive on supervisor time. An audio-pacing device which can be used by the trainee herself has now been developed by Toye and is being tested in a number of industrial situations.

PREVIOUS EXPERIENCE

The problem of disengaging from committed errors has some similarities with the problem of disengaging from previous work experience. It is often said that a trainee is handicapped by what he already knows. For example, in a training establishment where tuition was being given in television repairs, persons who had had some previous experience in electronics were found to be less successful than a group of ex-coalminers who were being retrained for a new job. Those with previous related experience were inclined to use their knowledge to pinpoint possible causes of faults in sets and this resulted in an unsystematic approach which consumed too much time. The coalminers, lacking this knowledge, took more readily to the use of the approved strategy in tracing faults.

Long-continued experience in a narrow field may result in a rigidity of mind which makes it difficult to eradicate not only habits but attitudes that have been acquired in previous jobs. For example, a man used to some form of precision work may find himself slow to establish the type of quick reaction required in a machining operation on output incentive. A demobilized army officer may find problems in adjusting to the different pattern prevailing in the conduct of relationships in industry between managers and subordinates.

Prior experience sometimes exerts a positive influence on performance and sometimes a negative one. The whole matter is also interrelated with age. A good illustration of the complexity of the subject is provided by Entwisle (1959), who cites the experience of a company which operated a fleet of horse-drawn service vehicles. These were replaced by motor vehicles and the 283 displaced drivers, covering a wide age span, were retrained. The results showed that, up to the age of 40, previous experience facilitated learning to drive a motor vehicle, but that after this age the opposite effect held and an increasingly negative influence was noted.

The effects of previous experience in learning are referred to by psychologists as the transfer effects of training. These transfer effects are said to be positive when they facilitate learning and negative when they impede it. The study of such effects has proved a very involved one and it is not proposed to discuss it here. The most pertinent question is what to do about the situation when negative effects are showing themselves, as they frequently do with adult trainees. Certainly the evidence suggests that older workers are not easily 'talked out' of their preconceptions.

DISCOVERY LEARNING

The problem of developing completely new concepts that are not in line with previous experience, or involve a new departure in thought, can sometimes be effectively tackled by employing 'discovery learning'. The object is to allow the trainee to develop concepts for himself.

Discovery learning differs from traditional tuition in several ways:

(1) Words are avoided, as far as possible, as the means of imparting information, and the emphasis is placed instead on *controlled* experience.

(2) The trainee learns by tackling problems that are within his reach. The solving of these leads to an insight of the principles or essential relationships that apply. The practical task is therefore problem-solving and never a demonstration of some principle that has previously been enunciated.

(3) The effectiveness of discovery learning depends on task design, whereas traditional tuition often depends on teacher flair. The trainer's main job in discovery learning is to diagnose the level of accomplishment of the trainee, to administer the appropriate task out of a number of graded tasks, to check the results, to ask the right question at the right time, and to act as consultant to the trainee only when help is sought.

The reasons why discovery learning seems to be of special benefit in training older workers are various. Amongst the foremost is the indication that the learning of adults consists of a conscious attempt to place new knowledge into some pre-existing framework of their own. It is here that the explanations and analogies of teachers may prove bewildering. It is often the case that the teacher, especially if he is an older worker himself, insists on putting forward his own framework into which the particular piece of knowledge fits and this interferes with the natural process of thought of the trainee. Discovery learning has the practical advantage of securing a natural way of learning to the mature adult, as a means of imparting an understanding of concepts and principles. It clearly has application in a fairly wide range of industrial training situations. It is currently being applied by members of this Unit in situations ranging from a project of training stonemasons to the training of adults in electrical and machine operating jobs.

It is worth noting that parallel trends have been taking place in the education of youth. In the teaching of reading, mathematics, languages, and science new and effective methods of training have arisen in recent years. Some of these new ideas have still not been fully exploited in industry and the difficulties experienced by older adults provide a favourable opportunity for their introduction. In this connexion it would seem that discovery learning offers to be a bridge between developments in the educational and industrial training fields.

FORGETTING

The next phenomenon which is worthy of special attention is the importance of what may be referred to as 'interference' effects on adult learning. Under ideal conditions the evidence would seem to suggest that differences in learning capacity between different age groups of comparable status are smaller than is popularly supposed. But under unfavourable conditions age becomes associated with decline in performance. The most unfavourable condition on this hypothesis is where items of knowledge that enter into temporary storage in the mind are subject to some external interference before they can be transferred into long-term storage. The results may be the same as those with any other unfavourable condition – a loss of learning ability – but if the cause of the loss is recognized there are prospects that the difficulties can be reduced by changing the condition of learning.

Many everyday examples come to mind: 'I forgot to bring what you asked me – someone spoke to me on my way here'; and how many of us forget a phone number just ascertained from the directory while we dial the code number?

In a study of training London postmen, it was noticed that part of the traditional procedure of learning to sort incompletely addressed letters was subject to this kind of short-term memory disturbance. During training, the recruits had to sort cards on which were written London street names into a 48-box frame bearing the name of the London postal district. Kensington Gore might appear on a card. The idea was to learn, while sorting, that Kensington Gore was in SW 7. If the trainee knew the appropriate box, he would 'post it'. If he did not, the procedure was:

> Read 'Kensington Gore'
> Turn card over
> Read correct postal district on back of card (SW 7)
> Search for appropriate pigeon hole in frame
> Sort card into pigeon-hole

It was often found on questioning the trainees that they had quite forgotten the original street name. Thus no associative learning could take place. The turning-over and search had provided a distraction which interfered with learning.

We commonly associate loss of short-term memory with ageing, but experiments have shown that it is not necessarily short-term memory deficiencies which are the problem. In a carefully planned experiment Bromley (1958) found that three matched groups of people aged between 17 and 76 years showed no differences in scores with age on a test of short-term memory span (that is the amount which could be remembered immediately after presentation). On the other hand, there is a good deal of evidence to show that a marked age trend exists in the disturbance to retention caused by events, especially unrelated events, that occur near to or at the time of learning.

The implications for training the older worker seem to be that where learning involves some degree of conscious memorization rather special conditions are required to ensure that rapid forgetting does not limit learning performance. In the case of the Post Office training problem cited above, the solution is straightforward – learn the frame locations first; put the 'answer', at least for the initial items, on the front of the card. In other industrial training situations, it may be necessary to pay much more attention to detail in task design.

The effects of interference on tasks of learning involving memorization have their counterparts in the learning of other skills where memorization plays little part. An instance might be cited from the early stages of learning of sewing machining (already quoted). The older trainee was observed from time to time to make fumbles: or she suffered the misfortune of having her thread break. The effect of these disturbances, however, was not merely to increase the time for the element of work affected, but to disturb the performance of successive elements with which she had not previously experienced difficulty. Again, on transfer to production work the older trainee was so much affected by the impact of the change that she seemed to lose what she had previously learned and had to be received back into the training school again before being reinstated in the production department.

The need to exclude interfering activities may also account for the evidence that older trainees show a marked preference for longer training sessions, whereas younger people prefer short sessions with breaks in between. For example, Neale* taught map-reading to teacher trainees of different ages by means of the Auto-Tutor Mark II machine. He found that for the age range 18–20 years, ten half-hour sessions (two on each of five consecutive days) produced the best results. On the other hand, with trainees in their thirties and forties, results from five one-hour sessions on the five consecutive days were significantly better than from the ten shorter sessions.

This appreciation of longer learning sessions by older learners may indicate that they are loath to engage in any other activity following recent learning that is in danger of interfering with or disturbing what they have recently learned. Perhaps it is part of the same problem that older trainees need to consolidate immediately what they have learned. These considerations have led to the development of a cumulative-part-learning method which has been shown to have a special application in teaching the over-35s.

Suppose a task may be broken down for training purposes into four parts, a, b, c, and d. It would be possible to learn each part separately and then to combine them: or to learn and combine them in various combinations. But what has been found with older learners is that they often have forgotten 'a' while learning 'b' – thus they never get to a stage of combination. Cumulative-part-learning aims to teach 'a', then 'b' in combination with 'a'; then 'c' in combination with 'a + b', and so on. Thus the original parts are rehearsed continuously and not forgotten while new aspects are being learned. If the most difficult 'part' to learn can be labelled 'a', so much the better, for it will ensure greater practice on that component.

SELECTION OF OLDER APPLICANTS

One of the factors upon which successful skill acquisition depends is the suitability of the trainee. This is particularly important in the case of older job applicants because there is good evidence that differences in capability within an age group increase with increasing age. Selection methods, therefore, have a special importance.

It has been found, however, that methods of selection of acknowledged success with young people are often unreliable predictors of the abilities of mature adults. Older people often react unfavourably to novel material or to the use of paper and pencil tasks so that what is being scored is uncertain. More practice with tasks of any sort might improve performance quite considerably. Even a limited period of return to education or training can exercise a major influence on test results. For example, in some studies in the United States on the use of the General Aptitude Test Battery – which is applied to adults accepted for training under the Manpower Development and Training Act – it has been shown that scores can rise as much as twenty points for the 45-year-olds after twenty weeks of vocational training on activities seemingly unrelated to those abilities measured in the test.

Most tests treat the abilities they seem to measure as static, and the assumption is made that the abilities (or general factors of ability) demanded in the work situation can be related to corresponding test scores of these abilities. This seems reasonable enough, apart from the fact that one factor is left out of consideration: the matter of potential. We can measure specific abilities as they are now, but we are perhaps more concerned with how these abilities grow and develop during training. It is often this capacity for growth and development which interests us more than the abilities displayed at the onset of training.

During the early stages of industrial psychology some attempts were made to measure trainability, but by the 1930s these endeavours had been largely abandoned in favour of special aptitude testing. Viteles (1932) describes the original idea as being based on the *analogous* test – 'an attempt to duplicate in one test the essential activities of the job'. This was accomplished by reproducing in miniature the pattern of the job, by constructing a test which simulated the job without actually reproducing it, or by using 'the Work Sample which requires the subject to perform either all the operations of the job or certain selected operations'. The criteria for selection were then the rate and amount of improvement of the subject with a given amount of practice. While these tests were stated to be reasonably successful, in practice they were difficult to administer and to fit into an industrial recruitment programme.

A start has now been made in re-exploring this field. A useful lead was gained in the study of manual sorters in the London Postal Training School. For experimental purposes, unconnected with selection, the trainees were given some tasks in which they were required to learn the association between hamlets and counties. Performance on this *learning* task, however, proved a useful predictor for mature adults of their success and failure in the letter-sorting training programme.

The success of this approach to the selection of the higher age groups is now being considered by Downs* in relation to the selection of carpenters for courses of training at Government Training Centres. The 'trainability' test involves learning short tasks incorporating some critical elements of the carpenter's job. The rate and accuracy of learning is then assessed. As a test it is rather well received by mature adults since it is clearly related in their own mind to the job for which they are seeking training. The results have shown promise in detecting potentially unsuitable trainee carpenters. The same principle is currently being applied by Downs in trainability tests designed for the selection of welders and bus drivers.

Another promising approach to the selection of the middle-aged for retraining is to consider the extent to which an applicant has maintained learning activity since leaving school. From an analysis of some results of Coal Preparation examinations it was found that those older students who maintained some form of learning activity after leaving school were by far the most successful in their theory examinations, even though this learning consisted of subjects quite unrelated to the course of instruction (First Aid, music, languages, wireless telegraphy, and so on).

TABLE 2: *Average Marks for Coal Preparation Examination 1965*

| Age | 'Continuers' (those who had attended un-related courses) | | | 'Non-Continuers' (those who had attended no courses since leaving school) | | |
	Theory	Practical	Number	Theory	Practical	Number
20–29	71·3	72·3	4	53·6	72·9	7
30–39	71·7	73·7	14	60·4	76·8	14
40–49	69·8	76·8	15	54·7	70·9	14
50+	62·3	65·3	3	48·5	63·8	4
			36			39

If this is so, the collection of personal history or biographical items should offer possibilities in diagnosing potentially successful trainees in the older age range. In fact, Mottram* and Crinnion have found such a method suitable in the selection of older trainees for a number of courses in a training centre. Ninety-three trainees completed personal-history questionnaires as well as a battery of intelligence and aptitude tests. The results suggest that for those over the age of 30 a combination of test score and 'active' spare-time interests was a useful predictor in training. This was not so with the younger recruits, where test score alone offered a fairly useful predictive validity. This difference between results with age is no doubt due to the fact that the relevance of spare-time interests changes from being an indication of occupational inclination in youth to an indication of continued application of intellect (and thus trainability) as we age. Thus the value of information afforded by 'active interests' lies more with vocational guidance in youth and with selection as we get older.

The importance of active interests for trainability as revealed in Mottram's and Crinnion's study is in line with some recent theories about the ageing process. Thus K. U. Smith (1966) writes: 'In cybernetic theory, learning involves changes in the detector neurons and systems of receptor and sensorimotor control. To become functional early in life, such neurons must be activated. To retain their precision of control, they must be reactivated repeatedly. We believe that ageing involves deterioration of neuronic control which proceeds more rapidly if the cybernetic control systems are not used.'

There are a number of other factors which have a significant bearing on the success of mature adults in training. One of the most important is the attitude of the trainees themselves. In several countries where Government-sponsored programmes have been designed to assist and promote vocational training it has been noted that the number of adults aged 40 and over availing themselves of the opportunity has been disappointingly low. Indeed, there is plenty of evidence that, where opportunities arise for vocational retraining, older workers often show signs of avoidance behaviour. Of 331 men rendered redundant by the closure of two British Railways workshops, not one accepted offers of retraining. In Arizona it was necessary to contact 900 migrant families in order to enrol seventy-five adult trainees.

Many mature adults are deeply imbued with notions that in effect circumscribe their behaviour. For some, it is that they are 'too old to learn'. Such stereotypes seem to be most easily broken down when adults find their peers setting a pattern that serves as an example. New patterns seem to spring up quite readily in the appropriate socio-economic setting. There are a number of instances both in Great Britain and abroad of firms that have established themselves in remote townships where they have often formed the only important source of local employment. In these cases, groups of mature adults have generally adapted themselves to new jobs and skills with a marked enthusiasm and readiness to learn.

ADJUSTMENT AFTER TRAINING

Changing jobs in middle age involves problems of selection and entry into training programmes and of performance in these programmes. Less well known is the cluster of problems arising after training. The fact that older workers have more stable employment records may be partly a function of a long period of adjustment to the requirements of the job and the firm. The same degree of stability cannot be assumed in the case of an older worker who enters into a new occupation for the first time following retraining.

Newsham* has found that after successful completion of training there occur what she characterizes as 'critical periods of adjustment' to the work situation. It is at these times that older trainees are very liable to leave. The problem of adjustment may be that of adapting a newly acquired skill to actual workshop conditions or of developing personal relationships in a new environment. Sometimes inadequate knowledge of shop-floor conditions and preconceived notions may lead to disappointment ('we never thought a job requiring full-scale medical examinations and selection tests would turn out like this'). Examples can also be cited of older workers having difficulty in adjusting to the 'rejection' standards of the inspectors.

The critical period of adjustment may differ according to different jobs and firms. The period may be immediately after or some weeks after training. If no account is taken of this critical period, training the middle-aged can often prove to be uneconomic. However, where adequate attention is given to the problems that occur during these periods, the ultimate survival rate of older worker trainees is generally higher than that of juveniles and young adults.

Many of the more successful attempts to train older workers for new skills have been those undertaken for existing personnel *within* a firm, where, for example, unskilled labour has been upgraded to semi-skilled jobs. In such situations the potential trainees are already well known to the employer; the training methods have often been designed to take account of their special needs and due care is given to problems of placement. The most successful programmes seem to be those where the changing nature of the company's product has demanded a policy of periodic retraining for all employees. Such a situation leads to the development of facilities carefully attuned to the special needs of adults.

RETRAINING IN PERSPECTIVE

We can conclude with some observations on a few general points.

First, changing jobs in middle or late maturity still tends to be regarded as a freak event. In practice, the older trainee is nearly always a victim of forces outside his control: it is quite likely that his former place of employment will have closed and that retraining offers his only job prospect. At all events it is very rare to find adults entering into courses of training on their own volition. This is a measure of the deep-seated prejudice that exists against retraining in mature adulthood.

Secondly, it is incontrovertible that there are significant problems involved in training older people. These problems have hitherto been avoided because the age structure of the working population was such as to provide an adequate number of new recruits for all the training vacancies available and because there have always been an adequate number of unskilled menial jobs into which older drop-outs from the work force could be fitted.

Thirdly, the changes that are now taking place in the occupational structure of society demand that many middle-aged workers will need to be upgraded to learn more difficult skills than those to which they are accustomed if they are to maintain their hold in the labour market.

What *is* becoming apparent is the possibility of coming to grips with these problems. This makes one realize just how many men and women are in occupations far below their potential.

PART THREE

Ergonomics

ERGONOMICS originates from the researches of experimental psychologists and physiologists and the more practical work of time-and-motion study experts. Ergonomics, or human engineering as it is sometimes known, has been described as the psychologist's extension of motion study. More correctly, the term embraces the many applications of sciences such as experimental psychology, anatomy, and physiology to questions of fitting the job to the worker. It therefore complements the effect of training, which is to fit the worker to the job. The purpose of ergonomics is to facilitate effective performance of man–machine systems by ensuring that the worker's capacities and inclinations are given due recognition. To do this, the ergonomist may, for example, apply himself to human factors in building design, the control of high-speed vehicles, and the manufacture or operation of industrial equipment and machinery.

As technology itself begins to emphasize the mental rather than physical requirements of jobs, so knowledge of psychological processes in the operation of elaborate engineering constructions assumes critical proportions. As Whitfield points out in Chapter 8, the identification of ergonomics with advances in engineering and its potential for predicting human performance in novel situations are among its most attractive features.

The ergonomist's work is relevant to a wide range of management activities. For example, he grapples with the questions of allocating operations between man and machine, investigates the computer's function as an extension of human mental skills, and draws attention to the physical environment in which the employee is required to work. It is not difficult to imagine how each of these facets may eventually be extended to provide a basis for fitting the technical systems of work to the social organization. The contributors to this section of the book have worked together closely in drawing attention to some aspects of their subject which have particular importance today.

CHAPTER 8

Ergonomics as a Management Technology

D. WHITFIELD

M OST of the social sciences applications discussed in this book are aimed at problems which arise from the interactions of individuals, or of groups of people, in industrial or commercial contexts. Ergonomics, on the other hand, is an attempt to come to terms with the relationships between human beings and the non-human constituents of industry – the machines, working methods, processes and physical environments which impinge upon men and women. And, just as human interrelationships contribute towards the success or otherwise of an industrial organization, so the ease of communication and cooperation between man and machine influences the ultimate efficiency of the system to which they both belong. It is on this interdependence of man and the rest of the industrial scene that ergonomics focuses; all industrial systems embrace a human contribution, even, as we shall see in Chapter 10, those processes which the engineer would describe to the layman as 'fully automated'.

The ergonomist takes as his frame of reference our scientific knowledge of human capabilities and limitations. Further, he accepts that, outside certain limits which are reflected in the development of training facilities, these capabilities and limitations cannot be modified. It is obvious that a labourer will never be able to lift unaided a casting weighing half a ton; it is no less true that the controller of a chemical process plant has a (fairly low) maximum rate for assimilating information from his instruments and making consequent decisions. Thus, reasons the ergonomist, since man and machine must be integrated into an efficient working unit, then it is the machine which must change to fit in with the man. In fact, there are two complementary objectives implicit in this engineering of work to match human characteristics. First – and this positive objective deserves more emphasis than it has had in earlier treatments of ergonomics – we must recognize and use to the full the enormous range of abilities which human beings do possess. Ignoring the emotional undertones of the word, we can talk about the 'exploitation' of the versatility of human behaviour, which can cope with unpredictable situations by learning and modifying its approach to new events. We can accept man as a valuable component of any industrial process and plan his activities so that he performs valuable tasks. Second, as a constraint on this utilization of human resources, we must avoid overloading the operator – his task must always remain within safety limits for physical or mental effort. If we can maintain the optimum balance between these dual objectives, then we shall be using human beings both efficiently and humanely.

THE AFFINITY OF ERGONOMICS AND ENGINEERING

Thus, ergonomics is a product of the frontier between the applied social sciences and engineering. It is also a direct result of the sophisticated achievements in engineering over the past few years – one could not have expected such studies to emerge as a separate technology when the engineers themselves were still grappling with basic problems of their own. Today, the picture is different, in two complementary respects. On the one hand, complex equipment and working procedures increase the demands on human beings; probably the first widespread recognition of this came during the Second World War, when several examples of advanced military equipment fell short of expected performance because of difficulties experienced by normal operators. On the other hand, with his new skills and specialized techniques, the engineering designer is more able to meet the real challenge of designing systems to 'fit' people; in machine tools, for example, the application of electrical or hydraulic techniques gives flexibility in arranging layout of controls for optimum human use which was unattainable with mechanical linkages. The affinity with engineering can be pressed even further when we consider the impact of technological advance on an industry; the emphasis changes from art to science, and the evolutionary process of trial and error in solving problems has to be discarded. As with other technologies, so with

174

ergonomics – the development of hand tools over centuries of use is a fascinating illustration of evolutionary 'human factors engineering', but current man–machine systems, representing enormous financial investment, must work first time, with little allowance for running modifications of man–machine interactions.

It is of great significance to ergonomics that modern technological achievements are changing the role of human beings in industrial systems. In general, people are being used less as sources of energy or physical work, and more as instruments of judgement and decision. Specialized branches of engineering, such as mechanical handling, provide elegant and efficient solutions for tasks which once required long and arduous human participation. The *control* of such devices, however, is predominantly a human responsibility and human beings generally perform a vital role in both day-to-day decision making and long-term planning in complex technological systems. The implication for ergonomics is that we need to know a great deal about how people behave in such situations; for instance, how operators make use of pattern perception or long-term memory in arriving at decisions. We are thus beginning to emphasize human *mental* capabilities and limitations rather than their *physical* characteristics, and so our knowledge of psychological processes becomes extremely important. Work study has shown that much can be achieved in the optimization of physical work, even with little understanding of the basic human processes involved; for tasks with a high psychological content, the problems are more complex, and their solution depends on the application of strict scientific evidence.

ERGONOMICS AS A MANAGEMENT TECHNOLOGY

Such arguments make a good case for the inclusion of ergonomics in the modern battery of management techniques. Its identification with current engineering developments, and its potential for predicting human performance in novel situations, are probably its most attractive features. The ability to predict derives from its basis in the theoretical concepts and accumulated knowledge of the experimental human sciences. Much of this chapter will be devoted to the demonstration of some of the theoretical framework of experimental psychology which guides the ergonomist's activities. This seems the best comparison to draw with work study, whose operations and objectives are, of course, allied to this newer technique. Indeed, ergonomics can be seen as the latest in a line of 'scientific management' techniques descended from such pioneers as F. W. Taylor, who first overtly 'fitted the job to the man' by designing a range of constant-load shovels for labourers loading materials of varying density. But, whereas work study and its predecessors depend on a mixture of individual experience and systematic though arbitrary procedures, ergonomics has this foundation in experimental evidence and theory.

In essence, ergonomics is a way of looking at problems of man–machine compatibility, within the framework of what we know about the functioning of human beings. Like all technologies or problem-solving disciplines, its practice comprises three broad divisions: a body of carefully collected and classified facts, techniques and concepts for analysing specific problems, and a creative element for producing unique solutions. The last is not amenable to exposition here, and the first is too detailed for general reading and is, in any case, available in the standard text-books. We shall therefore concentrate in this and the two succeeding chapters on the working models and analytical techniques which the ergonomist brings to his work. We shall attempt to convey his general approach to problems, and the flavour of his contribution. This chapter gives a broad survey of the scope of the subject, and the other two concentrate on the two areas most relevant to general management – problems of production techniques and the impact of automation on human tasks.

BASIC CONCEPTS

Three human sciences

A convenient way of defining the scope of ergonomics is to outline the three human sciences on which it is based. The three are anatomy, physiology, and experimental psychology.

Anatomy is concerned with the structure of the body, and is applied to ensure that the working postures required of operators, and the general accommodation of the body, are adequate for human comfort and efficiency. In particular, the branch of *anthropometry*, the study of body and limb dimensions, has many direct applications to work-place layout. The 'average man' is just as misleading here as in economics, for we ought to cater for a range of different-sized people within the dimensions of a standard layout. Anthropometry tabulates this variation of body sizes in the form of statistics, from which can be deduced the minimum or maximum dimensions to suit a proportion of a given population of users. This detailed information, together with general recommendations on working posture, can be found in any of the ergonomics text-books, and certain widespread applications, such as the design of office furniture, have been accepted as standards by the British Standards Institution.

Physiology is the study of the physical functions of the body. From this point of view, the human being is an engine capable of performing work. The physiologist's contribution to ergonomics is to define the safe limits of physical effort which can be expected from the human operator. To this is allied the study of human capabilities under various types of environmental stress, such as extremely hot or cold working situations. Related areas cover human reaction to, and optimum levels of, the thermal environment, lighting, noise, and vibration, though these are departing from purely physiological considerations and involve psychological functions as well. There are also the 'temporal' stresses involved in fatigue and the organization of working hours, in the problems of shift work, and in the effects of 'vigilance' tasks such as inspection – again, a complex of physiological and psychological factors. In the next chapter, B. A. Lacy will outline the salient features of these aspects of human work, and the ergonomics literature contains much relevant information. Moreover, as already emphasized, the dominant human factors problems in current and future industrial contexts are more likely to centre on the operator's mental, rather than physical, functions.

Thus, *psychology* – or to be more precise, *experimental psychology* – is the primary constituent of ergonomics. The label 'experimental' indicates that we are restricting ourselves to those aspects of human behaviour which can be controlled and observed in a laboratory setting. Questions of attitudes towards work situations, for instance, are better handled by other specialists (though we would hope that current trends towards inter-disciplinary studies will encourage the sharing of techniques and theoretical concepts on such topics). The experimental psychologist is trying to build models of human behaviour, precise descriptions of performance under specified conditions; the ergonomist's main contribution is predicting human performance in engineering systems, by making use of such models. Broadly, the models are meant to cover the ways in which people take in information from the outside world, the processes by which decisions are reached, and the strategies for implementing these decisions. The decision may be an inspector's acceptance of a component from a quality control sample, or a charge engineer's shutting-down a faulty nuclear reactor, but the same sequence of information–decision–action applies in any man–machine interaction.

The influence of systems engineering

Before developing any further the psychological content of ergonomics, we must acknowledge another powerful influence on the field. The early workers in ergonomics were enthusiastic, but they tended to take a narrow view of their responsibilities. Man–machine compatibility was the ultimate goal, with – as we can now see comfortably in retrospect – little attempt at evaluating whether the man–machine combination was in fact achieving the desired objectives or was put together in the best way. Thus attention might be centred on the detailed design of a meter scale, perhaps on the relative merits of different pointer designs, when no one had questioned the necessity for conveying that particular information from machine to man or its presentation in such a form. Fortunately, contact with the equally new discipline of systems engineering helped to dispel any tendencies to 'make mountains out of molehills' and injected a new ordered approach and a sense of priorities.

Systems engineering is a product of the need to cope with engineering design problems of increasing complexity in the shortest time possible. The complexity arises from the sheer size and detail of the tasks which face engineering designers – for instance, individual hand or machine tools are being replaced by integrated production lines – and the time limitation implies that iterative design and development must be cut to a minimum. The approach is to concentrate first on defining precisely the objectives of the system; all subsequent design decisions must derive from this statement of what the system has to achieve. Second, in expanding this definitive statement into a form which enables decision about the component parts of the system, the designer sticks to *functional* descriptions as long as he can. That is, he produces a complete and detailed description of *what* the various parts of the system have to do before considering *how* these various functions are to be achieved. The point is that it is all too easy to jump to a conclusion that 'we'll have to use a hydraulic device there' or 'it needs an automatic control system' before the complete set of individual requirements, and their inevitable interactions, have been enumerated. (This applies equally when considering functions which will possibly form part of human roles in the system – the 'amateur ergonomist' finds it difficult to take a disinterested, objective view of these.)

A comprehensive and searching functional specification of the whole system is an invaluable foundation for deciding on its physical realization. This, of course, is where the ergonomist first has a contribution to make (if he hasn't already been involved in the functional specification, which often happens); a crucial decision is: which functions are to be performed by human operators, and which by the hardware? Allocation of function to man or machine, to use the jargon, is a most important stage, to be considered in terms of what man *ought* to, and what he *can*, be asked to do. The decision obviously depends on the relative capabilities of man and of machine, and on the relative costs of having each perform the required functions. But consideration of human participation also forces us to assess the nature of the resulting operator's task. If the person is to fulfil any role other than that of a 'trousered ape' – an apt, if not felicitous, description of many industrial jobs – then his functions ought to be chosen so that they create an integrated and meaningful task. If we are to depend at all on the human resources of invention and flexibility, then we must provide conditions which enhance learning and understanding of the complete system. Moreover, this principle is to become more important as machines take over more routine activities and leave the human contribution as that of supervisor and decision-maker.

The importance of allocation of functions to man or machine was first stressed in the United States and originated in the military field, like several other ergonomics developments. There are signs that it is now a useful concept in British industry – for instance, computer control of power stations is seen not as the computer eclipsing ultimate human control, but rather assisting the operator in his task of management. And examples of incorrect allocation are not hard to find: the elaborate conveyor lying idle because it can't be adjusted to a new product, or the computerized production control system which needs frequent manual 'intervention' because of changed input or output data – both opportunities missed to incorporate the flexibility of human beings properly into the system.

The influence of systems engineering is, then, to put first things first in designing man–machine systems. By following this series of specifications and decisions, we delineate the part which the operator (or operators) have to play in the system. And, after the allocation of function stage, we have a full description of the interactions between the operator and the rest of the system, from which we can take up the problems of compatibility. The 'systems approach' continues to influence these further decisions, as we shall see. It is perhaps appropriate to remark here that, although it was originally intended for large-scale systems being developed 'from scratch', its application to even small man-machine systems or to modifications of existing set-ups has proved to be most useful and not unwieldy. Some further discussions can be found in Gagné (1962), Singleton (1966), and in the proceedings of a recent conference (Singleton, Easterby and Whitfield, 1967).

The operator's task

Having 'allocated functions', we are now at the stage where the operator's responsibilities are defined, and it is necessary to design his task so that he works in harmony with the rest of the system.

The problems of man–machine compatibility are essentially problems of communication – just as efficient communication is essential to any social group with a specified objective, so must the man and the machine exchange information to achieve their common aim. Thus, the basic concept of the *display-control loop* (Figure 11) has arisen. The machine must send information to the

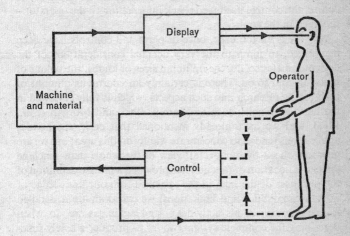

Figure 11. The display-control loop. The operator receives information from the machine displays, mainly in the visual and auditory modes. He transmits information through the machine controls, by means of hands and feet. He also receives feedback information, by way of the 'feel' of controls. These three links are essential to any efficient man–machine system

man so that he can monitor its progress and know when to do what; in many cases, however, the appropriate form of information for the machine may not be as appropriate for the operator. One can see difficulties in trying to apply a typical machine output such as an electrical signal directly to the operator! So the information must be converted, or *transduced*, into a different form. In our example, we might feed the electrical signal into a meter with a graduated scale, or on to a chart recorder. This *display* must enable the operator to perform his task properly, and its information must be presented so as to conform with his perceptual capabilities. Similarly, when the operator has made a decision based on this information, so we must enable him to communicate the right sort of information, in the most efficient way, to the rest of the system. To this information link we give the generic term '*control*' – a handwheel or a lever are typical examples. In addition, of course, the control itself feeds back information to the operator – the 'feel' of the control.

Now, it is all too easy, once displays and controls have been mentioned, to jump to the very detailed considerations of the design of meter scales, the optimum sizes of knobs, the colour of labelling, and so on. There is certainly an enormous amount of painstaking research into such aspects (which is fully reviewed in the basic textbooks, such as Murrell, 1965, and Morgan *et al.*, 1963), and we have already mentioned that early ergonomics applications tended to concentrate wholly on this area; but we are now influenced by our overall view of the whole man–machine system. Allocation of function has provided a precise definition of the purposes of the man in the system. From our knowledge of human capabilities and limitations, we can draw up a detailed *task description* of his activities – and again, as we do when describing the complete system, we try to produce a solely functional description before deciding on specific ways in which the operator will achieve these aims. The task description may take several forms, depending on the sort of functions. A sequential series of activities may be represented best by a block diagram or flow-chart of the work-study type. A non-sequential task, where each operator decision is based on a reassessment of the state of the system, may lead to a 'decision matrix' linking possible states with possible actions. Other examples are shown in Figure 12.

However it is presented, the task description is our starting point for ensuring good cooperation between operator and equipment. It is also the basis for personnel selection and training – an analysis of the skills involved will indicate what kind of operators are needed, and hence the selection standards and training needs, given the available population. It is obvious that there is an intricate relationship between ergonomics, selection, and training –

an increase in the amount of effort devoted to one area will allow more leniency in the others – but we shall not be able to explore these trade-offs here. It is also obvious that a given task description may suggest such excessive demands on the operator that we have to go back and re-allocate functions between man and machine; nevertheless, design is inherently an iterative process, and at least the systems approach, by having us adhere to a priority of decisions, emphasizes these problems at the earliest possible stage.

With the task description complete, and some of the relationships with selection and training defined, we can begin to think about the details of display and control design. Here again the importance of an exhaustive task description is emphasized, as we consider the 'off-line' displays, as well as the more obvious 'on-line' displays such as the indicator lamps, meters, and gauges which actually appear on equipment. 'Off-line' displays are sources of information which the operator may need, but which are not being continuously generated by the rest of the system. Instruction manuals, calibration charts, and check-lists, for instance, are not often thought of as being within the scope of ergonomics, but in many situations their content and organization affect the operator's efficiency. It is fair comment that computer manufacturers sometimes have to organize courses to teach people how to read programming manuals, and any laboratory technician will tell you how rare is the really good instruction handbook for a new piece of apparatus – far too little effort is devoted to this area of equipment ergonomics. Figure 13 shows the improvements which can be made even in a very familiar job-aid. Once again, we can see a close link between off-line displays and the instructional materials used for training – yet another instance of the close relationships between ergonomics and training techniques.

Operators' 'models'

Another useful principle combines with the task description to help us select and design displays and controls for the operator. Operators seem to base their decisions on various 'conceptual

CAPSTAN LATHE

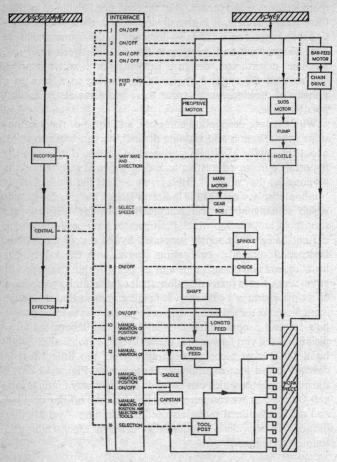

Figure 12. A task description for the operator of a capstan lathe. The operator's task is presented here in two different ways. The *interface chart* shows how the machine controls enable the operator to modify the flow of power through the various units of the lathe. The *link design chart* analyses in detail the two-way transmission of information between operator and machine

LINK DESIGN CHART

OBJECTIVE   Make king-pin
SYSTEM   Capstan lathe & skilled operator
DATE   September 1961   OBSERVER   W. T. S.

No	PURPOSE	TRIGGER Previous Check / Next Action	NA	Control No or Letter	ACTION (Both Hands / Right Hand / Left Hand / Foot LF RF)	BH	RH	LH	CHECK (Vision / Hearing / Touch Kinesthesis / Taste Smell)	V	A	K	S
1	Provide Power	Start		1	Up isolator lever		✓		Pressure, Position	✓			✓
2	Preoptive motor on	✓		2	Press button		✓		Red light				✓
3	Suds motor on	✓		3	Press button				Suds run		✓	✓	
4	Main motor on	✓		4	Press button				Noise		✓		
				15	Capstan feed	✓							
5	Position bar	✓		8	Release clutch		✓		Position Impact				
				5	Feed motor R.F								
6	Provide first tool	✓		15	Index capstan				Pressure, Position			✓	✓
7	Adjust spindle speed	Experience		7	Speed control & knob	✓							
8	Provide lubrication		✓	6	Adjust nozzle	✓			Stream				✓
9	Apply first tool	✓		15	Bring capstan fwd			✓	Pressure, Position, Noise	✓	✓		✓
10	Apply powered feed			14	Lift control	✓							
11	Adjust preoptive speed	Experience		7	Speed control		✓		Reading				✓
12	Provide next tool	Powered feed thrown out		15	Index capstan		✓		Pressure, Noise	✓	✓		
13	Adjust spindle speed	✓		7	Preoptive knob				Appearance				✓
14–19	as 18–13	for 2nd tool											
20–25	ditto	for 3rd tool											
26–30	ditto	for 4th tool											
30–35	ditto	for 5th tool											
36–38	as 8–10												
39	Remove capstan head	Capstan cycle completed		15	Index capstan		✓		Pressure, Noise	✓	✓		
40	Provide 1st saddle stop		✓	A	Stop control		✓		Position	✓			✓
41	Provide correct post tool		✓	16	Tool post control				Position	✓			✓
42	Bring tool into use	✓		12	Cross feed control				Position of tool with saddle against stop	✓			✓
				10	Longt feed control					✓			
43	Provide lubrication	✓		6	Adjust nozzle				Stream				✓
44	Use 1st post tool	✓		10	Longt feed control		✓		Pressure, Reading	✓			✓
45	Withdraw tool post	✓		12	Cross feed control				Away from				✓
				10	Longt feed control		✓		Work piece				✓
46–51	as 40–45	for second tool and stop											
52	Provide 3rd saddle stop		✓	A	Stop control		✓		Position				✓
53	Position parting off tool	Tool post cycle completed		12	Cross feed control				Position of tool with saddle against stop	✓			
				10	Longt feed control		✓						✓
54	Use parting off tool	✓		12	Cross feed control	✓	✓						
55	Remove work piece	✓			Catch piece and control		✓	✓	Appearance, feel	✓		✓	✓
56	Remove parting off tool			12	Cross feed control		✓		Away from	✓			✓
				10	Longt feed control		✓		centre line				✓

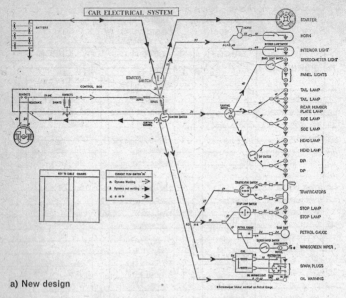

a) New design

Figure 13. The redesign of an automobile wiring diagram (by K. W. Tilley, of the R.A.F. Technical Training Command). The new diagram is not organized according to the physical layout of the various components of the car (note that the old one attempted to do this, somewhat unsuccessfully). What *is* emphasized in the redesigned diagram is the flow of current from power sources to the separate units, and the branching of circuits to serve various units. This will help fault-finding

models', or personal interpretations of how their equipment works. Thus, at a very simple level, we have the phenomenon of *motion stereotypes*, in which a given direction of movement of a control is expected to produce a certain direction of display movement. Thus, a machine-tool operator expects a cross slide to move away from him if he turns a handwheel on the front of the machine clockwise. Some expectations of this sort seem to be consistent over a wide range of people (Figure 14), and so the designer who chooses an inconsistent relationship, or reverses a highly consistent one, cannot blame the operator who turns the handle the

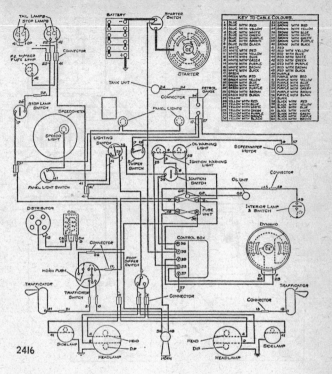

b) Old design

wrong way in an emergency. There, the conceptual model is the product of long experience with similar apparatus; in modern central control rooms, such as in power stations or chemical plants, we may have to create a model for the operator. In advanced situations like this, the controller lives in an 'artificial world' of specialized displays and controls, and a significant disparity between artificial and real worlds may have serious consequences. Here again, we emphasize *functional* aspects. Very often, the actual geographical layout of the plant is unimportant to the controller – the features of the real world which must be represented

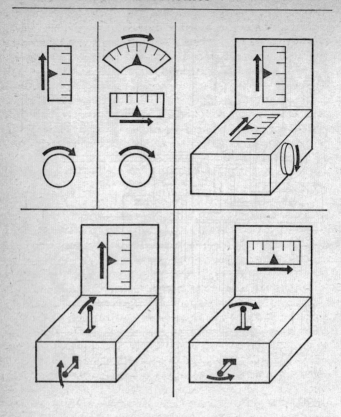

Figure 14. Examples of some expected relationships between control and display movement. (*Reproduced by permission from the Ergonomics for Industry Series, No. 2, H.M.S.O.*)

to him are the important interactions in the process. If he shuts down a supply line here, how will this affect preceding and subsequent stages? If one piece of equipment develops a fault, how can the flow of material be re-directed to prevent a general stoppage? The organization of displays and controls to reflect the functional arrangement of plant, and the representation of the relative importance of different controls and displays, are vital to this 'understanding' of the whole system. A good everyday example of the benefits of functional displays as opposed to geographical displays is given by the traveller's map of the London underground railways. Compared with the actual geography, only the features of direct relevance to getting from A to B have been retained. As an example of a functional off-line display in industry, R. S. Easterby's re-design of the legend plate for a centre lathe (Figure 15) is an excellent reminder that the design engineer's model is often at odds with the operator's.

APPLICATIONS OF ERGONOMICS

The industrial applications of this approach may be conveniently divided into *product* and *production* ergonomics, although the same broad principles of understanding the human being's role in the system are basic to both.

Product ergonomics covers applications in engineering design, where the company is producing a range of equipment. Techniques of mass-production have now reached the stage where the economies achieved enable much more detailed investigation of design principles such as ergonomics, and create the opportunity to have the finished product better tailored to human needs than with traditional design and production. Recent examples of applications include electronic equipment, laboratory apparatus, commercial and private vehicles, machine tools, aircraft, and various types of consumer goods. There is increasing evidence that attention to the human factors aspects of products is being given more weight, perhaps especially in highly competitive industries where technical performance specifications are often virtually identical from one company to another. This emphasizes the management responsibility to encourage the application of ergonomics to company products; for instance, the initial stimulus might well come from the sales manager in interpreting customer requirements. The successful exploitation of a new technique like ergonomics depends largely on the lead from upper management, and so this initial chapter, while painting the broad outlines, has been biased towards engineering design applications.

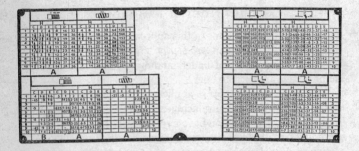

Figure 15. The redesign of the legend plate for a centre lathe (by R. S. Easterby, of the University of Aston in Birmingham). The legend plate helps the operator to convert his requirements for cutting a particular thread or gear into a setting of levers on the lathe gear-box. In the original design (below), the lever settings – indicated by capital letters and numbers – were presented as the independent variables, along the margins of the tables. The resulting gear or thread for any particular combination of lever settings is shown as the dependent variable, in the body of the table. Thus the operator has to scan the body of the table to find his required value, and then read back to the margins to find what lever settings are required.

In the new design (above), the required value is presented instead as the independent variable, systematically arranged along the margin. The associated lever settings appear next to it in the form of a simple code. Thus the legend-plate structure has been 'turned inside out' to suit the mode of thinking of the operator. The general appearance and legibility of the display has also been improved, but this is less important than the fundamental reorganization.

Production ergonomics is the primary concern of Chapter 9 and covers situations where the major human interaction with the company's product is in making it rather than in using it. New problems, including inspection, fatigue, and repetitive operations arise here. Specific applications have been carried out in 'heavy' industries, such as iron and steel and chemical process, and in light industry such as shoe production. The close interaction of production processes and operators in a wide range of industries offers many opportunities for ergonomics, and such applications will be discussed in detail in the next chapter.

FUTURE DEVELOPMENTS IN ERGONOMICS

The selection of these three chapters on ergonomics reflects our judgement on those aspects which are becoming increasingly important for the industrial manager. We are emphasizing, above all, the appreciation of the proper role of human beings in a technological environment; this is essential for coming to terms with increasing mechanization in industry. The problems of production management and of the effects of automated processes seem particularly pressing.

The close relationship between ergonomics and engineering should be quite obvious by now. In fact, like any technology, ergonomics thrives on contacts with other disciplines and techniques. The methods of operational research have great potential for the analysis of human functions in industrial processes, and cybernetics – the formal theory of systems – adds to the mathematical tools available. There are relationships too with the industrial designer, part of whose brief is to satisfy human operations and needs. Another aspect, which ought to have been represented in this book, but which awaits joint exploration by the two

---

It should be noted that the original structure fits the engineering designer's mode of thinking about the gear-box – he works from a combination of gears to a resulting value. This is the opposite of the operator's 'model' (*Reproduced by permission of the Council of Industrial Design*)

disciplines, is the overlap between sociology and ergonomics; the artificial separation of human group interaction from person–machine interaction cannot be maintained much longer. This area of common interest ought to be particularly relevant to production problems.

Another fruitful area of application seems to be in the information procedures and systems of commerce and industry – to apply the American jargon, 'soft' systems rather than the 'hardware' systems with which we have been primarily concerned in this chapter. We have referred to the development of 'off-line' displays, such as instruction manuals and charts, as an integral part of the approach to man–machine system design. The clerk in an office, or the manager at his desk, continually receives information from such sources, and his ability to make decisions obviously depends on the content and presentation of the information. Certainly, the overall design of 'soft' systems has been extensively investigated by specialists in systems analysis and organization and methods, but there has been little overt attention to the role of the human beings, clerks or managers, inherent in them. In particular, the design of management information systems is analogous to the problems posed by the high-level operator in a central remote-control room. The manager, too, must be supplied with the right sort of information in the best form, he must be encouraged to build up a useful conceptual model of the real-world activities he is trying to control, he must be provided with the best job-aids, and so on. These applications have hardly been explored at all, but they offer important opportunities to gain much from ergonomics principles.

It is but a short step to consider the interaction of human beings and the most sophisticated of technological achievements – the computer. Just as mechanical handling devices enormously extended man's physical capabilities (and at the same time created the problems of man–machine compatibility), so the computer extends his mental capacity. We are just beginning to recognize some of the problems which arise from close communication between man and computer, where the computer is regarded not as a substitute for routine clerical operations, but as a complement to human mental skills. The creative activities of computer-aided design, or of 'conversational' operation of computers, will require the application of our knowledge of human thought-processes and problem-solving behaviour, and the extension of our knowledge in these areas. Ergonomics history is repeating itself, even at this early stage – advances in technology create the need for new knowledge of human capabilities and limitations.

CHAPTER 9

Ergonomics in Production Management

B. A. LACY

PRODUCTION management is the organization of the work of people to achieve economic objectives. Everything the manager achieves he does by getting people to work in some particular way. His task is more difficult if he is trying to get people to do things which are not well matched to their abilities. If the environment is also not suited to the work which he is asking them to do, he will have still greater difficulty in achieving his production objectives.

There can be little doubt that the scientific study of human characteristics and abilities has a bearing on the problem of production management. But can the information provided by such studies really help to design work and factories which are better suited to people? Can it be done economically? The answer to both these questions is certainly yes, if it is a new job or a new factory. The application of ergonomics to existing work is likely to be more difficult to justify. There must be a tangible management problem which can be shown to have a solution in a change of working methods or organization, equipment used by people, or some aspect of their physical environment. There are occasions when the application of ergonomics will reduce the cost to the worker in terms of his general well-being, without impinging on any identified production problem. In this case, if the price of the application is low, it is probably sufficient to argue that some economic good will result from improving the operating conditions. If the price of application is high then obviously more forceful arguments are needed. Ultimately, society decides what are reasonable demands to make on the individual. The ergonomist can try to ensure that society knows what demands it is making.

To understand how ergonomics can be used in a factory requires some discussion of how ergonomics fits into the concept of management services and particularly its relationship to work study.

Any ergonomist who tries to work solely within the framework of his knowledge of human characteristics will not be effective in the industrial situation. He must get to grips with the whole problem and understand the cost centres involved. He will do this best by working in a management services team. In a large team he can provide a service to the other members of the team, particularly those practising work study. He himself must become proficient as a systems analyst and designer and he must absorb the practical, change-seeking, attitude inherent in good work study.

In many ways ergonomics and work study have proved to be an embarrassment to each other. Work study has been reluctant to apply its critical questioning technique to itself. It has largely been satisfied with the time study dogmas it has inherited from Taylor and Bedeaux and has paid lip service to the motion study of Gilbreth. Beyond this it is pragmatic, with little in the way of established theory or codified knowledge on which it can draw. The ergonomist finds it difficult to accept such an approach, and the danger is that he will assume that the work-study man's conclusions are wrong because his methods and stated reasons for arriving at his conclusions can be shown to be wrong. Work-study men are often right for the 'wrong' reasons. The ergonomist must appreciate that work study is effective in spite of certain aspects of its approach. If one can point to a fundamental difference in concept between ergonomics and work study it is this. Work study conceives a standard man doing work in a standard time, taking a standard amount of relaxation, using a standard method of working. The ergonomist deals with a man who varies, and he regards the measurement of this variation as central to the solution of problems involving man. A standard man may well be an effective concept for management control but it is unrealistic for job and factory design. Gradually the ergonomist and the work-study man are ceasing to regard each other with disdain, they are seeing virtues in each other's approach. The human factors specialist of the future will be part ergonomist, part work-study man, and part operations researcher.

It is hoped that this introduction will have given a view of the background against which the writer wants now to describe ergonomics in production management. The application of ergonomics generally requires great attention to detail. The dilemma in providing a broad appreciation of the subject is that this aspect of the fundamental nature of ergonomics will be missed, yet if a detailed but narrow account is given, the scope of ergonomics is missed. In reading this summary of the ergonomist's knowledge as it applies to production, the reader should bear this dilemma in mind.

AN ANALYSIS OF THE PROBLEM

The basic role of people in a factory is to sense information, process it, and take action. People as sources of energy are of course no longer a viable proposition. Occasionally it may not be possible to split the energy requirement of an operation from the control task and this results in a heavy manual job, but such jobs become fewer every year.

The ergonomist is helping to bring people to a high level of effectiveness and to do this he must identify:

(i) The real objectives of the job being studied.

(ii) The information that the operator can use so that he knows how far he is from his objectives.

(iii) The resulting control actions which can be used to bring the work to a successful conclusion.

This is the approach to job design which is outlined in Chapter 7 and is taken up again by John Beishon in the next chapter. With this understanding of the work, the ergonomist will try to structure the job so as to eliminate things which people do not have the capacity to do well. Detailed design can then commence.

The spatial layout of the work needs to be arranged to suit the dimensions of various shapes and sizes of operators. The task information must be presented so that it is easily distinguished, and this involves consideration of the background against which the information must be sensed. Since much task information is obtained through the eyes and ears, light and sound feature prominently in task design. If the task is a heavy manual one it becomes necessary to pay special attention to the temperature of the job surrounds. Man uses fuel inefficiently and so creates heat which he must lose to the environment.

HUMAN PHYSICAL DIMENSIONS

Designing the dimensions of equipment and relating these spatially to the user must be a compromise. A knowledge of human dimensions enables a compromise to be achieved which will inconvenience only the smallest number of users. It is not a matter of designing for people of average dimensions. Indeed, doors so designed, that is 68 inches high, could prove painful for half the male population.

In any situation there are a number of critical dimensions and it must be decided whether least inconvenience to the total user population will be caused by fitting the smallest or the largest user. The seat of a chair which has a fore-and-aft measurement short enough to enable a small person to sit comfortably against the backrest will also be suitable for a large person. The reverse of this would not be true. A space large enough under a workbench to accommodate a long-legged person would similarly accommodate a short-legged person. In some cases the use of an extreme dimension is not the solution because it inconveniences either the large or small user. It is then necessary to provide adjustment or alternative equipment if discomfort is to be avoided. Chair height is such a case.

It follows from the foregoing that what the designer needs are data showing the distribution of human measurements. These data are available. A comprehensive presentation is given in Morgan, Cook, Chapanis, and Lund (1963).

While data are available about the static dimensions of people, much less valid information is available about dynamic dimensions. For example it is difficult to specify even such an apparently simple matter as how far people can reach in various situations. Consequently there is the temptation to take a very mechanical approach to job design which does not really do justice to the versatility of human movement. Analysis of human movement is a complex problem since it involves consideration of defining degrees of comfort and stress when making the measurements on which design data will be based. At least one research project is at present engaged on collecting dynamic anthropometric data.

As yet there is not a general awareness in industry of the need to design the dimensions of equipment so that it will suit the people by whom it will be used. Tens of thousands, maybe hundreds of thousands, of women try to sit for hours working at conveyor bands or machines which were designed with almost total disregard of the fact that women even exist below the waist. The distance between a woman's elbow, with the upper arms relaxed, and the upper surface of the thighs is about 3 inches. It is just not possible to sit with any degree of comfort at a conveyor table which is, say, 8 or more inches thick. This, though, is the rule rather than the exception.

Factory chairs are designed for cheapness and strength rather than comfort. Purchase tax is payable only if the chair has padding and this encourages the use of unpadded seats and backrests. All the necessary information about human anatomy and dimensions is available to design a comfortable chair. Surely modern technology must be capable of producing a factory chair which will be comfortable over long periods of use, yet is nevertheless strong and reasonably priced? The writer knows of no such chair.

Because people are adaptable and they cope somehow with all but the most impossible arrangements, management tend to be unaware of the price they are paying for this adaptability. A person has a limited work capacity. Some of this capacity is used in overcoming aspects of the task which have been made unnecessarily awkward. This is really spare capacity which could be available to meet emergency situations. It could prevent the near accident from becoming an accident. It could enable quality to be maintained when, for example, a process variation has created a situation which requires extra concentration and effort from the operator. This spare capacity could be available to bring the work within the abilities of a greater range of people, older people, disabled people, or just people who have less ability than others. The ergonomist can show by such techniques as electromyography that quite small changes in equipment dimensions have a marked effect on the static activity of muscles which are maintaining posture (see Figure 16). Continuous activity in these muscles leads to the early onset of fatigue. There is also evidence that poor postural habits are a cause of such complaints as backache and sciatica, which in turn are a cause of absenteeism.

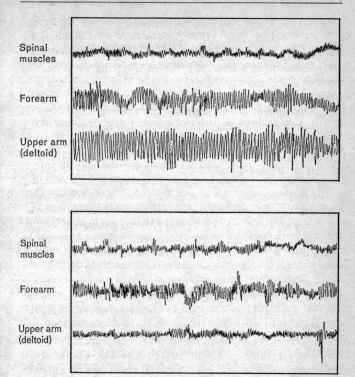

Figure 16. Electromyogram showing reduction in muscle activity with a two-inch lowering of desk height. It shows the muscle activity of a person writing seated at a seventeen-inch high chair (*above*) at a thirty-inch high desk, (*below*) at a twenty-eight-inch high desk

If the problems of human dimensions involved in equipment design are considered right at the start, they can be solved without much trouble. If considered later the solution becomes difficult. If left until after the equipment is built, unless one is very lucky, only a costly modification will remedy the all too usual situation of the operator having to adapt as best he can.

THE VISUAL ENVIRONMENT

Illumination of a factory should satisfy three basic requirements:

(1) Sufficient light must be reflected from the work piece or machine to the operator's eye to enable the necessary detail to be distinguished.

(2) The amount of light reaching the operator's eye from the various surfaces in his field of vision must not be in excess of that which is compatible with the state of adaptation of his eye.

(3) The provision of a pleasing environment conducive to interest and a sense of well-being.

The lighting engineer and architect of course consider these requirements, but probably in a rather generalized way. The ergonomist will start by analysing the visual task to be performed and will work outwards to the overall environment. The need for this approach will depend very much on whether the work being done requires fine detail or shades of colour to be discriminated.

It is important to appreciate that a human being's response to illumination is different to that of a light-meter. The eye adapts to variations in the available light by allowing more or less light to pass through the iris. Then the retina, on to which the light falls to form the image, alters its sensitivity to suit the ambient illumination. A room will appear inadequately lit if the eye is adapted (perhaps by a view of the sky) to a level of lighting much higher than that in the interior of the room. When one is out of doors, adapted to the high brightness prevailing there, things inside a room, or even inside a shop with a big glass window, appear dark and obscure. Once inside the shop or room, the eye adapts itself and things will look well lit. But in a deep room, or in one with a low ceiling, parts remote from the window may look dark. This is because the eyes may still be adapted to the bright sky seen through a big window from inside. In this state of partial adaptation, the remoter parts of the room may very well appear dark and gloomy even where a light meter would give a high reading in lumens per square foot.

Conversely if the eye is adapted to a low level of illumination, and a source of brightness insufficient to raise the adaptation level

(1963) which gives an excellent account of the human factors involved in providing a good visual environment.

THE AUDITORY ENVIRONMENT

Sound is useful in industry for communication, but industry also produces sound that is unwanted. Such unwanted sound is called noise.

The physical properties of sound can be measured in terms of the intensity of the pressure wave which causes sound, and also in terms of the frequency at which the pressure wave is vibrating. The frequency of sound may be referred to as the pitch.

The intensity of sound is measured in decibels. It is important to remember that this is a logarithmic scale. A doubling of the sound intensity adds about 3 decibels to the sound measurement. The frequency of sound is measured in cycles per second, usually in octave bands.

The subjective perception of sound is affected by the intensity and the frequency. But even for a given frequency a human being does not perceive sound in a manner which would provide a one-to-one relationship to the intensity of the sound. That which is perceived as being twice as loud is in fact of ten times greater intensity. This is an important consideration, because if the physical intensity of a noise is reduced by tenfold, a person will only perceive this as halving the noise.

Noise has both physical and subjective effects. The physical effects of noise are to interfere with communication and to cause damage to hearing. The subjective effect is to cause annoyance.

Interference with communication

If communication is to take place, the background noise must not be so loud as to mask the signal or sound (information sound) to be heard. The masking of one sound by another depends on the frequency characteristics of each as well as on their relative intensities.

Most industrial sources produce a wide band type of noise of which only the frequency band corresponding to (but slightly wider than) the frequency band of the information sound has any masking effect. Thus, a given sound intensity will be less easily masked if it is a pure tone than if it is spread over a wide frequency range.

Damage to hearing

Prolonged exposure to high noise levels will cause permanent and incurable loss of hearing. The problem of what noise levels and times of exposure are safe is complicated by several factors.

(1) A temporary loss of hearing occurs even after a short exposure to noise. This may disappear in a matter of minutes or weeks or the loss may persist for months. This temporary loss of hearing is superimposed on any permanent loss that may be present.

(2) With advancing age the sensitivity of hearing decreases, particularly at high frequencies. This loss is independent of any loss due to exposure to noise.

(3) There is a wide variation between individuals in the noise levels that produce permanent loss of hearing.

(4) The intensity and frequency range that are to be considered significant must be decided. The hearing of high-frequency sound, around 4,000 cycles per second, is more sensitive to damage than sounds of lower frequency. Excessive sound seems to cause damage to hearing in the next octave above the sound itself. Thus noise at 2,000 cycles per second will be the most damaging. But from the point of view of hearing speech, for which the most significant frequencies are 600 to 2,400 cycles per second, noise in the range 300 to 1,200 cycles per second will be most critical.

(5) A given intensity of noise is more damaging if it is concentrated in pure tone or narrow band.

Several criteria for assessing the effects of continuous exposure to noise over a period of years have been put forward by various authorities. It is generally agreed that the risk of damage is slight if the level in any octave band between 300 and 4,800 cycles per second does not exceed 85 decibels. If the levels in these bands are 95 decibels or over, hearing damage is to be expected. Some authorities would put the level at 80 and 90 decibels. If the noise contains a pure tone, such as the whine from a machine, the critical levels are 10 decibels lower. (See Figure 18.)

The problem of deciding whether an environment is causing damage to hearing can be approached directly by measuring the hearing of people exposed to the environment, or indirectly by measuring the sound intensity of the environment and comparing the results with the levels which are known to cause damage.

The direct method, audiometry as it is called, involves measuring the hearing of employees when they are engaged and at inter-

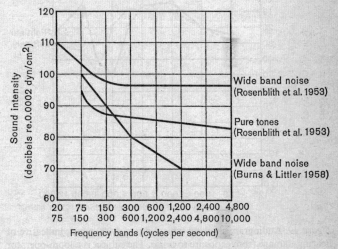

Figure 18. Proposed criteria for hearing-damage risk

vals of say six months. This measurement is a relatively simple procedure and losses characteristic of damage due to excess noise can be detected before they become serious. (See Figure 19.)

Annoyance

There is some evidence that regular noise levels above 90 decibels lead to increasing numbers of errors in a task. Generally speaking it seems that noise is annoying at first and causes a reduced performance, but in a short time people become accustomed to the noise and their performance returns to normal. These remarks, of course, do not apply to the question of damage to hearing.

So much for the thumb-nail sketch of the effects of sound, but what of the practical application of this knowledge in a factory? It is usually difficult to forecast that a noise problem will be caused

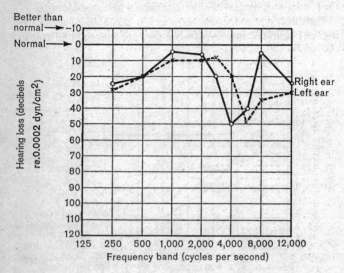

Figure 19. Audiogram showing typical dip at 4,000 c.p.s., indicative of hearing-damage from exposure to noise. The subject is a loom-operator after twenty-eight years of exposure

by the installation of new machinery. Unfortunately once machinery is installed and found to be excessively noisy the cost of quietening it may be prohibitive. If new plant is expected to be noisy the layout can sometimes be arranged so that the control operators can be isolated from the plant if necessary. If the operators cannot be isolated a detailed study of the noise sources must be made. It may then be possible to reduce the cause of the noise or to contain it. The techniques involved in such a study are described in Harris (1957).

If, despite efforts to reduce the noise, the ambient noise levels recorded are of the frequencies and intensities to cause hearing damage, then the operators should be provided with ear protectors. At present there is a reluctance on the part of operators to wear protectors, and management usually will not enforce their use. In the future there will probably be legislation specifying safe noise levels and the management action which must be taken if these levels are exceeded. As mentioned previously, it is society and not management which must decide what are reasonable demands to make of the individual.

THE THERMAL ENVIRONMENT

The human body generates heat through the metabolic process. This results in an excess of heat, and this heat needs to be dissipated in order to maintain the body temperature in a state of equilibrium. If the rate of dissipation is too fast, we feel chilled; if it is too slow, we feel warm.

The body is continually in a state of adjusting to its environment to maintain the heat balance. Various physiological processes are involved in the adjustment, but it is regulated principally by the rate of blood circulation and the activity of the sweat glands.

The four physical methods of transmitting heat must be considered when designing environments in which people will feel comfortable.

(1) *Convection*, as applied to the human heat-exchange process, relates to the heat carried away from, or to, the body by the moving air around the body.

(2) *Conduction*, as applied to people, is the transmission of heat by direct contact with cooler or warmer solid objects. Conduction is of limited importance however, because clothing helps to keep such heat transmission at a minimum.

(3) *Radiation* is the exchange of thermal energy between two or more objects. This process does not require an atmosphere; it is a surface phenomenon only. The warmer of two bodies will lose heat by radiation to the cooler body. A person will receive radiant heat from a fire, but will lose it to the surface of a window in winter.

(4) *Evaporation* of perspiration from the skin and moisture from the lungs is the fourth method of heat transmission.

From the preceding paragraphs it will be noted that the factors concerned in the provision of the correct thermal environment are: the rate at which a person is working and so generating heat; the speed and temperature of the air flow in the vicinity; sources of radiant heating or cooling; and the humidity of the air, which will affect the rate at which perspiration can be evaporated.

The significance of these things depends on the particular situation. At high working rates and high temperatures, the strain on the body is considerably greater than with similar working rates at lower temperatures. In extreme situations heat stroke occurs if these factors are not carefully controlled. In more temperate situations one is concerned with providing a stimulating and pleasant environment rather than with physiological stress.

There is evidence to suggest that people work more efficiently and with a lower accident rate when thermal conditions are kept within certain comfort zones.

Much work has been done in order to try to assess the effect on comfort of varying combinations of air temperature, air speed, humidity, and radiant heat. This has resulted in the construction of a number of combined temperature scales. Thus, if one measures the various components of the environment it is possible to combine these measurements into a single index. This enables one environment to be compared with another and the effect of changes in the components to be forecast.

In a study of 2,000 factory workers, Bedford (1936) recorded their sensations of comfort against a series of carefully worded criteria along with various components of the thermal environment. This investigation showed that 70 per cent of people engaged on light work wearing indoor clothing will feel comfortable if the effective temperature is between 57°F and 63°F. These temperatures would be obtained with an air temperature of 60°F to 68°F (dry bulb) under most average factory conditions. In the warm summer months these temperatures would need to be 3°F to 4°F higher. People's reaction to cool factories on hot days depends on the humidity. If the factory is significantly cooler than outside, perspiration may condense on the skin and clothing on entering unless the humidity of the factory is low.

While the concept of a combined index of environmental warmth is useful, the individual components of the environment must not be ignored.

If the air speed is less than 20 ft per minute a room will feel stagnant, and not less than 40 ft per minute is desirable. At 100 ft per minute the air movement starts to be felt as a draught and this speed should not be exceeded. Some fluctuation in the air speed has been shown to produce comfort, at a higher temperature, than would normally be acceptable.

Radiant heat, such as that of the sun shining through a window, cannot be combated by manipulation of the other components of the environment. The air speed required to remove from the body the heat that is being received from the sun becomes excessive. The correct action is to deal with the radiation component itself by suitable screening. Conversely, if excessive air movement cannot be avoided, a radiant heat source can provide a comfortable environment more economically than by heating the air. Another effect of radiant heat is that with the same effective temperature a room with cold walls and warm air feels stuffy. Rooms are more often regarded as comfortable when the walls are at a higher temperature than the air.

Humidity is only important when temperatures are over about 75°F and/or heavy work is being done. In these circumstances high humidity prevents efficient evaporation of perspiration and the body cannot lose enough heat. Manipulation of the humidity can in these circumstances be most beneficial.

The foregoing has concentrated on the comfort aspect of the environment, since this is the problem which is most frequently encountered. The more critical problem, though, occurs in such extreme situations as blast furnace or cold-store work. Here one is concerned with protecting the operator with clothing or heat shields and regulating the periods of exposure. Selection of personnel and their acclimatization is also relevant. Acclimatization is not merely a matter of the person being better able subjectively to tolerate the discomfort. There are, for example, physiological changes which occur that enable the acclimatized person to lose heat more effectively in a hot environment.

There is evidence which indicates that excessive heat is more likely to cause performance to deteriorate in older than in younger people.

The amount of time spent in an extreme environment, between rest periods, should take into account not only the temperature conditions but also the energy expenditure required by the job. The problem in a hot environment is that it restricts the rate at which the body is losing heat, hence this is aggravated as the energy expenditure increases. In a cold environment the need is to restrict the loss of body heat, and so the problem is eased if the job involves a high energy expenditure.

Tasks in a cold-store, such as stock-taking or fork-lift truck-driving, are likely to be more arduous than manual shifting of goods. Clothing and working periods which were suitable for cold-store work in the past may be inadequate for high-efficiency modern stores using mechanized handling and air-blast cooling.

Work has been done on the design of protective clothing and a unit of clothing insulation has been developed. This is the 'clo unit', equal to the amount of clothing needed to sit comfortably at rest with an ambient temperature of 70° F. The required insulation value of clothing for an environment can be calculated and specified in terms of the number of clo units. Four clo units is about the practical maximum insulation. Beyond this the clothing is too bulky for active work.

There is an extensive work physiology literature setting out methods for calculating stress resulting from working in hot or cold environments. The production manager or work-study man who is concerned with organizing the work of people in these environments would certainly increase his understanding of the problem by studying some of this literature.

THE ORGANIZATION OF WORKING HOURS

It is broadly true to say that today's industrial worker must get his pleasure from the material results of his work rather than from the work itself. This being so it would seem reasonable to try to maximize leisure time and material achievement. From this premise follow a number of questions. How many hours a week should be worked? How many hours per day? How should the working day be divided between work and rest? Does the time of day during which the work is done have an effect? There are no easy answers. This is to be expected with the variety of work situations which exist, manned of course by a variety of people.

As long ago as the First World War, Vernon (1920) showed that a reduction of the working week from 66 to 47 hours resulted in an increase of 13 per cent in total output. More recently a survey in the United States covering 34 factories, showed that maximum efficiency was occurring with a 40-hour week and an 8-hour day (Kossoris and Kohler 1947). The survey showed a decline in output, an increase in absenteeism and accidents when the working week was longer.

It is worth commenting that in British industry despite nominal 40-hour weeks, in practice 50 hours is common and even 60 hours is not all that uncommon. The managers in factories working these sort of hours should consider whether they are in a positive feedback situation, that is longer hours may be reducing efficiency and so be giving rise for the need to work longer hours.

Many research workers have examined the rate of output during the day and have observed the effect of inserting rest pauses. A commonly found work pattern has a period during which speed is built up, then peak performance is held until boredom, muscular, or mental fatigue causes performance to fall off. Sometimes there is an end of task spurt anticipating a period of rest. If organized rest pauses are inserted at about the time when performance is expected to decline, the overall output increases.

The production manager needs to study and experiment with the hours that his operators work if he is to find the optimum arrangement. In doing this he must not be impatient for results nor accept beneficial results too readily. Many months may elapse before working rates increase to meet shorter hours. A person used as it were to spreading his effort over a longer period needs time to adapt to a new situation. Conversely, people react to management showing interest in their work, and this in itself rather than the change introduced may temporarily increase output.

The final question posed was: how does the time of day affect working efficiency? Does it make any difference whether a person is required to work during the day, or the evening, or at night? Basically the answer is no, providing the person has adapted. Certain physiological functions of the body follow a daily rhythm. The body temperature reaches a peak in mid-afternoon and is at its lowest in the early hours of the morning.

The activity of the endocrine glands, blood pressure, pulse rate, and the secretion of urine follow this rhythm.

There is evidence that human work performance efficiency is also related to this diurnal rhythm.

If a person is required to work during the time when the physiological functions mentioned are at their lowest activity, he is less effective, he makes more errors, and is more liable to have an accident. If he continues to work at this unnatural time the body rhythm will, in most people, adapt to the new pattern of activity. This adaptation may take up to about six days, but in some people, will occur only partially or not at all.

Thus, from physiological considerations, an operator should not change his hours of work frequently. Shift work on a weekly rotation causes the operator to be in a state of continually trying to readapt. There are studies of workers on rotating shifts which show high error and accident rates. There are adverse effects on health. For example, it is more difficult to sleep during the period when physiological functions, such as the secretion of urine, are at a high level of activity. Not less than fortnightly rotation of shifts is likely to be more satisfactory. Sociological considerations may of course make infrequent shift rotation unpopular. This might well offset the physiological advantages. On the whole, though, the evidence points to better results from infrequent shift rotation.

Finally it should be remembered that there are some people who cannot adapt their diurnal rhythm to enable them to work satisfactorily at night.

TASK STRUCTURE

So far discussion has been confined mainly to the general conditions which will help people to work effectively. Earlier the claim was made that the ergonomist would structure the operator's task so as to eliminate the things which people do not have the capacity to do well. A brief account is now given of the sort of things for which the ergonomist will be looking.

Discrimination

Tasks which require absolute subjective judgements to be made will not be done efficiently. For example, an operator who has to judge whether coffee is roasted to the correct colour would produce a very variable product if he is not given an external reference so that he can make a relative discrimination. Better still, he should be given an upper and lower reference, one dark and one light, so that he does not have to make an absolute judgement of the relative difference from a single reference.

It is not uncommon to find operators not only making absolute judgements, but doing so without any clearly defined standards having been provided by the management. Studies on quite simple inspection tasks have shown that considerable differences occur between operators – what one rejects, another passes. Not only do different operators vary, but the same person will vary his idea of a reject. He will tend to loosen his standard if rejects are frequent and to tighten up if rejects are sparse. Subjective judgements will always tend to produce a variable response from the operator.

Short-term memory

Most people have looked up a telephone number, only to forget it or its sequence in the few seconds necessary to pick up the phone. In the same way a person getting information from a schedule, to feed weighing instructions into a mixing machine, also has a short-term memory problem. He will occasionally insert incorrect figures – in particular he will tend to reverse the order digits, 24 will become 42 for example. Even if the probability of making an error is very low, the occurrence of errors can become a certainty. If a task is performed ten times per hour, the 1 in 1,000 chance of an error will be happening once or twice a month. Operators should not be used merely as information channels. In the task just mentioned, a punched card would be a much better way of transferring information from the source data to the machine.

Repetitive work

As people become skilled at a repetitive task they are able to relegate control from their conscious attention to lower levels of the nervous system. The task tends to become a series of reflex actions. Providing the operator is not isolated, she can converse or watch what is happening in the room and the onset of boredom will be delayed. If, however, the motion pattern of the task has been made complex with perhaps many precise positionings being needed, a high mental load may result and even a long period of training may not enable the operator to shed this load. These tasks become irksome and boring. They rarely lead to the levels of output which can be calculated from time studies, or predetermined motion-time syntheses of the work. There is evidence that operators dislike being changed frequently between jobs. This is probably because it upsets the ease with which they can shed conscious control of their work.

Paced work

There are research studies which show that when a skilled operator can work at her own chosen speed she produces a greater output than when her work is linked to a machine cycle time. The basic reason for this is that people do not work at a constant speed, and if they are to keep pace with the machine it must be set at the longer of the operator's cycle times. Hence the operators's full potential is not realized. This disadvantage can be overcome by providing flexibility between operator and the machine; she must be able to drop behind and to get ahead. Variation in motion pattern and speed of movement is an essential feature of skilled performance. The idea that skilled performance is clockwork-like is incorrect. The skilled person maintains a constant achievement of objective, despite variations of input of one kind or another which will always occur. The unskilled person attempts to place an unchanging set of motions on to a variable situation. A further reason for providing flexibility between machines and people is that people make mistakes which they should have the opportunity to rectify.

Level of activity

If people are employed to take some action which is needed only infrequently, they will do it inefficiently. It can be shown on inspection tasks, for example, that the percentage detection of a fault is positively correlated to the frequency of occurrence of the fault. What this means is that all jobs must sustain a minimum level of arousal in the operator. On vigilance tasks, for example, the less the operator has to do, the more rapidly will his attention deteriorate. When he is required to take action he is likely to be out of touch with the situation. Whenever operators are being used merely as a safeguard against some improbable thing going wrong, an attempt should be made to measure objectively what is being achieved by using an operator. If an operator must be used, then his job should be properly thought through and the level of activity should be raised even by giving him work which could easily be automated. In this way when things do go wrong he will be orientated to take the needed corrective action.

Freedom of movement

The desire to move the body and getting pleasure from movement are natural features of human behaviour. The task which has been designed to restrict, or 'economize' movement will tend to increase the stress on the posture-maintaining muscles and overload small groups of muscles which will need to be used continuously. Work should be arranged so that the operator can move freely, using the largest appropriate muscle groups. This will not, as might be thought, lead to longer work-cycle times because more movement has been allowed. Freely made movements tend to be overlapped, resulting in higher effective speed of the body extremities. The use of large muscle groups reduces the time required for relaxation. A muscle can only be held at full contraction for a matter of a few seconds, whereas 15 per cent of maximum contraction can be maintained almost indefinitely. To take a rather obvious example, lifting a small weight by the fingers only will be more tiring and necessitate more relaxation than if the complete hand and forearm are used.

Knowledge of results

People work because they are motivated to achieve some objective. They work more effectively if they know whether they are achieving their objective. In a limited sense there must be an immediate feedback of information to the operator for a task to be done at all. But further than this, it is beneficial to give the operator a knowledge of his results beyond that needed to close the control loop of the task.

Laboratory studies have shown increases in speed and accuracy when the subject has been told how he is performing. In factories output has risen when targets are displayed and output is recorded against the target. This has been shown to occur with and without the payment of financial incentives. This is not to say that output will always increase if a knowledge of results is given. The work must have been organized to provide scope for an increase and the operator's interest in results must be aroused.

Wherever a job or jobs are arranged so that the operators have little idea of how well or badly they are doing, it would certainly be worthwhile for the manager to make quite considerable efforts to improve communication of results to his operators.

*

The speed of technological change in the production function does not usually allow time for the rigorous approach of the academic research worker to be used to find solutions to problems. This does not mean that we must always go to the other extreme and merely put our faith in common sense. What is called common sense is so often, unfortunately, a common lack of sense. Even when time is short the broad approach and concepts of ergonomics are an effective way of seeing the fundamental nature of the problem as it affects the people in the system. We must expect time to be short – this can be the very reason for the problem. There has not been time for a trial-and-error approach in which people can adapt or opt out of the situation.

When people are reluctant to behave in the way which would seem best for the production manager, the too usual complaint is that supervision and operators are not like they used to be. It is more likely that our troubles are caused for want of applying some factual knowledge about the design and organization of work.

CHAPTER 10

Ergonomics and Automation

R. J. BEISHON

WHAT IS AUTOMATION?

AUTOMATION is a word which has been widely used in the last ten years, yet it is still difficult to find a definition which is acceptable to everyone. Most people are agreed that automation has to do with an extension of the use of *machines* to replace or add to human labour, a process which started with the industrial revolution some 150 years ago. It is the *replacement* of human labour which generally arouses most interest, since this usually has important social consequences affecting the labour market. Originally the word 'automation' was used in the 1930s to refer to the use of transfer machines in the car-making industry; here machines carrying out specific functions such as drilling and planing were linked together by devices which passed the work piece from one machine, or work station, to the next. However, since then other ideas have been put forward about automation. Basically there are two schools of thought. The first maintains that automation is no more than a continuing extension of the use of machines to replace human manual labour; cranes and fork-lift trucks, for example, replace or add to human muscle power, and calculating machines replace human mental labour. A second school of thought distinguishes between the replacement of physical labour, termed *mechanization*, and *automation* which is primarily concerned with *automatic control devices* and the replacement of human *mental* labour. The idea behind this second approach is that the production process needs *three* basic ingredients:

(1) materials;
(2) labour or physical energy;
(3) information.

We are familiar with the handling or processing of the first two ingredients, but the importance of information processing has only lately been recognized. Until comparatively recently information was only handled and processed by human beings, but we now have information-processing machines and it is suggested that the replacement of human information processing by machine processing is the distinguishing feature of automation. This view of automation is becoming more widely accepted and will be the one adopted in this chapter.

It may be helpful to begin with some comments about the nature of machines. Most machines are designed to work on materials (for example a lathe) or on energy (for example an electrical transformer) and it is difficult at first sight·to think of machines as processing information. The idea of information-processing machines has come from the development of the large, general-purpose, digital computer, and the word 'machine' is now used to refer to all devices which do things, and not just mechanical 'machines'. No doubt the idea of a 'computing machine' arose because the first computing devices of Babbage were mechanical, and hence when electronic computers were first introduced the idea of their being 'machines' stuck on.

As mechanization has proceeded over the last hundred years men have gradually been released from manual labour and have been employed more exclusively for information processing or *mental work*. This change has caused many social problems associated for example with movement of labour and redundancy but has, over the years, largely been accepted by society. It seems now that we are facing a new kind of industrial revolution where machines are taking over many human *mental* functions (the automation revolution), and this has aroused a good deal of fresh alarm, possibly because it is likely that machines will be able to replace human labour completely, if not in the immediate future then at least within a fifty-year span. It may not be true that *all* human mental work can or will be taken over by machines, but nevertheless it is increasingly becoming clear that a wide range of functions involving information processing is being done better by machines. Furthermore, these machines are getting more sophisticated as our knowledge increases.

KINDS OF MENTAL WORK

It is convenient at this point to distinguish two kinds of mental work associated with industrial production:

    (1) on-line control behaviour;
    (2) off-line activity.

The first of these is directly concerned with the control of an on-going process and the information processing involved is concerned with a specific piece of plant, such as a paper-making machine or steel-melting furnace. The second kind of work is that which we usually associate with supervisory or managerial functions and is concerned with overall planning, budgeting, and so on. This work is also control behaviour in a sense except that the process under control is probably a department, or even a whole factory, rather than one machine and the controller or manager has to deal both with plant and also the *men* who run it. This distinction is not fundamental, but it is a useful one here because automation has had different effects on human skills in these two areas. We shall discuss these two activities briefly in the next two sections.

On-line control

Here men or machines are actively responsible for the operation of an on-going process – usually one piece of plant. The operation procedures are generally well defined and the technical aspects of the process are fairly well understood. Many control functions in such a plant can be automated. For example, the regulation of the weight of paper from a paper-making machine can be achieved by a device which measures the current weight, compares this with the desired weight, and makes any necessary adjustments from time to time according to rules which relate control settings to output weight. For many control functions sophisticated devices can keep the output of a machine within very close tolerances. These devices have many advantages over human operators: they do not get tired; rarely, if ever, make mistakes; and can work at high speed with great precision.

Control devices mostly work on the basis of *feedback*, and it is important to note that they only take action when something is wrong or starts to go wrong in the output. Very few such devices can 'anticipate' a fault condition and take action to avoid it, but feedback systems generally work so fast that adequate control can be maintained under most conditions. Where a man has been working in a feedback control mode it is usually advantageous to replace him by an automatic device, always provided that the *sensing* part of the operation can be carried out by a machine. For example, it is not easy to fit regulatory devices to baking ovens since it is difficult to build a sensing machine which will 'recognize' a correctly baked tray of cakes. It is of course also necessary for engineers to know enough about the technical aspects of the process so that suitable control strategies can be formulated. This is not always true by any means, and many plants are still run by men who somehow can pilot a process although engineers do not know in detail quite how it works or how they do it. Operators in these situations cannot usually explain to anyone else how they do their job, just as we find it difficult to explain to someone else how we ride a bicycle.

Any survey of current jobs in industry will provide a wide range of examples where enough is known about a process for automatic controls to be used, but where the situation at present is such that the economic advantage still lies in employing men. In time, it is said, most of these jobs will be taken over by machines, thus saving expensive human labour and producing a more consistent and accurate product. Closer examination of the situation suggests that things are not quite so straightforward as they seem. Firstly, where automatic control devices have been installed it is usual to find that, contrary to expectation, the number of men employed in the plant has not gone down. Control rooms of automatic plant still have men in them for monitoring, checking, and inspection work, as well as to take over in emergencies. Furthermore, numbers of skilled maintenance men, instrument engineers, and fitters have to be employed.

Secondly, feedback control devices are inherently limited by any time lags which exist in a situation and they cannot take effective control action faster than process dynamics allow. Men can

221

however foresee and predict a new situation arising and, on the basis of past experience, take anticipatory actions beforehand. This is called *open-loop* or *feed-forward* behaviour and there are very few automatic control devices which can do this at present. In fact this kind of control behaviour would need a large and complex computer system to generate predictions and to test them.

A third consideration is that automatic control devices cannot usually be fitted directly to existing plant, and detailed information about how the process works must be obtained and often extensive modifications made to the plant to enable sensing devices to be installed and to check on variables within the process which were not hitherto recorded.

The consequence of these and other considerations is that, although automatically controlled plant may produce a more consistent product, the savings in manpower and increase in efficiency expected do not always follow. It would be fairer when considering the possible benefits of automation to start by comparing the performance which could have been achieved by a *man*, had the same time and trouble been devoted to supplying him with appropriate information about the plant variables as would be done before installing an automatic control device. When a comparison is made between a man *aided* by suitable information sources, explicit control rules and strategies, the advantages of the automatic system may be far less apparent. Even so, the gain in speed and precision with feedback control devices may still outweigh an *aided man*.

We can however consider a further step before going to full automatic control; men are nearly always retained in automated plant to cope with emergencies and to monitor fault detection, but they could take an active part in control activity by using their superior predictive abilities. Men do have many advantages over machines, and vice versa, so it is sensible to consider a planned use of the two in combination. This leads us to the idea of an *augmented man* who is responsible for those activities he can do best and who has machine aids to improve his functioning in those areas where he is weak. For example, men are poor at remembering exactly what has happened in detail in a plant and slow at complex arithmetic calculation; computers are good at these things. On the other hand men can filter and smooth out information, picking out only relevant features from a 'noisy' signal, and can also store large amounts of data and retrieve certain aspects of this enormous mass of information very quickly; computers are not very good at this kind of thing. Clearly there is tremendous scope for cooperation between man and computer, each doing an essential part of the total job. We know relatively little about the possibility of this 'marriage' between men and computers partly because we are only slowly developing ways in which the two can communicate with each other. This is undoubtedly a field where much progress will be made in the next few years and further reference to this will be made in a later section.

To some extent the undoubted success of computer-controlled plant has led some to suppose that it is only a matter of time before computers will take over all human functions, but it is worth pointing out that even at the process-control level there are still many functions that only men can carry out. This is not only true of complex problem-solving or trouble-shooting work but also of more mundane, but still important, activities, such as picking out a relevant signal from background 'noise'. A mother can identify the cry of her child from that of others or from a background noise, and an experienced mechanic can identify a faulty component by listening to an engine 'knock'. No machine or computer is at present available which will do things like this, and where such skills have to be replaced the issue is 'avoided', in the sense that the job is redesigned, often radically and at high cost, so as to remove those activities which machines find difficult. Typical of these problems are perceptual identification of patterns such as signatures on cheques or written postal addresses. Clearly this is sensible when redesign is simple and not too costly, but attempts are often made to remove men from control activity by automating the obvious part of the man's function, with the result that many more subtle checking and monitoring activities done by men are lost. Men have then to be re-introduced to monitor and check the automatic device with little, if any, overall saving.

This discussion of on-line control suggests two preliminary conclusions:

(1) Before embarking on automation it is well worth examining the performance to be expected from *aided man*.

(2) It is also worthwhile looking at the more sophisticated use of an *augmented* man working in *cooperation* with automatic systems.

Off-line activities

So far we have discussed the on-line control behaviour associated with the mental work needed in process control. When we look at the mental information processing activities associated with planning, long-term decision-making, and so on, we find that little or no attempt has been made to automate these activities. Some of the reasons for this are clear: high-level supervisory and managerial skills involve many face-to-face human situations which depend on the influence or interactions of one personality on another, and it is difficult to see how machines could take over here. Much of the mental work involved at these levels is concerned with estimating probabilities, taking risks, and with making decisions under conditions where all the factors affecting the situations are not known. As yet we do not have machines which are very good at this kind of activity although they may well be developed before long.

Although there is little immediate prospect of taking over all managerial and other off-line skills and activities, there are good prospects for augmenting human decision making and planning. The topic is too large to be developed here but, as with on-line control, we can identify the imperfections in human mental activity (weakness in large-scale calculations, limited memory, slow speed of working, etc.) and use computers to supplement human mental work.

EFFECTS OF AUTOMATION ON SKILLS

Automatic control devices and computer-controlled plant are increasingly being used in industry, since they have many advantages over control by human operators. The introduction of such devices does not *replace* men so much as *displace* them. Men are still needed in the automated plant but now for different functions – the kinds of skills required of men are changing. This raises many questions for management and is, as we have seen in Chapter 8, directly the concern of 'Ergonomics'. These changes in skill requirements are complex and to some extent depend on the industry and type of work done, but basically the changes fall into the following categories:

(1) Plant and process setting-up and programming activities become more important than on-going control behaviour.

(2) Many perceptual activities which machines cannot do, for example judging quality and recognizing patterns, still have to be done by men. These men will now have to work in close coopera-tion with a control device or computer.

(3) Where man can be released from on-line control he is still usually retained to *monitor* and *check* the plant or process. Two additional functions are generally included in this: (i) Emergency conditions must be quickly detected and responded to so that plant and personnel are protected; (ii) At certain times manual control has to be resorted to, for example if a control device breaks down.

(4) *Maintenance* and *repair* skills become of increased import-ance.

The first of these is generally one-off activity and we shall not refer to it further here. We have already briefly dealt with the question of man working in cooperation with a computer or con-trol device in an earlier section, and the remainder of this chapter will be concerned with further discussion of this and of items 3 and 4 above.

MONITORING AND CHECKING ACTIVITY

It is convenient to refer to this kind of activity as *control-room* behaviour, since it includes the emergency actions mentioned above and virtually all automated plants have a control room or centre from which the overall supervision and control is done. The operator is concerned with monitoring the states of the plant and process mainly to detect fault conditions. He is also there to take appropriate action in emergencies and to take over control where possible to keep the plant running. At present these tasks are usually done by operators who have had experience with the earlier, non-automated plant and although they may have some difficulty in adjusting to the new conditions they have sufficient detailed knowledge of the plant and its characteristics to cope. New operators trained in the control room will lack this direct experience on the plant, and because they may be relatively isolated from the plant by the control room, which could be some distance from the plant, they may build up very different mental 'models' of the process. Inevitably if the men are not involved in direct-control activity they tend to think of themselves as being isolated from the plant and two worlds will emerge, one 'in here' and the other, the plant, 'out there'. This isolation may have serious consequences and the more important of these are dealt with in the following sections.

Boredom and reaction to emergencies

In an automated plant there is frequently very little for the operator to do, the rooms are usually kept at comfortable temperatures and the noise levels are low. It is a common experience that as the environment becomes more comfortable and stimulation is reduced so men become drowsy or bored and inattentive. This condition reduces efficiency in the sense that quick and effective responses to emergencies suffer, and it also means that danger symptoms are often not spotted until it is too late. A number of techniques for overcoming these problems are available and active research is going on, for example, into methods of improving the efficiency of signal detection, that is the ability to pick out an important signal from other, less important or irrelevant signals.

One widely used method is the *false alarm*. Here artificial fault conditions are signalled to the operator who does not know at the time whether there is a real emergency or not and he must take the appropriate action as if it were a real crisis. This cannot be used in certain plants without the operator immediately being aware that it is a false alarm, and in any case too many false alarms build up a negative attitude in the operator. A certain number of test alarms can be useful but they must be very carefully planned so that they are indistinguishable from the real thing and are relatively unpredictable. Experimental studies of men doing watch-keeping tasks have suggested a number of other methods for improving alertness: for example, a certain amount of noise or background music and variations in temperature and humidity are useful. Much more attention could be paid to making the environment in control rooms more stimulating without distracting the man from his primary task. One important factor often overlooked is the beneficial effects of social contact with other people – even telephone contact is valuable. It may, for example, be worthwhile using a man to deliver a message which could well be done by an electronic link, since letting the man do the task enables him to meet other people.

The problem of ensuring appropriate actions in an emergency are in many ways more difficult to solve. Many fault conditions can be anticipated and suitable emergency drills prepared, but the very nature of modern complex plant means that it is virtually impossible to predict all the different things which can go wrong. It is still necessary to rely on the operator recognizing the presence of danger conditions and taking the appropriate actions. This means that operators may have to have a much more detailed knowledge of the plant and how it works than may be apparent at first sight; this point will be discussed further in a later section.

Sampling and monitoring behaviour

One immediately obvious feature of modern industrial plant is the complexity and extent of the instrumentation, which reflects to some extent the large numbers of variables which have to be measured and checked during operation. A certain number of automatic alarms can be built into a system, but there is a limit to this and we usually have to depend on an operator for the overall checking of displays, to see that everything is working normally. Since a man finds it hard to attend to more than one thing at a time he has to divide his attention among the various sources of information about the plant or process. Information is then obtained by *sampling* one source after another. The sampling procedure may be rather more complicated than just searching a display panel and may require a man to make a telephone call or send a sample for analysis or possibly go to some other part of the plant to look at a particular machine. Where the collection of information about one source of data takes an appreciable time it means that the man cannot, during that time, sample or attend to any other sources. This may lead to his missing a serious fault condition on another information source. The way an operator goes about collecting information may be called his *sampling strategy* and this may be very important in determining whether or not he will be able to detect danger conditions rapidly enough.

Very little work has been done on sampling behaviour, and it is known that men often adopt or carry over from previous experience inappropriate strategies. For many information sources there is a theoretical *sampling interval*, that is a maximum time between two successive samples on that source which if used by an operator will enable him to get all the required information from the source. Often a suitable sampling interval can be arrived at by plant engineers if consulted. This value can then be used by the operator, or he could fit such values for a number of sources into a routine logging system which will automatically ensure that the sources are looked at in the right proportion. This process can be carried to the point where the operator sits in front of a single screen on which can be displayed many different instruments; he can either select different information sources himself or initiate an automatic sequence of displays which brings the appropriate displays in front of him at the correct sampling frequencies. This technique has many advantages: the operator could call up plans or circuit diagrams of the system on to his displays should something go wrong with a part of the plant; or some form of educational material could be interspersed with the technical information about the plant. Since he has only one display source, alarm signals which would override other material would be speedily dealt with.

Manual take-over

In the event of a breakdown in the control system for part of the plant it is often possible, and desirable, that the operator should take over manual control for that part and keep the whole plant running. This need raises problems which have not been fully recognized by designers of control rooms. In normal manual operation of a process or plant an operator is directly concerned with the decision-making and control activity needed over long periods of operation. He builds up during the working period a picture of the way the plant is working and of the particular trends and variations which are occurring. In short he has a detailed knowledge of the immediate past history, over a period of say several hours, of the process. In an automated plant he may well have much of this information in front of him, but since he is not concerned in the on-going detailed decision-making he is not likely to take in the necessary history of what has been happening. If in these circumstances he is suddenly called on to take over he will not be able to act appropriately if his decisions depend at all on the recent history of the process. He needs to have readily available a record of what has happened to the important variables. Unfortunately this kind of information is rarely supplied to operators, and it is not surprising to find that plant engineers often prefer to shut down a whole plant rather than to allow an operator to take over part of it when something goes wrong. An operator may not be able to perform at a sufficiently high level to match an automated system but, as has been mentioned earlier, operators are frequently blamed for poor performances which are hardly their fault. Another reason for poor manual-control performance is that in normally reliable automatic plants men rarely have a chance to practise their skills and they become 'rusty'. The solution is to run the plant under manual control from time to time even at the expense of some production loss. This may well be repaid when some of the machines fail and the whole plant would otherwise have to be stopped.

Some implications for training

There is a new generation of operators coming up who have never experienced the old manual-control days and their experience is confined to control-room running. In the normal operation of the plant these men may well be capable and competent, but there is a danger that their lack of broader training on the plant, and on manual control techniques, may have serious consequences when emergencies arise. Men in control rooms build up mental pictures of the world 'out there', but these may not bear a very close relation to the actual plant or the ways in which it works. Normally it may not matter that their picture is wrong in some details or even in a gross way, but when some unexpected situation arises the operator may be faced with making decisions which require a knowledge of the process, and he could, for example by alerting the appropriate repair crew and directing them immediately to the right area, save much time and money in repairs and 'down time'.

A particular difficulty in complex plant is that training cannot usually be carried out on the plant itself – it may be too costly or too dangerous to let a trainee loose on the real thing. One solution, used widely by airlines for example, is to use simulators; here the plant or process is simulated on a computer and the trainee is presented with controls and displays similar to those of the real plant. The simulation has the advantage that it can be run at different speeds, slowly at first as the subject learns and then increasingly faster until the real time speed is reached. Often in process plants the real time changes are very slow and here training time can be saved by speeding up the simulation.

MAINTENANCE AND REPAIR SKILLS

Automation inevitably means more modern and more complex plant. The automatic-control devices required to run the equipment need information gained from a complex array of sensors and instruments. One of the great advantages of automated plant is that processes are linked together so that a whole series of operations can be carried out on materials without human intervention – often the raw material is completely converted into the finished product in one series of operations. This has however the disadvantage that a breakdown in one part of the plant can bring the whole process to a halt. Even worse, a malfunction in one part could cause serious damage to another part of the equipment. Naturally safeguards are built into the system as far as possible, but nevertheless all eventualities cannot be guarded against. In these circumstances 'down time' can be very expensive and the importance of maintenance increases. Automation does not particularly change the nature of the maintenance work required compared with older plant, but it does mean that any method of minimizing breakdowns assumes greater importance. In one sense maintenance problems are more complex because with large integrated plant the problem of tracing faults becomes more difficult, but this is really no more than an extension of the problems which have faced repair teams before.

It is important to distinguish between *preventive* maintenance and *repair* maintenance. The former is concerned with the regular checking and upkeep of plant to avoid breakdowns and to detect possible failures before they occur, whereas the latter deals solely with the consequences of a failure. Clearly preventive maintenance has much to recommend it and it has proved its value. Fortunately it can be carried out by relatively unskilled labour and does not normally make very heavy demands on the personnel concerned. In most cases routine procedures can be laid down which are followed by rote, and provided that certain simple precautions are taken it is easy to apply. Many principles of design for ease of preventive maintenance have been laid down by ergonomists and engineering designers (see Morgan *et al.*, 1963). In general these preventive maintenance procedures do not raise any special problems, but one point may be overlooked: in automatically controlled plant men are much less likely to visit the machinery and in consequence the more or less incidental checking of the equipment which occurs when men are actively concerned with direct control of the machines does not occur. For this reason it is probably well worthwhile using the perceptual abilities of the preventive maintenance crew to spot unusual plant conditions. These men will be passing among the machines regularly, and provided that they know something about how the plant works, and the way it should behave, their normal observational abilities can be used to advantage. This means that training in aspects of plant behaviour and operation should be given to these men and they should be encouraged to report unusual events even at the expense of a few false alarms. The operating crew could well be used for some maintenance tasks as well, since this would bring them into contact with the equipment and might well enable them to improve their behaviour in emergency conditions, as discussed in a previous section.

Repair and fault-tracing

In many ways fault-tracing is similar to the problem-solving situations we devise for our leisure-time amusement. Anyone who has had to trace a fault in a motor car will be aware of the intellectual effort required and the time saving possible when a systematic search technique is used. Automated plant poses similar, but much more complicated, problems for the fault tracer. Much research has gone into the improvement of fault-finding procedures, and the results suggest that logical, split-half techniques are the most efficient. These methods employ tests which eliminate one half of the equipment, then half of that, and so on. In large and complex systems this procedure is very time-consuming, and it is often worthwhile looking first at the parts which it is known from experience are most likely to go wrong. Every attempt should be made to provide the fault tracer with adequate aid; proper diagrams and suitable test equipment should be available and *symptom* charts which set out the possible causes of the various faults should be built up. Even so, the problem can assume enormous proportions and the best solution is to tackle the problem at the design stage. For example, suitable test points should be provided for inaccessible parts and the system should use standard components which can be readily replaced. These and many other useful principles are given in the references listed in the bibliography.

MAN–COMPUTER COOPERATION

In the next few years we can expect rapid developments in this field of men assisting, or being assisted by, a computer. The move towards these combined systems comes partly from a recognition of the advantages to be gained by augmenting man's abilities, as discussed in previous sections, and partly because although designers would like to do away with men in automated plant, it is usually found that operators are still needed to do those tasks which cannot be done by computers. Whatever the reason for this need for man–computer systems, we are faced with a new range of problems which arise from the combination. These fall roughly into three categories:

(1) How to allocate the different functions to man and computer.

(2) How to match the high speed of the computer with the slower speed of man.

(3) How to convey information rapidly and efficiently across the interface between man and computer.

The first of these problems has been mentioned in Chapter 8, where some indications have been given how it might be tackled. There are many difficulties associated with this kind of system design, because the abilities of men seem to change when they are faced with new kinds of task situation. Human beings are often able to produce ingenious and novel ways of behaving after some experience on a job, and it is difficult to predict ahead just what a human being can do in a complex interrelated system. One particular problem which is receiving attention at the moment is how much mental work a man can do in given circumstances. No method of measuring mental work is known at present, and we cannot predict when a man will become 'overloaded' with mental work as we can when dealing with physical work. This is one important area where ergonomics can hope to make a valuable contribution to the planning and design of new systems as well as to possible rational methods of payment for jobs involving 'mental' skills.

Matching computer and human speed is not so much of a problem now, since computers can be used in a *time-sharing* fashion. Here the computer rapidly does its part of the task and, while waiting for a man to check the result or carry out some further processing on the data, gets on with some other job or another aspect of the current task. In this way one computer can be used to control several processes or to carry out off-line functions such as wage calculations or schedule preparation while still actively being part of some other man–computer system. Large computers employed on work for research organizations can have dozens of input–output stations where individual research workers are carrying out different calculations – the computer spends a fraction of its time on the work being put in at each station but does enough each time to keep the human 'component' continuously busy.

Getting information into and out of men and computers is a difficult task in itself. Men are much better at receiving large amounts of information when they are contained in visual patterns or in spoken or written languages such as English. Computers deal with vast quantities of simple numbers and the interface problem is to convert one form to the other quickly and accurately. The most satisfactory technique used so far is to use the computer itself to generate displays of information which are easily assimilated by man. This is being done now in several sophisticated ways. Computers are used to generate patterns, graphs, and diagrams and to display them on screens in front of operators. The man can draw directly on to the screen with special pens and ask the computer questions or alter a design or a diagram. The computer can then work out what the alteration would do to the performance of the system. There is virtually no limit to the kinds of display which can be produced, and the ergonomic problem comes back to deciding which kind of display is most effective and provides the information the man really needs.

Cooperation with computers can be achieved at various levels. For example a relatively simple use is to have the computer correct drafts of articles and reports. The writer types the first draft directly into the computer and the print-out is then studied. Any alterations can be fed into the computer as instructions, and a new print-out of the revised draft obtained immediately. The computer is simply acting as a typist would, but with a considerable saving in time. At a more advanced level, computers can be used to predict ahead from the current state of affairs what is likely to happen in a plant or process. They can do this very quickly and are currently being used to supplement human control of many industrial processes, for example in steel-making.

One particular case where this has been successfully applied is the Bessemer converter. The conversion of iron to steel takes place in a large vessel where oxygen is blown through the molten iron. The process takes about 20–30 minutes and it is important to finish blowing at a particular time to give a desired carbon content for the steel. The finishing temperature is also important, and the computer can predict from the starting conditions what the blowing time and control actions for the process should be to achieve the desired end-state. Industrial processes are rarely as predictable as we would like – one reason of course why we still need men to control them – so the computer predictions, which will be based on a mathematical model of the process, may be wrong. The computer can be given information during the blow which will enable it to check its predictions, and, if necessary, suggest control actions to take account of unexpected changes. Operators are valuable here, since they can often spot that something has changed by looking at the colour of flames for example. They can also decide whether process information is correct before it is fed into the computer. In some applications of this system the computer can take control actions directly, such as changing the flow rate of oxygen, without human intervention.

Full computer control is always being talked of, but while the industrial processes are so complex and subject to variation men are indispensable for assessing information and interpreting the occasional odd or peculiar occurrence. Man–computer control systems of this kind are currently in use in the steel industry and are proving successful.

So far we have barely begun to tap the possibilities of man–computer cooperation, and it is likely that this area alone will lead to some of the most impressive advances in industrial and commercial practice in the near future. At the managerial level the computer will be able to give the manager information about the current state of processes, stock levels, production rates, etc., and then, in response to suggestions from managers, it will be able to produce rapidly predictions for the outcome of various control actions which may be contemplated. At present computers are being installed in many industries and in the course of their on-line control activity they are producing valuable facts and assessments about the process. Much of this information would be valuable to managers, but it is not being given to them because the existence of the information and its value is not recognized and also because the display devices being developed are not utilized. Managers understandably find computer print-outs of tabulated figures difficult to assimilate, but with a little planning the computer can easily produce information in more acceptable forms.

*

The proponents of automation often claim that we already possess sufficient knowledge and have the necessary technology to build the automatic or 'electronic' factory. This case has been forcefully put by Beer (1965) and Diebold (1965). These writers make a particularly important point: the slow piecemeal application of automation to production processes may well be hindering the real progress which computers and control systems could achieve for us. This is because we try to replace men by automating their purely human functions and therefore we retain the 'limitations of hand, eye and brain' (Beer 1965). For various reasons we are not prepared to make the radical changes in our ideas and industrial methods which the computers and automation experts claim are necessary. It may be due to lack of foresight or courage, but also possibly to forces governing the pace of change which are beyond our immediate control. The result however is that we are faced with 'partial automation' rather than full automation for some time to come. There are also those who feel that, despite the claims of the automation experts, men do have many abilities which cannot be replaced and which are essential to the business of industry. In this situation we must recognize the respective abilities of the men and the machines and try to use them to best advantage, bearing in mind that we must accept certain limitations on the extent to which we can ignore social and human considerations in employing people.

Perhaps the most important conclusion to be drawn from this chapter is that fairly drastic changes are taking place in the skills required of men but that we have not clearly recognized the nature of the new skills. Because men are adaptable they are finding ways of dealing with new situations, but these are often inefficient and uncomfortable. It is also possible that we are a little in danger of throwing a useful part of our 'baby' out with the 'bathwater' when we try to replace men in automated plants. There are many things men can do efficiently and cheaply – they may also even *enjoy* doing some skilled tasks. For many reasons we have to have men in automated plants, and it seems foolish not to consider using their unique abilities to the full. Much ingenuity has gone into producing sensing devices and into methods of redesigning production processes to replace men which, had it been directed at using men effectively in cooperation with the machines, might have paid off handsomely.

PART FOUR

Organization Behaviour

ORGANIZATIONS are fundamentally biological entities; they go through the process of birth, growth, stabilization, decline, and death. The growth of an enterprise we usually associate with a period of excitement and challenge, whereas we see stabilization as a concomitant of order and the ascendancy of habit and custom. We are also accustomed to perceiving organizational growth and stability as opposites, for, once past the initial period of expanding activity, the concern and its systems of management sooner or later begin to fossilize: they become, as we are likely to say with scorn, 'bureaucratic'. Real success and achievement are replaced by reminiscences and the ritualization of past achievements; striving for goals gives way to the dominance of method. Few industrial concerns with us today have followed this course, as for example have the church and civil service, because, in the context of economic viability, it is the way to ruin.

In recent years there have been intensive efforts to arrest the natural processes in the organization's life, largely because the functioning of organizations and man's behaviour within them have assumed critical significance for the stability and continued prosperity of our industrialized society. Indeed, a noticeable feature of successful enterprises in our time is the engagement of their owners and managers in a search for ways of sustaining the features of growth while achieving some degree of internal stability. These attempts are leading us to recognize that any organization's survival depends on more than making an annual profit, it involves also having the capacity to adjust to an unstable market and to maintain a flexible internal order. The social scientist has an important role to play in helping concerns to achieve these objectives.

When industrial researchers first began to study man at work they concentrated their attentions on the individual, his job, and his immediate physical environment. Then sociologists and social psychologists widened our horizons and got us to recognize the influence on industrial behaviour of the work-group and the boss. Then, later still, social scientists began to realize that the behaviour of work-groups and the boss, in their turn, were linked with the firm's culture and its technical operations. At the same time we were being induced to recognize, as the market became increasingly competitive and unstable, that the firm's functioning is affected by social and economic conditions outside its own boundaries. In this way the focus of attention in industrial research has moved from the individual to the organization and from a preoccupation with techniques for solving localized problems to the exploration of the widest range of processes underlying behaviour. In both respects we can say that social research has become more realistic.

The study of organizations and of behaviour within them may take place from any one or more of the following points of view: the individual, the work-group, the firm's structure and controls (the ways of allocating work and responsibility and of coordinating human effort), its systems of management, technology, and its interaction with the market. One attitude characteristic of the younger generation of social scientists is that, whatever their own particular bent, they are likely to recognize that each of the aspects we have just listed interact with each other and are capable of influencing the functioning of the enterprise.

CHAPTER 11

The Industrial Manager*

D. G. CLARK

THE rapid changes in science and technology which the world is experiencing are nowhere having a greater effect than in industry itself. Here, the vast amounts of money spent on research, the trend towards the amalgamation of industrial units, and the increasing number of specialists have greatly enhanced the unique position of industrial managers as coordinators. Indeed, commentators like James Burnham predict that the overall influence of the shareholders will decrease, and also that managers will eventually rule society. Whether or not we accept this thesis, we cannot doubt the increasing importance of the manager's role in society and in this chapter we will be considering several questions about the industrial manager. Who is he? Where is he educated? From which strata of society does he come? In what ways is his career pattern changing with technological development and the increasing 'professionalism' of his role? However, before dealing with these questions and some of the evidence relating to them, we will briefly consider the growth of industrial management in Britain.

Traditionally British industrialists have had to overcome something of a social stigma, but as industry slowly acquired 'social respectability', so the public schools have had to change from turning the sons of entrepreneurs into gentlemen to helping the sons of gentlemen to become managers. It is in fact a common belief that the public schools have produced a large proportion of managers in the past, especially at the director and upper management levels. An attempt will be made in this analysis to judge whether they will play such a dominant role in the future. In this

* Material in this chapter is produced by courtesy of Business Publications Ltd from *The Industrial Manager*.

respect the emergence of British management has differed considerably from its American counterpart. In the United States, owing to a combination of factors – the protestant ethic, the absence of a traditional élite, and an expanding population – the controllers of industry have always found acceptance in 'society'. Consequently management became more professional and the large corporation emerged as an accepted part of American life.

With the development of the large corporation in Britain and increased American investment and participation, it is apparent that British management is beginning to move into line with that of the United States. This is especially so with respect to education. Today a manager is increasingly likely to have received a full-time higher education and also perhaps some form of management education.

It is possible to distinguish two broad areas of a manager's background; first his background outside industry (education and social, for instance); secondly his career within industry (as regards mobility, job changes, etc.). These two are obviously interrelated and a change in one will have some repercussion in the other. For example, a well-educated manager with good managerial education is likely to be more mobile than his less educated colleague.

It is in his educational and social backgrounds that the manager has changed most. The structure of management reflects the tremendous transformations in British society brought about in the last fifty years with the emergence of the Labour Party and the growth of the Welfare State. These factors, however, have not affected mobility to the same extent and it appears that industry itself has shown more resistance to change than society as a whole.

In spite of the apparent tendency towards amalgamation already mentioned, it is very difficult to generalize about the educational background of managers because of the large number of small firms and family firms which are still very important in Britain. (Two thirds of British manufacturing firms still employ less than 1,000 personnel; and half, less than 600.)

In these smaller firms nepotism is often rife and it is possible to find a high proportion of 'ex-public-school' managers, particularly as one goes further up the ladder. For example, the Institute of Directors (1965) in a recent study found that 66 per cent of their members, many of them from small firms, had attended public schools, whereas studies of larger firms suggest that a much smaller proportion of managers have been to public school. Similarly, small and large firms will affect the career patterns of managers in different ways. Family ties may restrict mobility between firms. The size of the smaller firms may necessitate less specialization, and the nepotism of their management restrict the promotional opportunities open to outsiders.

While the evidence concerning small firms is very limited, there have been several post-war studies involving large firms. The first to collect such data was Copeman (1955), who conducted a survey of directors in British industry in the early 1950s. This was followed by a more comprehensive investigation carried out by the Acton Society Trust (1956), which dealt in detail with the internal and industrial background of managers but was a little sketchy on their social origins. The third study of the 1950s was conducted by R. V. Clements (1958). This was essentially a regional study of managers in large industry in the Manchester Region. A recent study by the author (Clark, 1966), like the Clement's study, was primarily concerned with the Greater Manchester conurbation. Many of the firms sampled must have overlapped in these two studies, and in comparing the results certain trends of the past ten years can be discerned. In addition, the author attempted to compare the managers in the private sector with those of the nationalized industries. Much of the evidence used in this chapter is drawn from these two inquiries.

A further study, concerned solely with directors of large companies, has been conducted by R. Heller (1967), in which he reiterates suggestions made in previous studies that directors are older than the average manager, are more socially homogeneous, and have received a select education (71 per cent have attended public schools and 32 per cent Oxford or Cambridge). However one slightly surprising fact to emerge was that over half the sample were graduates. Heller argues that British management is gradually becoming professionalized, but nevertheless the director is still recruited from an extremely narrow social and educational stratum of society.

EDUCATIONAL BACKGROUND

The 1944 Education Act, born during the latter days of the war under the coalition Government, set out to provide secondary education for all and it has had a profound effect on the educational pattern of industrial managers. The educational background of managers has undergone considerable changes and the 'poor boy made good' managers who worked their way through night school are being replaced by those with at least a secondary education.

It has generally been assumed that the public-school-educated manager will have a considerable advantage over his grammar-school colleague, and evidence does suggest that this may be so in small and family firms. It is also becoming increasingly apparent that, in large firms, merit is at least as important as social background. In the highest echelons of industry, however, it is still true

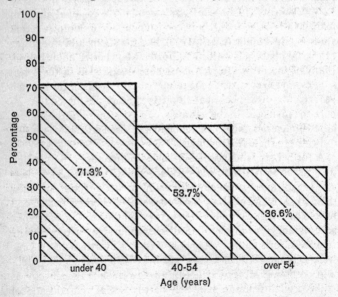

Figure 20. Managers with grammar-school education. (*D. G. Clark*, The Industrial Manager, 1966)

to say that one's chances are considerably better if one has been to the 'right school'.

The increasing importance of education for managers can be seen in the proportion of graduates holding managerial positions. The National Economic Development Council's Report (1965) shows that two fifths of all trainees and recruits on promotion to first management positions are graduates. Other studies back up this estimate and in the larger firms the proportion is almost certainly higher, keeping British managers in line with their counterparts in the U.S.A., the Soviet Union, and other countries in Western Europe.

Again, there is little evidence to support the tradition of Oxbridge Arts graduates predominating throughout industry. In fact the author's study found no less than 80 per cent of the graduates came from science or technological disciplines, although this proportion decreased the further up the ladder one looked. As is perhaps to be expected, it is in the very highest levels where the 'myths' best apply. Yet more evidence of the importance of education is the increasing number of managers who have acquired a host of other qualifications, some professional, others purely technical, in addition to their formal educational qualifications.

SOCIAL BACKGROUND

Whereas in the sphere of education evidence points to a more 'meritocratic' state of affairs, an analysis of the social origins of managers presents a less encouraging picture.

The concept of the upper social classes dominating the managerial world can be discounted particularly as university and college qualifications become more accepted as the means of entering industrial management. Nevertheless there is still evidence of 'discrimination' against the working classes, inadvertent though this may be.

According to investigations by a number of social reformers, the 'tripartite' system of education has tended to benefit the middle classes and enabled them to increase their domination of the grammar schools. Hence a close correlation emerges between the increase in the number of managers from grammar schools and those from the middle classes. This has been not only at the expense of the upper classes, as may be expected, but also of the lower classes. There is evidence that less opportunities exist for children from working-class homes today than thirty years ago. There is, in fact, a fairly rational explanation for this surprising state of affairs.

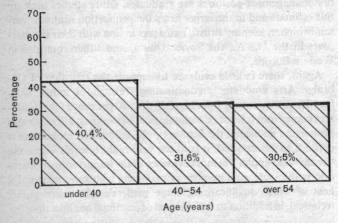

Figure 21. The social background of managers in the Registrar General's Class II (an intermediate grade which includes such occupations as teachers, managers, and supervisors in general, and which constitutes a large proportion of the English 'middle class'). (*D. G. Clark,* The Industrial Manager)

Management recruitment can broadly be satisfied by two methods: either upwards from the shop floor, or sideways from the institutions of higher education. In large firms, particularly, the latter is increasing at the expense of the former. If the 'tripartite' system does favour the middle classes then it would appear that both routes to management are partially blocked to working-class school-leavers. However, we can expect to find that if the working-class school-leaver has succeeded in an educational system which apparently works against him then he will probably be competing on equal terms with his middle-class counterpart in industry.

248

The champions of the comprehensive system believe that it will alleviate this problem, and, for the sake of social equality as well as industrial efficiency, we must hope that it is successful. Effective systems of management require that recruits be drawn from all sections of society and not preponderantly from the 'top' 20 per cent, that is the Registrar General's Classes I and II.

The position is different in smaller firms, where there are often more opportunities for promotion from the shop floor to junior management positions, and where, at the same time, the higher management positions tend to be occupied by those with family connexions and the 'old school tie'.

At the director level of industry, regardless of size, the distribution of the social background is more likely to be unequal. At this level even the middle-class manager has taken second place to those from the upper classes. However, it must be remembered that directors are usually older than the average manager, and the educational repercussions, felt elsewhere in industry, have yet to permeate the boardroom. In the future, it is likely that there will be changes even in the august boardroom, but it will nevertheless be many years before the 'meritocrats' can gain control here.

BACKGROUND WITHIN INDUSTRY

So far discussion has been limited to the external aspects of manager's backgrounds. Let us now turn to internal aspects, particularly mobility. With the decrease in the importance of the promotional ladder from the shop floor has come a consequent increase in the number of people who start their management careers as management trainees and technicians. This is partly the result of the growing technological complexity of industry as well as the more general, but obviously related, growth of educational awareness. It seems that only about one quarter of managers change functions during their careers. The author's study also showed that British managers do not move significantly either geographically or between firms. One third of managers had only been employed in a single firm, over a half in two firms or less, and over three quarters in three firms or less. The author also found two peaks when the managers are most likely to move firms. The first is in his early and mid twenties, often in order to undertake his first real management job. The second comes after a period of 15 to 20 years with the firm between the ages of 35 and 40. This is probably the time when managers can fairly accurately assess their prospects within a particular firm and also realize that they are reaching an age after which it may be difficult to move.

The overall impression is that in spite of the fact that management has undoubtedly become more professional, there is still a very strong conservative streak which prevents the expected increased mobility from showing itself to any great extent. It will be one of the prime functions of the management education services to remove this underlying conservatism and help to increase mobility.

MANAGEMENT EDUCATION

After the Franks Report of 1963 it was decided to create two institutions to deal exclusively with management training, one in London, the second in Manchester, financed jointly by government and industry. These perhaps symbolize more the acceptance of the need for this type of education than offer a practical solution.

Despite its growth since the 1950s, business education has suffered from both a lack of prestige and the intransigence of the traditional educational establishments. In the past, industry, whilst paying lip service to the concept of management training, was seldom prepared to release personnel for courses in any great numbers, and the educational institutions were not sufficiently flexible to make their courses viable and attractive to industry. The problem is even more acute with small firms who cannot afford to release their managers for four to ten weeks, simply because of replacement problems, and there have been few attempts to meet these particular needs.

The lack of cooperation between the industrial and academic worlds forced industry to take on the burden of business education often when it was not in a position to do it properly. As a consequence it has suffered from three major drawbacks. First, the fact that company sponsorship makes it unlikely that new ideas will permeate sufficiently from outside. Secondly, these courses lack prestige, and while it may be possible to impose them on junior management it is extremely difficult to get senior management to attend them. One result of this has been that the latter either neglect management training or go to outside courses, especially those of the various consultants and institutions such as the Administrative Staff College, Henley, and Ashridge Management College. (There exist in the field of management education several

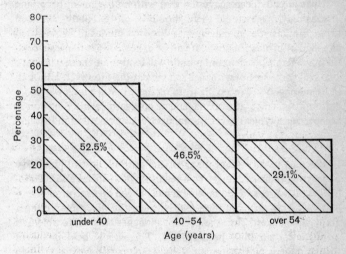

Figure 22. Managers with management education. (*D. G. Clark*, The Industrial Manager)

private organizations offering courses, two of the most important being at Henley and Ashridge. The former institution particularly has considerable prestige amongst British managers. In the author's study over 11 per cent of management education received by top managers and directors was provided by these two colleges alone.) The third main disadvantage facing industry in providing its own training is that only the larger firms have the necessary finances to run effective courses.

The author's study suggests that the battle for management education is being won. Over half of the younger managers are likely to have participated in some course, compared with one quarter of older managers, and they are also likely to have gone on longer full-time courses offering more scope.

A disturbing point is that even smaller numbers of top-management and director-level personnel appear to go on courses of this kind. At this level the attitude seems to be that management education is acceptable, even desirable, but it 'can't teach me anything'.

It has already been suggested that with management becoming increasingly professional there should be more mobility between firms. Similarly, as management education comes to be regarded as a sign of professionalism, it will be expected that those successful managers who are more mobile will tend to be those who have also had some sort of management education. However, although more managers are receiving training there is still a long way to go before attendance at a management course of some duration is accepted as a typical part of a manager's career pattern in Britain.

*

In the past twenty years many of the nation's institutions have undergone radical changes as a result of both social and technological pressure, and management has proved no exception. Comparisons with earlier studies and between the older and younger managers suggests that the present managers are more able and competent than their predecessors. The widely held image of British managers being amateurish, which may have been true in the past, certainly doesn't bear credence today as far as large firms are concerned. Nevertheless they still have a long way to go before they reach the professionalism that is found amongst managers in the United States of America.

It is in the sphere of educational background that the greatest changes occur. Not surprisingly the modern manager is far better educated than his earlier counterpart; the degree of improvement in his formal educational qualifications is surprising. He is likely to have received a good secondary schooling, probably at a grammar school, and to be a graduate from a science or technological faculty of a redbrick university.

This educational movement also has repercussions in a social sense, repercussions that were not intended by the social and educational reformers, for managers are being drawn from a *narrower* social stratum of the general population than they were previously. The reason for this is clear. On the one hand, industry has not continued to provide the suitable promotional ladder from shop floor to management that existed in the pre-war years; while on the other hand, the secondary educational system has tended to give great advantages to the child from a middle-class home at the expense of the working-class child. Thus industry's demand for educationally qualified managers leads to their increasing recruitment from the middle classes.

There have also been changes in career patterns. The laboratory and the drawing office are replacing the general office as the best place in which to commence work if management is the ultimate aim. Experience with the technical or production process of a firm is increasingly important. However managers do not seem to be any more mobile than their predecessors in spite of improved communications.

Thus it can be seen that the changes of a manager's career within industry are mainly the result of the technological pressure that inevitably affects industry. This is not a purely British phenomenon but, as Professor Galbraith and James Burnham, amongst others, have indicated, it is a trend found in all modern industrial countries whatever the prevailing political ideology. Moreover, ownership of large corporations doesn't appear to affect the position radically. A comparison of managers in the nationalized industries and those in large private corporations shows no appreciable differences in the backgrounds and career patterns of their managers.

In Britain, as in other countries, technology has demanded a well-educated management often with a technical bias; it is getting it. British managers are increasingly coming to resemble their counterparts in Western Europe, Soviet Russia, and the United States of America. Perhaps Burnham was correct and technology is achieving what certain political philosophers have dreamt of for centuries, a world-wide revolution – the 'managerial revolution'. But there is a considerable way to go yet in Britain, for, although lower and middle management positions are open to the meritocratic, this is certainly not the case amongst top managers and directors. Here, all too often, they are drawn from a tight, homogeneous social and educational group. Until merit becomes the criterion for selection, the philosophers' 'managerial revolution' can hardly be said to have arrived, and Britain will continue to waste a great deal of natural talent.

CHAPTER 12

Executive Leadership

P. J. SADLER

THIS chapter looks at management as a process of leadership and at the ways in which managers as leaders influence the performance and morale of members of working-groups. This is a topic which has long engaged the interest of social scientists; it is a field of study which carries important practical implications for management selection and development and which at the same time involves some of the most fundamental questions of human social behaviour.

Leadership takes many forms and the conditions under which leadership is exercised vary considerably. Some leaders are appointed to positions of authority over groups, others are elected by popular vote, still others arise spontaneously in informal groups. The manager is, of course, an example of the type of leader who is appointed to hold an office which carries authority. In the modern organization the appointed leader characteristically is responsible for the achievement of a more or less defined segment of the organization's task and carries authority which has been delegated to him by his organizational superiors. These characteristics make the nature of the role of the appointed leader rather different from those of the elected or informal leader. The leader who has been appointed to a position of authority cannot avoid the exercise of authority, whereas this *is* possible for the leader in the informal group setting. Douglas McGregor (1966) has expressed this in the phrase 'the boss must boss', referring to his experiences as President of Antioch College. He says: 'It took a couple of years, but I finally began to realize that a leader cannot avoid the exercise of authority any more than he can avoid responsibility for what happens to his organization.'

The leader who is elected to his leadership position receives his authority from those he leads and is responsible to them. The manager, however, receives his authority from his superiors and is responsible in turn to them. Not only, therefore, must he exercise authority but he must do so within the framework of an overall pattern of institutional authority in such a way that his own leadership makes a contribution to the achievement of organizational objectives. This will often mean, as McGregor points out, that 'since no important decision ever pleases everyone in the organization, he must also absorb the displeasure, and sometimes severe hostility, of those who would have taken a different course'.

Although managerial leaders cannot choose whether or not to exercise authority, they can often choose *how* they will exercise it – that is to say, they can choose a leadership style. Much of the social science research concerned with executive leadership has, in fact, been directed at classifying and describing different styles of leadership and assessing their relative effectiveness.

Although some early research in this field was directed at studying the personalities of leaders in an attempt to determine what type of individual is most suited to exercise the leadership role effectively, this approach has been largely abandoned since it has become clear that there is no one personality type which is associated with successful leadership under all conditions. It has come to be appreciated that effective leadership is a function of the type of group being led, its task and its total situation, as well as of the personality of the individual occupying the leadership role.

The main approach, particularly in recent years, has been to study not the leader as a person but the attitudes of leaders and their behaviour patterns and to relate these to other characteristics of the situation in which leadership is taking place.

One of the earliest studies of this kind was carried out in 1939 and 1940 by two American researchers, White and Lippitt (1959), and is now regarded as one of the classical experiments in social psychology. Their aim was to evaluate the effectiveness of different ways of exercising the leadership role. In their first experiment they compared two contrasting leadership styles – the *autocratic* and the *democratic*. These terms largely speak for themselves; the autocratic leader takes decisions and imposes them on the group, expecting group members to put them into effect without questioning the reasons for them. The democratic leader, on the other hand, encourages the members of his group to share in the decision-taking process and sees himself as a coordinator of group effort, rather than as the decision-taker. In a subsequent experiment a third style was also examined which was described as the *laissez-faire*. This third type of leader, as the use of the term indicates, plays a passive role in group affairs, and normally interacts with group members only on *their* initiative.

In this second study four groups of eleven-year-old boys were formed, matched as far as possible in terms of their personal characteristics and interests. Four adults were then procured to act as leaders to these groups of boys. Each adult was coached so that he could convincingly perform each of the three leadership styles being studied. The groups were then given tasks to do and worked successively under each of the four adults three times, with each adult using a different style of leadership on each occasion. In this way any personality differences between the three leaders which might have influenced the results were cancelled out.

The productivity of each group in each session was assessed by observing the boys going about their work and estimating the proportion of the total time during which they were actively working on their tasks. When overall ratings of productivity were compared, the groups were considered to have been most productive in the sessions in which they were autocratically led. The quality of the work done, however, was adjudged to have been best during the sessions under democratic leadership. An interesting further finding to emerge concerned the boys' behaviour while the leader was absent. In the course of each session the leader was called away for a brief period. In the sessions under autocratic leadership the activity level dropped sharply while the leader was out of the room, in the democratically led sessions there was no significant change in the level of activity, while in the *laissez-faire* climate productivity actually rose in the leader's absence.

This piece of research was carried out under laboratory conditions using young boys as subjects. It is not always the case that findings established in this way will hold good for the much more complex situation which obtains in later life. In this case the situation was to some extent artificial in that the boys were experiencing different styles of leadership in rapid succession from the same individual. It is doubtful, too, how far reactions of eleven-year-old boys provide a reliable guide to those of adult men and women who are earning their livelihood. However, since these experiments a considerable amount of further research has been carried out in the actual settings in which executive leadership takes place and much of this indicates that White and Lippitt's findings are, in fact, not at all irrelevant to the issues of productivity and morale in industry.

One criticism of their work which has been frequently made is that they looked at leadership styles too much in terms of black and white. The autocratic and democratic styles which they described are extremes, whereas in practice the behaviour of many, perhaps most, leaders in business will be somewhere between the two. Among those who have made this point are Tannenbaum and Schmidt (1958), who have suggested the idea that leadership behaviour varies along a continuum and that as one moves away from the autocratic extreme the amount of subordinate participation and involvement in decision-taking increases. They also suggest that the kind of leadership represented by the democratic extreme of the continuum will be rarely encountered in formal organizations.

At least four leadership styles can be located at points along such a continuum:

The autocratic. The leader takes the decisions and announces them, expecting his subordinates to carry them out without question.

The persuasive. The leader at this point on the scale also takes all the decisions for the group without discussion or consultation but believes that people will be better motivated if they are persuaded that the decisions are good ones. He does a lot of explaining and 'selling' in order to overcome any possible resistance to what he wants to do. He also puts a lot of energy into creating enthusiasm for the goals he has set for the group.

The consultative. The significant feature of consultative leadership is that the leader confers with group members *before* he takes his decisions and, in fact, considers their advice and their feelings when framing his decision. He may, of course, not always accept his subordinates' advice but they are likely to feel that they can influence him. Under this leadership style the decision and the full responsibility for it remain with the leader, but the degree of involvement by subordinates in decision-taking is very much greater than in the preceding styles.

The democratic. Using this style the leader would characteristically lay the problem before his subordinates and invite discussion. His role is that of conference leader, or chairman, rather than that of decision-taker. He will allow the decision to emerge out of the process of group discussion, instead of imposing it on the group as its boss.

Clearly there will be some situations in which each of the above styles is likely to be more appropriate than the others. In an emergency, for example, where an immediate decision is demanded, an autocratic style is likely to be most appropriate and would normally be considered justified by the group. The persuasive style would tend to fit situations in which the group leader, and he alone, possesses all the information on which the decision must be based and which at the same time calls for a very high level of commitment and enthusiasm on the part of group members if the task is to be carried through successfully. The consultative style is likely to be most appropriate when there is time in which to reach a considered decision and when the information on which the decision needs to be based is distributed among the members of the group. The democratic style is appropriate under similar conditions, with the important exception that this is likely to be appropriate only in those instances where the nature of the responsibility associated with the decision is such that group members are willing to share it with their leader, or alternatively the leader is willing to accept responsibility for decisions which he has not himself made.

The fact that different styles are appropriate to different situations would imply that the skilled leader varies his style according to the nature of the situation facing his group. Nevertheless, the research findings in this field indicate that individual leaders tend to employ one of the styles more consistently than the others, thus giving their overall pattern of leadership behaviour a 'flavour' which makes it possible to describe it as characteristically autocratic, or persuasive, or consultative, or democratic.

PREFERENCE FOR LEADERSHIP STYLES

Some recent work in British industry by the Research Department of Ashridge Management College has been concerned with exploring employee attitudes to these four leadership styles (Sadler, 1966). People at all levels and in all fields of work in two companies were questioned, involving a total sample of over 1,500. The four styles were described in a questionnaire and the employees were invited to say which type of leader they thought they would most enjoy working under. The styles were simply labelled (a), (b), (c), and (d) and the terms autocratic, persuasive, etc., were not used in case they should colour the replies. The preferences expressed by different types of employee are shown in Table 3 below.

TABLE 3: *Preferred leadership styles*

	Auto-cratic	Per-suasive	Con-sultative	Demo-cratic	No Reply
	%	%	%	%	%
Managers (n=126)	8	16	71	2	2
Professional and technical (n=660)	7	23	67	2	1
Salesmen (n=196)	7	30	61	—	2
Supervisors (n=61)	18	31	46	2	3
Clerical, secretarial (n=354)	14	25	39	16	6
'Blue-collar' workers (n=113)	15	19	47	17	2

In each group the consultative style is more frequently preferred than any of the others, although the proportion selecting it tends to decrease as one moves from the higher grades of employee to the lower. At the same time, there is a tendency for the proportions preferring each of the extreme leadership styles – the autocratic and the democratic – to increase as one moves down the hierarchy. It is also interesting that the vast majority of the respondents did, in fact, feel able to answer this question and to indicate a clear preference for one of the four. As can be seen from the table, in no case did more than 6 per cent avoid answering the question.

THE PERCEIVED LEADERSHIP STYLES OF MANAGERS AND SUPERVISORS

People were also invited to state which of the four descriptions most closely corresponded to the way their own immediate managers led their sections or departments. Here a fifth response was included as an additional alternative – 'he does not correspond at all closely to any of them'. The distribution of replies is shown in Table 4.

TABLE 4: *Perceived leadership styles*

	Auto.	Pers.	Cons.	Demo.	None of these	No reply
	%	%	%	%	%	%
Managers (n=126)	15	30	36	6	12	2
Professional and technical (n=660)	15	25	25	5	28	3
Salesmen (n=196)	22	23	27	1	21	4
Supervisors (n=61)	34	20	15	8	20	3
Clerical, secretarial (n=354)	26	19	18	6	20	10
'Blue-collar' workers (n=113)	23	16	16	5	36	4

The clear preference for the consultative style is not reflected in people's perceptions of the actual styles of their own bosses. In other words, many of the people in these two organizations who feel they would most enjoy working under consultative leadership do not believe that this is the kind of leadership they are actually experiencing. There is a tendency for the proportions who believe that they are being persuasively or consultatively led to fall, and for the proportion regarding the boss as autocratic to rise, as one moves down the hierarchy.

For the sample as a whole, approximately one in four could not place their managers under one of the four leadership styles described. It is interesting to speculate on the reasons for this and on the kind of leadership pattern employed by managers whose subordinates could not fit them into one of the four categories. The next set of data throws some light on these questions.

THE EFFECTIVENESS OF DIFFERENT LEADERSHIP STYLES

White and Lippitt demonstrated in their laboratory experiments that different styles of leadership produced differential effects on the quantity and quality of group output. Outside the laboratory it is not easy to design studies to arrive at such neat solutions. Output is not always measurable. Where it can be measured an additional problem is that within the whole complex structure of an industrial organization the leadership style of first-line management is only one among many important factors likely to be influencing the level of productivity. It is also the case that managers and supervisors are employed to do more than maintain the quantity and quality of output. According to the nature of the situation they may also be expected to build and maintain employee morale, and to maintain discipline. Consequently, any attempts to find simple associations between work-group efficiency and leadership style are unlikely to be successful. In the Ashridge studies which took place in a marketing organization and a large research and development laboratory, it was not possible to obtain objective measures of output. It was, however, possible to compare the various perceived leadership styles of managers in terms of four criteria – subordinates' job satisfaction, subordinates' satisfaction with the company, subordinates' confidence in immediate managers and subordinates' ratings of their immediate manager's efficiency. The results are shown below in Table 5.

In each case attitudes vary significantly with leadership style. The most favourable attitudes overall are associated with the consultative style, although the autocratic manager is most likely to be described as 'running things efficiently'. The least favourable responses, particularly in terms of confidence in management and the belief that the manager is running things efficiently, are associated with those managers who are not seen as falling under one of the four distinctive styles. In other words, in the light of the results shown in Table 5, it would appear to be very much better to have a clearly recognizable leadership style of some kind than not to have one at all.

This brings into consideration what is, in fact, a neglected aspect of the study of leadership – the question of subordinates' attitudes and expectations. Where a manager does not operate consistently in accordance with a recognizable style of leadership

TABLE 5: *Leadership style and subordinates' attitudes*

	Auto-cratic (n=320)	Per-suasive (n=352)	Con-sultative (n=367)	Demo-cratic (n=379)	None of these (n=381)
	%	%	%	%	%
High job satisfaction	72	81	84	81	66
High satisfaction with organization	86	90	93	87	82
High confidence in management	76	87	89	70	50
High rating of manager's efficiency	38	30	35	27	12

it is likely that he fails to provide his subordinates with a clear set of expectations concerning how they should behave and what his reactions are likely to be as various kinds of situation arise. Recent studies (Kahn *et al.* 1964) have shown that the lack of a clear set of expectations of this kind is likely to give rise to anxiety on the subordinates' part. To put this another way, although the subordinate may desire a certain type of relationship with his leader in terms, for example, of the extent to which he would like to be consulted about decisions, what he is even more in need of is a consistent relationship which enables him to know where he stands and which makes it possible for him to predict the boss's behaviour.

OTHER CLASSIFICATIONS OF LEADERSHIP STYLE

Several groups of researchers have studied the question of leadership styles from a slightly different point of view. Instead of examining the differences in the ways in which leaders handle decision-taking, they have turned their attention to the way in which the leader carries out his functions, with special reference to the amount of concern he shows for getting the job done, on the one hand, and satisfying the needs of his subordinates on the other.

For example, in a classic series of studies, research workers at Michigan University (Katz *et al.*, 1950) classified first-line supervisors under two headings – the 'production-centred supervisor' who gives greatest emphasis to task achievement and the 'employee-centred supervisor' who gives prior attention to people's needs.

One of the studies in this series was carried out in an insurance company. The supervisors were classified as production-centred or employee-centred on the basis of their own descriptions of how they approached their jobs. At the same time groups were classified as high-producing or low-producing on the basis of production records. Out of eight supervisors classified as production-centred, only one was in charge of a group with high output. On the other hand, of nine employee-centred supervisors, six had high-producing sections.

In interpreting these findings it is possible that the supervisory style is a result rather than a cause of high productivity. In other words, it may be the case that where a section is producing good work a supervisor can afford to relax and to centre on human relations but where a group is less efficient pressure on the supervisor makes him become more concerned with getting results.

One weakness in these studies which has attracted much comment is the somewhat artificial separation of managers into those who are employee-centred and those who are production-centred. For example, although a study in a tractor factory (Kahn, 1956) indicated that high-producing supervisors were those most skilled in satisfying subordinates' needs for information and support, these supervisors were no less concerned with the need to maintain high production. Kahn suggests the need to replace the employee-centred /production-centred continuum with a four-fold classification embracing two other kinds of supervisor – the one who is highly concerned both with production and employee needs and the one who is not very concerned with either.

THE MANAGERIAL GRID

The classification of leadership styles in terms of concern for production and concern for employees' needs has been taken further by Blake and Mouton (1964). They suggest the idea of measuring the degree of a manager's concern for production and concern for people. They employ a nine-point scale to do this in each case and plot the resulting scores on a *managerial grid*, which is formed by plotting the concern for production scores on a horizontal axis and the concern for people scores on a vertical axis. Thus a score of 9·1 indicates the highest possible concern for production, combined with a minimum concern for people. The score 1·9, on the other hand, indicates the reverse – minimum concern for production, combined with maximum concern for people. The style held out as the ideal is 9·9 in which maximum concern for both production and people are combined.

Blake and Mouton go further than Kahn and point to the existence of a fifth style at the centre of the grid (5·5) which reflects a kind of half-way concern for production, combined with a half-way concern for people. They suggest that in practice this is the style that best describes the way most managers lead their groups.

The most important contribution made by Blake and Mouton is that they have drawn attention to the fact that the goal of maximizing production frequently conflicts with the goal of satisfying people's needs. In practice the supervisor who wishes to achieve a production target may find that his attempts to do this involve unsatisfying experiences for his subordinates which in turn promote resistance to his leadership. The 9·1 type of manager resolves such conflicts in favour of getting the production targets achieved, while the 1·9 type of manager does so in favour of keeping people happy. The 5·5 manager or supervisor adopts a compromise approach; his guiding philosophy is not to go all out for either high production or high employee satisfaction but rather to try to achieve a reasonably satisfactory output along with reasonably satisfied employees.

The 9·9 managerial style is characterized by the belief that conflicts between production objectives and the needs of employees are neither necessary nor inherent. This approach involves utilizing people's needs in the interests of production, achieving both high production and high morale through the involvement of people in concerted team action. Blake and Mouton also point out that for managers to be able to employ 'the 9·9 style' and to perceive '9·9 solutions' to work problems special training is needed.

LEADERSHIP AND TECHNOLOGY

In recent years social scientists have increasingly turned their attention to the ways in which organizational behaviour varies according to technology. Joan Woodward (1965), for example, has demonstrated the ways in which different types of organization structure are appropriate according to whether firms are engaged in unit or small batch production, large batch or mass production, or continuous flow-process production. What is true for organization structure holds good for patterns of leadership, and this can be best shown by describing the salient characteristics of the role of the first-line supervisor under three types of production system.

Unit or small-batch production usually involves producing something to the precise requirements of a known customer. Such work normally calls for exercise of a high degree of craft skill. Quality of work is emphasized over quantity. Employee motivation springs from satisfaction in the exercise of skill and pride in the finished product. The expectations of subordinates are that the supervisor should himself be highly skilled and should be someone they can turn to for technical advice when needed. They expect general rather than close supervision and probably expect to be consulted about technical matters. The expectations of superiors are that the supervisor should maintain quality and meet delivery dates.

Mass production typically involves larger work-groups than unit production, with an average skill level considerably lower. Quantity and cost reduction are likely to be emphasized over quality. Motivation is likely to be lower than in unit production and to spring from factors external to the job – such as the pay packet, working conditions, and relationships with management. Workers do not expect their supervisors to be highly skilled technically so much as to be good at planning and organizing the work and ensuring a free flow of materials. At the same time, since their needs for individuality and human dignity are unlikely to be satisfied by the nature of the work, they look to the supervisor for satisfactions of this kind. Superiors, on the other hand, expect of the supervisor that he should raise output, reduce costs, and control absenteeism and labour turnover. To this end the supervisor under mass production is often under considerable pressure for results which makes it difficult for him to give enough attention to his subordinates as individuals with needs requiring satisfaction. The mass-production situation creates pressures which tend to push the first-line supervisor in the direction of autocratic, production-centred leadership which may be successful in terms of production figures but has less happy effects on industrial relations.

Flow-process types of production are usually characterized by the fact that shop-floor workers do not perform operations on the materials being processed, but rather monitor the equipment which carries out the operations with a lesser or greater degree of automaticity. The work is not highly skilled in the usual sense, but involves considerable knowledge of the equipment and its functioning and a high degree of responsibility. Interruptions to plant running are usually extremely costly and considerable emphasis is given to avoiding breakdowns and to getting production resumed as quickly as possible when they do occur. Work groups are typically smaller than in either unit or mass production. In these conditions the shop-floor workers themselves assume responsibilities and perform roles which in more traditional industries are allocated to supervisors. The role of the latter is perhaps better described as supervision of technology than supervision of people. The leadership functions of communication and dealing with crisis situations assume great importance, as does the ability to build and maintain group cohesion and effective team-working. Subordinates expect of the supervisor that he should provide them with technical support and advice and support during emergencies. Superiors demand smooth running of the plant.

These three types of work situation clearly call for different approaches and styles of leadership. They also demand differential emphasis to be given to the various functions which the leader can be called upon to perform. This fact is being increasingly recognized, leading to the development of training schemes for managers and supervisors which are closely tailored to the needs of particular technologies.

TECHNOLOGICAL CHANGE AND THE MANAGEMENT OF THE FUTURE

The social sciences researches into executive leadership which have been reviewed in this chapter have been concerned with the management process as we know it and which has developed over the last half-century in the industrialized parts of the world. Many authors, however, have pointed out that, owing to the increasingly rapid rate of technological change, the nature of management itself is likely to undergo considerable transformation within the next few decades. In looking ahead and considering what the nature of executive leadership will be in the future, it is not possible to point to firm conclusions based on empirical research. Nevertheless it is useful at this stage, in the light of the knowledge we already possess about the nature of technological change and its impact on human functions, to put forward some hypotheses which can be tested and modified by experience. In fact, several eminent social scientists have turned their attention to just this problem.

H. A. Simon (1965) has made a particularly extensive study of the impact of automation on managerial decision-taking. He points out that the problems facing managers vary in the extent to which they are well structured and can be precisely solved. At one end of the scale are decisions which he describes as 'highly programmed', such as the routine procurement of office supplies or the pricing of standard products. At the other end of the scale lie decisions which are 'unprogrammed', such as one-off decisions to enter new markets or develop new products or strategies for industrial relations negotiations. Between the two extreme points are decisions with every possible blend of precise and imprecise, routine and non-routine elements. Simon points out that the technological change which is currently taking place in industry is having a considerable effect on the decision-taking process. The use of computers and management tools such as operational research is making it more and more possible to take valid decisions at the programmed end of the decision-taking scale. It is likely that in a relatively short period of time it will be possible to automate all decisions of this kind, thus removing them from the functions of the manager. At the same time some progress is being made towards the automation of the more complex and less routine decisions which lie towards the unprogrammed end of the scale. The important implication of both these trends for the nature of the manager's job is that the manager will find less and less of his time is taken up by the processes of decision-taking and problem-solving. This in turn implies that he will have more time and energy to spare for other activities, with the possibility that leadership aspects of the manager's task may assume greater prominence than hitherto. Managers frequently complain that they have insufficient time to deal adequately with the important tasks of communicating with their subordinates, developing their subordinates' abilities and the like. Automation at the management level may well liberate the manager from the paperwork that binds him to his desk, enabling him to devote much more attention to the 'employee-centred' and 'group-centred' aspects of his task.

A particular example of the effect of technological change on a manager's job which illustrates this possibility has been described by Anshen (1965). The case involves a manager in a plant concerned with the processing of a number of raw materials which could be combined in various ways in order to yield a variety of end products. An important part of the manager's job was to schedule the operations of the plant. In taking his decisions he had to contend with a mass of information on changes in material costs and in customer demand and market prices, and the complexity of the problem was such that he had had to devote up to two thirds of his time to it. A computer was then introduced into the organization and after a year's automatic operation the manager found that the amount of time he spent on the actual decision-taking aspects of his job had fallen to 10 per cent. He reported that the time which was now available to him was spent in four main ways. First, he was enabled to spend more time conceiving and introducing changes in the system; in other words, he was giving greater attention to the exercise of managerial initiative. Secondly, he spent more time on personnel matters and, in particular, on developing better industrial relations within the plant. Thirdly, he found himself able to take an active role in affairs affecting the relationships between the plant and the neighbouring community. Fourthly, he was able to spend more time in developing the relationship between his department and other parts of the business. All four of these activities fall under the heading of leadership functions.

This particular example does, however, raise an important question. It is clear from the evidence Anshen presents that in this case the manager found himself with much more spare time than he had been accustomed to and then began to use this spare time in ways which seemed to him important. It certainly appears that he acted intelligently and used his spare capacity to good effect. It cannot, however, be taken for granted that this would always happen. As management functions change, and as the time spent on information-processing and decision-taking is reduced, more and more managers will be faced with the problem of deciding how to plan their activities. It is important that they should receive adequate help and guidance in doing this. The important task of management education and training in the current time of rapid technological change is to prepare managers to use wisely the freedom of action that the newer technologies are likely to bring in their train. It is also important that managers should be emotionally prepared for this transition. The change from a task in which the pattern of activity is largely determined by events and by external demands on the manager's time to a type of task which is relatively unstructured and which leaves the manager a great deal of choice is likely to involve considerable anxiety and uncertainty. Automation may be seen as a threat to the manager's power and status rather than as an opportunity to broaden the scope of the manager's job; managerial resistance to change may emerge in the form of attempts to cling to the familiar patterns of routine decision-taking and to avoid the challenge which greater freedom of action will bring.

LEADERSHIP AT THE TOP

It is noticeable that the great majority of the studies of leadership in industry have been focused on the role of the first-line supervisor. The reasons for this are several. First, there are more supervisors at this than at higher levels, thus providing sizeable samples of leaders. Secondly, research workers are more likely to be granted facilities to study the behaviour of the supervisor than they are to analyse the activities of top managers. Thirdly, it is perhaps at the level of first-line supervision that the nature of the leadership role is most clear-cut, since the situation involves a group of people with a specific task to perform being led in an immediate and personal way by one appointed to a position of authority over them.

Selznick (1957) has drawn attention to important differences between leadership at lower levels, which he refers to as *interpersonal* leadership, and the kind which takes place in the high echelons of large organizations, which he terms *institutional* leadership. Whereas the task of the former is primarily to achieve routine tasks and to facilitate personal involvement and group working, the role of the latter lies mainly in the field of developing and maintaining systems of beliefs and values. The institutional leader deals with issues in terms of their long-range implications for the organization. His major functions are to define policy, to build the kind of social structure which will put that policy into effect, and to maintain the values which will ensure its continuity. At this level of functioning the true contribution of the leader may be made in the course of two or three critical decisions in a year.

Among the few studies of leadership at this level one that stands out is the report by Guest (1962) on the leadership behaviour of the chief executive in an automobile assembly plant. This plant was first studied in 1953. At this time its level of performance compared with five other similar plants in the same company was very poor. In mid-1953 a new manager was assigned to the plant. Within a relatively short time its performance improved dramatically and there were indications of a considerable increase in the favourability of attitudes of employees at all levels. In 1956 a second study of the plant was made in order to trace the reasons for these improvements. It was found that there were few differences in basic organization structure, comparing 1950 with 1956. It was the view of the researchers that the main reason for the improved performance and morale was the effectiveness of the leadership style of the new chief executive. The findings were in line with Selznick's observations on the functions of high-level leadership in that one notable characteristic of the new manager's approach to his role was his concern with matters relating to future planning. This was in marked contrast to his less successful predecessor, who appeared to act chiefly in response to immediate emergencies.

*

It has become evident during the course of the social science research on leadership that the search for a best leadership style in general terms is futile. Leadership is a process which, to be effective, must be adapted to the needs of the group and the situation. In particular, the following aspects of the total situation have emerged as of critical importance in determining the requirements of the leadership role.

(1) The general cultural setting in which leadership takes place and the extent to which the values of society are ones which favour autocratic or democratic forms of social control. Western societies are characterized generally by movement away from autocratically controlled social institutions and towards ones which are democratically constituted. This trend has inevitable implications for people's attitudes to the legitimacy of leadership and authority in the work situation. Increasingly, autocratic styles of leadership are being challenged not only in terms of their effectiveness but on moral grounds.

(2) The nature of the objectives of leadership and in particular the extent to which the leader is concerned with the achievement of specific, short-term, routine objectives on the one hand or with the long-term maintenance of institutional values and traditions on the other.

(3) The type of technological environment and in particular the extent to which it provides the leader and/or the members of the group with means of control over group productivity.

The research which has been reviewed in this chapter has been mainly concerned with identifying different approaches to leadership and comparing them in terms of various criteria of effectiveness. Studies of this kind are important, and provide useful information, but will in future be the more productive the more attention is paid to these situational factors. A neglected field, however, has been the study of the contribution which leadership of any kind can make to overall organizational effectiveness compared with the contributions to be expected from such factors as organization structure and the use of management techniques. Currently most emphasis is laid on the organizational framework of behaviour on the one hand and the new tools which the computer is providing for management's use on the other. Leadership receives scant attention not only in research programmes but also in the content of management education. Guest's study of leadership in an automobile plant suggests that this emphasis may be wrong. We may still live in an age in which personal leadership can make not only a significant but in fact an overwhelming contribution to organizational effectiveness. Certainly, more research along the lines of Guest's study is needed in order to test this hypothesis.

CHAPTER 13

Training and Developing Executives

PETER B. SMITH

It has been argued that organizations are one of the most important inventions upon which civilization rests. They make possible productivity on a scale hitherto inconceivable and enable man to live increasingly prosperously in a wide variety of previously inhospitable environments.

One major aspect of organizations is that they are rigid insofar as they structure very many of their operations up to a point where far greater coordination of effort is possible than among groups of people who just happen to be working alongside one another. Sociologists such as Weber, writing at the turn of the century, saw this rigidity as a very important characteristic of organizations. More recently attention has focused increasingly on the flexibility of organizations. The technology of production and the available markets for a product have been subject to increasingly rapid changes. Those organizations which have prospered have been those which are most responsive to the environmental changes.

Every organization, then, needs firstly to make provision for changing itself and secondly to check that the changes made are indeed in a direction which leaves the organization better adapted to its environment than before the change. This chapter takes a look at attempts by organizations to develop or train their own managers at fairly senior levels either within the organization or by the use of a course provided by some external body. Management training in this country has passed in the matter of a few years from a neglected and sporadic activity to a rapid-growth industry in its own right. Only a handful of universities remain uninvolved in the training of managers in one discipline or another, while technical colleges, consultants, and staff colleges are even more heavily involved.

Before we examine the methods of training which are being

used and the aims towards which all this training is oriented, it is worth reflecting again on the contribution of Weber to the study of organizations. An organization is defined by numerous expectations in the minds of its members, some explicit, some implicit, about how each member of the organization ought to behave in various situations. Such expectations have considerable importance to the organization member, so that one should hesitate before assuming that training a manager is certain to achieve *any* long-term change in his behaviour within the organization. To achieve change in a manager's behaviour is in fact probably rather difficult, and from the point of view of the manager this may be no bad thing. He is protected from the passing tide of fashion among management trainers or among his superiors within his own organization.

THE PROCESS OF TRAINING

The directions in which organizations attempt to train their management range widely from specific training in a specialized skill appropriate to a particular task, to more generalized attempts to 'develop' a man's potentialities to the full, whether they are potentialities for taking added responsibilities, becoming more decisive, becoming more able to relate effectively to others, becoming more flexible, or what you will. Sometimes the goal of the training may be quite precisely defined, but rather more often it is expressed in diffuse terms. Organizations' plans for training managers are very often tied up with their intentions for promoting the same men. Participation in training is seen as part of the manager's preparation for his new responsibilities.

There are also a variety of ways in which an organization can attempt to train its managers. Firstly, one can dispense with the need to attempt training by hiring an alternative, more skilled man in place of the first. At the senior levels of an organization this may cause as many problems as it solves; the organization may be obliged or feel obliged to employ the displaced man elsewhere, where his existing skills are poorly utilized, while the new man certainly has much to learn about the specific job before he can utilize his skills.

A second way to train a man for taking some responsibility is to appoint him to it right away. The rationale behind this might be that the challenge of the new situation combined with higher management's evident trust in the new appointee provide optimal conditions for the development of the very skills the job requires. The difficulty arises here of course if the trust of higher management proves to be misplaced. Nonetheless this is a very widely used way of attempting to induce change.

The third way to train a man is to attempt to instruct him inside the actual situation in which he works. Most typically this is done primarily by the man's own superior, whether it be by hauling the man over the coals when he makes mistakes or by coaching him in the desired direction through some appraisal system or more informal contacts. One might argue that if this function were adequately performed, organizations would have no need of any of the training methods shortly to be discussed. The fact is, however, that many managers either do not have the time to coach their subordinates or do not have the skills which it would be good for their subordinates to develop.

The fourth way to train a man is to make use of some specialized training facility, and it is this which will mostly concern us. The facility may be within the organization, as in the case of a personnel or training department, it may be a service provided by a firm of consultants or an industry staff college, or it may be a specific course at a university or technical college.

When a manager ceases to manage and enters upon some more or less temporary programme of training, two things happen. Firstly the pressures customarily exerted upon him by his organization weaken. The training is quite likely conducted away from the factory and arrangements are made either to defer decisions or to pass problems over to others for their action. Secondly, the trainee becomes subject to the pressures of the training institution. The manager has become a student and his understanding of how a 'good' student should behave may be quite at variance with the expectations of those staffing the training institution. Senior managers frequently place a high value on their own previous experience as a guide to future action. But they may also feel that the 'good' student should adopt a fairly passive role, receiving instruction from the acknowledged expert. Combining these two points we can see that senior managers are likely to be willing to be influenced by those who they see as having a high degree of relevant experience, whether they be trainers or other course members; but they will be suspicious of generalized theory and of teachers with evident managerial inexperience.

The manager's stance toward the training is complicated by some further factors. When he returns to his job, receives his promotion, or whatever follows training, he is once more subject to the pressures of his organization. If his trainer has influenced him to behave in some new way or adopt some new technique, he must now convince his associates that the change is a change for the better. If they prefer him as he was, they will have plenty of ways of discouraging his innovations. The manager has also to make his peace with some questions that may be nagging him. Why was he nominated for this particular training course? Was it a sign of favour, or a sign that higher management saw him in some way deficient in the requisite skills for the job? Should he take higher management's explanations (if he was given any) at face value, or do they conceal unspoken reservation about his abilities? These anxieties concern many managers, and few courses give much help in resolving them. Organizations wield a great deal of power over their managers' careers and it need not be surprising if a man on a two-week course spends as much time pondering the nuances of the meaning to his organization of his presence there as he does pondering the nuances of course trainers' words when he may never meet them again.

The important contribution of the trainee manager's pre-occupation with the status implications of his being on the course emerges very clearly from an excellent study of the first year at the Harvard Business School conducted by Charles D. Orth (1963). Orth conducted an extensive programme of interviews with the students through the year. Two of his main conclusions were that the students' learning was influenced at least as much by the norms of the student group as by the demands of the instructors; and that the acceptability of the different courses was judged in terms of whether or not they were at variance with the norms of the business community to which group the students aspired. For example the more quantitatively oriented courses were preferred to those in administrative practice, in that they were·seen as more tough-minded and practical.

Turning from the manager-in-training to the management teacher there is little or no consensus among the teachers about the desired student role. There are some who see intellectual rigour as the foremost requirement, and who teach managers much as they would teach undergraduates. There are others who believe that managers are best educated by talking to other experienced managers, so that formalized instruction is minimized. And there are still others who are attempting to design new training methods based on various types of simulation of managerial situations. Although there is little consensus among management teachers, we shall see that the demand for training methods which relate to specific and practical experience has had a powerful and innovative impact on teachers' methods. It has pushed them well ahead of our knowledge about the effectiveness of different training methods.

TRAINING METHODS

Having examined some of the issues surrounding participation in any form of management training, it is now time to examine the actual methods currently in use. With each method it will be important to discuss how and where it is used, what effect it is claimed to have, and what independent evidence there is on its effectiveness. The more important training methods currently in use, together with some of their synonyms, can be arbitrarily classified as:

> Lectures
> Discussion groups (or syndicates)
> Case study groups
> Study projects
> Role-playing
> Business games (or business exercises)
> T-group training (or group dynamics)

Lectures

A good deal is known about the lecture as a method of instruction, although very little of this information is derived from studies of lectures to managers. The hallmark of the lecture is that one man talks more or less continuously, while the others either listen or make notes on what he says. It can be very economical of training staff resources, and it may enable a lot of information to be transmitted in a short time. Since the listeners respond little or not at all, it is easy to assume that they have understood all that they have heard and that they have heard all that has been said. The method is widespread and many lecturers enjoy lecturing. The assumption implicit in the method is that what the lecturer has to say will be interesting to the listeners and relevant to their needs. In practice of course a great deal of the lecturer's wisdom is not retained by the listener, either because he doesn't hear it, or because he doesn't understand it, or because he forgets it. Lectures are nonetheless valuable if they succeed in arousing interest in a subject, leading to later discussion or reading. A good deal of the information loss involved can be circumvented by supporting handouts or reading. One final criticism of the lecture in management training is that it is necessarily abstract. Even if the lecture concerns the way managers act, or the use of some technique, it is a description of the act and not the performance of the act. Thus the method is more appropriate to an intellectual understanding of a problem or situation than to the development of action skills.

Discussion groups

Lectures shade into discussion groups where the size of the audience permits extensive questions or discussion during or after the lecture. So long as the lecturer remains present in such discussions he is likely to be the focal figure. The implicit model of learning is left undisturbed – the lecturer *knows*, while the student must learn. Discussion can clarify misunderstandings, or enable the lecturer to explain why an apparently contradictory fact does not impair his argument. A syndicate or discussion group may be asked to discuss something they have read or to share their experience of some common problem they have each had to face. The basic method remains unchanged – abstract discussion of situations not present – but the learner's opportunities to participate actively and to steer discussion in the direction of his own interests are markedly increased. Research studies have shown that most managers spend a great deal of their working hours talking to other people, so it is not surprising to find that syndicate discussions are often valued highly by them. In one guise or another they find a place in most courses for senior management.

Research studies comparing lectures with group discussion as a source of attitude or behaviour change are numerous. A carefully conducted one was that of Edith Bennett Pelz (1959), who compared the effectiveness of various methods of inducing students to volunteer for psychological experiments. She found that group discussion was not necessarily any more influential than lectures, but that two other factors did differentiate those who volunteered from those who did not. Volunteers were defined as those who actually reappeared to participate in experiments. They were, firstly, those who had made a conscious decision to volunteer straight ·after the influence attempt, and, secondly, those who thought that most others had also decided to·volunteer. It didn't matter whether the volunteer's own decision was made publicly or privately. From this one might expect that management training would most readily lead to behaviour changes where a specific decision to behave in some way was involved and where a perceived consensus was achieved. These conditions may be quite often achieved in discussions, particularly of case-studies, but there cannot be many lectures which end in this way. These conclusions must not be over-generalized, since the behaviour changes examined in the Pelz research were conscious changes; plenty of the ways in which a manager responds to training may involve changes of which he is unaware, such as changes in the frequency of behaving in a particular way.

So far we have looked at lectures and at group discussion, probably the two most widely used methods. It is obvious that a mixture of the two methods is superior to either alone; lectures are best suited to relatively brief introductions of new concepts or information, while group discussion permits the testing out of these ideas in specific situations to the point where a manager can decide in the company of his peers whether he likes the idea sufficiently to give it a try.

In order to examine the remaining training methods in management education and to understand why they have become more or less popular, it will be necessary to digress for a moment and reconsider the purposes of training managers. Training was linked at the beginning of this chapter with provision for organizational change, but this goal is too gross to be very illuminating. Argyle and Smith (1962) interviewed senior managers from forty-five companies utilizing the Ashridge course, and found them rather uncertain of the goals, other than keeping up with other firms. In answer to suggestions they agreed that increase in knowledge, especially of administrative techniques and improvement of social skills, were important, and were somewhat less keen on attitude changes. From the viewpoint of management teachers, Fairhead, Pugh, and Williams (1965) suggest that the goals of management education should be:

(1) increase in analytic skills including quantitative aids such as operations research

(2) increases in awareness of the forces shaping management decisions, including politics, macro-economics and sociology

(3) increases in awareness of the functioning of organizations and in social sensitivity skills

If we accept these three overall goals, it can be seen that increase in knowledge is a component in all of them but only in the second is it the major component. The other two goals both concern increases of skill, and skill training requires practice. The combination of lectures and group discussion is likely only to be of value where increase of knowledge and its utilization are more important than increase in some analytic or behavioural skill.

Case study groups

The first method we shall consider whose purpose is skill practice is that of case studies. The case study is typically conducted as group discussion and is perhaps the method which is uniquely characteristic of management training. It differs from other forms of group discussion only in that it is focused on a previously prepared report on a specific and real managerial problem situation. The discussion group is typically required to recommend the future action of the principal actor in the report. The skill being practised here is plainly a diagnostic one; each man must weigh the evidence and choose between possible courses of action. A good deal of the method's cachet no doubt derives from its wholehearted use in the Harvard Business School and other prestigious American institutions. Elisabeth Sidney, in a recent survey of some representative management training centres in this country, found it used almost everywhere in every conceivable subject. But few if any institutions were using it to the exclusion of other methods.

Increase in diagnostic skill is a good deal less easy to measure than increase in knowledge; it is also a good deal less easy for the manager to transfer it from his learning situation to his job. Knowledge once learned or at least noted down is relatively imperishable. Skill in diagnosing cases may increase but the case material may differ in many ways from problem situations arising in a particular job. Some ingenious modifications of case-method attempt to make it more realistic; such as only providing the information asked for by the discussion group, or providing a great deal of information, much of it irrelevant, or presenting a sequence of cases based on development over time within a single company.

Considering the widespread use of cases, the research evidence of their utility is very disappointing. No evaluation studies of case-method in this country have been published. Observation of Italian case groups by Giattino and Volpe showed a decrease in stereotyped judgements and interpretation based on previous experience, and an increase in analysis of the situation in terms of the facts presented. Various American studies have linked case discussion with changes in attitudes in the direction of greater concern with human relations; but not one study has examined linkage between the case-method and the subsequent behaviour of managers in their jobs. The only plausible explanation for this oversight is their considerable popularity with the consumers, who may find familiarity in the case material without the need to open up new lines of thinking. In America as in Britain, many management teachers favour the use of cases prepared by the teaching institution rather than those derived from a book or centralized file. This rather suggests that the popularity of cases may also be linked with the teacher's need to establish his first-hand and continuing knowledge of industry, without which his contributions may not be credible to managers.

Study projects

This desire for 'tailor-made' cases can be taken a good deal further with advantage. Rather than have the teacher compile the case material the manager can be asked to do it himself. This procedure might be called a study project; a form of it was used on the Churchill College management course at Cambridge a few years ago. Participants on courses within a company are quite often asked to write up a problem which concerns them for discussion during the course. Within the company problems of confidentiality do not loom so large, although the manager may still be reluctant to reveal his difficulties. The use of study projects verges on consultancy; if a man goes on a course and spends his time discussing the problems of his own job situation one must ask how far he is 'learning' rather than getting outside help with his difficulties. As this chapter progresses we shall see that the boundary between training the individual and intervening in his organization can with benefit get yet more confused. Use of study projects certainly ensures that transfer of the new skill to the manager's organization is achieved at least once, even though he may later discard it.

The principal value of case discussion and of study projects within the manager's own firm is probably in the development of diagnostic skills; in other words the trained manager may understand better the situations in which he becomes involved, but there is no particular reason why he should have become any more skilled in dealing with these situations. It would be equally true of course that a manager with good action skills but faulty ability to diagnose situations would be ineffective. The remaining methods attempt to develop managers' action skills by attempting to reproduce or simulate managers' work situation in such a way that they are able to receive feedback on their performance and hence improve it. The methods in this group are the newest and the most currently controversial.

Role-playing

The term 'role-playing' describes a procedure whereby a group of trainees acts a hypothetical situation using assigned roles and improvising their behaviour. The procedure is also used to re-create, approximately, situations which actually occurred. It has been used a great deal in foreman training and to a lesser extent with senior managers, a good deal more in America than here.

This method has attracted the attention of rather more re-searchers, even if it has not been so popular with trainers. At least we can say what would be its effect if it were more widely used. The rationale is twofold: firstly, by acting a role in various ways a manager can take a look at the comparative effectiveness of the different ways, and get coaching from observers on how to improve his performance. Secondly, by acting a role other than his own a manager can get insight into the roles of those with whom he customarily interacts. For example, a manager might benefit from role-playing a union official or a sales manager by playing a pro-duction manager. This second procedure is termed role-reversal. It is interesting to reflect that case-method has a role-playing com-ponent. Trainers often note that participants take the part of one or other of the characters in the case.

The evidence is that role-playing causes considerable attitude change by the role-players and that this impact is enhanced if the role-player has to improvise his performance rather than having it scripted or planned for him by others. Other studies have suggested that practice in role-playing certainly increases the ability to do role-playing exercises, but that transfer of the learned skills is not so easy. As with some of the other methods already discussed, it no doubt depends a good deal on how similar the role-playing scenes are to the situations the manager is actually faced with. In an in-company training scheme reported in one study, changes in behaviour followed the use of role-playing where the role-plays were based on scenes in which the principal actor had earlier been involved in his actual job.

A much-discussed study which is very relevant to the problem of transfer of training was conducted by Fleishman (1953) at the International Harvester Company. Unfortunately Fleishman omits to state which training methods were used, but it was most likely a mixture of lecture, discussion, and role-playing. Fleishman found that the 124 foremen under training showed marked attitude changes toward greater emphasis on human relations immediately after the course. But when he measured attitudes again some months later he found that the foremen had not only reverted to their pre-training attitudes, they had actually become less favourable toward human relations than before the course. Fleishman was able to show that this reversion occurred only where the foreman's boss was himself opposed to greater emphasis on human relations. In other words by training the foremen in a way which contradicted the attitudes of the foremen's own bosses, the trainers had produced a sort of boomerang effect which more than wiped out the effect of the training. Only if the changes imparted by training key in at least partially with the way the manager's organization operates can we expect much transfer whatever the training method.

Business games

The business game is a specialized form of role-playing evolved during the fifties which attempts to simulate rather more of the complexity of organizational life than orthodox role-playing. A more or less realistic economic environment is constructed with several companies, each staffed by a number of managers. The parameters of the game are laid down either in tables or on a computer programme. The game is divided into a number of decision periods for each of which the participants must decide on allocation of resources in the light of their trading position. These games, like most of the methods under discussion, are enormously popular, for much the same reasons as the game 'Monopoly' is. The goal of most games is to achieve economic rationality, but they are frequently played under so much time pressure as to eliminate the possibility of sophisticated analytical skills. On the other hand one can enjoy the exercise of simulated power, making multi-million-pound investment decisions in a way that few managers are permitted in actual organizational life. Evaluation studies are again scarce and the impact obviously will depend on the time investment, as with case-studies. One cannot expect the same results from an afternoon or two of case discussion or business gaming as one can from Harvard's use of cases as the predominant teaching method, or from Carnegie Institute of Technology's game which lasts throughout the academic year.

Two studies of games used in Britain have been completed. Fairhead (1965) showed that attitudes on Castle's (1952) supervisory attitude scale were not changed by nine hours of business game; neither did the attitudes of the control group who had lectures instead change. The scale consists of items such as: 'If the supervisor loses the power to award pay increases, he loses the only incentive at his disposal. Agree/Uncertain/Disagree.' The other study was conducted within BEA, who have devised their own game and made extensive use of it. Not much detail has been published of the study, but it is claimed that students who played the game for two weeks did as well on an exam as students who had a six-month directed-reading programme. Those who did best were those who had a concurrent course in addition to the game. Another study at Harvard showed that ability to discuss cases was improved as much by playing a game as by discussing more cases. It seems unlikely that a full-blooded study linking game experience with behaviour on the job will be forthcoming for some time, if only because games are almost always used in conjunction with other methods.

T-group training

The final method oriented towards skill practice which we shall discuss is probably the most controversial. It is variously known as T-group training, sensitivity training, laboratory training, or group dynamics. This method asks the trainees not to act a simulated role, but to make a study of the way in which others respond to their customary behaviour. On the basis of this feedback from others the trainee is claimed to be able to improve his social skills in managerial situations. The method is based on group meetings which have no fixed agenda other than that of examining the development of their relationships. A T-group laboratory may last for up to two weeks. One might argue that such a training method is not a simulation of a real organization but rather a contrived or unreal situation. Typically however it emerges that the behaviours shown by the different group members bear at least a strong family resemblance to the way they behave on the job and that the experience is anything but unreal. The success of the method depends a good deal on the skill of the trainer in establishing a climate within the group where there is sufficient trust for the members to feel free to discuss their behaviour with one another. T-groups have achieved a fair measure of acceptance in American management education after a slow start, now being used in most of the major business schools, but in Britain they are still little used. The only T-group courses for senior managers currently available are those at Leeds University and the Tavistock Institute of Human Relations. One reason for slow acceptance is that T-groups probably require more skilled trainers than any of the other methods discussed, but a more important one is undoubtedly suspicion of a radical innovation.

A good deal of research has been conducted into the T-group, possibly in an attempt to overcome scepticism. Some participants report that the experience was one of the most deeply rewarding for years, others describe it as a waste of time. There tend to be many more of the former than the latter. Changes of attitude certainly occur; two controlled studies have been conducted in Britain. Elliott (1958) found changes toward more emphasis on human relations on the Castle scale in T-groups (the same scale that showed no change after business games; no change on it has also been reported for various foreman training courses). The second study, by the author, found changes in attitudes implying increased flexibility of behaviour after T-groups but not after syndicate-type discussion groups.

Changes in behaviour on the job after T-group training have been found by Moscow at Leeds University in a study not yet completed, and in a number of American studies. For example, Bunker (1965) compared two hundred T-group participants and two hundred controls eight months after training. Trainees were asked to describe ways in which their behaviour had changed and to nominate seven work associates. The associates then also described any changes. Verified changes were those independently mentioned by two or more describers. Sixty-seven per cent of the T-group trainees showed verified changes but only thirty-three per cent of the controls. The significant changes were categorized as increases in:

(1) Diagnostic understanding of self, others, and processes in groups

(2) Openness, receptivity, and tolerance of differences

(3) Operational skill in interpersonal relationships with overtones of increased capacity for collaboration.

Bunker's controls did not undergo any form of training, but Boyd and Elliss obtained similar results when they compared T-group with lecture and discussion courses among senior managers of the Hydro-Electric Power Commission of Ontario. Some critics of T-groups would not dispute that they have a powerful impact but argue that the impact is too often a destructive one to justify the use of the method. The research studies do not lend any support to this argument. For some a T-group may be a waste of time and money, but the follow-up studies do not show trainees to be less skilled in their relationships or more anxious than they were before. Since the critics' reports about the destructive effects of T-groups are not customarily based on first-hand observations but third-hand rumour, the most plausible explanation of the rumours is that they represent an expression of the critics' own fears of a new method rather than any verified evidence.

This completes the discussion of different training methods. Several generalizations seem in order. First, the amount of research varies inversely with the acceptance of a method; the methods we know most about are those which are least used while the more popular 'commonsense' ones are taken on trust. Second, training methods undoubtedly increase in effectiveness when used in various fruitful combinations; this is not to say that a little of everything gives the best results. Third, training methods are mostly selected on the basis of their acceptability rather than of any proven ability to respond to a particular need for training. Fourth and most important, not very much is known about the transfer of learned skills from course to job situation but most of what is known is discouraging; it is much more difficult to change a manager's organizational behaviour than to make a 'good student' of him. On the last point at least current practice and research findings are moving in the same direction: while research throws doubt on the efficacy of transfer, practice is moving towards greater utilization of training within the company in response to a specific need.

MANAGEMENT DEVELOPMENT

An increasing number of companies are aware that provision for change at the level of senior management does not begin and end with a few nominations for courses, however excellent the courses may be. Investment in the development of managerial skill needs to be as systematic as the investment of economic resource. This line of thinking is often termed management development. It is characterized by attempts to recruit, train, and maintain potential managers in such a way that the needs of the organization for skilled managers can be satisfied on something better than a hand-to-mouth basis. Attendance at courses could well form part of such a programme, but equally or more important would be a series of promotions or transfers which ensured that the man had the requisite experience to fill the position for which he was required. If such a programme is to be based on more than intuition, pre-requisites for its success are a valid method of selecting managers of high potential at a relatively young age, methods of diagnosing the needs for training or experience of a participant in the scheme at any time, and a method of assessing whether a man is in fact realizing his potential. Within such a programme one might expect transfer of training back to the job to be relatively good because the training is matched with a need for it.

Let us look in turn at the three prerequisites outlined. Selection or identification of managers of high potential at an early age is at present based on very diffuse criteria in most firms and it is difficult to see how it might become more precise. The construction of valid selection tests would involve very long-term follow-up studies, but more importantly it is not clear what attributes the tests would need to measure. A good deal of recent research has shown that styles of management which are the most effective in one industry are not the most effective in another. Just as social psychologists were able to show in the early fifties that effective group leadership was dependent on the specific situation more than on universal 'leadership qualities', so students of organizations have now built up powerful evidence that the same is true of managerial effectiveness in organizations. If different managerial tasks require different skills, it is clear that who enters a company's management training scheme is less important than the way the management development scheme is operated thereafter.

Diagnosis of the training needs of a manager requires a measure of his present skills and of those required in the job to which he is to be appointed, whether it is next month or in the far-distant future. When the two measures are compared it may be seen that the man has no experience of working in the sales function, or that he has had no contact with operations research techniques, or that he is a technically sound man who is unaware of the impact of his behaviour on those whom he works with. Each of these implies the need for further training or experience. The 'measures' which an organization typically has available of present skills and future job requirements are appraisals and job descriptions. Neither of these is a measurement in any but the crudest sense. Appraisals consist of written reports or ratings on a man's performance, typically written annually by the man's superior and only sometimes discussed with the man himself. Their value can be very slight if the climate of the organization is such that the superior hesitates to put anything but generalized compliments on paper. Kay Rowe (1964) studied eighteen hundred appraisal forms derived from six British companies and concluded that 'managers are reluctant to appraise and even more reluctant to interview' (that is, to discuss the appraisal with the manager concerned). In another study, Rosemary Stewart (1965) found that what was actually said in the appraisal interview tended to be a good deal franker than what was committed to paper.

The job description states in a few sentences or paragraphs the responsibilities of a manager in a particular role. Probably rather more companies have worked out a series of job descriptions than utilized a formalized appraisal system. But the great danger here is that the job description may become outdated or may be based on someone's conception of how the job ought to be done rather than how it actually is done.

We can see that there are formidable difficulties in the way of operating an effective management development scheme within a company. No company has grounds for certainty that it is selecting the right men, or that they are being accurately appraised, or that their job roles are accurately described. A progressive company can of course do better on each of these points than one which does not attend to them at all, but there remains much to be desired.

CHANGING WHOLE ORGANIZATIONS

The sort of management development scheme we have been discussing deals with the manager as a unit, no less than does the external training course which we discussed earlier. The scheme is an improvement on earlier thinking because it examines the progress of the manager towards his optimal utilization by the company over a very extended period of time. But it fails to give any consideration to the ways in which the manager's development is linked with the attitudes, values and experience of those with whom he works. A number of instances have already been cited where attempts to train individuals have been nullified by the climate of attitudes and values within which the trainee normally lives, for example Orth's study of the Harvard Business School and Fleishman's of the training programme at International Harvester. It is not at all surprising therefore that some companies are becoming increasingly involved in attempts to change the whole climate of their organization.

If these attempts prove successful, 'organization development' may supersede management development. Training programmes would then be more heavily concentrated within one company and even within one team of people who work together. In closing this chapter some of these organization change programmes will be examined. There is no doubt that such change attempts are both difficult and very expensive in terms of time and money. Companies which embark upon them must have high hopes of what is to be gained. Introduction of technological innovations, renegotiated wage-systems such as that at Fawley, mergers, and redundancies probably all leave their mark on organizational climate for a long time after; but the focus of attention here is on programmes whose primary goal is to modify the organizational climate. A central concept in such programmes is that of 'change agent', or someone whose task it is to facilitate non-routine changes in others. A foreman instructing a man to stop one job and start another is not a change agent, but consultants, managing directors, training officers, and research departments often are.

Change agents may operate by making diagnoses and feeding these back to the organization members: or by waiting until managers express a need for something they do not have, and suggesting ways in which the need could be satisfied; or, if they have the requisite power, by announcing that certain changes will take place and initiating discussion of how these are to be achieved. We shall consider examples of each in turn.

The work of the diagnostic change agent is well illustrated by case-study descriptions published by various workers associated with the Tavistock Institute of Human Relations. For example, Elliott Jaques (1951) has described his part in the fascinating series of changes carried through since the war at the Glacier Metal Company, while Cyril Sofer (1953) has described his work as a change agent in a technical college department of management. We do not have any quantitative measures of the changes involved in these projects.

The change agent who waits for the expression of needs before he acts is widespread enough, but again there are no studies published which measure the impact of such a role. Some of the large American firms now maintain departments of organization development, staffed by such people. General Electric for example names them 'catalysts' and uses a two-year spell as a catalyst as part of its management development programme.

Change strategies backed by executive authority have been subject to rather more research. Probably the most sophisticated organization-change programme yet on the market is that known as grid-laboratory training, based on a modified T-group and designed to transform an organization's climate from rigid and mechanistic to something more 'organic' and flexible. Robert Blake, its originator, is working within several British companies as well as many American ones. The impressive findings of a study of his work conducted at Harvard are vitiated by the absence of any concurrent control data. Finally, a real organizational experiment was conducted by Morse and Reimer (1956) within an American insurance firm. The management of two divisions participated in T-groups designed to spread decision-making more widely, while the management of the other two divisions received lectures and discussion designed to increase the degree of organizational centralization. Both forms of training achieved their goals. The results were a 20 per cent increase in productivity in all divisions, coupled with deteriorating morale and turnover in the divisions which became more centralized. Social scientists have argued extensively over what conclusions this study permits; one can say at least that organizational change was a practicable and indeed a profitable proposition. But it is not clear whether the changes result from the training methods or whether they derive from something related to the celebrated Hawthorne effect, whereby any intervention in an organization may cause at least temporary beneficial effects.

This survey of attempts at organization change should make it clear how little is yet known about their effectiveness. As we have seen rather more is known about some of the different training methods available; but this knowledge serves only to emphasize that the crux of training lies not in the classroom, but back at the firm. If progress is to be made toward better utilization of training methods, unravelling the dynamics of organizational change and stability is the top priority.

CHAPTER 14

Beyond Payment by Results?

TOM LUPTON

A CHIEF concern of the manager in the modern organization is to plan and coordinate the work of the operating staff effectively in pursuit of the objectives of the organization. His problems in this connexion are easy to identify but hard to solve. Amongst them is the difficulty of finding methods of paying for work done which will help maximize output per man-hour and which will be regarded as equitable. This essay assesses various systems of wage payment which have been tried and proposed, and refers particularly to those usually described as payment by results (PBR). It has become somewhat fashionable to decry PBR as anachronistic, and this contention will be examined as carefully and objectively as possible.

THE MEANING OF PBR

There is a general sense in which all methods of wage and salary payment are payment by results; it is expected that brawn and brain will be exerted in return for cash payments. However, the description PBR is usually used to describe schemes in which the relation between the exertion and the cash payment is direct. Under PBR the cash is not paid out *unless* the brain and brawn have actually been exerted, and it is the promise of extra cash which is supposed to call forth the exertion.

It would be mistaken to suppose that PBR relates cash reward only to physical exertion. There are schemes which directly relate pay to quality, to machine or material utilization, and to other factors. In a payment by results scheme, each piece of work produced, or each operation completed to the required quality, might carry a cash price; or it might have an amount of time allowed for its completion. Pay is then calculated according to a formula relating cash to pieces produced or to time saved. Many complicated formulas have been devised to take account of different types of work and working conditions, and for relating the scheme of PBR to the pattern of negotiated rates of pay. For example, in some industries pay is calculated from a complicated price list which is arrived at by industry-wide negotiation. Each job is then given a price by adding together the appropriate item prices from the list. In others a separate price is negotiated in the workshop for each piece and pay is calculated by straight addition (straight piecework). In yet others, a certain base rate of pay is negotiated at industry level, then at factory level allowed times are calculated for each job, and bonus is paid over and above the national rate in proportion to time saved. The complications are endless, yet the principle is simplicity itself. Payment by results schemes are devices for persuading people to take less time over their work, and/or to pay more attention to it than they would otherwise have done – by offering them extra cash for their trouble.

The alternative to payment by results is any scheme of payment which relates total task to total reward, in which pay is fixed by the hour, day, week, or year, and is paid regardless of the exact amount produced; or, more accurately, ways are found to make sure that the job is done satisfactorily other than the offer of extra bits of cash for extra bits of work. As compared to such schemes as this, the justification for PBR is that it increases output and keeps it at high levels. Yet recently there has been increasing criticism of PBR on the grounds that in fact it fails to do this, and it is often suggested that there should be a return to flat hourly rates of pay (Brown, 1962).

PBR AND MECHANIZATION

Payment by results might well be quickly superseded were there to be a dramatic and widespread increase in the mechanization of operative work. If the machine, rather than the man, controls the quantity and quality of the output there is obviously no point in calculating the machine-minder's pay by reference to it. The machine-minder might be paid very highly for the responsibility he carries for expensive plant; this is not payment by results, but it relates his responsibility for the task to the total pay he receives. It is, however, a narrow way of looking at payment by results to think of it only in terms of the quantity and quality of physical output. The operator of a modern chemical plant or automatic rolling mill may have little direct control over levels of output when the plant is working, but neglect of his tasks could lead to expensive maintenance operations and sub-quality output. A man might attend to these things more diligently were he rewarded directly for doing so. So long as things have to be made by men or processes monitored and controlled by men, there seems no obvious reason why they should not be paid by results.

But consider the man on the assembly line. If the speed of the conveyor which brings work to him and takes it away from him on completion completely determines the quantity and quality of it then plainly PBR is irrelevant. In this case surely no one would want to argue for it. So the case that PBR is anachronistic might rest on the ground that the more work is done automatically or controlled automatically the less need there is for PBR as a means of getting it done. In fact the argument for the abandonment of PBR is not usually based on technological determinism, but on judgements about the economic, moral, and social shortcomings of it.

THE RATIONALE OF PBR AND THE CASE AGAINST IT

PBR schemes rest on a social and psychological assumption that if a man is given the promise of more money and freedom to choose within limits whether to exert himself or not, he will choose to exert himself and get the money. He then gets the satisfaction of having more money in his pockets; the manager gets high outputs, lower unit costs, more intensive use of production facilities; society gets an improvement in economic welfare.

The first and most damaging criticism of PBR is that it is sociologically and psychologically naïve. The assumption that given freedom to decide whether or not to produce more pieces, to save time on operations, to attend to quality, machine utilization, and so on, the operator will in all circumstances choose that course of action which will give him more money and the manager more output (or whatever), is open to serious question. One of the first systematic observers of operative work, Frederick Taylor (1964), concluded that although the desire for more money is a compelling human motive, it is naïve to assume that left to themselves to decide men will necessarily make the effort to get more. Taylor therefore suggested that men should not be left to themselves to decide. Instead, the managers should say, after careful study of the work to be done, how much time it should take using the best possible method. This done, a worker selected and trained to the method should be offered a high total reward for the total task provided he agrees to submit to managerial control of his activities. Subsequent observers have confirmed Taylor's general conclusions but have differed from him in what they recommend. (Roethlisberger and Dixon, 1964; Roy, 1954; Lupton, 1963). Some of these recommendations will be discussed.

It is easy to fall into the error of supposing that because the desire for money is by common consent a compelling motive for working that it is also the overriding motive. Work is a social activity, that is it involves the worker in relationships with others. If the worker is faced with a decision whether to attempt to maximize income or to sacrifice possible gains for the sake of establishing or maintaining satisfying relationships with his workmates, he might well choose the latter course. There is ample research evidence that this is what often happens, and it is a common experience of managers who have installed PBR. Groups of workers often evolve a norm of a fair day's work, or an appropriate level of earnings under PBR. They then apply their own controls upon group members to ensure that they conform. Taylor described this as 'systematic soldiering'; it is more commonly described as 'restriction of output'. The mere existence of 'restriction of output' is cogent criticism of the basic assumptions of PBR.

This is by no means the end of the criticism of PBR. The technical apparatus deployed by management to translate the assumptions of PBR into practical schemes of wage payment is itself far from perfect. There is much room for argument, for example, between the work-study engineer and the operator, when the level of physical effort being put into a job is being assessed – and this is a crucial element in·the calculation of standards of performance.

One practical outcome of the crudity of the method is the exist-ence of what an American observer has described as 'gravy jobs' and 'stinkers'; that is, jobs on which high earnings are possible without undue strain and those which require great effort for inadequate reward. If the individuals concerned are out each one to maximize his earnings, then there will be a scramble for the gravy jobs, attempts to influence the supervisor who allocates work, and in general wasteful, morale-destroying competition and jealousy. If the cash motive is less than overwhelming then the result might well be (and often is) collective action unofficially to organize equitable job allocation, to conceal the gravy jobs lest management cuts the rates, and to pit wits against the work-study man so that there are always enough gravy jobs to make possible reasonable earnings for the weaker brethren in the group and so that the stronger ones can do well without great exertion. In con-ditions where the flow of work is intermittent the need to negotiate allowances for waiting time gives further elbow room for manipu-lation.

It might be said therefore, with justification, that there are con-ditions in which PBR could lead to unpleasant jealousies and competition, and perhaps losses due to high labour turnover and other outcomes of low morale, or to losses due to restriction of out-put, when the natural 'groupiness' of operatives is channelled into anti-management manoeuvres and manipulations.

To be sure, the fascination of the battle of wits against manage-ment is a factor providing satisfactions at work which would not otherwise be there, but it is a great indictment of PBR that it wastes the intelligence and organizing talent of operatives when, given more intelligent and sensitive management and supervision and a wage system that encourages positive cooperation, these talents might be harnessed for mutual benefit. But PBR inhibits the development of positive and enlightened management methods, and there are two reasons why this would seem to be so. In the first place, PBR wastes the energies of managers and super-visors in frequent disputes: and secondly, it encourages a belief that the system of wage payment will do the manager's job for him. Workers whose capacity to earn is impaired by poor work-flow, faulty materials, and sub-standard tools will call attention to these matters and relieve management of the necessity for close and continuous control and investigation. This is an ill-founded belief since, as we have seen, working groups might compensate for poor management by other methods, but it is a belief that has great persistence. At this point it might be prudent to remark that supporters of PBR will be quite unmoved by the formidable-looking criticisms so far arrayed, and by others which have yet to be stated, and we shall shortly see what may be said by way of rebuttal. But we have by no means finished yet with the case against PBR.

In conditions of labour scarcity and rapid change of product or production method, PBR is prone to add to the difficulties for management of maintaining a viable wage structure and of preventing runaway movements of earnings. In conditions of labour scarcity, operators will feel powerful enough to refuse to use new methods until the price is to their satisfaction, and management is under great pressure to meet these demands, and can probably afford to do so. Other groups of workers in the factory, observing that the new 'slack rates' have disturbed customary earnings differentials, demand, in equity, that the differential be restored, even though they have themselves experienced no change in method. 'Leap-frogging' of this kind is one source of the 'drift' of earnings from negotiated rates which has been characteristic of some industries in recent years. It has also produced in some instances a rise in earnings without corresponding increases in output and has thereby contributed to 'cost-push' inflationary pressure. It must be allowed that in conditions of labour scarcity, bidding up the price of labour is likely to occur whatever the method of wage payment, but when accompanied by rapid technical changes, a method of wage payment which demands frequent adjustments is more likely to resist administrative control than one in which adjustment takes place at regular but infrequent intervals and at the relative calm of the bargaining table rather than under the pressure of production.

Finally, and briefly, there are a number of other points in the indictment of PBR. It is often claimed, by those who dislike PBR for other reasons, that the administrative cost of running it far outweighs any gains from its installation, although there is little hard evidence to support this contention. Another criticism is that PBR as usually organized does not encourage workers to find better methods of working, nor rewards them if they do so. PBR assumes that operatives have to be persuaded by the offer of extra cash to aim at performance standards already set, not to seek better ones to aim for. Operators do in fact discover better methods under PBR than work-study engineers have been able to find, but are often reluctant, for obvious reasons, to reveal them. This is but one example of many which have been adduced to support the very general indictment that PBR is bad not only socially and economically but morally. It brings out the worst in people. It appeals not to worthy motives such as the desire to give loyal service, and to cooperate willingly and unstintingly with one's colleagues. Instead, it starts with the assumption that operative workers (not, by omission, be it noted, managerial workers and technical and professional workers) are by nature inclined to be lazy and avaricious, so what better than to use their greed to overcome their disinclination for exertion. It is not surprising perhaps that they sometimes make a point of living up to these expectations.

IN DEFENCE OF PBR

Earlier, the undertaking was given to examine PBR carefully and objectively. The reader has probably detected a certain enthusiasm showing through the presentation of the case against PBR reflecting the writer's opinions. The indictment is by no means as cut and dried as it seems. There are many logical weaknesses in it, and to say that the empirical evidence for it is anywhere near conclusive would be dishonest. The reasonable defender of PBR would probably respond as follows.

Any payment scheme can founder for lack of managerial competence and inadequate industrial relations procedures. PBR is not alone in this. Whatever one's views are about the assumptions about human nature which seem to lie behind PBR, the fact is that if properly applied it gives results. In the previous arguments the assumptions have been grossly caricatured. The first thing an intelligent PBR man would do would be to find a scheme from the repertoire of PBR which suited well the situation to which it was to be applied. It is not necessary, for example, to destroy social cohesion or hamfistedly to turn 'groupiness' against management. A group, as well as an individual, can be rewarded under PBR, and there are many group schemes. In situations where work is repetitive and individual, a simple straight piecework scheme may be right. If there are problems about uneven earnings due to problems of work allocation, then schemes can be 'geared' to iron out the consequences of an uneven incidence of 'good' and 'bad' work (Currie, 1964). In brief, PBR is not just one thing but many, and the professional work-study man is well able to fit a payment scheme to the circumstances as he finds them. PBR is infinitely flexible, not implacably rigid as its detractors suggest.

Many of the difficulties reported by anti-PBR people are due not to PBR as such but to badly designed schemes. No professional work-study engineer would, for example, claim effort-rating to be an exact science. He would, therefore, take good care to see that no performance standard was laid down until the worker and his union representative had agreed it to be reasonable. In some companies, where PBR has been successful, shop stewards have been trained to work with the work-study men while prices and allowed times are being settled, and there are numerous instances of cooperation in the search for better methods.

It is unfair to blame PBR for shortcomings of work-flow administration. If a time-rate system exists in a firm alongside poor management and supervision it is unlikely that the workers will be moved to seek improvement. Some of them might do so if they looked like gaining money as a result. Although PBR encourages criticism of poor management and probably makes for better management, this should not be twisted to imply that PBR encourages bad management. Bad management arises from many causes, and PBR is rarely to be found amongst them.

There is plenty of practical experience and some respectable academic evidence to show that the replacement of time-rate payments by PBR can make a great difference to output without great installation and running costs (Ross *et al.* 1958). As for 'earnings drift' and 'leap-frogging', the culprit here is an antiquated system of industrial relations and not PBR. If the employers and the unions are prepared to confine themselves to negotiating unrealistic minimum rates and to ignore the need for a rational system of job gradings and pay differentials, and to wink at the free-for-all at plant level, then the absence of any firm basis for the setting of job rates is bound to lead to drift and leap-frogging whatever method of wage payment is employed in the plants. The fact that working men exploit the free-for-all might be taken as evidence of a desire to improve their financial position, which, if it is properly harnessed and controlled by joint rule for the conduct of industrial relations, might well lead to a great improvement in efficiency and in management–worker relationships.

BEYOND PBR?

Is there any reason to believe that to replace PBR by other methods of wage payment would lead to significant improvement? To judge whether one alternative is better than another requires that acceptable criteria be established. We shall take it that any payment scheme that leads to the following outcomes is to be preferred to one that does not, always bearing in mind that a payment scheme is only one measure among many that could be employed:

(1) That the best available methods of working will be sought after and used.

(2) That waste of time will be avoided.

(3) That the rewards for work done are considered fair by those doing the work.

(4) That the work as well as the pay is regarded as providing satisfaction.

(5) That the relationship between pay and productivity is such as to prevent 'drift' and is under joint control.

(6) That change is not inhibited.

MEASURED DAY WORK

It has been suggested that a method of payment described variously as measured day work or controlled day work is superior to PBR and ought to replace it (Lupton, 1964), although the administrative problems of changing from PBR have not been over-looked and will be referred to presently.

Measured day work rests on a sharper separation (in time and place) of arguments about performance standards and arguments about what the job is worth in cash terms than is typical of PBR. It cannot be applied unless and until all the jobs in a plant have been graded according to the skill and training required, the physical effort needed, and so on. There are well-established methods of job description and evaluation which can be used jointly by management and unions to determine which jobs shall go in which grades and to establish appropriate pay differentials between the grades. The outcome of this procedure is to decide what will be paid regularly, by the hour or week, to whoever happens to be doing the job in the grade. It is assumed that the operative in question will be properly selected and trained for the job. It must be emphasized that job-evaluated grading schemes are also to be found alongside PBR, in which case the hourly rate for the job is used as a basis on which the job price or output bonus is calculated.

In measured daywork the relationship between the performance standard and the pay is different. Once the rate for the grade has been established, the management undertakes to pay it as a regular weekly wage as long as certain conditions are met, and these conditions are also the subject of negotiation. In return for his regular weekly wage the operative undertakes to meet the performance standard on whatever job he is called upon to do in his grade. The performance standard has to be agreed to by the operator and his union representative but will be first suggested after a careful study of the job, using time study and effort-rating in much the same way as under the best PBR schemes. The managers, for their part, undertake to provide the operatives with the work, the tools, and the services that he requires if he is to meet the standard.

In measured day work the wages bill becomes a kind of over-head cost for management which changes little from week to week. Managers will be interested, therefore, in seeing that performance standards are met and will make every effort to ensure that no one is idle for want of work or of the services that they (management) are in a position to provide. In measured day work managers also require an efficient system to provide continuous information of where in the factory performances are off-standard so that inquiries may be made to uncover the reasons, and appropriate action taken. For the operator's part, having been involved personally and through his union representative in setting the standard of performance, he will feel strongly obliged to meet it. He will feel confident that if he happens to fall short of it he will not be blamed until the machines, the materials, and the maintenance and supply system have been checked. The sanction in measured day work is that if inquiries show that the operator has fallen short of standard and the fault clearly lies with him, then he must expect that after due warning he will be either transferred to a lesser grade or dismissed. Some advocates of measured day work have suggested that the sanction should be a temporary drop in pay, but this would seem like a negative kind of PBR and a weakening of the moral obligation to keep contracts freely entered into which is the rationale of measured day work.

There is, at first sight, a family resemblance in MDW to the *task work* advocated many years ago by Frederick Taylor. Taylor was convinced that to leave the decision with the operator whether or not to expend effort was an abdication of the duty of management to manage. He therefore argued that the total task, the method, and the total pay for the task should be determined and men taken on who could and would perform the task for the pay. The sanction for failure was dismissal. Closer inspection of MDW and task work reveals more differences than similarities. Under MDW the task, the method, and the pay are the outcome of joint discussion and bargaining, and not of management *fiat*. The sanction in MDW, namely that management has in the last resort the right to dismiss a man for failure to meet standard, is balanced by a number of undertakings. These are: that dismissal will not happen unless it can be shown that the tools and materials are in good order, and that the work is flowing smoothly, and the worker still is shown to be consistently short of standard after an investigation in which his own representatives are involved, and which allows him the right of appeal.

What MDW does, in effect, is make the contract of employment more specific than it usually is, and spell out the rules of conduct for the parties to that contract. If it be objected that the contract is unequal in giving management the sanction of dismissal when the operative has no such sanction upon management, the answer must be that there *is* force in the objection and this is the reason for the stress in measured day work on the involvement of the trade union in the contract as a collective safeguard against management breach of contract, with the final sanction of the strike.

How does MDW stand in relation to the criteria listed on page 302 It is no better than the best PBR schemes on criterion 1, or on criterion 2 either. Both pay careful attention to methods and to accurate and acceptable performance standards. On criterion 3 we would judge that MDW is better. Whether MDW is any way superior to PBR on criterion 4 depends on so many factors outside the pay scheme that it would be unwise to pass general judgements. Since MDW lays such stress on joint rules and procedures for effecting changes in job grades and performance standards it is probably superior to PBR on criterion 6. We have argued that PBR tends to promote suspicion and jealousy and restrictive behaviour which would inhibit the calm joint consideration of the consequences of change and its smooth introduction. And finally, although there are many factors external to the firm which could promote drift, as for example employer bidding for scarce skills, MDW seems to offer better scope for control and therefore scores higher on criterion 5.

The crux of the matter lies in the nature of the relationship between the operative and the management which is implied in MDW. MDW gives formal recognition to the fact that the operative has a positive contribution to make in setting performance standards, it stresses parity of esteem in the bargaining relationship, and in the procedures that govern it. There is a risk, however, and this is not lost on the advocates of PBR, that the initial bargain in MDW about performance standards will be influenced by an existing conception of the effort–reward relationship. The result may be unacceptable to management on economic grounds and conflict will ensue. One reason why measured day work has not been introduced widely, in spite of its seeming advantages over PBR, is that it necessitates changes in attitudes as well as in formal procedures if management and operatives are to discuss and bargain freely and openly. Changing attitudes and beliefs is often a painful and difficult process. MDW also calls for administrative skills and procedures of a high order, and the effort to replace management by the wages system (PBR) by management by consent (to put the contrast at its simplest) is for this reason often avoided – if it is ever thought of. On the trade union side it is easier to allow 'drift' to happen than to accept responsibility for its existence, let alone for seeking means to control it.

A SCHEME BASED ON A PERSONAL CONTRACT

Measured day work is based on a performance standard *for a job* in a grade, whoever happens to be doing it. Some companies have introduced in place of PBR a system of payment based on a *personal* contract with each operative. That is to say each operative is separately assessed using the usual techniques of work study and is given a *performance rating*. The assessment is sometimes based on recorded past performance of the operatives under PBR, sometimes on recorded performance during training. Operatives with similar ratings are paid a similar weekly wage which does not vary so long as the operative performs at the agreed standard when work is available. This scheme avoids one of the main sources of discontent under PBR, namely that the operative's pay can fluctuate for reasons outside his control, and it has been introduced mainly for that reason. It also avoids the necessity for operatives to find devious and unofficial ways to offset the effects on their pay of what they perceive to be managerial inefficiencies

Under personal contract schemes, as under MDW, wages are an overhead and this encourages managers to see that workers are kept fully occupied and perform to the agreed personal standard. Similarly, shortfalls from standard are the occasion for an inquiry, with reduced performance rating and finally dismissal as the sanctions. Under personal contract schemes there is usually provision for operatives who can reach and maintain higher performance standards to be re-rated and receive higher pay; this might be regarded as a residue of PBR which does not feature in MDW.

A personal contract scheme would appear to score higher than

PBR on the six criteria and as high as, if not higher than, MDW. It has its shortcomings in practice, chief amongst which is the onerous personal responsibility laid on the operatives, but its advocates can fairly claim that it takes more account of differences between operatives in skill and personal characteristics and makes more use of these differences than does MDW, or indeed any system based on the assessment of a job, or a conception of an average trained operator working at it in normal conditions. Like MDW, personal contract schemes require a high order of administrative skill if they are to succeed, and they have probably not been widely introduced because of the same difficulties that accompany the introduction of MDW.

However, there may be other more compelling reasons why the two alternatives to PBR that have so far been mentioned have not been more widely introduced. It could well be that the persistence of PBR as a method of wage payment might be due to its suitability in some circumstances where methods based on a contract and the administrative control of it would be inappropriate. Later we shall be considering the question whether particular kinds of payment system persist or are introduced because of their appropriateness to a particular industry, or production system. It may be that theoretical arguments for the superiority of one system or another miss the main point, that is the 'goodness of fit' of the payment system to the problems of the firm or the industry. A discussion of *work simplification* schemes seems a good way of introducing this issue.

WORK SIMPLIFICATION

In every system of wage payment so far considered great stress has been laid on the importance of setting proper performance standards. The importance of a careful measurement of time and effort by trained specialists has been thought to be a *sine qua non* of successful operation. The best practice under PBR as well as MDW and personal contract schemes is to involve the operative in the process of setting standards. But, once set, standards are difficult to change and whenever there are job changes the whole process has to be repeated.

Advocates of work simplification argue that the emphasis is wrong, and should be placed not on performance standards but on the necessity for a *continuous improvement of working methods*. To organize this shift of emphasis is claimed to be fairly simple. In the first place it is necessary to stop arguing whether present standards are good, bad, or indifferent, and simply just accept them as the present standards whether they emerged from PBR, MDW, or whatever. It is not difficult to persuade people to stop arguing about the present method if they are handsomely rewarded for looking for and finding simpler, more effective methods. To find improved methods does require some knowledge of the procedures developed by methods engineers, so the operators must themselves be trained by the firm in the techniques of methods study. This is an essential part of a work simplification scheme. Most of the complex technical and administrative apparatus of work measurement, at least as it affects the payments system, can now be dismantled at a saving much greater than the expense of training the operators to be do-it-yourself methods engineers.

Operatives who are trained to look for ways of making changes, and who are rewarded for doing so, are, it is claimed, less likely to resist changes when management wants to introduce them. Further, because of their intimate minute-to-minute knowledge of the job they are doing, operatives who are moved to seek improvements and trained to find them will probably find more than any methods engineer could. To look systematically for improvements also adds interest to the job, so that job satisfaction is combined with the prospect of cash reward. Finally, if it can be arranged to reward the innovators especially well but to ensure that everyone benefits from the innovation then a competitive spirit can be engendered that does not inhibit group cohesion and management–group cooperation.

Although the principles underlying work simplification schemes are attractive, simple, and direct, such schemes are difficult to administer. Suggested innovations must be carefully considered, and a system of rewards devised according to technical merit and cost-saving potentiality. If the rewards are considered unsatisfactory, or the system of assessment unfair, or if there are delays in introducing the suggested improvements, as there might well be if amendments to machinery or layout, or new jigs and fixtures are suggested, then the operatives' enthusiasm for the scheme might rapidly cool off. But, given the will, management could make administrative provision to prevent this from happening.

On all our criteria, work simplification schemes score highly. They train and tap the worker's innovative flair, make the job interesting, relate pay to productivity, encourage change, and so on. However, they can surely only succeed where jobs are changing fairly rapidly. If conditions were stable, workers would soon come to the end of their ideas for improving jobs. There must be a limit to the improvements that can be made to a given job, and they must become less dramatic as one succeeds another. Operatives would soon become frustrated if, after having been trained and encouraged to seek improvements, and promised rewards for them, they find none. There is also the risk that healthy competition among workers might degenerate into envy or jealousy. But these seem to be minor criticisms compared with those that can be made of PBR. However, it has to be said that it is mostly in firms where rapid change of product and technology are common that work simplification schemes have been introduced with apparent success. There is no experience that the writer knows of where they have been introduced in more stable conditions. Nor is it likely that work simplification schemes could be appropriate for other than fairly repetitive manipulative operations. When work is technically complex it is not easy to see how operators could be trained to suggest improvements continuously. One thinks of the crew of operatives on a modern chemical plant. The expense of training operatives to the point where they are capable of making significant improvements in the design and operation of complex and expensive plant would hardly be worthwhile. Such improvement must in the nature of things be a matter mostly for the scientist and the engineer.

'SCANLON TYPE' SCHEMES AND PROFIT SHARING

In the payment schemes so far examined the supposed desire of the individual to maximize his pay is linked fairly directly to his performance. Some schemes give less weight to the cash motive than others, but all focus on the motives of the individual or the small working group. But there are some payment schemes that acknowledge the cash motive but locate it quite differently in the scheme of things. Cash reward is here associated with a sense of identity with *the firm as a whole*, and the expectation is that operatives might feel committed to the firm's objectives, and by their efforts assist it to grow and prosper, if all can gain appropriately as a result.

One method of effecting this is to pay a bonus to workers at regular intervals which is related to the dividends paid by the firm to its shareholders. For example, if the firm declares a 10 per cent dividend the operatives might receive 10 per cent of their basic pay as a bonus. In some schemes a block of the firm's shares is given in trust for the employees and a committee comprising company and employee representatives decides the principles on which the earnings from the shares are to be distributed. Such a committee might well decide that the shareout should be uneven, long service or rank being admissible claims to a larger share. Yet again, a firm might simply issue a number of its shares free to employees with, say, over five years' service, and add more with every subsequent five years of service. These examples of profit-sharing could be multiplied to include the few schemes where the operators are partners in the firm.

The claims made for profit-sharing are that it encourages people to stay in employment with the firm, and to be interested in its fortunes while they are there. Also, since the firm is in business to make profit, it is surely right that the employees have some share in them. In return for this share the firm may hope to raise the general level of identification and gain commitment thereby to its purposes, and hence higher productivity; but it might do no such thing and either give the fund, the shares, or the bonus, without any expectations from that source of greater productivity and take other measures such as PBR to effect improvements. There are many firms with profit-sharing schemes which also have PBR schemes or one of the other alternatives proposed so far. Experience seems to show that workers find their periodical bonus very welcome, indeed they might even decide to stay with the firm because of it, but it is unlikely that they will find the relationship between the bonus and profits easy to comprehend, or the relationship between their own productivity and their profit-sharing bonus. A worker whose earnings, or some of them, are based upon decisions over which he has little or no direct control will not have much sympathy with profit-sharing if it is introduced instead of, rather than merely as an addition to, an existing scheme of PBR, measured daywork, or whatever.

It has often been shown that the proportion of the national income which goes in wages is fairly stable. The discovery of the fact that certain outgoings of individual firms, wage costs amongst them, also exhibit regularities and stand from year to year in a nearly similar ratio is attributed to Scanlon (Lesieur, 1958). The stable share of wages in the national income has often been used to sustain arguments that the bargaining activities of trade unions have little long-term effect on real wages. Whether this is so or not is difficult to determine, and whatever is said is unlikely to stop trade unions from bargaining. But if a firm's wage costs stand in a regular relationship to other costs then it might be argued that there is no need for costly and complex payment systems and that these *can* be got rid of. Attention can then be turned to increasing total activity so that there are more incomings which can be turned into outgoings, that is to swelling the total wealth from which shares are to be taken. All that is needed is agreement between workers, managers, and employers as to the formula which is to be applied each year to determine the shares.

In the type of scheme just outlined it appears as if the best interests of the operative lie in cooperating with management to further the interests of the firm. It does not seem difficult, *prima facie*, to demonstrate the connexion between these efforts and what should go into the pay packet. The division of the total share going to labour need not be enveloped in the noise and fury (signifying nothing?) which is so often characteristic of bargaining under PBR. Instead, all that is required is a set of agreed criteria for grading jobs, and agreement about performance standards. However attractive they may look there is a difficulty about such schemes. They require for their success, as do profit-sharing schemes, a knowledge of what is going on; what the formula is, why for example the shareout is less this year than last year.

It must be difficult in a large firm for the individual to be kept completely and continuously informed so that he is always aware that the success of the firm rests upon his efforts, and results in higher earnings for him in the future. It is, perhaps, optimistic to suppose that the calculations on which the total shareout is based will be understood and accepted. Therefore, such schemes as the Scanlon Plan probably work better in the small firm than in the large one, or in small accounting units of larger firms. However well understood and accepted the economics of the scheme, there remains the problem of grading jobs to establish relativities in the shareout and setting standards of performance, even if these latter are used only for scheduling production.

Indeed, in all the schemes discussed grading and standard setting are quite crucial. How is it to be decided how much one job is worth relative to another? And what is reasonable to expect the man who holds the job to do? The difficulty in deciding such questions is that they seem to invite conflicting judgements, and there are no clear common criteria against which to assess these. Grading schemes when systematically planned are commonly based on a full description of the jobs involved and an attempt to list and weigh the qualities and qualifications required of the incumbents. This done, the jobs are ranked in order of their scores on the various qualities and qualifications and are then grouped into grades to establish pay relativities. To minimize dispute, the evaluation of jobs, in the best current practice, is done or checked jointly by managers, and the trade-union officers and operatives involved. This is not easy as there are so many factors to be considered. It has recently been argued that job-evaluation can now be done objectively, using a single measure, rather than subjectively, using many. The grounds for this argument have to be examined carefully, for if they are justified they undermine most existing theories of equitable payment.

JAQUES AND THE TIME-SPAN OF DISCRETION

To Jaques (1961) all the payment systems we have reviewed in this essay are to be deplored because they produce unnecessary conflict. In the absence of objective criteria for deciding the worth of one job relative to another which is characteristic of these schemes, the world of work is an undignified scramble for what can be got by hard bargaining, exploiting tight labour markets, contriving scarcities of particular skills, and so on. Men are locked in a prison of their own contriving; but they feel uneasy because they are able to judge intuitively the worth of their job in relation to others. They know, or rather feel, when they are equitably paid, underpaid, or overpaid. Jaques' researches have been directed towards defining this intuitive criterion of 'felt-fair' pay and to working out a means of measuring it.

To establish his measures Jaques has distinguished between work which is prescribed for the employee by someone else, and work which leaves discretion as to what is to be done to the employee himself. All jobs, with certain exceptions, have work of both kinds in them. The work of an industrial operative will usually be high in prescribed content and low in discretionary content. The reverse will be the case, for example, with a university teacher. But it is not just the *amount* of discretion (the number of things that can be decided on without referring to someone else) which is significant in Jaques' theory; it is the *frequency* with which the results of exercising discretion are assessed. The time-span of discretion is the single test of the relative worth of work, which Jaques claims he is now able to measure.

If this claim were justified there would be no difficulty in grading jobs; it is a simple matter to measure anything once a neutral and efficient measuring instrument has been invented. The numerous criticisms of the time-span measure have left its originator unmoved. His reply is that the test of a measuring instrument is not so much the explanatory power of the theory from which it derives, or even the validity of the data that supports the theory, but whether the instrument is of practical value. Simply, the test of the time-span instrument is whether it does or does not measure the relative worth of jobs to the satisfaction of those who do them. To date, we do not know whether it does or does not, since those whose pay is arrived at by complicated horse-trading seem reluctant to abandon it in favour of a supposed neutral measure.

*

313

If the reader is convinced by the foregoing that PBR is in general anachronistic there is no lack of alternatives from which to choose, or of keen advocates for each of them. Controversy about systems of payment becomes as heated as arguments about pay. It would probably be less so if attention were to be directed to the question whether there are systems of payment which 'fit' one set of circumstance, and others which 'fit' other circumstances, rather than to the question which system is best in all circumstances. The reason why the question of 'fit' has not been much considered is probably the result of a too great concern with psychological factors in motivation to the neglect of the context of organization and industrial relations in which the motives are activated.

What seems to be required is a set of aims for a payment scheme such as were set out on page 302 and a check list of conditions in which a particular kind of payment scheme or combination of schemes is likely to fulfil these aims. Only if having done this there are no possible circumstances in which PBR is likely to fulfil the aims, or if there are, that such circumstances will soon disappear, one would be justified in claiming that it is anachronistic. Plainly, this is not so. There is no good reason why, given repetitive work, in a slowly changing situation, where care has been taken to grade a simple job structure and modern work study has been applied to setting methods and standards, PBR should not give results, especially if there is effective joint machinery for periodic review. PBR will probably be inappropriate where the flow of work is irregular, where there is a diversified structure and where changes are rapid and where there is a lot of shop-floor bargaining.

In these circumstances measured day work, work simplification methods, or individual performance schemes could be examined for their relevance. Given a detailed collective bargain which set upper and lower limits on earnings and could control them, even a well-designed PBR scheme might serve very well. In small or medium-sized firms where people are personally known to each other, and can genuinely feel a sense of identity with and commitment to the firm, a profit-sharing or Scanlon-type scheme alone might serve. But, here again, provided that the collective bargaining machinery is adequate to exercise some control, PBR might well be used to advantage as a way of attaining and maintaining high outputs.

The unhealthy competition or collusion which has been linked with PBR could partly be the result of the fact that the rules governing the performance of work have not been drawn up well enough and jointly enough, and this in turn could have arisen from the structure of the collective bargaining arrangements. But some of it could well be due to the nature of the production technology, or the rate of change.

Much more research is needed before it can be said with any certainty what the circumstances are which make one scheme more appropriate than another. What can be said with more confidence is that the circumstances which fit PBR are diminishing with changes in technology and the structure of occupations. Therefore there *is* point, when changes of wage payment system are contemplated, in examining the wide range of alternatives in search of a good 'fit'.

However much one looks for a 'fit' that promises job satisfaction, equitable pay, good performance, etc., one is often tempted to say that one also ought to seek amongst the alternatives one which not only gives good results for productivity but which is 'superior' on other grounds, for example that it appeals to 'higher' motives than the quest for money. But this is a matter for people to decide for themselves.

CHAPTER 15

Individual Growth and Strategies of Trust

DENIS PYM

WHY PSYCHOLOGICAL GROWTH IS IMPORTANT

WORK, in the sense of having a job, is very nearly a universal experience. Yet it means something different to each one of us. Work is a joy, a game, or a way of life. It is a drudgery, a bore, or a means of living. It is a source of anxiety, of prestige; a means to worldly success or a way to escape from reality. Faced with having to categorize our many attitudes to work, we might say that man works because he wants to, because he has to in order to live, because society expects him to, and because he must from inner compulsion.

Working for the joy of it calls for the opportunity to exert control over what we do and to explore and make use of our talents. These features of work provide us with scope for positive mental health or, more simply, *growth*. The remaining categories of attitudes to work are largely concerned with establishing equilibrium or with making good our *deficiencies*. The necessity of working to support oneself and one's dependants has always been with us. Society too expects us to work, partly because its functioning is based on our efforts and partly because, within western society's system of values, industriousness is associated with virtue. This belief is linked with our tendencies to engage in compulsive activity, a relatively new phenomenon. The development of this attitude towards effort, Fromm (1960) observes, 'may be assumed to be the most important psychological change which has happened to man since the Middle Ages'. The freedom which man gained with the collapse of the old order affects him simultaneously in two ways. It gives him independence and it makes him feel alone and isolated. In this context of increased independence, both survival and worldly success grow more closely associated with man's efforts, and by burying himself in ceaseless toil he does not need to feel alone. So work assumed a form of adaptive behaviour, the means for reconciling conflicting impulses. It was the very important role of work in the doctrines of the non-conformist churches and the business achievements of their members which led Weber to postulate a causal link between religion and the rise of capitalism.

The extent and importance of compulsive effort in our lives today is masked by the fact that work is still necessary. Our attitudes to retirement, the proportions of industrial waste, the growth of the non-productive sector of employment, even the way we 'work at' leisure, are but the visible signs of the iceberg of compulsive effort. Compulsive effort is more than a consequence of the fear of freedom, it found an ally in the early technologies of the machine. These sped the processes of fragmentation and rationalization, so dismissing feeling from a wide range of man's tasks and dissipating their intellectual content. In this way more and more tasks have called for routine unthinking effort on man's part. However, new technologies and industrial changes are bringing now, to the work-place and to life itself, those very features of ambiguity and uncertainty which man was previously able to dismiss from his conscious life by burying himself in ceaseless toil. We can no longer ignore compulsive activity or escape from freedom.

Put in another way, man's fear of freedom, the available means for doing work and economic instability have lessened in the immediate past the opportunity for the importance of working for the joy and pleasure of it. The development of large-scale organizations, to which we are apt to attribute the meaninglessness of work, is part of this depressing story but perhaps a less important part than we think. Size is less important than the simple fact that in the history of the world so far no civilization has had the means to fashion, with lasting success, institutions and modes of social intercourse which sustain the variability of the human personality. The electronics revolution certainly enables us to exert more control over our environment. It also reverses much of what has gone before and it may even allow a greater degree of variability in social behaviour.

Our thesis is that man's desire for independence and his desire to use his talents and temperaments to the full (that is, to aspire for

317

growth) is becoming a vital factor in the continued prosperity and advancement of western society. The adaptability of each organization depends on the versatility of its employees and both are linked with the concern's system of management. It is our contention that management strategies based on trust, which underlie a philosophy in keeping with the technical developments of our time, will nurture individual growth and contribute to organizational success. Furthermore, it is also our contention that the individual himself is able to play a part in shaping these strategies. It may be asked how we reconcile this argument with the de-skilling and de-humanizing processes which are occurring in the workplace. In the continuing separation of functions between man and machine, our arguments apply to the kinds of work for which man himself is needed. When it is pointed out that this represents a rapidly contracting segment of production, distribution, and exchange, then our reply is that the attitudes implied in the concept of growth are becoming increasingly relevant, outside the narrow bounds of employment, in contemporary life itself.

These ideas are not new. They have been postulated many times before. A number of organization theorists are showing a timely interest in the relationship between the individual and the concern which employs him. We will follow here the work of McGregor (1960) and Argyris (1964), two American psychologists. They observe that modern organizations are as unsuccessful in meeting man's needs for growth (independence and self-realization) as they are successful in providing for his deficiencies (the needs for support, security, conformity, and compulsive activity). The problem, as they see it, is how to integrate the employee's own needs with the goals of the concern to achieve success for both. They postulate a link between the psychological health of the employee and his own effectiveness and the organization's success. The psychologically healthy individual aspires for growth and given the opportunity will increase his contribution to the concern. If many employees experience psychological health in their work then the organization will be better able to perform its key activities effectively. These are, according to Argyris (1964), achieving its objectives, maintaining its internal order, and adjusting to its environment. These theories are not 'soft' in the sense that they don't expect the organization to give the individual everything he wants. Argyris, for example, looks upon the lack of fit between the individual and the organization as the basis for energy which will enable both to survive and grow.

Let us now bring into our discussion the management strategies which link the individual with the organization. By management strategies we mean the various methods for coordinating the individual employee's efforts – the system of rewards and punishment, rules and regulations, methods of deploying manpower, financial controls, leadership styles, and so on. The distinctions between growth and deficiency we find characterized in McGregor's Theory X and Theory Y. In the view of McGregor, most management strategies are based on Theory X, which assumes that man dislikes work, does it for its compensations, is self-interested, and therefore must be directed and controlled. This is a theory of *distrust*, which still pervades every aspect of life. Our society proliferates with an ever-increasing army of pen-pushers, countless different kinds of inspectors, traffic-wardens, and machines each of them checking on the rest of us and each other. A vicious circle is sealed by man's natural response to these controls which justifies their enforcement. The more man is treated like a child the more he behaves like one.

As we have noted, the need to regulate man's behaviour is interwoven with defects in the mechanical technologies. In the cruder methods for doing work man's efforts and those of the machine remain an integral part of the same process. But the development of unstable markets, of automation and electronics, also bring opportunities for social systems based on integration and self-regulation: systems based on *trust*. Unfortunately our methods of social organization lag far behind those of technology.

Managerial systems based on trust, which give the employee the opportunity to achieve growth at work, underlie McGregor's Theory Y: namely the assumption that man will exert self-discipline and self-direction in serving objectives to which he is committed. But the kind of commitment which we desire is itself partly a consequence of being in control of what one does and enjoying one's work. We are back in the same familiar circle. It is the job of management to break that circle. The task may be arduous but the rewards are high.

The reader will have reason to be sceptical about the workings of social systems based on trust, for it suggests a state of anarchy. But we are contrasting two basic strategies, one of distrust, the need for externally enforced laws, and the other of trust, which calls for the internalization of uncodified laws. The last could be viewed as a refined form of anarchy. It may be argued that policies based on trust are viable among senior personnel, but the worker on the shop floor has neither the ability nor inclination to give them a fair trial. This attitude of 'I can vouch for myself and my own people but not others' is typical of the cynical thinking which underlies the concept of distrust. Yet, there *are* very obvious limitations to the amount of responsibility and the size of job each one of us can handle. A change from strategies based on distrust towards increasing trust will run into difficulties and perhaps even chaos in the early stages. For man engaged in routine fractionalized tasks, increased responsibility may in the first instance mean that he has to face again those distasteful activities he was previously able to avoid by repressing them from his conscious thoughts. For this reason job enlargement and rotation often meet with opposition from the worker. If we are out of practice at any activity we do not do it well. By the same token, employees who are suddenly required to think for themselves, to take on some degree of self-responsibility and to make use of their talents after years of unthinking, instinctive effort are bound to find the experience stressful. It is precisely for this reason that man when faced with freedom found a palliative in ceaseless toil. Sometimes when man's aspirations for growth have been inhibited, the acquisition of new responsibilities has led to abuse. A child does not become an adult overnight much as the parent, in the form of father or factory manager, would like.

There are many reasons why policies based on trust run into difficulty. It is our contention that short-term disadvantages will precede long-term successes. Indeed, in this matter of increasing responsibility it is doubtful whether, in the long run, we have any choice. Technical change is transforming the basis of work. Tasks are becoming less physical and more mental. These new demands on man are for responsibility rather than industriousness. Before we begin to seek out some of the limits of strategies based on trust and to see how the individual can influence them, let us link our ideas with other approaches to the study of organization behaviour. Our purpose is to help the reader to recognize the similarity in theme and content of much social research in this field although subjects, terminology, and approaches may appear dissimilar.

SOME OTHER APPROACHES TO THE STUDY OF ORGANIZATION BEHAVIOUR

Studies of organization behaviour are variously conducted from the point of view of the individual, the group, the structure, and the technology. We will cover one or two examples from each point of view to illustrate their similarity with the argument outlined so far.

The distinction we make between attitudes to work which contrast man's growth and deficiencies is derived from the work of Maslow (1960), a clinical psychologist. His theories are particularly important in our discussions because he postulates a link between growth and deficiency motivation. Maslow maintains that man's motives are ordered in a hierarchical way and each particular need or group of needs becomes critical in influencing behaviour as the one below it is satisfied. The lower or most basic of man's requirements are his deficiencies:

Physiological needs (for food – sleep)
Safety and security needs
Social and affiliative needs
The higher-order needs are those for growth, and these are:
Needs for recognition
Needs for autonomy
Needs for self-actualization

According to Maslow, man's deficiency needs must be satisfied before his desire for growth is likely to influence his behaviour markedly. It is the two highest order needs which interest us most here. Maslow's concept of *autonomy* is self-explanatory. *Self-*

actualization he describes as 'the process of continual realization of one's potential capacities and talents, as a fuller knowledge of oneself and one's own intrinsic nature as an increasing trend towards unity or integration within the self'. The distinctions between *growth* and deficiency overlap differences between the *flexible* and rigid personality, the *open* and closed mind and perhaps even *divergent* and convergent thinking.

The same points are observed in the study of work groups. The researches of Lewin (1951) and Likert (1961) and their associates show that the extent to which the group is able to *participate* in the making of decisions is a critical factor in work performance and adjustment. In this case trust is placed in the group.

In the Introduction to this volume the *scientific* and mechanical technologies were compared and contrasted. The differences are also observed in the process and batch productions technologies as they are described by Woodward (1965). The basic features of the new scientific technologies, we noted, were that they called for social systems based on *integration* and *self-regulation*. This is precisely how Maslow describes man's growth needs.

In the study of organization structure, the work of Burns and Stalker (1961) is given prominence by some social scientists. They contrast two systems of management, *organic* and mechanistic. In the organic system any problem requiring a decision sets up its own unique requirements. There are no prearranged rules for dealing with it as in the mechanistic framework. Control is accorded to those with the greatest knowledge. Communications run in various directions and take the form of information and advice rather than orders. Jobs and responsibilities are continually being redefined. The organic firm is one where the strategies are based on trust.

ASPIRATIONS FOR GROWTH AND PERFORMANCE

When we argue that the extension of trust in employees will lead to greater success for the individual and the concern we do so on the assumption that every man has the capacities and inclinations to cope with that trust. But, just as we go along with the view that in every soul there is a responsible and an irresponsible being, so we know that individuals, through the course of nature and nurture, come to differ in the extent to which they possess these propensities. It is this fact which presents us with difficulties in ascertaining the extent of our adaptability to jobs which offer increased responsibility. Theorists like McGregor and Argyris have been criticized for failing to show that independence and self-realization always fall within the scope of the worker's aspirations. We will take up this question in the course of outlining two inquiries.

Aspirations among factory workers

First, let us recount a study of worker reactions to innovations in a footwear factory (Pym, 1965). We will begin with the circumstances which prompted these changes. The shoe industry is faced with fairly unstable markets, the result of trade cycles, cut-price foreign competition and changing fashions. It is a business in which firms need to be internally adaptive. However, in this traditional industry the internal structure of many firms was unsuited to meet these demands. In a number of ways this observation also applied to the firm in which our inquiry was undertaken. Production control was poor and procedures for moving the work through the factory were often manual and fairly haphazard. Over the years, agreements between employer and unions added to the inflexibility of work practices. For example, according to a long-standing agreement, operatives engaged in machining tasks contracted to undertake only a limited range of footwear lines, a fact which increased the difficulty of meeting rapid changes in fashion. The innovation we will now describe was designed to improve the fit between the new market requirements and the internal functioning of the factory. Principal among the changes affecting the machinist was the installation of a mechanical conveying system which replaced the fetching and carrying of work by operatives and indirect labour. Following detailed union–management negotiations, the old system of contracted work was replaced by one in which each machinist had to do *all* the lines of shoes sent to her by the feeder operating the conveyor. Responsibility for quality was largely taken from the hands of inspectors and returned to the operatives. By reducing waiting and unproductive time, the conveyors enabled each operative to increase her production if she so desired and, in addition, piece rates for the work were increased. Management hoped to gain greater control over the production process by *increasing* the operatives' involvement in their work. Their responsibilities were enlarged, greater emphasis was placed on versatility in machining skills, and some of the disincentives of the jobs were removed.

The investigator's part in this exercise was to ascertain each operative's level of aspiration for growth, using paper and pencil questionnaires, and to see if this information would predict the effects of the innovation on output. As a result of previous researches, growth was measured by diversity of leisure interests and aspirations for: independence, varied tasks, and work which emphasized skill and judgement. Concern for security, in contrast with growth, was measured by the extent to which the operative preferred economic security, and predictable and routine work. From the scores on these measures each operative was classified in relation to the rest of the machinists as having stronger aspirations for *growth* or for *security*.

The output of the two groups is compared over a 2½-year period in Figure 23. Predictably, following the change the growth-oriented group's output rises faster and to a higher level (an increase of 33 per cent) than the deficiency-oriented group (an increase of 13 per cent). Output immediately prior to the innovation is also shown to be rising and could be attributed to the anticipation of the change and approaching holidays. The differences between the groups are negligible before the operatives became aware of the impending changes. We interpret this and the subsequent divergence of the two groups in terms of the initial lack of variety and opportunity for independence and the increasing scope in both these respects for the machinists following the changes. Taking the inquiry in total, this innovation proved to be most successful. Enlarged opportunities for psychological success enabled the 99 operatives to increase their output by an average of 22 per cent. Furthermore, 89 indicated that conditions were better 20 months after the event than they had been before. The company also benefited. According to reports from the work-study department, between July 1962 and July 1964 the overall productivity of the section had risen by 51 per cent and standards of quality were higher. But most important of all, by this and similar changes the factory was developing a more organic internal structure in harmony with the realities of the market.

Our interest in the success of this exercise must not allow us to skate over the problems. Like most work reorganizations, the

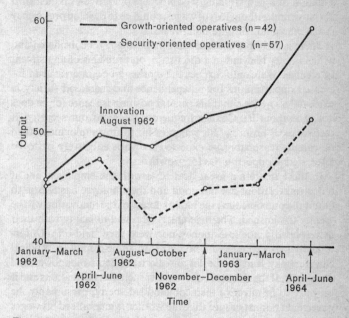

Figure 23. The output of growth-oriented and security-oriented operatives before and after an innovation

immediate effects of these changes were not altogether favourable. In fact some months passed before the machinists, as a group, regained their pre-change level of performance. There were a number of casualties. Some of the nine who left during the course of the inquiry did so because they were unable to cope, and the eight inspectors had to be transferred on to work elsewhere in the factory. Eleven of the women were still having difficulty with the new scheme twenty months after its inception. The fact is that one third of the operatives, most of them in the 'security oriented' group, took quite a long time to readjust themselves, and if management had neither been patient nor prepared to help them it is unlikely that the project would have been such a success. One example of management's enlightened policy was the instigation of a new training school where operatives, on their own initiative and without loss of wages, could go to develop proficiency in the machining of unfamiliar tasks.

There is an important question we have not yet considered and which is very relevant in a discussion on problems of adjustment to change. We cannot expect the worker to be interested in increased opportunities for independence and increased variety in work unless he feels that his general position is secure (or he does not care about it). Change frequently threatens our security. If the worker is unsure of his wages or his future employment, then he cannot reasonably be expected to work effectively or to be interested in opportunities for growth.

In these matters a great deal rests with the employer, and if industrial relations are not good and the employee has reason to doubt the outcome then the likely success of the innovation will be greatly diminished. The machinists who had difficulty with their new roles did not lose money nor were they 'laid-off'. Unfortunately many changes are not like this; some cannot be. Radical changes may lead to the large-scale transfer of manpower and dismissals. If the worker is not to resist such transformations and if they are to be effective then some outside body, presumably the government, must ensure that the worker is guaranteed his wages and future employment together with the necessary training facilities to ensure that he can become proficient at his new task. Just what is being and can be done about these questions and the adequacy of the measures are analysed elsewhere in this volume, particularly in Chapter 3.

Aspirations among professional engineers

We have seen that as jobs become more complex so those workers who aspire for growth are able to perform the new tasks more effectively and to derive greater satisfactions from them. Some jobs contain a high discretionary or responsibility content. In a way they permanently simulate the ambiguous conditions of many changes. After the study just reported a short attitude scale, derived from the items which best predicted versatility among the machinists, was completed by 274 mechanical engineers engaged in professional work in industry. The scale is shown below and is called a measure of growth or work flexibility. Most of the items illustrate the idea that the predisposition for growth can be detected by the extent to which the respondent is prepared to tolerate ambiguity, take risks, do things on his own and consider several things at the same time.

Here are some statements aimed at measuring your attitudes to aspects of your work. Please indicate your opinion by placing a tick in the appropriate place for each statement.

Key: SA   Strongly agree   SLD   Slightly disagree
     MA   Moderately agree   MD   Moderately disagree
     SLA   Slightly agree   SD   Strongly disagree

	Agree			Disagree		
	SA	MA	SLA	SLD	MD	SD
1. You like your work to be predictable	1	2	3	4	5	6
2. You feel that there is usually one best way to solve most problems	1	2	3	4	5	6
3. You prefer a job which is always changing	6	5	4	3	2	1
4. You like taking risks in things you do at work	6	5	4	3	2	1
5. The best job for you is one in which you work under instruction	1	2	3	4	5	6
6. You dislike having to change your plans in the middle of doing something	1	2	3	4	5	6

Scores inside the rectangle are not included in the questionnaires. The higher the score the more the respondent is growth oriented.

The scores on the scale above were then related to each man's effectiveness. This was ascertained from a composite measure based on estimations of his own competence and his salary corrected for age and kind of job. On the basis of these two sets of information the engineers were then categorized as being high, average, or low in job competence. Figure 24 illustrates the obvious link between growth and effectiveness among these engineers.

The results of these two inquiries confirm our earlier contentions; namely that people who aspire for growth in their work are likely to be numbered among the more effective in mentally demanding jobs and in situations where changes increase the uncertainty of work roles. Probably the most important observation

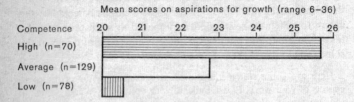

Mean scores on aspirations for growth (range 6–36)

Figure 24. The relationship between aspirations for growth and competence among 274 mechanical engineers

that we might make, from the management point of view, is that the encouragement and nurturing of the worker's aspirations for growth depend very much on the extent to which management is able and prepared to pursue policies based on increasing trust in employees.

THE INDIVIDUAL AND MANAGEMENT STRATEGIES

We have seen how unstable market conditions played a part in the introduction of factory changes which increased the variety and scope of work being done by the machinists. In the kind of conception of the organization we follow here, change can take place anywhere within the system. Our definition of organizational effectiveness includes the notion that changes in the market can be forestalled, that, in one sense, a cause can be anticipated by the effect. Anticipatory action is normally more effective than action forced upon us because we have all the advantages of time, one of which is that the necessary changes can be more carefully considered and introduced.

All this depends on management itself, and our attention in this respect is directed towards the individual manager. We postulate that the greater the amount of choice open to the individual in his job, the better placed he is to change it. By the same token, the greater the individual's influence over the firm the more able he is to shape and form its policies and development. We are familiar with remarks about the way great men have left their mark on firms, institutions, or even countries. For example, Lord Reith is said to have set his seal on the British Broadcasting Corporation; Lord Nuffield played a major part in the formation of the motor industry. The social scientist has to be sceptical about such claims. He is aware that a multitude of factors influence the life and growth of every enterprise. Sometimes it is possible to control for some of these variables so that particular events may be traced to the personality of an individual. Let us briefly outline one such attempt.

A comparative study

Consider three automatic data-processing (ADP) units providing a service to industry and commerce, each belonging to one company and under the same senior management. In their internal operation each is faced with the same serious problems. On the one hand, they need to be flexible, and yet on the other hand their operation calls for a high degree of rationalization. Let us expand on these conflicting requirements. These ADP units have to be flexible because they pursued a policy of taking on all kinds of work brought to them by customers. In a sense, they have minimum control over the input of work. Furthermore, the key jobs of the systems analyst, fitting machine specifications to customer requirements, and the programmer, writing instructions for the way the computer is to analyse data, cannot be carried out within strict time limits. Although it is possible to estimate how long the systems analyst and programmer will take to do a job, these estimations can often only be expressed in terms of weeks and months.

Rationalization of the work processes is important because computer operating time is very expensive and there are always a number of hard and fast customer deadlines to be met. Payroll calculations, for example, must be completed on a specific day each week. This discussion leads us to the popular misconception that the ADP unit is an example of automation. In fact, with the variety of skills involved in its processes and the differing methods for doing work, little of which is automated, it much more closely resembles the technology of mass production. The insatiable appetite of the computer systems and the stringencies of customer requirements are continuing and strong influences on all behaviour in the ADP unit.

To return to our three units, in many ways they are remarkably similar. Their similarities include size, formal social structure, and standards of operation. Their staff are equivalent in numbers, skills, and educational experience; only in technical structure do they differ slightly. Let us call the units A, B, and C. Although A and B possess comparable ranges of machines and computer systems, C has, in addition, two more sophisticated computers. Yet the ways in which the three units cope with the conflicting demands for flexibility and rationalized procedures diverged radically. The informal organization of A could easily be distinguished from B and C and the determinants of these differences are to be observed in the personalities of the respective managers of each unit.

In Unit A, the manager is a friendly, direct, and approachable man, admired by his staff. He is confident of his own abilities and those of his subordinates. He is, as Likert (1961) describes, employee-centred. Indeed he seems to be deeply involved in the problems we have just underlined. He uses the strategies of trust in building up systems of operation which are highly organic. Few demarcations are observed between the various sections. For example, if a programmer is found complaining about a machine operator he is known to resolve the problem by sending the former to work in the machine room for a week or two. Internal recruiting is also high. Each level provides a pool of manpower for the one above it. Successful key-punch operators can be promoted into the machine room and computer operators to programmers. In the machine room itself, operatives are required to be proficient on all machines.

In Units B and C, by contrast, the managers maintain some distance between themselves and the rest of the unit. They associate less with the men and their contact with them is more formal. The manager at C continually emphasizes the objectives of the unit at meetings with his senior personnel. Both attempt to resolve the basic incongruities of the internal system by regulation. In B, no programmer can enter the machine room without the supervisor's permission. Recruitment seldom takes place internally in either unit: no key-punch operators have been promoted and only a small number of computer operatives in either unit has moved on to programming work. Job roles are fairly strictly defined; for example, in the machine room, the operators specialize on limited ranges of equipment.

Predictably, the differences, we have observed, are reflected in the work dissatisfactions of the personnel (see Table 6). The more organic system of management at A is associated with better passing of information and greater freedom of action but it does not facilitate the steady flow of work through the unit.

TABLE 6: *The differing dissatisfactions of personnel in three automatic data-processing units*

Unit	A	B	C
Management strategy	Trust	Distrust	Distrust
Numbers in unit	75	79	65
DISSATISFACTIONS	%	%	%
Excessive work-load	33	32	21
Poor communications	11	44	49
Unsatisfactory scheduling and organization of work	42	29	40
Rigid rules of conduct	0	39	21
Excessive emphasis on objectives	6	8	44

It could be said that each strategy has its strengths and weaknesses from the employees' point of view, but what of the relative effectiveness of each unit? Senior management reports that all three are achieving their annual targets, though operating costs in B are higher than they should be. There are other criteria of effectiveness, one being that the organization should be adjusting to its environment. There is a serious shortage of data-processing personnel. It might therefore be argued that the unit most likely to retain its personnel is also in a better position to maintain itself internally and go on achieving its objectives. Each member of the three units is asked if he sees himself still working with the company in two years' time. Those answering in the affirmative are as follows: Unit A 94 per cent, Unit B 75 per cent, and Unit C 77 per cent. This study shows how differing styles of behaviour are available to managers in dealing with their work problems and that in the situation we have just observed strategies based on trust appear to be marginally better than those based on distrust.

The inquiry we have just outlined was conducted in units which were new and therefore it might be argued amenable to the influence of people running them. It is more difficult to change the procedures and practices in well-established organizations, but not impossible. Guest (1962) describes a study of changes in a car-assembly plant which he attributes largely to the successful leadership of one man. Under the old management the style of leadership was inclined to McGregor's Theory X, in our terms, to strategies of distrust. Operations were controlled by one man, the manager, and the interdependence of departmental work was largely ignored. Working relationships in the plant began to fossilize in such a way that it became impossible to make the kinds of changes needed to maintain its internal order. As a consequence, morale and commitment were low and on a number of performance criteria this plant had the worst record in comparison with five other plants. A new manager was then appointed who brought a different philosophy of management to the plant. He stressed the dependence of functions and increased the influence of people at all levels over the plant's operations. The resulting improvement in performance placed the unit in the top three on each of the criteria of efficiency and its direct labour costs became lower than all other plants. As with our study of ADP units these differences were achieved without any changes in the formal structure of the plant.

One of the best-known examples of a radical change in methods of coordinating employee performance is the simplification of paperwork exercise initiated by the late chairman of one of Britain's largest chain stores, Marks and Spencer. The story goes that it was triggered off through a chance observation by Sir Simon Marks of two sales girls carefully completing stock inventory replacement cards while customers waited for service. There followed a company-wide purge on all paper work. Clock cards were banished, sales girls were given access to store rooms; stock controls, order records, wage and staff records, and head-office procedures were either simplified or abandoned altogether. Within three years it was estimated that 26 million pieces of paper weighing 120 tons had been eliminated annually. The savings were reckoned in millions of pounds and, in conjunction with this exercise, Marks and Spencer reduced their staff, by normal wastage, and cut the prices of their merchandise while increasing sales and profits. To put it crudely, they found it cheaper to trust their employees; cheaper in fact to allow pilfering and dishonesty than to apply stringent controls on employee conduct and work procedures. Despite the success of policies like this it is remarkable how few organizations have been prepared to take similar courses of action.

Technical change itself is increasing the influence of personnel, traditionally in subordinate positions, over the functioning of organizations. One such example is the computerized control of information. At first glance such a system appears to increase the opportunity for senior personnel to manipulate employees. Activity-reporting procedures enable the chief executive of a firm to know in detail what his employees are doing, but in reality, if such a system is to work properly, it *must* be based on trust. Because the reliability and validity of the information received at the top depends on what people at the bottom feed into the system in the first instance, reprimand for deviant behaviour is more likely to bring about changes in reporting than in actual behaviour. As a result the information service provided to the chief executive can become distorted or downright untrue and action taken on such information may have dire consequences. We should look upon the improvement of such control systems in a different way. Through direct links with those responsible for decisions of the greatest importance to the concern, it will become possible for every employee to influence the internal workings of the concern.

*

We will retrace the arguments of this chapter by stating them as a series of points:

(1) Years of experience of submission and dependence at work, the result of fragmented and highly regulated work roles, man's fear of freedom and managerial systems based on distrust, lead to difficulties and stress for employees in dealing with job enlargement and work changes.

(2) Job roles, which become ambiguous as a consequence of change, and work which entails a high degree of discretion on the part of the individual, can be most effectively discharged by employers who are growth-oriented (that is, they seek independence and the opportunities to use their talents to the full).

(3) Employees who are initially unable to exercise much self-responsibility or to make greater use of their talents can learn to do so. A prior condition for the development of growth is the provision of security through guaranteed wages and employment and the availability of facilities for learning new skills. Beyond these prerequisites an organizational climate which encourages greater individual initiative will help also to nurture such values among its employees.

(4) Management strategies can be developed in a variety of circumstances to increase the opportunities for growth. The assumption underlying such strategies is one of trust. The extension of trust at all levels of the concern can lead to greater commitment to organizational objectives, and improved individual and organizational performance.

(5) Although the development of managerial strategies is dependent on features of the market, technology, and social organization, the individual in a position of authority can exercise considerable influence over them. Furthermore, new technical processes are increasing the opportunity for all employees to exert some influence over the broad scope of management activities.

CHAPTER 16

Technology, Control, and Organization

JEFFREY RACKHAM

THE EMERGENCE OF ORGANIZATION THEORY

SUCCESSFUL management depends upon the choice of appropriate action. One ever-present management problem is that of choosing actions in situations of uncertainty, and management theory represents an attempt to provide decision rules for such circumstances. Ultimately the purpose of organization theory is to provide guidance for managers faced with problems of the design of organizations. Each of these questions interests the social scientist, since each can be expressed in terms of relationships between people.

In different ages, managers of one sort and another have adopted different standards in deciding what to accept as reliable guides to the best ways to proceed. For example, it has been pointed out (Koontz and O'Donnell, 1959) that Moses delegated his judicial function according to advice given him by his father-in-law, who said that 'God command thee so' (Exodus viii, 17 f.). Belief in gods, chance, and fortune have produced an extensive variety of decision-rules (Cohen, 1964). Nor is this restricted to the ancients. A contemporary example of the use of chance in elections is to be found where 'an innocent child of San Marino draws from an urn one of three scraps of paper furnished with two names – and the republic has been provided with two new governors' (Aubert, 1959). Considerable importance was apparently attached to chance by the oil millionaire who is reported to have said, 'I'd rather be lucky than smart, 'cause a lot of smart people ain't eatin' regular.'

More characteristic of the early part of the twentieth century was the reliance upon the 'informed speculation' of men with extensive experience in particular spheres of management endeavour (Fayol, 1916; Taylor, 1911; Hamilton, 1921). Fayol, a mining engineer, became managing director of a large French mining and metallurgical combine. Taylor, a mechanical engineer, became a management consultant. Hamilton was a soldier. They were men accustomed to taking executive action; the situation of having to choose actions was familiar to them; and their writings predominantly take the form of rules to be followed when choosing actions. In Fayol's five elements of management – plan, organize, command, coordinate, and control – there was the beginning of analysis of management functions, intended to help the reader to understand management, or to clarify his thinking about it. The classic analysis of Weber, one of their contemporaries, of the bases upon which authority in organizations may be founded can be seen as an attempt to clarify thinking about organizations, rather than as a system of rules for action. But for the most part, the writing on organizations that dates from the early years of this century was aimed at providing decision-rules or guides to action. Fayol proposed 'General Principles of Management'; Taylor had 'Four Great Underlying Principles of Management'; Mary Parker Follett (1941) listed 'Four Principles of Organizations'; and in all cases these principles were expressed in terms not of description or of analysis but of what should be done.

'Until recent years, almost all of those who have attempted to analyse the management process and look for some scientific underpinnings to help the practice of management were alert and perceptive practitioners of the art, who could base their speculations on many years of experience. . . . Although not based on questionnaires, controlled interviews, or mathematics, the observations of such men can hardly be regarded as "armchair"' (Koontz, 1951). At the same time it must be doubted whether normative principles derived from the particular experience of even the most experienced practitioners of half-a-century ago are likely to continue to have universal relevance to current problems of organization design.

Between the two world wars, the principles of Fayol, Taylor, and Follett were made widely known in Britain through the work and writing of Urwick; and during this period organization theory comprised little other than the principles of organization. For example:

Principle of the Span of Control: The number of subordinates reporting to a superior should preferably be limited to no more than five or six at the executive level.

Principle of Definition: The duties, authority, responsibility, and relations of everyone in the organization structure should be clearly and completely prescribed in writing.

Principle of Organization Effectiveness: The final test of an industrial organization is smooth and frictionless operation (Alford and Beatty, 1951).

After the Second World War, a change of attitude towards the principles of organization began to emerge. As a result of studies in the United States by the National Industrial Conference Board (1946) and by the American Management Association (1951), some doubt was thrown on whether the Principle of the Span of Control could be stated in terms of precise figures. However, this principle was still being stated in text-books published as late as 1959, though its character had been radically altered by the qualifications attached to it:

... the practice of giving positive numerical definition to the principle has led one writer to state that the span of control principle is no longer valid since the effective supervision of the chief executive is much wider than that 'predicted' by the principle.

The attitudes toward the principle appear to represent a misunderstanding of its true meaning. The real underlying principle is that there is a limit to the number of subordinates a manager can effectively manage, but the exact number will depend upon such factors as the training possessed by and required of subordinates, the extent to which authority is clearly delegated, the clarity of plans and policies, the degree to which objective standards can be and are applied, and the effectiveness of the communication techniques used. Until these factors can be clarified and quantified, either generally, or in a specific instance, the principle cannot be given a numerical value. But the basic principle exists, has not been superseded, and is no fable. Moreover, it is a useful fundamental to give managers a guide for improving their quality of management to the end of effectively managing more subordinates and simplifying organization. (Koontz and O'Donnell, 1959.)

If one tries to paraphrase this new version of the principle, it transpires that it now says no more than that 'a manager can deal with the problems raised by no more than some unknown number of subordinates; but although no one can say what that number is going to be in any given situation, nevertheless it is prudent to remember that there is a maximum figure'. We perceive that the principle has undergone a significant change from its original, simple, numerical, dogmatic form.

The N.I.C.B. and A.M.A. studies revealed that spans of control were in practice much more variable than the original principle would allow; such studies were only descriptive, and offered no explanation for the variation. At the same time, writers had begun to suggest that some of the factors might result in different spans of control being more appropriate to different situations, but their statements were not based on systematic empirical study, nor were they reliable or exact.

This is not to say that those who propounded such principles, even when it had become clear that they were degenerating into dogma, necessarily merit unqualified criticism. The absence of alternative theories, explanations, or principles left a gap that many managers preferred to see filled. The situation may be compared with the use of work measurement, for example, where the techniques are almost universally recognized to have serious weaknesses, both theoretical and practical, but where the value of using a second-class tool is regarded as being greater than the value of avoiding error by using no tool at all.

It is probably also true that at the beginning of this century the principles of organization were more than merely the best available. For one thing, this was a period of industrial expansion, with marked characteristics of change and uncertainty, when decision-rules in as clear and unequivocal a form as possible served a purpose in helping to provide some stability and security. At the same time, much of this expansion was occurring (in Britain and the United States) in the area of production of high-output, low-cost, standardized articles to supply the demands of increasing material standards of living; and, in so far as the principles were devised and expounded on the basis of experience mainly within such a type of production, they may have done more than provide a system of beliefs to support those who were filling the emergent role of industrial manager. The principles may have been reliable because they were appropriate.

But in the years following the Second World War the situation changed. It is perhaps no coincidence that the studies by the N.I.C.B. and the A.M.A. mentioned above were both published during that period. Significant transformations occurred in the industrial scene, changes of social and economic as well as of a technical nature. Increases in the power and cost of labour and in business competition which created new demands for efficient management also led to the detailed scrutiny and development of management itself. With government support, courses in management training proliferated; and for lack of an alternative, the teaching on these courses was based on the handbooks of principles of industrial management. Managers and potential managers attended the courses and were taught the principles and they went back into their firms in all types of industry. Some found the principles made sense, and some found they made nonsense. Some found them fruitful, and some found them sterile. For some, the guiding light of nineteenth-century origin was still burning brightly; for others, it seemed to have been blown out by the winds of change.

It is in this context that we find the N.I.C.B. and the A.M.A. questioning the Principle of the Span of Control, on the basis of studies which described variations found in practice but which did not try to explain them. Also we find some writers beginning to suggest factors that might account for the variations, but without producing reliable or exact statements based on systematic empirical study.

The need for new ideas was evident, and the response was 'a deluge of research and writing pouring from academic halls', the result of which has been described as 'The Management Theory Jungle'. Where once there was only the school of Fayol, Taylor, and Urwick, known variously as the 'classical', 'traditional', or 'universalist' school, Koontz (1951) has identified six main schools of management theory. Yet within these factions, a common factor can be seen to have emerged. The classical school was predominantly concerned with 'rules of good practice' that were supposed to provide reliable guides to action in all circumstances. A common characteristic of current theories is that they are predominantly concerned with analysing management practice, and with assessing the effects of different management practices in different contexts. As most contemporary organization theorists would like to see it, the current approaches represent attempts at being scientific in a more sophisticated way than the 'scientific management' approach.

In consequence, many current writings about organization have developed a different tone. Systems of belief have largely been replaced by systems of analysis, and implicit *a priori* assumptions by hypotheses needing to be tested and verified. Ideas of what is good or bad have been replaced by ideas of what is appropriate or effective. Statements of principles, which are implicitly statements of cause-and-effect relationships, where the 'effect' is some desired objective of the organization, not necessarily specified, have largely been replaced by questions about how far one can expect to be able to demonstrate reliable cause-and-effect relationships in situations that are dominated by the complexity of human behaviour. Now, the interest is as much in questions as in answers, and theories tend to be in the form of suggestions about what factors managers will need to consider in looking for the answers.

So far, we have given the impression of a sad and destructive development. However unreliable the classical principles of management were, they did at least serve the purpose of providing answers to questions that managers asked. Sometimes decisions so arrived at may not have been the best decisions, by any criteria; but often a sub-optimal decision is preferable to indecision. And the impression given is that the inadequacy of the classical decision-rules has been demonstrated but that nothing has yet been produced to fill the gap that is left.

In some sense this is true. It is no longer accepted that there is any universal 'natural law' that 'the number of subordinates reporting to a superior should be limited to no more than five or six at the executive level'. There are no new alternative rules to suggest what the answer to such a question should be in any particular instance. At the same time, organization theorists concerned with the analysis of organization structure are asking what is meant by 'superior', 'subordinate', and 'reporting to', what is involved in a particular superior–subordinate relationship, how different such relationships vary according to different functional responsibilities of superior and subordinate and according to the nature of delegation, what is delegated, and so on. Whereas writers of the classical school proposed that by the clarification and quantification of such factors the Principle of the Span of Control can be given a numerical value, current work on organization analysis suggests that the complexity and variability of the factors involved may make it misleading to continue to talk at all of principles.

One can say that the basic problem has been re-formulated. Although the eventual aim of organization theory, in an applied sense, may be to provide guidance for managers faced with the problem of choosing organizational-design actions in situations of uncertainty, the emphasis has changed. The stress is now placed not so much on the provision of decision-rules – which are likely to be unreliable – as on the analysis of the situations, and on helping managers to understand the uncertainties they face, and so perhaps to reduce this uncertainty.

THE TASK ANALYSIS APPROACH

One factor in industrial situations has come to be recognized by industrial social scientists as having a particular significance in the study of social relationships at work. This is the nature of the work that the organization exists to perform, or the nature of the organizational task. During the past fifteen years, sociological research has produced a considerable body of evidence to indicate a relationship between the work done and both individual behaviour and organization structure.

In a classic study of automobile assembly-line work (Walker and Guest, 1952), characteristics of mass-production work – such as repetitiveness and mechanical pacing – were related to job satisfaction. In another study (Sayles, 1958), the ways that different occupational groups brought up their grievances with management were related to 'broad technological factors' – standardized, low-skill tasks; repetitiveness; and so on. Yet another study (Blauner, 1964) relates technology to alienation (powerlessness, isolation, and self-estrangement in the individual, and lack of meaning for him in his work).

More sophisticated than these three American studies is the socio-technical system theory arising out of the coal-mining study by Trist and others at the Tavistock Institute of Human Relations (Trist *et al.*, 1963). In this study for the first time it was stated that 'the social and psychological (aspects) can be understood only in terms of the detailed engineering facts, and of the way the techno-logical system as a whole behaves.'

In some measure this approach was present in the writings of Follett (1941), who noted that 'authority and responsibility should derive from the actual functions to be performed, and not from a place in the hierarchy'. Current thought might suggest that a person's place in the hierarchy should derive from the functions to be performed. Follett saw it as axiomatic that, from the joint study by those involved of the facts of a situation, there would emerge the 'law of the situation' which would determine what action should be taken. Brown (1960) also concludes that 'effective organization is a function of the work to be done and the resources and techniques available to do it.'

Probably the clearest and most conclusive studies demonstrating the link between the tasks of organizations and their structures are those of Burns and Woodward.

In a study based on the electronics industry, Burns (1961) found that management practice differed considerably in respect of conformity to the classical Principle of Definition and that non-conformity did not inevitably lead to failure to achieve business objectives. Rather, it seemed that in some circumstances confor-mity was less likely to lead to success than non-conformity. 'There seemed to be two divergent systems of management prac-tice. Neither was fully and consistently applied in any firm, although there was a clear division between those managements which adhered generally to the one, and those which followed the other. . . . One system, to which we gave the name "mechanistic" appeared to be appropriate to an enterprise operating under relatively stable conditions. The other, "organic", appeared to be required for conditions of change.' In organic systems, 'jobs lose much of their formal definition in terms of methods, duties and powers, which have to be re-defined continually by interaction with others participating in a task'.

This contrasts strongly with the classical management principles, and what is now interesting about this development is why the classical principles were accepted without serious question for so long. Part of the answer is to be found in a phrase which gives some insight into the basis upon which such a belief was founded: 'a machine will not run smoothly when fundamental engineering principles have been ignored in its construction'. Classical management theorists, many of whom had an engineering background, found it easy to consider the material that goes to make up a social system in the same way as they treated the material that can be used to construct a mechanical system. Burns' distinction between mechanistic and organic systems, suggesting by analogy a comparison of mechanical and biological systems, goes some way towards making up the deficiencies of the engineering analogy; but ultimately it may not have gone far enough. An understanding of social systems involves analysis at one level higher than that of biological systems. For example, an understanding of the growth and development of human beings does not provide a complete explanation of the behaviour of two motorists converging on a parking space in central London.

In a study of a hundred firms in south-east Essex, Joan Woodward (1965) collected information on a wide range of topics related to organization structure. The results showed that conformity with the classical principles of organization was not associated with business success. But when the firms were classified according to their production systems (unit production, mass production, and process production), the information about organization structure began to form patterns. Firms within each category were found to share similar characteristics of organization structure. The firms that more nearly conformed to the average figure for the various structural characteristics were likely to be the more successful, in business terms, while those that diverged most from the average figure for their category were likely to be the less successful.

These conclusions have formed the starting point for research currently being carried out at Imperial College.*

THE FURTHER ANALYSIS OF TECHNICAL VARIABLES

Before going on to see how Miss Woodward's study, 'Management and Technology', has been extended, let us consider briefly what the concepts and methods of that study were. The conclusion was that among commercially successful firms, different patterns of organization structure were used to deal with the 'situational demands' of different production systems. How did Miss Woodward identify and measure differences in these two variables, organization structure and production system?

For comparing production systems, a list of nine basic categories was compiled. These were grouped into three main categories as follows:

Unit and small-batch production
    Production of units to customers' orders
    Production of prototypes
    Fabrication of large equipment in stages
    Production of small batches
Large-batch and mass production
    Production of large batches
    Production of large batches on assembly lines
    Mass production
Process production
    Intermittent production of chemicals in multi-purpose plant
    Continuous-flow production of liquids, gases, etc.

Miss Woodward says these 'nine systems of production . . . form a scale; they are listed in order of chronological development and technical complexity; the production of unit articles to customers' individual requirements being the oldest and simplest form of

---

* The following section is based upon work being done as part of a research project on management control systems now being undertaken in the Management Engineering Section of Imperial College, London. The project as a whole is described in the Social Science Research Council's publication *Research Supported by the SSRC: 1967* (H.M.S.O.).

manufacture, and the continuous-flow production of dimensional products the most advanced and most complicated.'

The comparison of organization structures was made in a different way. There was no attempt to reduce the various factors to a single system of categories. Each of a number of selected factors – number of levels in the hierarchy of authority, span of control of the chief executive, and so on – was taken separately; and for each factor, the characteristics for firms in each production system category were grouped.

Within each category, similarities in organization structure characteristics were found. Eight of the structural characteristics varied progressively, increasing or decreasing from unit to mass and from mass to process production. This is shown in Table 7.

At the same time there were other respects in which unit and process production firms had similar organizational characteristics compared with a greater difference from the mass-production firms. Comparisons in terms of seven such characteristics are shown in Table 8.

This research provided a fund of rich and valuable empirical data and, in demonstrating that a link exists between the characteristics of the production system and the structure of the organization, it constituted a major advance towards understanding how organizations work. But as almost invariably happens, the new questions it raised were more numerous than the ones it answered. Miss Woodward says: 'If we could find answers to such questions as why unit articles can be produced successfully only where the lines of control are short, why mass production demands the definition of duties and responsibilities, and why the chief executive in a process production firm can successfully control more subordinates than his counterparts in other types of production, we would have come a long way towards the discovery of cause and effect relationships between systems of production and the forms of organization they demand. These cause and effect relationships might in turn provide us with a basis of reasoning in the field of management.'

Two particular areas for further investigation have been chosen in the current research project supervised by Miss Woodward and Professor Eilon at Imperial College. One concerns the nature

TABLE 7: *Organization differences between firms with different production systems (1)*

	Unit production	Mass production	Process production
The average number of levels in the hierarchy of authority	3	4	6
The average span of control of the chief executive, i.e. the number of people directly responsible to him.*	4	7	10
The span of control in the middle levels of management	highest		lowest
The relative part played by manual workers (represented by the average percentage of costs allocated to wages)	35	32	15
The relative part played by management and supervision (represented by the average ratio of managers and supervisors to total personnel)	1 to 23	1 to 16	1 to 8
Whether graduates are employed, and in which departments	perhaps a few, in non-production departments	rare	in production and non-production departments
The importance of production, relative to administration (represented by the average number of industrial workers per member of staff)	8	$5\frac{1}{2}$	2
The importance of productive jobs, relative to maintenance and service jobs (represented by the average number of producers per non-producer)	9	4	1

* Usually the managing director or general manager.

of the control systems instituted by management to deal with the problems thrown up by the nature of the production system. This will be mentioned in the last section of this chapter.

The other is to find a more precise method of comparing production systems. What Miss Woodward called a technical scale is not of the simple type of classification based on a single parameter

TABLE 8: *Organization differences between firms with different production systems (2)*

	Unit production	Mass production	Process production
The average span of control of the first-line supervisor	23	48	13
The proportion of manual workers classified as skilled	high	low	high
The skill level of the typical production worker	skilled	semi-skilled	semi-skilled/ skilled
The person in whom technical competence is found	production management	specialist	production management
The type of organization structure, using Burns' categories*	organic	mechanistic	organic
Production control procedures	used less	elaborate	used less
Predominant mode of communication	verbal	written	verbal

* Op. cit.

that can be expressed numerically. It is, rather, a system of categories based upon a complex conceptual idea of production systems. It includes a range of factors relating to the equipment used; the extent to which processes and sequences of processes are standardized and repetitive; the extents to which the total manufacturing task is mechanized and the human activities specialized, fragmented, and standardized; and the level of market demand. Placing a particular firm into one of the categories involves a sophisticated but largely intuitive choice and of course there were problems with mixed systems. Miss Woodward's wide experience of industry enabled her to place each firm into its appropriate category.

Like most theoretical concepts, when one tries to express it in terms of some explicit indicator, 'technology' turns out to be multidimensional. This may go some way towards explaining why some of the organizational characteristics were found to vary from unit to mass and from mass to process production systems, while others show similarities between unit and process compared with mass-production systems.

The first attempt to find a more refined measure of technology was undertaken by Brewer (see Appendix of Woodward, 1965). He worked on the assumption that when the conventional scale of production – unit, job, batch, mass – was arranged in ascending order, it implied an increasing rate of production. It might therefore be possible to define a production rate index in terms of the ratio between (a) the time interval between the completion of one article and the completion of the next and (b) the manufacturing time, that is, the time taken to produce the article or component concerned. When this production index was applied to the firms studied in south Essex, an interesting fact emerged. Firms that had been classified as unit and small-batch were grouped closely together at one end of the production index scale and those classified as process were grouped together at the other. The batch production firms were distributed over a wide area in the middle of the scale. Thus it seemed that the variations in behaviour and organization revealed by the research might be explained by reference to technical differences.

As suggested above, another factor entering into the differentiation between production systems is the extent to which processes and sequences of processes are standardized and repetitive. Eilon suggested that this might be measured in terms of the variation in a firm's product range from year to year. An index was devised, so that a value of 1 would signify maximum variation, with no product common to two successive years; and a value of 0 would indicate no variation, where all the products made in the first of two years were also made in the second. Values ranging from about

0·1 to about 0·8 have been obtained in a number of firms, and these differences appear to be related to differences in the nature of the management tasks in these firms.

It was found for example that two batch-production firms in the electrical industry, which would have been classified in the same category in any previous classification, differed considerably in this respect. This difference provided an explanation of why one had a number of characteristics in common with mass production as far as patterns of organizational behaviour were concerned, while the other resembled unit production. (It would be interesting to compare this with Burns' assessment of innovation.)

To supplement this, it is necessary to assess the degree of interchangeability of components between a firm's products; but one finds severe practical limitations to doing this in firms making computers or aircraft or even cars. Smith-Gavine (1963) has published a 'Percentage Measure of Standardization' for attempting to combine a number of factors relating to product standardization, but this leaves a number of problems still unsolved. Easterfield (1964) has published a useful paper on the general questions of the effects of variety on organizations.

But while these and many other methods of comparing the technical characteristics of industrial organizations are in their way useful and illuminating, their value will not become fully apparent until a clear and cogent theoretical framework has been put forward.

Examination of the various factors listed above, and others that have been set out elsewhere (in particular the current work of Emery at the Tavistock Institute of Human Relations on the nature of the unit operations of which the total production process is made up) suggests that the basic characteristic of interest to the social scientist is the extent to which knowledge about the production process and its constituent operations enables effects to be calculated and predictions made.

Such a theoretical basis would also relate the analysis of technical variables to the other main area of interest being pursued in the current research at Imperial College – the nature of the control systems instituted by management to deal with the problems thrown up by the production system.

ENCOUNTERING THE FUTURE

How, then, does one tackle the study of management control systems? If one regards these control systems as being instituted by management to deal with problems thrown up by the nature of the production system, how does one investigate the ways problems are so dealt with?

Eilon (1966) has produced a theoretically comprehensive scheme for the classification of control systems, identifying all the possible factors that could vary from one control situation to another. This classification is based upon the analogy of control theory as applied to mechanical and electronic systems. It is at present too complex for use as a tool for sociological research. However, it does suggest a conceptual framework for the analysis of all forms of control of production systems, and not merely the personal control of subordinate by superior that forms the basis of all the classical discussion of control in industry. Traditionally, control in industry has been exercised through the personal hierarchy of an organization structure, and the concept of a pyramid of authority has become so much a part, both of management ideology and sociological conceptualization, that, without a framework such as that suggested by Eilon, it is easy to overlook the increasing part played by mechanisms of a non-personal nature in the control of an ever-widening area of routine action.

In particular, control theory calls for investigation of the operation of feedback in the control of production processes. In feedback systems, actual achievement is compared with a desired result, and information about any discrepancy is signalled to a controller for use in deciding what corrective action should be taken. Control theory suggests that the operation of feedback enables a system (*a*) to deal with uncertain knowledge of the likely outcome of a particular action, and (*b*) to stabilize or otherwise make predictable the outputs resulting from variations in input.

In production systems, these two factors pose real management problems. Since a production system is a socio-technical system, subject at least to the unpredictability inherent in the existence of a human component to the system, the outcomes of particular actions are invariably uncertain. This is the bread and butter of the industrial engineer and the operational researcher. But even apart from the intrusion of the human factor into the engineering system, the outcome of action may remain uncertain. Where manufacturing processes are being carried out near the boundaries of engineering knowledge, predictability and calculability may not be complete. And in practice, whatever the sophistication of the process, in terms both of the manufacturing operations being performed, and of the associated control function, some human monitoring duty invariably remains (see Chapter 10).

So also with the problem of variations in input to a production system, the relevance of considering the operation of feedback is clearly apparent. Since a production system is operating within the environment of a market, the input in terms of demand can be seen to be very rarely predictable in exact terms. But even given the most effective market research, most production systems face the difficulties arising from the fact that the total manufacturing process is made up of a number of operations or stages. As a result, manufacturing objectives have to be divided up into sub-objectives or departmental plans, and each of these is subject to disruption through the unforeseen or uncontrolled variations or fluctuations in the performance of the others.

Such a way of looking at management control systems is still vastly over-simplified and far removed from the complexities of the everyday, real industrial world. But even if it does not yet provide any answers to managers' questions about organizational design, it does begin to suggest a framework within which some of the important questions can be asked.

It suggests that in considering the design of organizations one should begin by asking questions. These questions would concern the following: what the firm's products are and its processes of production; the factors of uncertainty and unpredictability inherent in these processes; the human contribution needed for effective control; and the kinds of personal relationships best suited to satisfying simultaneously both the needs of this control function and the social and psychological needs of the people involved. Clearly this is the beginning of a story and not the end, but one can take heart from the contributions to such an approach made by Wiener's (1950) analysis, *The Human Use of Human*

Beings, and by the current work on socio-technical unit design by Emery and others at the Tavistock Institute of Human Relations.

And not the least of the possible values of such an approach is that it may help to explode some of the myths surrounding the question of the effects of automation. There is still a fairly widespread fear that automation will result in unemployment. But if we regard automation as increasing the adaptability of production systems in dealing with situations of uncertainty, then a different outcome seems more likely. The more adaptable production systems become, the greater variability they will be able to cope with. It seems likely that where the nineteenth century was characterized by increased standardization in the production and supply of manufactured goods, the twenty-first century will be characterized by an increase in the extent to which manufacturing industry caters for individual differences in demand. This, together with the likely continuation of the tendency for manufacturing processes to be pushed towards the boundaries of engineering knowledge, would produce a situation of greater variability and uncertainty in production processes, requiring associated control systems of a sophisticated nature, geared to dealing with the greater uncertainty. In such a situation, the characteristically human contribution in both the design and the operation of the systems could well require a fuller use of human capacities than at present, and lead, as a result, to a greater development of the capacity for individual satisfaction.

CHAPTER 17

The Nature of Morale

ROGER HOLMES

'THE term *Morale* refers to a condition of physical and emotional well-being in the individual that makes it possible for him to work and live hopefully and effectively, feeling that he shares the basic purposes of the groups of which he is a member: and that makes it possible for him to perform his task with energy, enthusiasm and self-discipline, sustained by the conviction that, in spite of obstacles and conflict, his personal and social ideas are worth pursuing.'

THREE MEANINGS OF 'MORALE'

IN this chapter we are concerned with the nature of 'Morale' – perhaps the most frequently invoked of all motivational concepts in occupational social psychology. But what is morale? The frequency of its use would sometimes seem to be rivalled only by the number of different meanings attributed to it. What we shall try to do here is to describe some of the uses to which the word is put and then to show the ways in which these uses can be seen to be interrelated. In the course of such an analysis we shall argue, in the context of a somewhat wider discussion of group relationships, that the kinds of uses we shall outline are indeed interrelated and that the confusion surrounding the term is due to the fact that one kind of 'morale' can lead to another.

But what are these various meanings? The above quotation (which shall remain anonymous) seems to include within its span most of them. We shall therefore use it as an anchor point in this discussion. At least three meanings are implied, and we shall take these three meanings one at a time. In the first place it refers to what we shall call 'identification with the group goal'. In the words of the quotation, an individual feels 'he shares the basic purposes of the groups of which he is a member', and a man with 'high

353

morale' is 'sustained by the conviction that his personal and [more to the point here] social ideas are worth pursuing'.

In the second place, and somewhat differently, the quotation implies fairly strongly that the man with high morale is somehow euphoric, or at least is generally hopeful and enthusiastic. 'Morale' is 'a condition of physical and emotional well-being in the individual', an emotional well-being that allows him to perform his task 'with energy, enthusiasm and self-discipline'.

Lastly, the quotation implies that the individual with high morale is not just identified with the group goal and satisfied with his identification, he is also effective. The implication in the passage above that those with high morale work better than those without is fairly clear.

We will now take these definitions and give them labels. Later we hope to show their interrelationship. First, then, some definitions.

Aims morale. This is the name I give to the first meaning distinguished in the above quotation – that of identification with the group goal. 'Morale' is frequently used in this sense. It is, for instance, the definition that Viteles (1954) used in his *Motivation and Morale in Industry*. 'Morale,' he quoted, was a state of 'satisfaction with, desire to continue in and willingness to strive for the goals of a group or organization'. The meaning of this kind of morale – if it means anything at all – lies in the fact that the individual renounces his direct, personal, advantage for the sake of the common good. It describes, in other words, a form of altruism. The individual with high aims morale is concerned to 'give' and not to 'get', to support the group cause, not to maximize his individual return. Put like this it sounds somewhat extreme – but this is the implication nonetheless. Indeed if we examine the consequences of this particular state of mind, it is hard to resist the assumption (and I shall not attempt to do so) that the 'group cause' or the 'common good', or the 'group' itself for that matter, is not only reified, in that it is seen somehow to exist as an entity 'out there' in its own right, but also to some extent idealized. The larger whole with which the individual is identified – be it the regiment, the school, the country, the firm, or the project – is considered to be not so much 'significant' as 'Significant'. It, and all its attributes, warrant capital letters. It is venerated and treated with awe. The individual belongs to an 'Important Firm' (not an 'important firm') – there is a discontinuity between an individual and the qualitatively superior entity, that he is 'proud to serve'. Most of this paper will be taken up with explication of this phenomenon – a phenomenon that, on inspection, has a very wide application indeed.

Progress morale. This is the name I give to the second meaning extracted from the quotation. It refers to the state of feeling that allows the individual (to quote again) 'to work and live hopefully', performing his task with 'enthusiasm'. It refers also to the commonly noted feeling of exhilaration that can come to those who are adequately pursuing a task that is within their powers. Hence the title I have given it, 'progress morale'. A sense of failure or inadequacy – defeat in battle, failure in one's examinations, failure to meet a production deadline – can put a very severe strain on morale in this sense; for it is, after all, basically a state of optimism and hope.

This form of morale seems to me to be different in one important respect from aims morale: aims morale, at least as described here, is of necessity a group phenomenon in that one must revere something outside oneself – one's God, king, discipline, profession, or institution. Progress morale, on the other hand, can be either an individual or a group phenomenon – one can get the corporate sense of progress that is known as 'team spirit', but one can get equally well an individual sense of progress or despair. We can talk of a student having 'high morale' or 'low morale' all on his own. He may get up early in the morning, whistling as he greets each day, confident of his First, or he can slump ever further into the slough of despond, growing for ever more certain that his present bafflement with his subject matter will later on be translated into an official verdict.

These are the only two terms we shall deal with, and before rejecting the third distinction we drew from the original quotation – the effectiveness of those who are committed – we shall return to Aims Morale for a moment and make a further distinction.

We shall distinguish between what we shall call 'vocational aims morale' and 'organizational aims morale'. In the former case one joins an institution because one already believes; in the latter case, belief is an emergent property, one believes because one belongs.

If one joins a particular school as a teacher because one wants to 'educate the masses', if one volunteers in wartime because one wants to 'do one's bit', if one enters a religious order because one wants to 'spread the word of God', then clearly one's identification with the cause comes first, and one's membership of the institution is an expression of that identification. This is 'vocational aims morale' – the aims morale of those who have a sense of 'vocation' or dedication before the event. Such 'prior dedication' may be totally pre-emptive, but on the other hand it may be almost totally lacking – particularly it would seem amongst those who enter a humdrum concern for the sake of private gain. The reader may have noted that there was no industrial example given just above. This was because it seemed to me unlikely that very many people would enter a firm to 'raise productivity' or to 'serve the cause of making biscuits'. Most people take a job in industry because they want to earn a living: such people are unlikely to feel any strong commitment before the event.

But must we therefore assume that there can be no aims morale outside the heady preserves of the remote and the ideal? I do not think so, for two reasons. In the first place vocational aims morale must always be a question of degree and so applicable to some extent; in the second place it seems to me that involvement can be the result as well as the cause of membership. If we join an organization (to take the first point) we are bound to see that organization as some sort of reflection, however pale, of our earlier authorities to which we may still in some measure be in thrall. Organizations, then, may be respected just because they are there at all. A measure of 'loyalty' may be natural rather than the reverse.

Important as such a diffuse kind of loyalty can be, we are not concerned with it in this chapter. We shall concern ourselves here with the second point – not with the legacy of a moral past, but with the emergence of a moral present, with the development of loyalty to a superordinate cause that is the *result* of working towards that cause. This form of loyalty, the loyalty that springs out of activity rather than itself determining it, we call 'organizational aims morale'. Organizational aims morale, unlike vocational aims morale, presents us with a difficulty: how is it possible to become loyal to a superordinate group goal, to be content, for instance, to work not just for one's own sake but also for the 'firm (or department, or work group) at large'? All this would imply a loss of autonomy and the recognition of the existence of something greater than the self. This, as already noted, is the main problem to which we address ourselves here.

Indeed, the main assumption can be stated at this point – we shall argue that organizational aims morale arises out of successful group progress morale – that dedication to a group cause will arise out of a common striving for that cause. The reader will note that this hypothesis – if it can be made in any way plausible – has the advantage of reconciling within itself the various uses of the term 'morale'. Indeed, the very confusion surrounding the term will in some measure have been explained – confusion is to be expected when the different meanings of a term can be shown to be causally related.

Before discussing this assumption in any detail, we must first make clear that we are not concerned with the third usage of the term 'morale' mentioned in the quotation – that concerning the euphoria and effectiveness of those who enjoy 'high morale'.

Morale is sometimes loosely used to cover a state in which those involved are simultaneously happy and hard-working. This indeed was implied in the quotation where the individual with high morale was said to be working both 'hopefully and effectively'. This type of usage has been particularly common where the 'objective indices' of morale have been used – lateness, voluntary absence, labour turnover figures, for instance, as measures of 'satisfaction' and output per man hour as a measure of 'satisfactoriness'.

We will not discuss morale in this sense at all – here we are solely concerned with aims morale and progress morale as we have defined them. There are already two acceptable terms, 'satisfaction' and 'satisfactoriness', and I see no reason why the confusion caused by giving the term morale indiscriminate meanings should be compounded here. (The reason it has come about is fairly clear – we can only measure what our measures let us measure and in our dissatisfaction after the event, we are all too prone to deny

357

ourselves this fact: since morale is 'there' – after all people talk about it – we must somehow have measured it.) It is quite true, in my view, that 'satisfactoriness' and 'satisfaction' can be closely linked, but they need not be so, and the use of any term which suggests that they somehow must coincide is but leading us into wishful thinking.

Not only is it silly because one may work for all sorts of reasons, but also because there is no good reason for assuming that a 'loyal' employee – as defined in terms of aims morale – is a better worker than one who is more mobile, more pragmatic, and more critical in his approach. There is no *necessary* relationship between committal and either satisfactoriness or satisfaction – committal refers only to *why* you do something, not how much you do or how happy you feel about it. Committal can certainly lead to constancy in the face of adversity (a 'loyal' employee may not leave the firm so soon), but against that it may equally well lead to parochialism, conservatism, and a general ossification of the pragmatic spirit. Further – and this may sound odd – it can very well lead to outright insubordination. There are few more dangerous subordinates than those who are more identified with the group cause than are their masters. Such a subordinate, where he feels that his 'betters' are wanting in dedication and application, will attack the 'betters' not with a secret guilt but with the relish of those who see the presumptuous exposed. From the point of view of the Pope, Luther took Christianity too seriously.

'Morale', here, will then refer to aims morale and progress morale. Indeed we are only really concerned with one problem in this chapter – organizational aims morale, the nature and derivation of emergent group committal.

TWO DIMENSIONS OF INDIVIDUAL ORIENTATION

So much for the various uses of the word 'morale'. Before proceeding to the main point of our argument – the explication of my hypothesis that group progress morale leads to organizational aims morale – we shall have to analyse the notion of aims morale in some greater detail.

If aims morale is in any way relevant it is worth taking seriously, since it would seem flatly to contradict the notion (particularly dear it would appear to certain of the tough-minded) that man is a self-centred being who indulges (as far as he is able) in intelligent, in-strumental, 'problem-solving' behaviour in order to maximize his individual returns. To the extent that our description of aims morale holds, and to the extent that aims morale actually does exist, then man is, by that measure at least, not acting like this. An in-dividual who wishes to 'serve the group goal' in the way we have described fails on both counts. In the first place he does not wish to maximize his direct personal returns, he wishes to 'give' and not 'get' – to 'serve' not to 'make use of'; in the second place, he does not behave in an instrumental, 'problem-solving' way. He wishes to 'give', not 'get', because he regards the group goal – idealized and reified (that is, seen as existing in its own right) as it is – with awe. For him the apperception of the group goal is abstracted from those relational comparisons that are the basis of intelligence. To treat such a group goal in a rational, instrumental way – that is, to be loyal out of calculation, to profess devotion to a firm just be-cause they pay well – is to treat such a group goal with less rever-ence than it deserves.

What are we then to make of aims morale? Are we to consider it but an instance of aberrant behaviour only to be found amongst idealists, largely irrelevant to the general run of men? We might be tempted to answer 'yes' – but the state of mind that we have at-tempted to describe appears, on inspection, to be very widespread indeed.

If we look a little closer, it turns out to be coterminous with the concept 'group' – not a 'group' by geography or ascription (thus an experimenter will put four people round a table and claim he has a 'group', presumably on grounds of propinquity, or again one can define a group in industry in terms of the interlocking roles that one has prescribed), but a 'psychological' group that resides in the loyalties and in the sense of identity of its members. This form of 'group' can be of any size, but however large or small it may be, it can be shown to possess the lineaments of aims morale.

The industrial enterprise is not so useful for purposes of ex-position here, so the examples will be given from elsewhere. But we should remember, of course, that in industry too one can be expected to 'serve' – at least that is what the managing director says he is doing – in a somewhat static, undifferentiated way. But much clearer examples can be found. Thus we have a national 'group'. Certain people feel very strongly that they belong (psychologically) to a certain nation state. This state is reified and idealized in their eyes – they regard it as somehow 'existing' in its own right and they regard it with awe. The state is an entity they are 'proud to serve'. Anyone who tries to maximize his returns in an instrumental way – that is, goes over to the enemy when he is persuaded that the enemy has a better chance of winning – gets very short shrift. There are few more emotive words than 'treason', 'traitor', and 'betrayal'.

Our attitudes are similar when we consider such disparate groupings as the profession and the face-to-face 'primary group'. In the professions, too, one is expected to be loyal, and to 'serve'. This 'service', a reflection of a loyalty that may profoundly affect someone's sense of identity, involves again an idealization and a reification ('the standing of the medical profession'), and a suspension of any problem-solving behaviour that implies a preoccupation with direct, personal rewards. What, after all, is a swot, a rate-buster, or a deserter but someone who is attempting to maximize, as best he is able, his individual rewards? A deserter very sensibly puts his own life first, a rate-buster his own purse. What could be more rational – at least if one assumes a primal self-centredness – than that? With the face-to-face group, of course, the idealization and reification of a group as an entity *as such* is much less clearly seen than with the other example. Still, even here the skeleton of such a reification can be perceived. Thus group members may talk about the 'group' as if it somehow existed over and above the members composing it. In the same way people may talk about 'letting the side down' as if 'the side' was an entity in its own right.

There are similarities between states of aims morale and what might be called 'ordinary groups' – in both cases there is a 'psychological group' that is idealized and reified in the members' eyes, that evokes sentiments of loyalty and the need to 'give' and to 'serve'. All this can be opposed to the pragmatism of psychologically isolated individuals, who attempt to maximize their individual returns, who try to 'get' not to 'give', who regard the corporate entity, as such, to be an irrelevance. Are there, then, any differences between aims morale and 'ordinary groups'? There are, and we must now look at the peculiar quality of aims morale.

The state of aims morale is essentially a 'dynamic' state. The 'group goal' – winning the battle, finishing the corporate task – is a problem that must be solved. Those with aims morale face the future – a future that is clouded in doubt. Where the battle is wholly assured, there would the characteristic element of 'striving' be somehow lost: 'Onward, Christian soldiers, marching as to war'. When the war is won, where will the soldiers march? This is the question we must not ask, for then we would no longer feel the exhilaration of those who rejoice in the enemy *being* defeated. Aims morale, in other words, as suggested in the hypothesis, is compounded of progress morale – a corporate sense of movement or purpose.

But there can still be committal where the battle is won – but it is a committal of a different order. It is the quietist 'renewal' of those who have already 'arrived'. This is best exemplified in ritual. Ritual is surely the opposite of aims morale. In ritual, one is not facing the future, one is facing the past – a past that holds the moment of our acceptance and tells us before we start how our conduct should go. There is no 'problem' facing us in the same sense – instead of doubt we find certainty, instead of the clear-cut criterion of success, there is the conformity implicit in cleaving to precedent. The exhilaration of achievement is replaced by the reaffirmation of those who testify their faith anew.

Thus there are two dimensions, not one, of individual activity. There is the 'commitment–self-sufficiency' dimension that distinguishes all forms of 'group behaviour' from non-group behaviour, and there is also a 'static–dynamic' continuum that distinguishes between an orientation to the past and an orientation to the future. These two dimensions can be set out as in Figure 25.

Point A reflects pure ritual, point B, pure aims morale. Point C gives us an individual indulging in solitary, compulsive behaviour, point D, the pragmatic individual facing the future alone.

Before discussing the problems posed by the existence of these two dimensions, two further observations must be made.

In the first place, a 'group' can find itself, not just in one of the four corners of Figure 25, but anywhere on the space described by the two axes – thus none of the four 'ordinary groups' we described would find themselves all the time at point A. A group may find itself on different points at different times. Thus at times of corporate reaffirmation – such as religious services and military parades – groups may well be at position A, but the same group

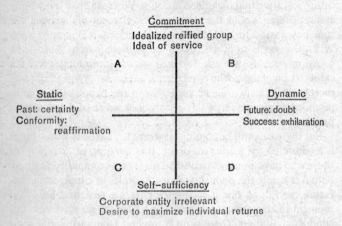

Figure 25. Two dimensions of individual orientation

in times of challenge and doubt – the church 'militant', the army 'in war' – will move to position B. But the compound of conviction and pragmatism that probably characterizes all groups may be differently constituted in different cases. All groups (national, religious, professional, and face-to-face, for instance) have their problems and their rituals. However, certain groups seem to be of their nature more 'problem-centred', others more 'ritual-centred'. Thus it may not be altogether fanciful to regard the Fascist (for all his super-manic pretensions) as one who is nostalgic for a pure and primitive past, while a Communist looks forward to the dawn of a new era. But what happens if the Communist succeeds? 'Doubt' may not last for ever and with 'certainty' a reaction may set in – the successful Communist runs the risk of becoming indistinguishable from the Fascist, defending the *status quo* for its own sake. Either that, or he may resort to such hysterical re-evocation of 'battles-yet-to-be-won' as seen in the behaviour of the Red Guards in China in the mid-sixties.

'Red Guards' are fortunately rare – particularly so in industry. Most organizations, on achieving success, go the other way. Instead of getting more exercised, they get more somnolent; instead of raising their standards to loftier and loftier heights, they become, on the contrary, more and more readily satisfied. They relapse, in other words, into a comfortable, uninspiring, undemanding routine, in which all is predictable and yet all is in some way revered. For the God of the Past has defeated the God of the Future and all now worship at the altar of Tradition.

The movement is usually not from B to an ever more hysterical B, but from B to A. In the literature of organization theory, this moral encrustation of the rational arteries has been clearly expounded by Merton (1940). In discussing the 'pathology of bureaucracy' he shows how the most 'rational' and pragmatic of all organizational systems (Weber's 'legal–rational' bureaucracy) becomes ritualized through sheer success. Where the problems can be anticipated, so will 'means' become 'ends in themselves'. Bureaucracies are not geared for challenge – there is no challenge left where the work has been adequately codified – they are geared to continuity and the self-righteousness of quiescence. Where the future cannot surprise there can we grow our roots into the past. All this is perhaps inevitable and not very surprising. What is surprising, however, is the complacency with which this change is greeted. Torn from the sanction of failure, actions come to derive their legitimacy from precedent. Filling up the form correctly becomes more important than getting the job done, and as a result we can get the total triumph of ritual – every act can become normative, valued in and of itself.

The import is clearly this – aims morale may be something of a sensitive, and even a self-defeating plant: what could be more self-defeating than to be frozen by one's very success? Which brings us to the second observation. Norms – all norms – are essentially conservative. A norm implies an equilibrium, that is a state of affairs which is psychologically valued in and of itself, and in which there are resident forces that will reassert this balance when the balance is disturbed. Thus, in the 'ordinary groups' we cited – the national, religious, professional, and face-to-face groups – one is not supposed to give 'aid and comfort' to the enemy, blaspheme, advertise, or 'grass'. If one does, sanctions, designed to re-establish the *status quo*, will follow – one will be shot, sent to hell, struck off the register, or ostracized. Now the oddity lies in this – a state of aims morale, although facing the future and not the past, is nonetheless heavily normative. One is expected to 'muck in' and 'pull one's weight'. There is a clear code of 'what must be done' despite the fact that 'what must be done', since it is conditioned by an evolving situation, may be constantly changing.

This is odd enough, but there is a similar contradiction in the static situation. Aims morale is characterized by 'purpose', and 'purpose' implies a future state of affairs that it is intended to reach. (An act is said to be 'purposive' if it is better described by its end point than by any of the specific measures used to attain that end.) Since 'purpose' is forward-looking, ritual and tradition cannot be said to have a 'purpose' in the same sense that instru-mental, problem-centred behaviour can. And yet – and this is the oddity – ritual and tradition *are* said to have a 'purpose'. Ritual, which in strict learning theory terms can be explained in terms of pure reflex chains, is sometimes said to possess the qualities of more forward-looking complex behaviour.

THE GROWTH OF COMMITMENT AND THE VICTORY OF TRADITION

So much for a description of the problem; now for explanation. However, we have set ourselves several further problems since first explicating the hypothesis put forward, and the total range of the issues raised is now something like the following:

(1) We must attempt to account for the growth of aims morale – movement from D to B on Figure 25. We must further justify the assumption that this movement comes about through group progress morale.

(2) We should simultaneously account for the development of ritual and tradition – movement from C to A.

(3) We have mentioned a further problem when speaking of the self-defeating nature of aims morale – movement from B to A.

(4) There are the two oddities we have just outlined – that of B being 'normative' and A being 'purposive'.

(5) For reasons of parsimony (and perhaps cynicism) it would be pleasant to explain the growth of commitment through a 'self-centred' non-commitment assumption. Commitment cannot in any event be explained in terms of itself.

We shall attempt to deal with these problems in two stages. First, we shall be concerned with the vertical axis of Figure 25 – the problem of the growth of commitment. Next, we shall turn to the horizontal axis, the peculiar nature of aims morale and its distinction from ritual. We shall try to explain the growth of commitment in the simplest possible way. We shall make the overall working assumption ('hypothesis' is too grand a term) that we are all anarchic and self-centred in our preoccupations, that we are at root indifferent to any higher-order law and morality and are primarily concerned to control our environment and maximize our individual returns. (The reader will note that this comes very close to the tough-minded assumption we said was held by certain observers.) Such narcissism is our ideal – but it is an ideal that can never be realized. It cannot be so, for we must live in the company of others – others as narcissistic and as self-centred as ourselves. How then can we gain our solitary victory – a victory that we will not be denied? We can do so by forming an alliance with those whom we cannot ignore. With their cooperation we erect a code that is revered by one and all. This code is then identified with and each group member can see such a code as 'his own', as an extension of himself. Each is then granted the illusion that compliance to this code is compliance to himself. Each can gain a vicarious victory and thus can we all re-attain, in the bosom of our group, our earlier lost self-sufficiency.

We are reduced to morality. Where we cannot gain our victories alone we will erect a common code that prescribes the behaviour, not only of ourselves but of others as well. This code is idealized, for it is seen as an extension of that which we hold most dear – our narcissistic selves. We are then prepared to 'give' and to 'serve' this code, for we are but 'giving' to that which is our own. The conflict between primitive narcissism and corporate 'service' can be reconciled if we talk in terms of an extended rather than a bounded self.

A 'group' in these terms will be a collection of people who use each other for the creation of a corporate self-justifying myth. By this argument, 'groups' should arise under certain circumstances rather than others – namely when there is a large enough (or at least a powerful enough) number of those present who have an interest in the creation of such a myth. This should occur where people are dependent upon each other but have common interests. Thus we would expect, for instance, a code of restriction of output in a face-to-face group to arise where there are a sufficient number of those present who would fear a genuine state of free enterprise. The fastest worker will not be in favour of such a code, since he would lose money, but the 'average' worker would – he would not run the risk of being 'shown up' by those who are better than himself.

This principle has a very wide application. Thus it could not only explain the growth of a 'professional ethic' by exactly the same logic, but it could also account, for instance, for laws against murder and adultery. These laws can be seen as the result of a coalition of the weak – those of doubtful physical and sexual prowess – against the strong. After all, what the weak man has to forgo is very much less than he gains. He forgoes the problematic right to take the law into his own hands, he gains security from such unilateral behaviour on the part of others.

This code is the inheritor of our primitive narcissism and so it attains that state we all seek – indifference to others. There are none so heartless as those that believe. To each other, group members may well feel a warm sympathy, but this is not surprising, for each group member can see the compliance of the other as a compliance to himself. It is in their attitude to those 'who do not belong' that this heartlessness becomes manifest. Our code has the arrogance of an absolute – 'our' law is above all. Those who do not obey – the heretic, the deviant, or the alien – must be proscribed (or at best despised) because they call our unreal pretensions into doubt. In a very real sense they challenge our power.

Hence the most tragic and common of our failings – our intolerance of those who do not share our convictions.

If what we have said is given credence – if there really is a war of all against all, personally self-centred as we are – then suspicion of the other must be endemic. It will only be when we are able to see for ourselves that the other is equally obedient that we will be able to form a relationship with him, and accept him as 'one of us'. This is easy in the face-to-face group (and hence, in my view, its psychological importance), but how will we form such a relationship in the large group – in the national group, the religious group, the group of those who have forsworn murder?

This brings us to the position of the leader, a position of central importance in any account of 'group' life. The leader must 'serve' the code, for an exhibition of unlicensed narcissism is something that we could never willingly accept. Indeed he must give so much 'service' that he must become, in a strict sense, its outright 'servant'. The leader is expected before all else to enforce the dictates of the group. Only thus can we have an extended group: we must rely on other 'leaders' – the government, the police force, public opinion – to do our enforcement for us. We rely on the traitor being caught and the heretic being arraigned, by those to whom we have granted power to do our will. Were it not for this consolation, a larger 'group' could not form at all.

But what of the strongest man of the tribe, the fastest worker? Why should they accept a code that can but hinder them in their pursuit of their goal? They will accede because, provided the code is enforced, they may well have no alternative. They may choose to rebel against the code of their fellows, but then they must risk the persecution reserved for those who do not obey. Why not join the big battalions if one has no hope of winning? Why not identify oneself with a morality that can in any event not be evaded and see its power, not as an alien force that constrains, but as an extension of one's own will, providing opportunities for a wider glory upon the social scene?

Those confronted by an ongoing morality, then, are grievously tempted to join. A law that is enforced will probably always find its willing adherents. Workers today, at least by this argument, may well be less willing to obey, more factious and preoccupied with immediate personal reward, just because management is unable to enforce its laws. But workers too will demand a price. Managers also must pay, they too must 'believe' and devote themselves to some higher-order cause. Obedience was never 'willingly' given to an individual who did not himself conform. If our betters do not 'obey' how can we be repaid the advantages that derive from our altruistic concern?

In this short account we cannot hope to follow the implications at all adequately. Certain features of the 'commitment' end of our vertical dimension have been described – we will have a 'group' where we find a collusion in a joint fantasy of power. We will 'give', for we will be but giving to that which we are intimately dependent upon for the maintenance of our illusions; we will idealize for we will have found, in corporate means, a return to a primitive narcissism. But should we *reify* the object of our reverence? There is no problem here; what could be more self-centred than to assume that our fantasies really exist as discrete objects in the world of a higher reality? What could conceivably be more narcissistic than to make the jump from 'I like' to 'it is good', from 'I think' to 'it is so'? Reification is but part and parcel of reading the outside world as an extension of the self.

So much for the first problem, the movement to commitment from self-sufficiency, described in terms of the explanatory predilection we avowed – that of an explanation which did not imply an anterior commitment for its force. We now turn to the horizontal axis and deal with the distinction between aims morale and ritual, and the relationship between them. In this account we are also concerned with the 'oddities' mentioned earlier – that the two states may have more in common than we have any right to expect – that aims morale can be normative, and ritual purposive. We will first deal with aims morale in isolation, then turn to its relationship with ritual.

The development of norms under 'dynamic' conditions – conditions that present one with a problem and where the future is in doubt – must be an exceedingly precarious affair. In the first place those confronted by a problem must use their brains, they must be resourceful in anticipating the future, they must be prepared to be flexible and to adapt their actions to moving necessities.

Behaviour must, as we have already said, be 'problem-centred' and, in terms of the end point, rational. Now the difficulty in this state of affairs – where what is 'right' cannot easily be laid down before the event and where conduct must be judged by its results rather than by conformity to procedure – lies in the perennial problem of stilling suspicion. Shorn of our knowledge that certain behaviour has already been legitimated, our problem of ensuring to ourselves the compliance of others is considerably increased. It is perhaps for this reason that conditions of aims morale – unlike those of ritual – will probably always be found at their most intense in small, face-to-face groups, amongst those who know each other intimately and are able to see for themselves – as no one outside the group can ever see (even perhaps with the very best of leadership, although that can help) – the dedication of the other to the common good.

Secondly, this difficulty is rendered the more acute by the very nature of a 'norm'. As we have seen, a 'norm' is essentially static, an equilibrium, to which there are ever pressures to revert. Norms, all norms, are at bottom reactionary and conservative. How, then, can there be a norm at all in a changing situation? The answer is that there cannot – not in any ordinary sense. What one is enjoined to do is to enter into a higher-order committal with a wider application. One is expected to 'enter into the spirit' of it, one is expected to give 'willing cooperation and not count the cost'.

These are vague prescriptions, difficult to define and so difficult to enforce. It seems to me that the precarious nature of any 'dynamic' situation is that which accounts for its peculiarly exhilarating qualities while it lasts, and accounts also for its ossification into ritual when the pressure is released.

The exhilaration will be that of a perilous victory. Where compliance is the more difficult to exact, there will that compliance be the more valuable to us; where we are reduced to relying on 'good will', there will that 'good will' be greeted with the greater gratitude. Hence the camaraderie of those who fight together and do not defect. But such a camaraderie must be precarious while it lasts and, of necessity, short-lived.

It will depend, for its very existence, on the continued success of the joint enterprise. Only with continued success can this unstable fusion of volitions be preserved. Organizational aims morale (to come to the hypothesis we outlined at the beginning of this chapter) must be based on group *progress* morale: while group progress is being maintained, doubts may be stilled in the light of the overwhelming evidence of objective achievement. But only so long. Failure will put a very severe strain on the relationship, for it can well imply that some other has been disloyal. Particularly incensed will be those with vocational aims morale who arrive armoured in their committal, whose loyalty has a stronger wind and is not so dependent upon outside success. These may all too easily convince themselves of the weakness and turpitude of others.

But failure is not the only predator upon the spirit of corporate venture; success itself can pose an equally dangerous, although different, challenge. *The corporate goal must be constantly renewed.* Any firm that wants to remain mentally alive must seek new goals, must, in a sense, wantonly engender stress. For great is the seduction – once the problem is solved, and 'what needs to be done' becomes more and more explicitly known – no longer to tolerate a resort to the discretion of others. We may thankfully withdraw to a safer, if less exhilarating, set of relationships where prescriptions can be more explicitly laid down and compliance more readily enforced. 'Loyalty', committal to the over-riding 'group cause', is – by the terms of this chapter at least – but the moral extension of a hope for power. Those most 'loyal', those most identified with the *status quo*, will be the most reactionary and the most confirmed in their rejection of the new. For the *status quo* will be 'their' *status quo* and criticism thereof will be taken personally.

This movement from 'dynamic' to 'static' conditions is the re-establishment of the equilibrium to which all groups will return once the pressure of the environment is removed. This development, provided it is not taken too far, is by no means all sheer loss. Some measure of formalization allows of a much wider identification with the firm itself. A measure of continuity can become the very bones of the wider society, it can provide us with an external conceptual framework to which we can relate our corporate existence. It is difficult to see how, without such continuity, the individual could come to have any feelings about the larger organization at all. (Indeed some such certainty of ground, coupled with a residual vocational aims morale, or at least a predisposition to venerate authority, may serve well enough for most individuals. They may even come to evince feelings of diffuse 'loyalty' to the firm at large.)

However the outcome may not be so fortunate – not where this process is taken too far. Where the adventitiousness of the environment is wholly removed, we may, through our insatiable appetite for power, reattain that equilibrium to which all groups will tend. We may demand greater and greater dominion over the minds of others and thus attain the total, satisfying 'pathology' of bureaucratization that we in our hearts desire. Everything – but everything – will have become traditional. Instant status will now be possible with the minimum of effort. Our curtains, cars, procedures, dress (and, worse still, production methods and design policy) will be conformist (that is, undemanding of thought), a symbol of our obeisance – that which grants us an inner victory – to that which we have neither the energy nor the will to question.

But hardly any firm is as exalted and as reactionary as that. Thought is usually needed at some stage and there is usually lurking in even the very safest of markets the ultimate sanction of possible failure. Such a 'consummation devoutly to be wished' is as a rule attained only in high ceremony. Only there can we gain our final, solitary victory. But even then we may have doubts, and it is for this reason, in my view (and to come to my second 'oddity'), that those engaged in ritual may yet talk in terms of 'purpose'. The 'purpose' of a ritual is that of winning our battles anew, of reassuring ourselves of the continued dedication of others. Indeed, were this not so, were the behaviour of the other to be totally predictable, there might we very well ignore the compliance that can offer us no triumph. No sect, as far as I know, has ever prescribed that its members should sometimes sleep.

This discussion of ritual throws into relief a problem of aims morale that we have not yet tackled directly. The problem is that of the nature of the 'cause' around which the group is polarized. Certain causes are attractive and will readily appeal, but others are less so. How can we be inspired by the humdrum? How, we asked somewhat superciliously, can one be dedicated to the cause of 'making biscuits'? The answer is now clear – an injunction or a cause derives its power to inspire us, not because of its nature or the objective purpose of that required behaviour, but because of the relationship with others that that behaviour implies. This is particularly clear in the case of ritual, for there we see wholly automatic behaviour, surely reminiscent of ant societies, invoking in us the profoundest feelings of significance and reality. Such an effect upon us is not due to the acts themselves – these acts can be of any kind – but to the total victory of each over all that is symbolized in our enactment. The same argument can be said to hold for 'dynamic' conditions (only slightly less clearly because of the greater prominence of the 'objective' task) – it is not 'making biscuits' that is revered, it is the compliance of others in the making of biscuits that we value.

*

We have considered the problem of morale as a special case of the wider problem of commitment, the underlying need of us-all to gain a victory over all others. Aims morale is but a perilous and exhilarating example that requires, for its maintenance, continued success – or 'progress'. Once the pressure of circumstance is removed, we shall return to that quietus – whether it be found in industry or elsewhere, in the tradition of the workshop or in court ceremonial – in which all shall obey. That such a quietus has on the whole been so little reached in our own Western civilization, is, in my view, due to one of the two desiderata of norm formation not being met. Although we are interdependent, we do not have common interests. Competition, so often despised by the more idealist – the war of individual preferment and a larger share of the market – may well (provided it is adequately harnessed and controlled) be the saviour of the open society. Even war, for all its brutalities, may well have had a part in reorienting us to external realities, in posing us problems for which there is no wishful solution. However, the elaboration of these ideas would require more space than is available, and anyway they have already been covered to a certain extent elsewhere (Holmes, 1965), and so will not be pursued here.

In conclusion, we can revert to our original quotation and show how the argument given here would invert the sequence there suggested. The members of the organization do not 'work and live hopefully and effectively' because, as the quotation suggests, each one 'shares the basic purposes of the groups of which he is a member'. Rather, does each one share the basic purposes of his group *because* he (and what the quotation missed out, others as well) works hopefully and effectively; again each one is not 'sustained' in performing 'his task with energy, enthusiasm and self-discipline' by the 'conviction that, despite all obstacles and conflict, his personal and social ideas are worth pursuing', rather are such ideas worth pursuing *because* each (again with others) performs his task with energy and enthusiasm and (above all) self-discipline.

This chapter is incomplete and much more could be said. We have consistently left out anything that might relieve the gloom. The warmth of camaraderie, the possibility of a heartfelt generosity and a love for, rather than a mere use of, the group cause has not been taken into account. This is true. Nevertheless, this approach, incomplete as it is, allows us to relate together a fairly wide area of somewhat disparate material and gives us a possible set of relationships for the various meanings of the word 'morale'.

CHAPTER 18

The Comparative Study of Organizations

D. S. PUGH AND D. J. HICKSON

IT is a commonplace of discussions among administrators and managers to hear that all organizations are different. Frequently the implication is that there can be little in common between them and consequently no coherent description of organizations. Even so, administrators continue to forgather to discuss their problems in a way which suggests that, after all, they find they have common interests and value each other's experience and advice.

For even if all organizations are indeed different it is possible to state these differences and to classify them so that something useful can be said about various kinds of organizations and the ways in which they function. This field of study has become known as 'organization theory'. It is a meeting ground for the managers of privately owned business, administrators of state-owned ministries and agencies, economists, sociologists, and psychologists. The practitioner wants to know how to run his organization to best advantage, and how to cope with the human problems that arise in doing so. The attention of social scientists has been caught by the proliferation of work organizations in modern society. Problems of size have been investigated; the characteristics of organization known as bureaucracy are increasingly studied; and there has been research on a variety of human behaviours at work.

ANALYSIS OF ORGANIZATION STRUCTURE

All organizations have to make provision for continuing activities directed towards the achievement of given aims. Regularities in activities such as task allocation, supervision, and coordination are developed. Such regularities constitute the organization's structure, and the fact that these activities can be arranged in various ways means that organizations can have differing structures.

Indeed, in some respects every organization is unique. But many writers have examined a variety of structures to see if any general principles can be extracted. This variety, moreover, may be related to variations in such factors as the objectives of the organization, its size, ownership, geographical location, and technology of manufacture, which are associated with the characteristic differences in structure of a bank, a hospital, a factory, etc.

The concept of structure is thus central to modern organization theory. Yet despite its importance it remains primitive in empirical application. So far neither manager nor researcher has any means other than personal intuition of knowing how far the structure of Company A is the same as, or different from, that of Company B, or State Agency C. Very often differences are assumed or taken to be obvious; whereas the crucial question is exactly how much they differ. In what respects do they differ, and in each characteristic do they differ a very great deal, a lot, a fair amount, a little, or hardly at all? Even then, phrases like 'a fair amount' or 'a little' are extremely vague. What is needed is precise formulation of characteristics of organization structure, and development of measuring-scales with which to assess differences quantitatively.

The Industrial Administration Research Unit at the University of Aston in Birmingham, whose work is more fully described in Pugh *et al.* (1963), Hickson and Pugh (1965), Pugh (1966), Hickson (1966), and Hinings *et al.* (1967), has been concerned with the problems of such measurements. This has involved (*a*) discovering in what ways an organization structures its activities and (*b*) seeing whether it is possible to create statistically acceptable methods of measuring structural differences between organizations.

Measurement must begin with the ideas as to what characteristics are to be measured. In the field of organization structure the problem is not absence of such ideas, for there are many books and papers discussing what organization is, but rather disentangling from such discussions those variables which can be clearly defined for scientific study. We will take three influential writers, Fayol, Brown, and Weber, as representative sources for our variables.

Henri Fayol (1949) was managing director for thirty years, until 1918, of a French mining and metallurgical combine. From his long experience he distilled a time-honoured definition of what management is: to manage is to forecast and plan, to organize, to command, to coordinate, and to control. In discharging these functions, management should abide by certain principles, one of which is the Principle of Centralization. But Fayol did not mean by this that organizations should always be centralized, for he argued that: 'The question of centralization or decentralization is a simple question of proportion, it is a matter of finding the optimum degree for the particular concern.' Here, then, is an interesting variable capable of empirical study: *Centralization of Authority*. Which organizations in what circumstances are more centralized, and which less so?

Wilfred Brown (1960), like Fayol, writes from his own experience of management and organization. For over twenty years until 1965 he was Chairman of the Glacier Metal Company, which manufactures bearings, and he was also Managing Director for most of this period. As a theorist he aims at clarifying what he believes happens in organizations by stressing that they carry out three distinct functions, executive, representative, and legislative. Discussing the executive or working organization, he subdivides its activities into operational work, which is development, production, and sales, and specialist work, which is in general terms personnel, technical, and programming. Specialists such as personnel officers, engineers, production controllers, chemists support the development, production, and sales departments. There are also specialists in operational work – specialists in research and development and specialist salesmen, etc. Here is a second interesting variable: *Specialization of Roles*. Which organizations in what circumstances break down their activities into the most, or the least, number of specialisms?

Pride of place among sociological theorists in this field goes to Max Weber (1947). He presented a typology of organizations in terms of the sources of the authority on which they are based. Why do subordinates accept the power of their superiors as legitimate? In 'charismatic' organizations, Weber suggested, it is because they have faith in the superlative personal qualities of the leader. In 'traditional' organizations it is because they accept long-standing custom without question. In 'bureaucratic' organizations it is because they submit to the law of rules and procedures.

Each source of authority corresponds to a type of organization.

Weber sees his third type, bureaucracy, as the dominant institution of modern society. In common usage bureaucracy is synonymous with inefficiency, emphasis on red tape, and excessive writing and recording, but Weber pointed out its strengths. In it authority is exercised through the official positions which individuals occupy by a system of regulations. These official positions are arranged in a hierarchy, each successive step embracing in authority all those beneath it. Rules and procedures are drawn up for every conceivable contingency. There are 'bureaux' for the safe keeping of all written records and files – it being an important part of the rationality of the system that information is written down. The system thus aims to develop the most efficient methods by depersonalizing the whole administrative process. Written rule-books, routine procedures, formal training and qualifications for appointment, fixed salary scales, all minimize capricious differences in the handling of the same problem at different times, eliminate nepotism in promotion, and set and maintain standards of efficiency. In modern computer jargon, a bureaucracy is an organization which is completely 'programmed'.

Weber's description of bureaucracy as an 'ideal' or perfect type (very much as economists often postulate 'perfect competition' whilst recognizing that this never occurs in practice) has led to a tendency to assume that an organization either *is* or *is not* bureaucratic. But thinking need not be so confined. It is far more useful to regard organizations as ranging from *more to less* bureaucratic in their activities, so that some have more routines and procedures and paperwork and files, and some have less. Here then are two further variables: *Standardization of Procedures* and *Formalization of Documentation*.

All three authors, Fayol, Brown, and Weber, assume a structure of related roles or positions. Fayol has his principles of 'one man one boss' and limited span of control. Brown has his executive system, Weber, his hierarchy of offices. They all have in mind what is usually summed up in the organization chart. This, too, can be regarded as a variable – or rather a series of variables. It has a 'height', from the man at the top to the man at the bottom; it has varying spans of control of subordinates to each superior, and so on. This 'shape' of the role structure we call its *configuration*.

Thus we have elucidated five primary variables or dimensions of organization structure:

> Specialization
> Standardization
> Formalization
> Centralization
> Configuration

RESEARCH DESIGN AND METHOD

The dimensional method of analysis has a major advantage over classification by types. If scales are devised to measure the dimensions, then the positions on these scales of a particular organization forms a 'profile' of its structure. Even with a comparatively crude analysis we obtain a very large number of theoretically possible profiles (with five dimensions each a ten-point scale, for example, there are a hundred thousand theoretically possible profiles). Of course, many of these theoretical profiles may never appear in reality, and those that are found may cluster into bunches of similarly structured organizations. These bunches may well be labelled 'types', but with the knowledge that these types have not been postulated *a priori* but have been evolved with reference to the empirical data. We can now go beyond individual experience and scholarship to the systematic study of existing organizations.

To begin with, and for convenience, we have limited ourselves to work organizations in the West Midlands employing more than 250 people. A work organization is defined as one that employs (that is, pays) its members. We have constructed scales from data on a cross-sectional sample of fifty-two such organizations. These include leading firms making motor-car bumpers and milk-chocolate buttons, municipal organizations repairing roads and teaching arithmetic, large department stores and small insurance companies, and so on.

We have written first to the chief executive of the organization, who may be a works manager, an area superintendent, or a chairman, and begun by interviewing him at length. There has followed a series of interviews with department heads of varying status, as many as were necessary to obtain the information we required. Interviews have been conducted with standard schedules listing what had to be found out; but since this was descriptive data about structure, and not personal to the respondent, no attempt was made to standardize interview procedure. Wherever possible documentary evidence was sought to substantiate verbal accounts.

It is the strength and weakness of this current project that we use no items unless they are applicable to all work organizations, whatever they do: several possible interesting items have had to be sacrificed to this end. As our research strategy has been to undertake a wide survey to set the guide lines, we have had to pay for this by the superficiality and generality of the data. Further, we have in this project dealt only with the formal organization – the administrative machinery for getting things done. The informal processes of organization have not been considered.

Since organization structure is a construct derived from activities, some concepts of the activities of work organizations are needed which can be applied to both manufacturing and non-manufacturing organizations. We have found the analysis given by Bakke in *Bonds of Organization* to be very useful as a generalized description of the processes of work organizations, and we have relied considerably upon his formulations of the work-flow, perpetuation, and control processes, among others (Bakke, 1950). Bakke's concepts have the merit of being applicable to every work organization whatever its purpose, whether industrial, commercial, retail, public service, etc. So the danger that we would only be concerned with work-flow activities (those involved in the direct production and distribution of the product or service) is avoided if attention is also drawn to perpetuation activities (such as those about buying materials or engaging employees) and to control activities (quality, inspection, budgeting, scheduling, etc.), and so on. By this means a list of items pertinent to each variable was built up. The method was then to ask of each organization, for which of the given list of potentially specializable functions it had in fact a specialized role, for which of the given list of potentially standardizable routines it did have a standardized procedure, and so on.

Our approach to scaling has been guided by techniques of psychological test construction in the main (see also Chapter 19). The major task in this connexion is the demonstration that the items forming a scale 'hang together', that is, they are in some sense cumulative. If this is so, we can represent an organization's comparative position on a characteristic by a numerical score, in the same way as an I.Q. score represents an individual's comparative intelligence. But just as an I.Q. is a sample of a person's intelligence taken for comparative purposes and does not detract from his uniqueness as a functioning individual, so our scales, being likewise comparative samples, do not detract from the uniqueness of each organization's functioning. They do, however, set the guidelines around which the unique variations take place.

THE MEASUREMENT OF THE FIVE PRIMARY DIMENSIONS

Specialization

Analysis of data from a pilot survey of organizations in terms of the Bakke activity variables enabled construction of a list of sixteen activities which are assumed to be present in *all* work organizations, and on which any work organization may therefore be compared with any other. These activities or functions exclude the workflow activities of the organization, and so are not concerned with operatives in manufacturing, sales clerks in retailing, etc. The question is whether an organization has a specialism responsible for an activity, that is, whether it is performed by someone with that function and no other, who is not in the workflow superordinate hierarchy (line chain of command, in management terms). Table 9 lists these specialisms, which form a functional–specialization scale from which a score for each organization can be derived. A range of organizations is found from those where all sixteen activities are performed by non-specialists (for example, in an agency of a central Government department) to those where all the activities are performed by specialists working in a functional relationship to the work-flow management who are left with considerably restricted duties (for example in the vehicle industry and electrical equipment manufacturing).

TABLE 9: *Functional specialization*

(n = 52)   Scale No. 51·01

Specialism Number	Activities to:
1	develop, legitimize and symbolize the organization's charter (Public Relations and Advertising)
2	dispose of, distribute, and service the output (Sales and Service)
3	carry outputs and resources from place to place (Transport)
4	acquire and allocate human resources (Employment)
5	develop and transform human resources (Training)
6	maintain human resources and promote their identification with the organization (Welfare and Security)
7	obtain and control materials and equipment (Buying, Stock Control)
8	maintain and erect buildings and equipment
9	record and control financial resources (Accounts)
10	control the workflow (Production Control)
11	control the quality of materials and equipment and outputs (Inspection)
12	assess and devise ways of producing the output (Methods)
13	devise new outputs, equipment, and processes (Design and Development)
14	develop and operate administrative procedures (O and M)
15	deal with legal and insurance requirements (Legal)
16	acquire information on the operational field (Market Research)

Scores: Range –   0–16
        Mean –   10·19
        Standard deviation – 5·19

Given that an organization has a specialism for an activity (that, for example, it has salesmen for Activity 2, or personnel officers for Activity 4) and so it scores on the functional–specialization scale, then scales of role specialization indicate how far the tasks *within* a functional specialism are differentiated and the role of the specialist narrowed down. As an example Table 10 shows the scale for specialism no. 8: activities to maintain and erect buildings and equipment, for which forty-nine of our organizations have specialists. On this, scores range from two up to ten different role specializations within the functional specialism.

381

TABLE 10: *Role specialization – Specialism No. 8*

(n = 49)   Scale No. 51·09

i	Specialized engineer
ii	Specialized machine maintenance
iii	Specialized building maintenance
iv	Specialized electrical maintenance
v	Machine maintenance specialized by process, etc.
vi	Specialized new works force
vii	Specialized surveyor or architect
viii	Specialized instrument maintenance
ix	Specialized research into maintenance
x	Electrical maintenance specialized by process, etc.

Scores: Range – 2–10
       Mean – 4·29
       Standard deviation – 1·89

Standardization

The empirical problems here revolve around defining a procedure and specifying which procedures in the organization are to be investigated. A procedure is taken to be an event that has regularity of occurrence and is legitimized by the organization (no assumption is made whether the procedures are used or not). We have used the Bakke (1950) activity headings to guide the construction of a list of potential procedures. For example:

Control: Quality inspection, ranging from none at all, through haphazard inspection and random sampling, up to the extreme of standardization, 100 per cent inspection of all outputs; and standardized techniques such as statistical quality control.

Financial control, ranging from historical costing through job costing, budgeting, and standard costs, to marginal costing.

Maintenance of equipment from repairs as needed to standardized routines of planned maintenance and programmed replacements.

Perpetuation (of necessary resources): buying routines such as standardized procedures for seeking and evaluating tenders for supply of materials.

Employment procedures such as standardized interviewing by central boards, automatic internal advertisement of vacancies. A range of scores from 30 to 131 is obtained, the extremes being marked by a chain of retail stores and a metals processing plant.

Sub-division of the overall standardization scale enables further differences to be traced among organizations. Bringing together from among the items in the original scale those procedures concerned with selection, discipline, and the like, a scale is constituted of Standardization of Procedures Controlling Personnel Selection and Advancement, etc. This is found to make a crucial distinction between kinds of organizations which will be discussed later. It is constructed in such a way that a high score on it signifies both that an organization *does* standardize procedures controlling the recruitment, selection, advancement, and discipline of employees, and that it *does not* have standardized procedures such as routine quality inspection, production scheduling, and work study.

Formalization

Formalization denotes the extent to which rules, procedures, instructions, and communications are written down. How does the weight of documentation vary from organization to organization? Definitions of thirty-eight documents have been assembled each of which can be used by any known work organization. They range from (for example) organization charts, memo forms, agendas, minutes, to written terms of reference, job descriptions, records of maintenance performed, statements of tasks done or to be done on the output, handbooks, manuals of procedures.

Further analyses can be made, such as the number of categories of employees using documents. Scores are found to range from 4 in a single-product foodstuffs factory where there are few such documents, to 49 in the same metals processing plant that heads the standardization scores and where documentation parallels the routine procedures. As with standardization, this dimension can be broken down into various aspects. The data suggest three which are conceptually separate: formalization of role-definition, of information-passing, and of role-performance recording. Linked together in the formalization of role-definition sub-scale are all those documents whose primary purpose is the prescription of behaviour, as shown in Table 11. Information-passing documents are those which are intended to pass from hand to hand (memo forms, house journal, etc.). Role-performance records notify or authorize the accomplishment of some part of a role (carrying out inspections, maintenance of equipment, etc.).

TABLE 11: *Formalization of role-definition*

(n = 52)   Scale No. 53·01

Examples of items:
Written contracts of employment (including 'legally drawn' contract, formal letter of appointment, and terms of engagement or rules signed by employee)*
Proportion of employees who have handbooks
Number of handbooks
Organization chart
Written operating instructions available to direct 'worker'
Written terms of reference or job descriptions
Manual of procedures or standing orders
Written policies (excluding minutes of governing bodies)
Workflow ('production') schedules or programmes
Research programmes or reports

Scores: Range – 0–20
        Mean – 9·15
        Standard deviation – 5·65

* It will be noticed that this item cannot be used in future studies since all organizations are now legally required to have such a document. If all organizations score the same on any item, then it cannot be used since it is of no help in telling the differences between organizations.

Centralization

Centralization concerns the locus of authority to make decisions. 'Authority to take decisions' is defined and ascertained by asking 'who is the last person whose assent must be obtained before *legitimate action* is taken – even if others subsequently have to confirm the decision'. This picks out the level in the hierarchy where executive action can be authorized, even if this remains subject to a 'rubber stamp' confirmation later by, for example, a chairman or a committee. A standard list of thirty-seven recurrent decisions has been prepared covering the range of organizational activities, and examples of these are given in Table 12.

TABLE 12: *Overall centralization*

(n = 52)   Scale No. 54·00

(Examples of decision items used)
Which level in the organization has authority:
1. to decide on appointments to operative level jobs
2. to decide on promotion of operatives
3. to spend unbudgeted or unallocated money on capital items
4. to decide when overtime is to be worked
5. to decide on delivery dates or priority of orders
6. to decide what shall be costed (i.e. to what the costing system, if any, shall be applied)
7. to decide what shall be inspected (i.e. to what the inspection system, if any, shall be applied)
8. to decide what operations shall be work studied
9. to dismiss an operative
10. to lay down training methods to be used
11. to lay down buying procedures
12. to decide the price of the output
13. to alter responsibilities/areas of work of functional specialist departments
14. to alter responsibilities/areas of work of line departments.

Scores: Range   –   108–173
        Mean   –   134·38
        Standard Deviation – 13·47

For each organization the lowest level in the hierarchy which has the formal authority to take each decision is determined, and Table 13 gives a generalized paradigm which then enables levels to be compared across organizations. This overcomes the endemic problem of deciding whether a foreman in factory A is at the same level as a shop-buyer in retail store B or a head clerk in commercial office C. Levels are equated in terms of the scope of the work-flow segment (the proportion of the production activities) which they control. Centralization scores are formed by scoring a decision taken outside the unit of organization (at the head office of an owning group, for example) as 5, a decision taken at chief executive level as 4, and so on, down to 0 for a decision at operating level. Thus a high score means high centralization, and a range has been found from the most decentralized organization with a score of 108 (an independent manufacturer of transporting equipment) to an extremely centralized organization, where a considerable majority of the decisions are taken right at the top or above, which has a score of 173 (a branch factory).

TABLE 13: *Centralization – levels in the hierarchy*

Score	Level	A metal manufacturer	A chain of retail shoe-repair shops	Local Authority Education Department
5 =	Above the chief executive	Board of group	—	City Council
4 =	Whole organization level	Managing Director	Chairman	Chief Education Officer
3 =	All work-flow activities level	Production Manager	Sales Manager	Assistant Education Officer
2 =	Work-flow sub-unit level	Plant Manager	Area Manager	Headmaster
1 =	Supervisory level	Foreman	Shop Manager	Head of Department
0 =	Operating level	Operator	Repairer	Teacher

Configuration

Configuration is the shape of the role structure. Its data would be contained in a comprehensive and detailed organization chart that included literally every role in the organization. The assessment of the configuration of this hypothetical chart requires the use of a combination of selected dimensions. Each of these provides a measure of the development of a particular aspect of the structure.

The vertical span of control (or height) of the workflow superordinate hierarchy (line chain of command) is measured by a count of the number of job positions between the chief executive and the employees directly working on the output, and by the proportion of managers and supervisors (workflow superordinates). Lateral 'widths' can include the chief executive's span of control; the ratio of subordinates to first work-flow superordinates (first-line supervisors) and the percentage of direct-output employees to total employees. Note that in a savings bank, the cashiers are direct-output employees, as are drivers in a bus company, and so on. The total of work-flow employees (those directly responsible for the output, including management) can be compared with the number of those engaged in other activities ('functional specialists' or 'staff' departments). Totals of employees in each of the sixteen specialisms (cf. specialization) can be calculated and related. Here the size of the specialism in terms of the number of those engaged in it is taken account of, as distinct from their specialization which is measured under that heading. And so on.

For example, a symptom of increasing bureaucracy may be the percentage of clerks employed. A clerical job is defined as one where the main prescribed task is writing and recording, but where there is no supervisory responsibility for subordinates other than typists. This definition excludes office managers with authority over other clerks, but would include both a clerk and his typist. For fifty-two organizations, the percentage of clerks ranges from small manufacturing firms with 2 per cent to a commercial office with 29 per cent.

STRUCTURAL PROFILES

Equipped with scales for the analysis and measurement of organization structure, we can now construct 'profiles' characteristic of particular organizations. (For comparative purposes, all raw scores are transformed into standard scores based on distributions with a mean of 50 and standard deviation of 15.) Figure 26 shows the profiles of six organizations which we have studied and it will be seen that they each have a distinctive pattern.

Organization A is a municipal department responsible for a public service. But it is far from being the classic form of bureaucracy as described by Weber. By definition such bureaucracy would have an extreme high-score pattern on our scales. That is,

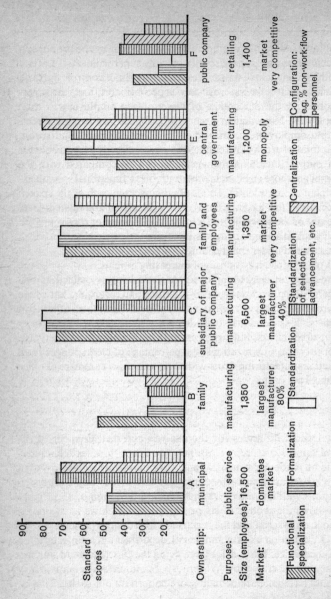

Figure 26. The structural profiles of six organizations

	A	B	C	D	E	F
Ownership:	municipal	family	subsidiary of major public company	family and employees	central government	public company
Purpose:	public service	manufacturing	manufacturing	manufacturing	manufacturing	retailing
Size (employees):	16,500	1,350	6,500	1,350	1,200	1,400
Market:	dominates market	largest manufacturer 80%	largest manufacturer 40%	market very competitive	monopoly	market very competitive

Standard scores

90 80 70 60 50 40 30 20

Functional specialization

Formalization — Standardization — Standardization of selection, advancement, etc. — Centralization — Configuration: e.g. % non-work-flow personnel

388

it would appear as highly specialized with many narrowly defined specialist 'offices', as highly standardized in its procedures, and as highly formalized with documents prescribing and recording all activities and available in the files as precedents. If everything has to be referred upwards for decision, then it would also score highly centralized. In configuration it would have a high proportion of 'supportive' or administrative or 'non-workflow' personnel. But of fifty-two organizations, *none* shows such a profile. Perhaps extreme total bureaucracy exists only among the bureaux of central government – which are not represented in our provincial sample.

Organization B represents a relatively unstructured family firm, relying more on traditional ways of doing things. Although it has the specialisms usual in manufacturing industry (and hence a comparatively high specialization score) it has minimized standardized procedure and formalized paperwork.

Organization C represents 'big business'. It is the subsidiary of a very large company, and its profile shows the effects of size; generally very high scores on specialization, standardization, and formalization, but *de*centralized. The distinctively different relationship of centralization is typical. Centralization correlates *negatively* with almost all other structural scales. The more specialized, standardized, and formalized the organization, the *less* it is centralized, or to put it the other way round, the more it is decentralized. Therefore these scales do not confirm the common assumption that a large organization which develops specialist offices and the routines which go with them 'passes the buck' upward for decision; in fact, such an organization is relatively decentralized.

But it is not only a question of size, as the profile of Organization D shows. It has the *same* number of employees as Organization B and yet its structure is in striking contrast and is more nearly that of a much larger firm. Clearly the policies and attitudes of the management of an organization may have a considerable effect on its structure, even though factors like size, technology, form of ownership, etc., set the framework within which the management must function.

Organization E is an example of a manufacturing unit owned

by the Government, and is characterized by a high centralization and a high formalization score. Comparison of the profiles of D and E brings home the fact that two organizations may be 'bureaucratic' but in considerably different ways.

Organization F is included as an example of the relatively low scores often found in retailing.

Scrutiny of all the profiles suggests that there are numbers of organizations which have similar structural characteristics, a suggestion which reflects the associations between measures shown by intercorrelations among them (Table 14). This impression is confirmed by the statistical method of principal components analysis, as a result of which the structural characteristics of each organization can be summed up in a comparatively few composite scores. Plotting the composite scores for all the organizations discloses various clusters which have certain pronounced features in common. These distinctive clusters extend from a core of comparatively undistinguished 'average' organizations which tend to have scores around the mean points. As might be expected, the one third of the total fifty-two organizations which can be roughly classed as 'average' make a very mixed collection. There are retail shops, a brewery, an omnibus undertaking, a development organization, and a variety of factories manufacturing anything from gears to machine tools. On the other hand, the clusters of organizations with more pronounced features are found to be comparatively homogeneous. Three among these several clusters will be outlined.

The first is sufficiently obvious in the data that the reader may already have discerned organizations of this kind in the six profiles in Figure 26. High specialization, high standardization, and high formalization is a pattern that prevails in large-scale manufacturing industry. Among the examples are factories in the vehicle accessory and vehicle assembly industry, those processing metals, and those mass-producing foodstuffs and confectionery. Organizations like this have gone a long way in the regulation of the work of their employees. They have gone a long way in *structuring* activities; that is, the intended behaviour of employees has been structured by the specification of their specialized roles, of the procedures they are to follow in carrying out these roles, and of

TABLE 14: *Intercorrelations among structural variables between forty-six organizations in Birmingham* (a random sample stratified by size and purpose)

Scale No.	Functional specialization	Overall standardization	Standardization – selection, etc.	Overall formalization	Role definition	Overall centralization	Chief executive's span	Subordinate ratio	Vertical span (height)	% Work-flow superordinates	% Non-work-flow personnel	% Clerks
51.01 *Functional* specialization	—											
52.00 *Overall* standardization	0·76	—										
52.02 *Standardization – selection,* etc.	−0·15	0·23	—									
53.00 *Overall* formalization	0·57	0·83	0·38	—								
53.01 *Role* definition	0·49	0·79	0·45	0·94	—							
54.00 *Overall* centralization	−0·64	−0·27	0·30	−0·20	−0·15	—						
55.08 Chief executive's span	0·22	0·28	0·04	0·32	0·25	−0·10	—					
55.09 Subordinate ratio	0·25	0·13	−0·46	0·04	−0·07	−0·14	−0·16	—				
55.43 Vertical span (height)	0·57	0·57	0·23	0·48	0·52	−0·28	0·24	−0·05	—			
55.47 % Work-flow superordinates	−0·53	−0·37	0·39	−0·24	−0·13	0·52	0·12	−0·50	−0·01	—		
55.48 % Non-work-flow personnel	0·58	0·51	−0·02	0·46	0·48	−0·40	0·10	0·01	0·21	−0·43	—	
55.49 % Clerks	0·17	0·31	0·31	0·29	0·36	−0·04	0·12	−0·24	−0·01	−0·05	0·46	—

the documentation involved in what they have to do. In short, the pattern of scores among specialization, standardization, and formalization denotes the range and pattern of *structuring*. So manufacturing industry or 'big business' tends to have highly structured work activities – production schedules, quality inspection procedures, returns of output per worker and per machine, forms recording maintenance jobs, etc., etc. We can call this the *workflow structured* kind of organization (see Figure 26, Organizations C and D).

This kind of organization usually has a high percentage of 'non-work-flow' personnel (employees not directly engaged in production). Many of these are in the large specialized sections such as production planning and scheduling, quality inspection and testing, work-study, and research and development, which generate standardization and formalization.

It will have been noticed that the workflow structured organization is relatively *de*centralized. Perhaps the explanation is that when the responsibilities of specialized roles are laid down, and activities are regulated by standardized procedures and are formalized in records, then authority can safely be decentralized because the organizational machine will smoothly run, as it has been set to run, and decisions will be made in the way intended with less need for referring to the top.

But while centralization correlates *negatively* with standardization in general (Table 14), it correlates positively with that particular aspect measured by the scale termed Standardization of Procedures Controlling Personnel Selection and Advancement, etc. (see p. 383). Therefore high centralization is associated with high standardization in this respect *only*, that is, with the structuring (or regulation) of employment activities. This means central control of recruitment, central interviewing by formally constituted selection boards, fixed staff establishment figures, procedures laid down in writing which are to be followed in cases of employee discipline or dismissal, etc. Such an organization we call *employment structured*. It should be remembered that it has not structured the *daily work* of its employees to the same extent as is found in workflow structured organizations. This kind of structure is especially common in local and central government, for example, a municipal education department or public transport department. Its centralization is accentuated by public ownership, where the need for public accountability requires many decisions to be referred upwards to committees and councils. Probably for similar reasons, the same structure also occurs in the smaller branch factories of large companies (see Figure 26, Organization A).

The cartoonist's stereotype of bureaucratic public departments proves to be very near the mark in so far as they are employment structured. Here are all the desirably equitable *but* unavoidably cumbersome procedures for control of employment and for uniform practices in taking decisions. But if public departments have a characteristic brand of bureaucracy, what the cartoonists have *not* spotted is that so has workflow structured 'big business'. However, here we are interested not in lampooning bureaucracy but in exploring the different forms structure takes in organizations with different tasks to perform.

One question that jumps to mind is: 'What is manufacturing organization like if it is also publicly owned?' The hypothesis being that it will be *both* workflow structured and employment structured. Our sample includes only one such organization, a medium-sized state-owned engineering factory (see Figure 26, Organization E). Examining its scores, we do indeed find that it shows both these forms of structuring – though one case does not justify generalizations, and further work is needed.

Thirdly, a number of organizations are found to have relatively low scores all round. Low on specialization, low on standardization, low on formalization, and low – but not too low – on centralization. Typical of this cluster of organizations are smaller factories in the size range from 250 to 750 employees, whose ownership is concentrated, that is, a comparatively small number of individuals are large shareholders and often are also directors. The low scores of such factories do not mean that they have no structure and career along in a state of anarchy. Rather, their kind of structure gives low scores on the characteristics measured and with the particular scales used. To label them unstructured would be a misnomer, for it is rather that for these measures their structure is latent. We might therefore cautiously call them *latent structured* (see Figure 26, Organizations B and F). A hypothesis would be that these organizations are run not by explicit regulation but by implicitly transmitted custom, a hypothesis which appears very plausible but is not adequately tested by these results alone.

FURTHER DEVELOPMENTS

All scientists, and particularly social scientists, are continually faced with the problem of having to identify with some precision the characteristics they have described and measured; that is they have to tackle the problem of validity of data. To some extent this is a semantic problem, as is illustrated by the famous non-definition that 'intelligence is what intelligence tests measure'. At this level, if it is thought that our scales of, say, specialization and centralization do not in fact tap these characteristics then other names would have to be found for them (since they have an *internal* consistency which makes it unlikely that they would be complete artefacts). But this is hardly adequate and some form of *external* validation is required. This we are at present undertaking.

The way that we obtain external validity is by testing acceptable hypotheses that there are relationships between the characteristics of structure that we have measured and other characteristics of organizations. Figure 27 gives a paradigm which relates an organization's structure to aspects of its context, its performance, and to the behaviour within it. If we can postulate relationships between the four boxes shown and obtain data to support our hypotheses, then we have gone a considerable way towards demonstrating that our scales do measure aspects of structure which are relevant to organizational functioning.

If we can predict to a considerable degree, from a knowledge of an organization's context (for example its size, technology of manufacture or service, ownership pattern), what its structural scores will be, then we have evidence that its scores are meaningful. Again, if we can demonstrate that in given contexts an organization's structural scores will be directly related to its performance (productivity, profitability, etc.), then we can have that much more confidence in our scales. If, in addition, we find that given structural forms are correlated with characteristic behaviour (specialization with interaction patterns, centralization with power and influence, standardization with rigid thinking, etc.) then we have added to the data on the external validity of our measures. Our work is geared to an examination of these topics.

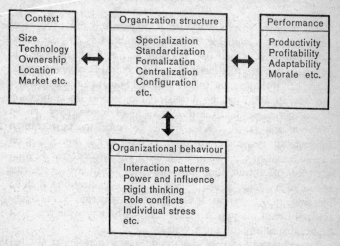

Figure 27. A scheme for organizational functioning

POTENTIAL APPLICATION

The manager of the future will have available to him ever increasing amounts of information, and will be anxious to know what signals he should primarily attend to. If he knows what is crucial to organization functioning he can manage by exception. What types and amounts of environmental change can occur before internal adjustments must be made in order to maintain performance? How much internal change will be required, and in what direction? What sequence of compensatory changes is likely to be triggered off by any specific decision? The precepts of the classical management theorists have proved inadequate to deal with such questions as these. The contemporary social science approach to organization theory may yield a more useful set of criteria to help the manager to take important decisions. Use of the profiles as developed here enables direct comparison between organizations, as shown in Figure 26. Closer analysis of typical organizations may lead to a better understanding of the patterns we have found. At least it should enable future theory to be firmly grounded in fact.

Many possibilities are opened up if relatively exact means of comparison are available. There is, of course, no political or geographical limit to their use. It would be feasible to measure the specialization of structures in French as against German organizations, or for that matter Indonesian and Soudanese. If degrees of bureaucratization can be represented by scores on empirically based measures, then the development of bureaucracy can be systematically studied. As a further instance, the businessman interested in systems of costing may have to rely completely on guesswork as to whether such a system will succeed: but if measurements of centralization have shown that such costing systems have a high rate of failure in decentralized organizations, then he has something to go on. If Company X's structure is more centralized than Company Y's, Company X may provide the most favourable setting for a new system.

To take another example, many researchers have studied 'restriction of output' among workers. We would like to be able to relate this type of behaviour to the sort of factory and the sort of economical and social context in which it does, or does not, occur. The same approach is possible for studies of many other kinds of behaviours – absenteeism, labour turnover, sociability among fellow employees, or neuroses among managers. The incidence of the factor studied can be related not merely to a vague description of the work-place in which it occurs, but to a precise and standardized characterization. We can then consider another firm, perhaps identical or perhaps different, and, knowing precisely the identity or difference, can see whether the same behaviour occurs. In this way the causes can more clearly be pin-pointed.

If these processes can be better understood, then a manager can predict better what changes are likely to take place in the structure of an organization and plan for them. Knowing which structures operate more efficiently in which situations, we can look forward to designing organizations appropriate to the tasks they face.

PART FIVE

Market Research

THE ultimate success of a firm, no matter how technically sound its products, is decided in the market-place. Here the questions it has to face may extend beyond winning a share of an established market for its products to creating a demand for them. The major operations in the distribution of products include market research, advertising, and selling. The capacity of production to outrun demand and the growth of large-scale business, which increases the gulf between the producer and the consumer, underline the need for scientific and systematic means for measuring consumer needs and habits. Market research is concerned with the evaluation of consumer attitudes to products and advertising and with providing answers to questions such as how a particular product is selling, who is buying it and why? The manufacturer may want to ask similar questions before his product is released on the market. When we realize that one seventh of the products on sale today were not available five years ago, we can begin to grasp the importance of new products and of understanding the personal and social needs which place a high value on innovation itself. Market researchers secure their information about the consumer through a wide range of social science techniques and methods like sampling, questionnairing, and interviewing and they have founded their own professional bodies, partly with the purposes of ensuring that adequate standards are maintained in the use of such techniques. A number of social scientists working in this field have outstanding academic reputations indeed, university research has benefited from techniques of classification and attitude measurement originally developed in the marketing setting.

The contributors to this final section have worked together to present us with an exciting picture of some of the activities engaging the market researcher.

CHAPTER 19

Empirical Techniques in Consumer Research

J. A. LUNN

CONSUMER research has become a vital part of modern marketing. This is due largely to the increasingly scientific nature of management. Marketing decisions are tending to form part of an overall strategy throughout the development and life-cycle of a product, and to be based upon facts about the market, not upon speculation, however inspired. The point is not that entrepreneurial flair is outmoded. On the contrary, a thoroughly compiled picture of the market may suggest several possible courses of action, and provide even more scope for flair and judgement than before. It is rather that marketing men cannot afford to remain uninformed about the consumer needs and habits they are trying to cater for. The penalties of mass-produced failure are too great.

At the same time there have been far-reaching changes in society, one of the most important for marketing being the vastly increased purchasing power of the lower-income groups. This has been accompanied by an erosion of traditional class-determined patterns of behaviour, including purchasing behaviour: the factory girl may dress indistinguishably from the deb, the home help may take her holidays in Majorca. The result is an ever-widening range of consumer needs for the marketing man to satisfy.

Consumer research has responded by taking a more systematic approach to marketing problems, and by evolving more sophisticated techniques. Social scientists are contributing to both. An example of the former can be seen in various attempts that are being made to build models or analogies to increase the understanding of the consumer process. At first these were based almost entirely upon concepts drawn from disciplines such as economics and psychology; more recently efforts have been made to derive models empirically from the study of consumer behaviour. A valuable résumé of work on consumer model building can be found in Nicosia (1967).

The emphasis in this chapter, however, will be recent developments in research techniques. Emphasis is placed on work on which the writer has been engaged during the past few years. No attempt has been made to provide an overall review of current progress in consumer research. For this the interested reader is referred to recent articles by Treasure (1966) and McIntosh (1966). The following section gives an outline of certain principles of attitude measurement; the remaining sections deal with the application of these principles to current marketing problems.

ATTITUDE RESEARCH

The examples given below are all from the field of attitude research. This field has produced some of the most exciting recent developments in the social sciences, and is symptomatic of their general trend towards quantification and precise measurement. It is hoped to show that the techniques, although sophisticated in themselves, have clear and practical applications to marketing decisions.

To begin with, some general points about attitude research that apply to all the examples.* Firstly, definitions. There are many theoretical definitions of the term 'attitude', some of them conflicting, which need not concern us in this chapter. We shall take a broad view of this concept, and shall provide operational definitions as we go along; we shall make clear in what senses 'attitude' is being used in each particular case. However, most theoretical definitions do agree that an attitude is a state of readiness, that it reflects the tendency for a person to act or react in a certain manner when placed in particular situations. For instance, if John Brown changes his seat on the bus when an Indian sits next to him, starts looking for a house in a new district when a West Indian family moves in opposite, declares that the immigration laws are too lenient when asked for his opinion by a survey inter-

---

* Only a few of the more important points are covered here, often in a rather cursory manner. The following references are recommended: Jahoda and Warren (1966), Oppenheim (1966), Green (1954), and a forthcoming book by McKennell (1968).

viewer, and so on, we infer that he has a hostile attitude towards coloured people. This information may put us in a better position both to understand other aspects of his past behaviour, and to make predictions about his future behaviour.

'Attitude' is thus an abstract concept. Attitudes cannot be directly observed. But they are necessary in order for us to account for both the consistencies and the apparent inconsistencies that we find in people's behaviour. This is just as important in consumer research as in any other applied social science. It is not sufficient for marketing men to know people's habits, choices, and preferences. It is also important to understand these phenomena in order to predict and cater for them.

Secondly, it would seem that attitudes are not qualitative – things you either have or have not – but quantitative. People hold them in varying strengths.

Thirdly, attitudes can be characterized in the following three separate but connected ways: they may be relatively enduring or transitory, relatively fundamental or superficial, relatively general or specific. The connexion lies in the likelihood that more general attitudes are deep-seated in the personality and therefore unlikely to change, at least, in the short term. And vice-versa. For consumer research, it is usually attitudes of only medium generality, or high specificity, that are the most predictive, and therefore of primary interest. However, a further important distinction in the consumer field is between fairly general attitudes that seem to belong to the person, rather than to anything in the environment, and attitudes that are directed specifically towards some object. The former describe a person's values; for example, the extent to which she is concerned with being economical. The latter refer to her opinions of particular objects, in terms, perhaps, of these values; for example the extent to which a product is thought to offer good value for money. Instances of both types of attitude are given in later sections.

Finally, attitudes cannot always be measured simply and directly. Whether deep-seated or superficial, they are often highly charged with emotion. In consumer research, it is rarely much use asking people why they bought a particular product or prefer one brand to another. They may not know. Even if they do, they are not always willing to say. Motives can be socially embarrassing. More-over, people on the whole like to appear reasonable, both to them-selves and to others, and direct questions are apt to elicit plausible but misleading answers.

Methods of assessment

An implication of the previous paragraph is that attitude assess-ment is a complex task. But it is by no means an impossible one. Social scientists have devoted considerable effort to it, especially during the past two decades, and a number of promising methods are documented in the text books.

Some of these take their origin in the field of mental testing, others in social psychology. Most are concerned with problems of grading people along an attitude dimension, selecting the best items to do this, and ensuring the soundness of the resulting measuring instruments.

These methods have usually to be modified to the circumstances under which consumer research operates. In particular respon-dents are not as 'captive' as the university students, hospital patients, and prisoners who so often figure as respondents in social inquiries: the doorstep or kitchen respondent is apt to be intolerant of lengthy questionnaires. Nor is it feasible in large-scale consumer studies to use interviewers with professional social-science training. The need, therefore, is for techniques which, although sound, are relatively short and simple to administer.

Fortunately, the main interest in marketing is in making broad comparisons between groups, for instance between buyers and non-buyers of a particular product, and not, as in much of social science, in the precise assessment of individuals: for instance in predicting the response of clinical patients to different forms of treatment. Thus slightly lower standards of accuracy are often permissible.

Given the circumstances in which commercial research is carried out, the most suitable method of attitude assessment is that of self-report. People are asked to respond in some way to items that have been chosen to reflect the attitude in question. For instance, they may be asked to indicate the extent of their agreement or disagreement with sets of statements. The stages involved in a typical inquiry may be broadly categorized into three – identifying the relevant attitude dimensions, developing suitable measuring instruments, and establishing the exact relationship between attitudes and behaviour. Failure to attend fully to all three stages may be the reason for the disappointing results of some attitude studies in the past. A few points about each will be made below.

Identifying attitude dimensions. It is all too easy for a researcher to assume that he understands both what main attitude dimensions are important in a particular inquiry, and how to phrase statements to express them. He may be wrong on both counts. And it is becoming customary to precede the main inquiry with an exploratory pilot. This usually takes the form of informal, conversational interviews, in which the respondent is encouraged to talk as freely as possible about the topic in question, the interviewer saying little except to probe areas of apparent importance. Additional aids such as projective pictures* may be used as ways of eliciting especially deep-seated or socially embarrassing attitudes.

These 'depth' interviews, as they are often called, are invaluable as a means of defining the main attitudes surrounding a particular activity. There was a time when they would form the only stage in an attitude inquiry. This is, however, a dangerous procedure. The unstructured form, which is their main advantage, results in rather imprecise information and lends itself to somewhat speculative interpretation. They also require highly skilled interviewers, and are therefore rather expensive to carry out on a sufficiently large scale to permit confident generalization from the findings. Consequently, the increasing awareness by consumer researchers of more precise forms of attitude measurement has led to these interviews being regarded essentially as exploratory tools. Verbatim transcripts are usually made – most people are willing nowadays to have an interview tape-recorded – which are submitted to a thorough content analysis. These transcripts provide a rich source of colloquial statements that crystallize the ordinary person's point of view.

* See Oppenheim (1966).

Developing suitable measuring instruments. It is customary to seek several statements to express any one attitude dimension. It might well be asked why the researcher is not content with one statement per area, particularly in view of the reference above to the need for short and simple techniques.

There is, however, a danger in over-simplicity. It is possible that a single item might mean different things to different people, and might, therefore, be answered from a variety of viewpoints. There is no means of telling this from the distribution of responses. The safeguard is to take a set of items, each of which expresses the underlying attitude slightly differently, and to see whether they elicit consistent responses. If they do, we can have confidence that we are measuring what we think we are.

This, then, is a fundamental principle behind the development of attitude scales, as these measurement tools are often called. There is another related and no less important principle. Many attitudes cannot be adequately expressed in a single statement without making the statement so direct as to maximize the risk of arousing defensive responses. So instead of asking a housewife outright whether she is economy-minded, one might instead obtain her responses to statements such as the following:

(*a*) 'A good housewife always buys the least expensive kinds of food.'

(*b*) 'You should always use up left-overs.'

(*c*) 'Everyone should give themselves an occasional treat.'

Each of these statements has both a specific and a general meaning: specific, in that people agreeing with (*a*) will not invariably agree with (*b*) and disagree with (*c*); general, in that they will tend to. As more items are added, the effects of the specific elements cancel each other out, and a better measure is obtained of the underlying theme, economy-mindedness.

This process of searching for consistencies amongst statements is a basic principle in attitude measurement; it is often referred to as testing for unidimensionality. Items brought together on grounds of apparent similarity may in fact contain more than one dimension. Statistical techniques are required to identify which items are measuring a common dimension, and which of these do so most efficiently.

Two techniques particularly appropriate for consumer research, and rapidly gaining acceptance, are factor analysis and Guttman scaling. Discussion will be largely confined to the former.

Factor analysis rests on the basis of the correlation coefficient. This is basically an expression of the degree of relationship between any two items. Thus, if everyone who agreed with item (*a*) above also agreed with (*b*) there would be a correlation of 1·0 between them; if it was impossible to predict response to (*b*) from responses to (*a*), the correlation coefficient would be 0.

Factor analysis* is essentially a means of summarizing a set of correlation coefficients (or correlation matrix) into a smaller number of factors that help to explain these correlations by identifying the main threads running through them. In consumer research it is used mainly as a fast and systematic form of cluster analysis. That is, it summarizes items into clusters so that those in any one cluster show a much higher level of correlation with one another than they do with items in other clusters. This procedure involves complex mathematical calculation and it is a tedious and time-consuming task by hand. It can now be performed cheaply and quickly by computer, with the result that factor analysis is becoming a key tool in attitude research.

Most computer programmes produce both principal components and rotated factor solutions. These have separate functions in attitude measurement. Which is used will depend on the nature and stage of the problem, as indicated below. Principal component analysis proceeds by extracting factors essentially on the criterion of mathematical importance: the first factor extracted will account for the highest common variance, the second for the second highest common variance, and so on. This analysis is an excellent test for the hypothesis that there is mainly one attitude dimension present. It is also a means of establishing which of the statements tested hang most closely together, and therefore form the best scale. The mathematical ratio of the first to the second

* A useful introduction to factor analysis can be found in Fruchter (1954).

factor can be used as a criterion of unidimensionality.* McKennell (1968) recommends a ratio of 3:1.

However, where there are several separate attitude dimensions present, that is, several quite separate clusters of items, principal component analysis is not the best means of identifying them. And it is customary to rotate the factor axes, in order to search out these clusters more accurately. Here factor analysis is being used as an exploratory tool. It clarifies the hypotheses about the main attitude dimensions present, built up after the depth exploratory stage. Each of the identified clusters can then be tested by principal component analysis.

A simplified example of this exploratory function can be seen in Figure 28. These are all items included to measure a general attitude to thriftiness. It can be seen that the first six items (those in triangle x) correlate highly together, as do the other six (those in triangle y); but there is a much lower level of correlation between any of these items and any of the other six (those in box z). By thus grouping the items, the factor analysis revealed two quite separate components of attitudes to thrift, namely economy-mindedness and bargain-seeking (see also p. 418). Figure 29 shows an example of the opposite kind. Exploratory interviewing had suggested four quite separate attitudes: factor analysis revealed that three of these (triangles a, b, and c) amounted to the same thing, and that there were therefore basically two consumer attitudes to consider.

Figure 29 illustrates another aspect of factor analysis, the demonstration of item redundancy. If a number of statements are highly correlated we can dispense with most of them for purposes of practical measurement. Indeed, just as good a measure of the attitude can often be obtained with three or four statements – those with the highest overall level of correlation - as with the total number that have been found to define the attitude (sometimes as many as fifteen).†

---

* Here factor analysis is used as an up-to-date version of item analysis. Unlike the latter, it does not *assume* a unidimensional total score against which the items are tested.

† This has led to the strategy of preceding a large-scale inquiry, in which 1,000 or more respondents may be assessed on a dozen or more attitude dimensions, with a scale development stage. Here, a relatively small sample,

Sometimes one finds that a set of statements are not only inter-correlated but also form a gradient of difficulty. That is, there are some items, the most difficult, that are endorsed by only a few people; others, the least difficult, that are endorsed by most people,

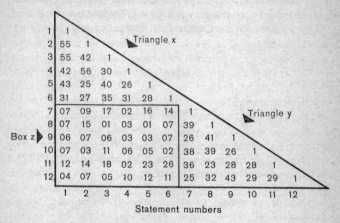

Figure 28. Twelve statements, thought to reflect a single dimension, are shown by factor analysis to contain two separate dimensions, namely items 1–6 and 7–12. (In this and the following figure, the numbers are coefficients of correlation between each pair of statements. Decimal points and positive and negative signs have been omitted)

and items in between of medium difficulty. Where this tendency is found, and where people who endorse the most difficult also endorse the less difficult items, the conditions of cumulative scaling are being fulfilled. The most popular cumulative method is that propounded by Guttman (see Green, 1954).

Cumulative scaling has certain advantages over methods such

---

will be asked a large battery of questions reflecting the hypothesized attitude areas. Statistical refinement of these responses will reveal a much reduced set of statements for the main inquiry. McKennell and Lunn have validated a short-cut version of Cronbach's Coefficient Alpha, which works directly from correlations and is an improvement on factor analysis for exploration, scale testing and item selection.

as principal component analysis which are based on correlations. From the knowledge of a person's scale score one knows which statements he endorsed rather than, as in correlation methods, merely the number he endorsed. Consequently, cumulative scaling allows small sub-sets of items to be used with greater confidence. Its chief merit for consumer research is in helping the researcher to extract maximum use from a small amount of data. It is being

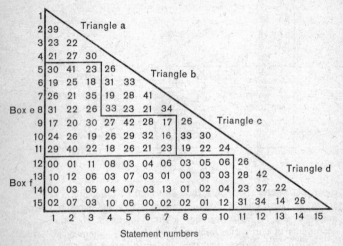

Figure 29. Fifteen statements were thought to form four separate attitude dimensions, as indicated by triangles *a*, *b*, *c*, and *d*. However, factor analysis, while confirming dimension *d*, and its separation from the three other dimensions (box *f*), showed that items 1–11 really reflected only one dimension, where the correlations are virtually as high as in triangles *a*, *b*, and *c*

increasingly used as a way of further refining clusters of items revealed by an exploratory factor analysis. It is inappropriate where the items do not fall easily into an order of 'difficulties'.

The reliability and validity of attitude scaling will be dealt with only briefly. These two concepts are basic to all psychological measurement. Reliability refers to the consistency of a measuring instrument – the extent to which it would achieve identical results on repeated use. There are a number of standard procedures for testing reliability;* on the whole, attitude scales achieve highly consistent standards.

Validity refers to the extent to which a scale measures what it purports to measure. This is much more difficult to assess, largely because there is rarely one clear external criterion.† There is no single way, for instance, in which housewives highly concerned with economy differ from those who are not. Behaviour is more complex than this. However, it is possible to adopt the principle of 'construct validity', that is to build up a network of relationships between the scale and other variables. This can be done either by examining correlations of the scale with other appropriate questions in large-scale surveys or by re-interviewing respondents identified by their high, medium, and low scores on the scale.

Relationships between attitudes and behaviour

This is a topic more for the future than for the present chapter. It is an issue that is perhaps only just being fully appreciated. The assumption has often been made in the past that attitudes should show clear one-to-one relationships with behaviour. However, as was mentioned above, behaviour is more complex than this. There will usually be a variety of pressures bearing upon an individual sometimes combining to reinforce or deter an aspect of behaviour, sometimes conflicting with each other to make it a marginal action.

A lot of research has been done in the past few years to identify and measure the individual pressures. But attempts are only just starting to be made to interrelate these pressures in ways that provide full understanding and prediction of consumer behaviour. A keen interest is being taken in various forms of multivariate and taxonomic analysis. (Cooley and Lohnes, 1962, and Joyce and Channon, 1966. See also p. 417 below.)

This section has briefly examined some important issues in attitude research and some developments in techniques that are gaining ground in marketing. The next three sections illustrate

* See in particular Cronbach (1960).

† For an excellent discussion of validity, see Vernon (1965).

ways in which these developments are being applied to practical problems.

NEW FORMS OF CLASSIFICATION*

Marketing men are becoming increasingly interested in directing products not at the total population but explicitly at certain *types* of people. This strategy of market segmentation recognizes that people's needs and circumstances differ, and that, consequently, so do their purchasing patterns. Any given brand or product is unlikely to be purchased by everyone: rather, it will make an appeal to a specific sub-group. Efficient marketing, it is argued, should capitalize on these appeals. It should, for instance, identify the key target group when the product is being tested, so that this group's preferences are not swamped by the irrelevant, possibly misleading preferences of people for whom the product is not intended. The same considerations apply throughout the research process, for example in selecting a sample for testing possible advertising appeals, in deciding which media should carry the advertisement, in selecting optimum distribution outlets.

But the problem is to identify critical sub-groups. For years, consumer research data has been analysed, almost ritualistically, in terms of a standard repertoire of classifications, such as age, social class, region, household size. These so-called demographic characteristics have an obvious value. They identify important differences in people's circumstances, which are often reflected in their purchasing behaviour: size of disposable income sets certain limits on what can be bought, larger households have more mouths to feed, and so on.

However, demographic classifications alone are inadequate for segmentation. They leave unexplained too many clearly identifiable differences in consumer behaviour; they fail to reflect the varied pattern of important needs. Consequently, there is a demand for new classifications that will provide a sharper description of present and potential buyers and will at the same time increase the understanding of the market situation. In particular, attempts have been made to examine the possibilities of psychological dimensions.

* For a fuller discussion of this topic see Lunn (1966).

In recent years, two approaches have been adopted, the *a priori* and the empirical. The former has involved trying out various instruments developed in other fields. Particular favourites have been standard personality tests. Probably the best-known study in the U.K. is *The Londoner* (1961). This survey compared the purchasing and media (reading and viewing) habits of people differing along dimensions such as extroversion (briefly, the tendency to be outward looking and sociable) and neuroticism (briefly, emotional instability). The results of this and similar studies have been disappointing. They illustrate the dangers of taking over, without clear hypotheses as to their probable value, concepts developed for quite different purposes. Certainly, the more *general* personality characteristics seem to have little relevance to consumer behaviour.

The alternative empirical approach is the one favoured by the writer, who has adopted it in a number of studies during the past few years. The principle is not to try to fit the consumer to a predetermined set of classifications but rather to derive new classifications from a study of the consumer. Three main stages are usually involved, as described in the previous section; namely, identifying the relevant attitude dimensions, developing suitable measuring instruments, and establishing the precise ways in which the new classifications tie in with behaviour. To give the maximum opportunity of finding relevant classifications, the initial interviewing may be carried out on groups of respondents with known differences in purchasing, for instance on heavy, medium and light buyers of a given product. The results so far are very promising. They will be briefly discussed under two headings: firstly, the new classifications themselves, and secondly, their relationships with consumer behaviour.

The new classifications

Characteristics that have emerged as most relevant are basic attitudes close to the context of product usage and purchase; in particular attitudes to such tasks as cooking, housework, and shopping. A large number of these classifications have been developed. Some have been very specific, and mainly applicable

to the product field in question (for example a concern with fresh-
ness in the mouth, in the toothpaste market). Others, however,
have been of a more general nature, clearly applicable to a much
wider span of consumer behaviour. These latter are regarded as
the first steps towards a final objective, namely the establishment
of a small repertoire of consumer personality scales, each of
proven value to several product fields.

For illustration, a few of these more general dimensions will be
outlined.

Firstly, the area of *thrift*, which was used for illustrative purposes in the previous section. It has been found possible to develop
measures reflecting a concern with thriftiness that apply to a wide
range of purchases. This does appear to be a general housewife
characteristic. There are, however, at least two clearly distinct
facets.* Firstly, there is 'economy-mindedness' – the tendency to
buy cheap rather than expensive goods, to keep within a strict
housekeeping limit, to deny oneself luxuries. This is quite different
from 'bargain-seeking', which reflects the satisfaction of saving a
few pennies by shopping carefully and comparing prices, and the
relish of hunting for bargains. One way of putting the distinction
is that whereas the economy-minded housewife abhors extrava-
gance, the bargain-seeking woman may welcome it – but she looks
for the cheapest shop in which to be extravagant.

The distinction has been confirmed on a number of occasions –
the two scales have been found to have a quite distinct pattern of
correlates. For example, the more economy-minded housewives
tend to come from the lower social classes, but not from any particular family size group. However, the more bargain-seeking
housewives are found amongst all social classes, but tend to come
from larger households. The two scales also identify quite separate
aspects of consumer behaviour.

This distinction has a clear practical value. Quite different
marketing and advertising action would be taken, according to
which scale was shown to be important. For example, the advertising appeal to economy-minded housewives would be quite
different from that to bargain-seeking housewives.

* Correlations within and between the two sets of statements can be seen
in Figure 28.

Another area is that of *Experimentalism*, which may be defined as an interest and enjoyment in buying new and different things. This again appears to be a very general characteristic. It does, however, have two quite distinct opposites. On the one hand are the rigid people who have an almost compulsive need to do and buy the same kind of things. On the other hand are the people who are afraid to buy something new or different, unless, say, it has been strongly recommended; they also tend to be anxious in case a purchase turns out to be a mistake.

A third and quite different area is *Traditionalism*. Here we mean the people who have relatively old-fashioned tastes and habits. For example, in housework they like doing things by hand, and enjoy cleaning and polishing the hard way; in cooking, they prefer traditional methods and recipes; they have a general abhorrence of modern values, and quick, easy, labour-saving methods.

Interpretations of the scales are based to a certain extent on the statements that comprise them. This is, however, reinforced by the approach of 'construct validity' mentioned in the previous section. From the use of a scale over a number of studies it is possible to accumulate a rich collection of ways in which high-scale and low-scale scorers differ. In time, concepts like 'economy-mindedness' and 'experimentalism' may become just as clear and familiar to marketing men as age and social class.

Classification and consumer behaviour

Results are very encouraging. Pronounced relationships are being found between the scales and consumer behaviour. There is only space for a few illustrations, which have been chosen from scales mentioned in the previous section.

The *traditionalism* scale was tried in a field where there are two distinct types of product: type A requires considerable effort in its usage, whereas type B is very much a labour-saving product. Analyses by demographic breakdowns had shown no significant discrimination between regular buyers of the two products. Analysis by 'traditionalism' showed quite marked discrimination. (Figure 30.)

The second example is from a product field of fairly recent

origin, but in which a high proportion of housewives purchase. There is a slight tendency for buying to vary with age and social class. But much sharper relationships were found between heaviness of buying and each of four psychological classifications. The most pronounced of these was *Experimentalism*. Analysis by product type proved even more illuminating. In Figure 31, type

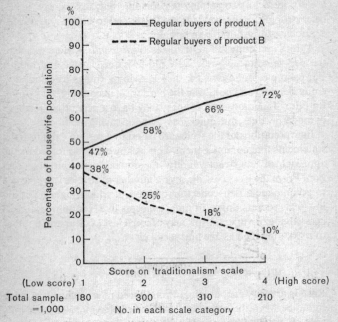

Figure 30. Segmentation of a market by the 'traditionalism' scale

A is a new launch, type B a fairly recent launch, type C one of the earliest launches. It can be seen that types A and to a lesser extent B are achieving sales chiefly to keen experimentalists. However, a disinclination to be experimental is no longer a barrier to buying C. It has also been found that high experimentalists show much more brand switching and, correspondingly, less brand loyalty over a range of product fields. Moreover, there are indications that this scale may help to identify 'new-product buyers' or even

'Innovators', whose possible existence has intrigued marketing men for some time.

The first two examples showed simple relationships between a single scale on the one hand and a measure of consumer behaviour on the other. Clearly, the situation is more complex than this. It is

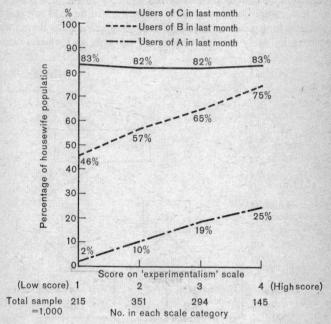

Figure 31. Relationship between 'experimentalism' scale and three product types

often necessary to group consumers in terms of combinations of characteristics. These profiles provide more meaningful descriptions of target groups than do characteristics taken singly. Moreover, by taking into account the interactions amongst psychological and other factors (see p. 411 above), they lead to much closer relationships with behaviour. There are two main approaches here, natural and predictive. The first establishes groups of people who are similar in terms of their scores on a set of characteristics. Relationships with behaviour are calculated only after the groups are formed. The second approach forms groups in terms of their prediction of an aspect of behaviour. Both approaches often show how the same behaviour may be carried out by different sub-groups of people for different combinations of motives.

An example of the predictive approach can be seen in Figure 32. It is for a product field where demographic variables do in fact correlate highly with purchasing. In this case all variables were

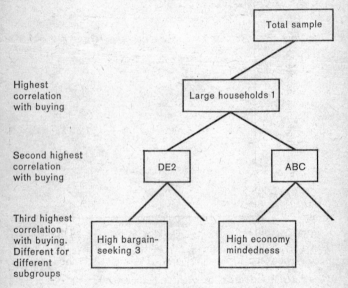

Figure 32. Segmentation of the market into sub-groups in terms of correlation with heaviness of buying

dichotomized, and their correlations with heaviness of buying examined in a series of stages. The highest single correlation was with household size, large households being the heaviest buyers. Within large households, the next best correlate was social class, proportionally more people from the lower socio-economic classes (DEs) being heavy buyers than those from other classes (ABCs). At a third level of segmentation, the highest correlation differed according to the sub-group: amongst DE large households it was bargain-seeking, amongst ABC large households, economy-mindedness.

The increasing precision gained from this kind of analysis can be seen from the following figures:

Proportion of heavy buyers amongst sub-groups

Large households	41 per cent
DE large households	54 per cent
High bargain-seeking DE large households	73 per cent

The value of classifications for marketing and advertising

The kinds of classification discussed above are quantitative – they enable us to divide people into groups in terms of their different positions along the dimensions concerned. And they are beginning to be used throughout the market research process in the same way as demographic classifications. Moreover, being directly expressed in terms of consumer needs, they increase the understanding of the market, suggesting possible courses of marketing and advertising action. Take the example in Figure 30. Here it seems that there are two distinct sub-markets separately catered for by product types A and B. If one's brand was an A type, attention would be focused upon the more 'traditional' groups and one set of product-benefits stressed. If it was a B type, attention would be focused upon the least 'traditional' groups and a quite different set of benefits stressed. (There might, of course, be benefits common to the two types.) The kind of action suggested can range from modification of product and pack design to the creation of more persuasive advertising copy. Leads may also be obtained for new products to satisfy needs not at present catered for (see also Chapter 20).

BRAND IMAGE RESEARCH

So far this chapter has dealt mainly with person-centred attitudes. However, object-centred attitudes play an equally important part in consumer research, and an especially familiar concept is that of the brand image. Indeed, 'image' has become an everyday term. It refers to the stereotypes, often well defined if inaccurate, that are held of different nationalities, politicians, pop-singers, and so on.

A brand image is simply the stereotyped view of a commercial product. It is the total set of impressions, feelings, and associations surrounding a particular brand. These impressions arise from a variety of sources – personal experience of the product, advertising, hearsay. It is generally considered essential that a brand should have a favourable image; that it should be perceived by intended consumers to have the characteristics that they require. And it is customary for a manufacturer to commission periodic checks, which place him in a position to take appropriate corrective action. Brand image research as such is not new. It has been carried out for several years, using a variety of techniques, all concerned with obtaining reactions to competing brands in terms of apparently important characteristics. Past research, however, has often been defective; in particular, it has often failed to show significant differences between the image profiles of apparently quite dissimilar brands.

New research developments

During the past few years, in an attempt to refresh and sharpen up image measurement, consumer research has turned to the kind of developments outlined in earlier sections of this chapter. There are, however, detailed differences in approach, which will now be briefly referred to.

As with person-centred attitudes, it is dangerous for the researcher to assume that he knows either what aspects are relevant, or how best to express them. These assumptions have often been made in the past, and brands have been compared on attributes like 'performance', 'quality', and 'hygiene', vague terms that may mean different things to different people, or indeed have little importance for brand discrimination. (An example of the latter point: good braking power may be an important characteristic of motor-cycles as a whole, but may not enter into the choice of a particular brand of motor-cycle; this may not be the kind of characteristic on which brands are expected to differ.)

Bearing the latter point very much in mind, unstructured exploratory interviews are coming to be supplemented by a technique adapted from clinical psychology, namely the method of triads.* Brand names (or any other objects) of interest are presented to a respondent in threes, with questions such as the following: 'In what important way are any two of these three alike and in the same way different from the third?' This basic procedure may be adapted in various ways. Chief interest has been not so much in the way the brands are grouped, although these can be illuminating, as in the grounds given for grouping them.†

As a result of a series of perhaps thirty such interviews, the researcher will have two sets of data: a series of hypotheses about the basic concepts by which people discriminate between brands; and sets of phrases which crystallize these concepts. Now comes the stage of measurement and item reduction. Here, the semantic differential technique devised by Osgood (1957) is becoming common practice. Phrases are presented to respondents in the form of seven-point bi-polar scales, for example:

soothes the skin   irritates the skin
reasonably priced   not reasonably priced

Respondents rate all brands of interest to the inquiry on the total set of scales. Responses are intercorrelated and factor analysed to indicate the main dimensions running through them. This procedure tests out the hypotheses concerning the basic concepts, perhaps suggesting modifications. It also indicates the best subsets of items to measure each concept in future inquiries.‡

* This is part of the 'Repertory Grid' approach put forward by Kelly (1955).

† Is is often valuable to probe beyond the first response to a triad. For example, if a respondent singled out one brand from the other two on the grounds of 'quality', one would ask what she meant by quality. 'It kills the grease.' Can she tell us more? 'With the other two you tend to get a scum left after washing-up, but not with the better-quality one.'

‡ Where there are several brands in the product field, say 10, and a large number of attributes, say 100, it is preferable to have two measurement stages, the first, a pilot, involving a smallish sample, perhaps 300 people. Each respondent will rate only 2 brands, but will use all 100 phrases; all 10 brands will be covered. The factor analysis will be performed on these

Much more sensitive and reliable brand discrimination is being obtained by these methods than previously. Characteristic results can be summarized under three headings:

(1) *Concepts*. For each product field, the concepts important for brand discrimination are established. Some of these concepts may have been known before, others may be quite new.

(2) *Consumer language*. Whether new or familiar, each concept is defined operationally in terms of a battery of highly correlated phrases, rather than vaguely by such abstractions as 'efficiency' and 'quality'. These phrases, being expressed in consumer language, provide much more meaningful guides for marketing action. For instance, the concept of glamour in the hair-spray market might be represented by the following phrases:

> Keeps you glamorous
> Gives a well-groomed look
> Used by top models
> Gives a silky look
> Makes you more feminine
> Holds your hair in place

(3) *Assessment of the market position and of marketing action*. When used as rating scales, these phrases can be turned into measuring instruments which permit precise assessment both of the current market position and of the effects of corrective action.

Figure 33 is a hypothetical illustration, based on actual figures from a different product field, of the position of two competing brands in the hair-spray market on two concepts, glamour and nourishment. B appears to have a slight edge on its rival A on nourishment, but to be considerably weak on glamour. Appropriate corrective action might be taken to make B more glamorous. The effects of this action could be measured by seeing how ratings on the glamour dimension improved as a result of, say, a redesigned package: several packages might be tested, and the one that brought ratings closest to A accepted.

responses. In the second stage, the full brand image inquiry, each respondent will rate all 10 brands, but on a much reduced set of attributes.

However, before any action is taken, three further considerations, vital to brand positioning, would normally be examined. These can be only briefly referred to here. Firstly, it would be pointless spending much effort on making B more glamorous if this is a relatively unimportant concept. Importance can be established by calculating the summed distances between the score for each brand and that for an 'ideal' brand (see below), and

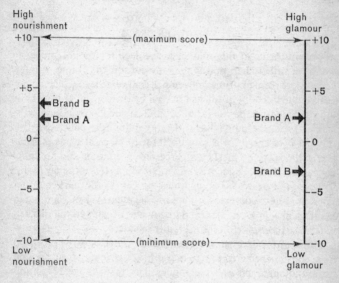

Figure 33. The rating of two competing brands on the concept of 'nourishment and glamour'

correlating these with overall brand ratings. The factor with the highest correlation is taken to be the most important, and so on.

Secondly, the optimum score on a concept is not necessarily 10. It is possible for a brand to be seen as too glamorous – perhaps meaning too 'flashy'. A rough but useful guide can be obtained by asking respondents to rate an 'ideal brand', and to compare these ratings with those for actual brands.

Thirdly, both relative importance of concepts, and optimum score on any one concept are not necessarily the same for all consumers. The hair-spray market might be divided into two broad segments: those who valued glamour and were unconcerned about nourishment, and vice-versa. Here it is important to carry out analyses by the kind of value characteristics outlined in the section 'New Forms of Classification' (p. 412).

MAPS OF PRODUCT SUBSTITUTION AND MARKET GAPS

A central theme of this chapter is the need for the researcher to establish rather than presuppose the consumer's frame of reference. A problem of prime importance is the extent to which apparently quite different products are seen by the consumer as equally appropriate for a particular need; and to which apparently quite similar products are seen as satisfying quite different needs. It is obviously essential for a manufacturer to be as clear as possible about the way the market is perceived by present and potential consumers. If he produces a *range* of products it is more profitable for these to be directed to separate segments of the market, rather than allowed to compete for the same segment. When planning to launch a new product, he should be aware of gaps in the market, in terms of consumer needs currently uncatered for.

Maps of product substitution, which describe with precision how consumers perceive the market, are coming to be plotted using the approach and techniques described above for brand image research. These can be plotted in n dimensional space, n being the number of important consumer dimensions. In practice a series of maps are usually drawn in either two or three dimensional space. An example of the latter is given in Chapter 20. As with brand image studies, we also require indications of the relative importance of various dimensions, of the optimum position for a product to achieve on each dimension, and of the different perceptions by different target sub-groups.

*

An attempt has been made in this chapter to show that the social scientist can help market decision-making in a highly systematic manner. Insights derived from unstructured interviewing can now be turned into precise variables: these variables can be interrelated both with each other and with consumer behaviour. This kind of information not only increases the understanding of the market, suggesting courses of marketing action, but also provides precise measuring instruments in the form of attitude scales by which to evaluate this action.

CHAPTER 20

New-Product Development

COLIN GOLBY

CONSUMER industries are becoming more and more concerned
with the development of new products. Product change is so rapid
in certain fields that some companies will not be able to survive
unless they can develop successful new entrants into their existing
markets or deploy their existing skills into new markets.

Whilst it is difficult to assess accurately the rate of new-product
development, a study carried out in 1965 by J. Walter Thompson
estimated that out of a total of 501 company names entered in 29
product categories in Shaw's Price List in 1954, *only half were still
in the same category in* 1964. Put in another way, in the total of
534 company names entered in 1964, over half had become involved in these categories since 1954. Moreover, between 1955 and
1963, 402 entries were in product categories which to the companies were new markets and 41 *per cent of these entries failed to
survive into* 1964. Not only is new-product development, therefore,
essential to the survival of many companies, but it involves a great
deal of trial and error. For example, it is reported that Bird's Eye
has rejected ten products for every one that it has marketed, and,
even so, the British housewife has rejected a hundred of the firm's
marketed products.

Trial and error may in fact be a necessary part of the process of
new-product development for many years to come. However,
because the consumer is human, it is reasonable to suppose that
the social sciences have some role to play in developing new
products as a means of reducing uncertainty. It is the purpose of
this chapter to attempt to define the limits within which the human
sciences can contribute to the development of new products. We
will be largely concerned with the role of the social scientist *qua*
market researcher in the field of consumer manufacturing industries.

NEW PRODUCTS AND SOCIAL CHANGE

Some of the more important social changes today are reflected in the ever-increasing development of new products – particularly in the consumer product field. For example, the public's growing involvement in leisure activities and the increased importance to the housewife of having part-time employment are, amongst other factors, reflected in the ever-increasing proliferation of convenience and snack foods. The growth of social mixing and entertaining in a context of rapid social mobility, particularly among the young and the middle-aged, is reflected in the increased popularity of the wine market and in the sales of new forms of social drinks, such as sherry, vodka, etc. Moreover, the greater opportunities for travel have increased the consumer's demand for food of a non-English origin. Children 'grow up' earlier and the family itself breaks up earlier – creating both a teenage and a pre-teenage culture which demand their own products and their own forms of dress and apparel. At the same time, and owing partly to the same maturing influences, the young wife learns more and more for herself – using her mother less and less as a model – and tends to imitate and take advice from her peers, who are her equals in age but not necessarily in status and experience. One of the reasons, therefore, for the demand for new products is the changing personal and social needs of the consumer. Older products carry older associations. What mother did and used needs more and more reinforcement and justification if it is to survive as a product and as a habit. In many product fields, old-established brands have a remarkable ability to survive; but they are suffering a constant erosion from competition which makes their owners search harder for new sources of profit in the future.

NEW PRODUCTS AND TECHNICAL DEVELOPMENTS

In spite of the powerful influences which broader social changes have on product development, it would be a great mistake to think that new-product development simply follows the paths outlined by other forms of change. Clearly, one of the most important factors, and in some fields *the* most important factor, is the development of technical skills in the creation and mass-marketing of new products and new forms of presentation. For example, the invention and mass-production of refrigeration equipment has almost certainly had a powerful influence on the role of the house-wife, enabling her to spend less time in the kitchen and so make a greater contribution to family life. Also, by going out to work, she can provide more income for the family, so adding to its possessions and thus increasing her own power and importance in relation to her husband. Similarly, technical developments, like the invention of detergents, the mass-production of washing machines, and even the marketing initiative involved in the mass selling of drinks like Babycham, have themselves made significant contributions to social change.

It is important to get into proper perspective the relative roles played by social change and technical development in order to understand the kind of contribution which the social scientist can make to new-product development. It is quite wrong to suppose that new-product development consists simply of the social scientist investigating the market, looking for latent or unsatisfied consumer needs and then reporting back this information to the research and development staff, who then produce the product to satisfy the need. Only very rarely does this occur in practice – and it is very rare for three main reasons.

Firstly, as we saw in Chapter 19, the tools of the social scientist, particularly in analysing and predicting behaviour (that is pur-chasing behaviour), are still in the process of development. Most of the investigatory methods have been based on inadequate attitude research techniques using preconceived concepts, and not enough is yet known about the role played by attitudes in the formation of behaviour change – and the extent to which certain attitudes are the causes or the results of behaviour – to enable sufficiently accurate predictions to be made.

Secondly, there is a creative component in new-product develop-ment to which social scientists are only very slowly learning to make a contribution – for example, in postulating hypothetical products as possible solutions to the satisfaction of consumer needs. Many market researchers still regard their role as only investigatory and analytical – whereas it could be just as much their task to formulate hypothetical solutions as it is to analyse problems.

Thirdly, and probably the most important, the success of a new product in many fields, particularly in the food and household product fields, will depend primarily, even if decreasingly so, on the intrinsic physical qualities of the product itself. This means that the role of the social scientist is bound to be secondary to that of the physical scientist and, although the experimental psychologist can play a complementary role in developing methods of measuring perceived differences in physical products, this work is still in its infancy.

Because of the limitations of investigatory techniques, the lack of creativity among market researchers, and the primary role of technical skills in innovation, new-product development is, and will remain for some years, largely a matter of experiment. The role of the social scientist will be to help reduce uncertainty, at the same time improving his understanding of behaviour and becoming more skilled at offering hypothetical solutions.

ANALYSIS OF TYPES OF 'NEW' PRODUCT

Before discussing how the social scientist, in the role of market researcher, can help in the development of new products, it is essential to make a brief analysis of the different meanings of the word 'new' in product development. The term, 'new products' can imply anything from minor changes in formulae to the invention of completely new products in completely new markets – the latter being very rare and almost always depending on technical breakthroughs. If we include not only objective product changes but 'subjective' changes, such as pack and advertising changes, we obtain a whole spectrum of change which probably covers most known examples.

One important lesson from this analysis is that most product innovations consist of changes to existing products. In fact, the majority of new products in most mass consumer markets are modifications of existing products. It is, therefore, better to regard new-product development as part of a cycle of change rather than as a series of radically different innovations.

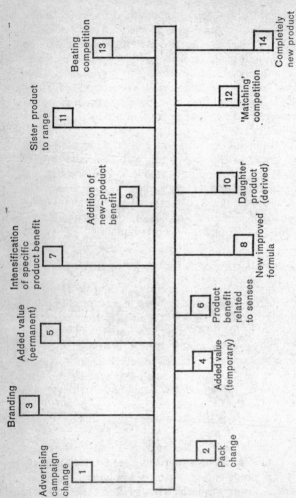

Figure 34. The spectrum of product change. Stages 1–5 may be regarded as 'subjective' changes – the physical product remaining unaltered. Stages 6–9 involve modifications to products already owned by the company. Stages 10–14 involve more radical changes both to formulae and often to plant and production. (*Reproduced by kind permission of the New Product Development Unit of J. Walter Thompson Co. Ltd*)

With this spectrum in mind, it will now be clear how the social scientist can help. There are three main areas:

(1) Origination of new-product ideas, mainly through analysis of the consumer
(2) Screening and evaluating these ideas
(3) Testing physical products representing these ideas

(1) ORIGINATION OF NEW-PRODUCT IDEAS

There are three main ways in which the social scientist can help in the origination of new-product ideas – by analysing behaviour, by measuring attitudes, and by the systematic creation of new ideas.

Origination by analysis of behaviour

It will probably be clear by now that, by reference to the spectrum of product change, it is possible to examine behavioural data provided by market research in the search for new-product ideas which correspond to existing behavioural patterns. The following example is provided by British Market Research Bureau Ltd.

As part of a programme of research in the household cleaning product field, a behavioural survey of brands, materials, and cleaning operations was carried out. This was on a national quota sample of 3,000 women with equal numbers being interviewed on different days of the week because of the different cleaning operations taking place on different days. The most important aspect of this survey was that it included a study not only of product usage, but also of the use of non-branded materials and, in addition, an account of the detailed aspects of the cleaning operations which accompanied the use of each product and material. In this way, it was possible to examine the role of the client's product (A) in relation to the whole cleaning activity. The results of this survey showed that product A had three main uses, each accounting for about one-third of sales:

Usage 1 – where it was used on its own
Usage 2 – where it was used on its own *but a usage known from other studies to be declining*

Usage 3 – where the product was used 50/50 in accompaniment with another product (B) marketed by a competitor.

One clear recommendation as a result of this analysis was that a second product should be developed to fulfil Usage 3 and so increase the total franchise of the brand. A 'sister' product was therefore produced.

This clearly demonstrates the way in which an analysis of behaviour can help to produce product ideas – particularly those which involve a combination of existing products and/or materials. But it also shows that it is important to analyse not only products, but whole operations. A simple analysis of products used would not have revealed the combined use of products A and B.

A completely different method of behavioural analysis has been used by Marketing, Advertising and Product Studies Ltd, where housewives have been filmed carrying out everyday domestic activites (cleaning, cooking, etc.). An analysis of the sequences revealed 'difficulties' and inefficiencies of performance which were not only capable of analysis, but, when played back to the housewives, caused them to have greater insight into their behaviour and to suggest remedies in the form of product and pack modifications.

Origination by measurement of attitudes

The second, and perhaps the more obvious, method of origination is to carry out studies of consumers' needs, using attitudinal research techniques and then to map out gaps in a given market, where there are needs but no products, or where competitors have products but not oneself. Examples of the application of this approach to new-product development are given in the following pages. A full description of the technique and additional examples in established product fields has been given in Chapter 19.

One example of the generation of new-product concepts through consumer research is outlined in a paper by Skelly and Nelson (1965). The first stage in such a research programme is to elicit consumer satisfactions and dissatisfactions by the use of group discussions and depth interviews. Women's frustrations, hurdles, and problems are explored in relation to a given type of activity. Techniques like the reconstruction of particular activities and play-acting are employed. From the solution to the problem thus diagnosed, new-product concepts are evolved. Attitudinal factors derived from this qualitative stage are factor-analysed and then, through a process described as 'segmentation analysis', the segments of the market are defined in respect of attitude differences, which are much more helpful for the detection of the unsatisfied needs than the more traditional break-downs of age, sex, social class, etc. The use of 'segmentation analysis' in the cold remedy market revealed three critical attitudinal segments.

SEGMENT 1. People who believe in taking medicine for colds (pills, capsules, etc.) and who have no real concern about the side-effects of taking such medicine. These are people who are essentially very active, confident, and usually healthy. They feel that the taking of any medicine will not jeopardize their general health. Relief from cold symptoms is their prime concern. This group was found in general to be takers of the available cold pills on the market – in fact takers of virtually every cold pill on the market.

SEGMENT 2. People who believe that, because there is no way to cure a cold, there is no point in trying to relieve the symptoms to any degree. This segment is composed of people who take to their beds with hot toddies and perhaps go as far as taking aspirin. In general, this segment is very unresponsive and, in fact, fearful about cold pills.

SEGMENT 3. People who want to feel as though they are taking something for their cold, but at the same time do not want to take anything strong or that would have potential side-effects. The very action of taking a pill is something they want to do in order to feel that action is being taken because inaction is intolerable. It was found that this third segment was *not* being served by any existing products on the market. A mild cold pill, that is one that did not promise great efficiency but rather promised slow relief, was clearly something that might have real appeal for this segment.

It was concluded that Segment 1 is a logical target for a new cold remedy positioned along existing lines. Segment 2 is not really in the cold remedy market, whilst Segment 3 is receptive to a new-concept cold remedy – *contingent on its size in the population* – which could be subject to a validation study.

It is necessary to quote these findings in some detail since they clearly demonstrate the way in which attitude research can both produce and eliminate target groups and also (in the case of Segment 3) point to an unresolved need. It is also possible, although not discussed in the paper quoted above, that a modified product might be developed for Segment 2 – modified not necessarily from a cold remedy product, but from some other source.

A second method of attitude measurement, using the Kelly (1955) Repertory Grid and factor analysis* in the origination of new product ideas, is employed by Advertising Assessment Ltd.

Imagine a manufacturer of confectionery who already markets a range of confectionery products. He wants to know how far the products currently available satisfy the consumer's requirements. Do the existing products span all the range of requirements? Are there any requirements satisfied by his competitors but not by himself? Take, for example, the texture dimension of crunchy/ soft. Do competitive products bunch and overlap on this dimension and are there gaps – gaps which may intersect with, say, the light/dark dimension? For example, the need for a crisp/dark chocolate may be satisfied by an existing product but the need for a crisp/light chocolate may not. The starting point in this analysis is the use of the Kelly Repertory Grid on a small sample of consumers to establish the dimensions. Advertising Assessment believe that, although this method may be reinforced by the more traditional group discussion, on its own it is superior to the group discussion, since the triad administration technique tends to have greater power to force out attributes of which the consumer was not previously completely aware. The attributes which evolve from this study undergo factor analysis and then are matched against existing, new, and even imaginary ('ideal') brands in the market in question, using a brand/attitude survey. The kind of information which emerges is a multi-dimensional model which relates both the attributes and the brands. A three-dimensional

* For explanations of Kelly's Grid and factor analysis see pp. 421 and 407 respectively.

version in the confectionery field might look like Figure 35.

Brand A being 'filling', 'sweet', and 'soft' has a considerable market as has Brand B, which is 'hard', 'light', and 'sweet'. Meanwhile, there is a market for a non-existent brand, Y – which is 'medium hard', 'filling', and 'not so sweet'. This can be a useful method for charting attitudinal constructs, particularly in fields where the relationship between attributes may be complex – that

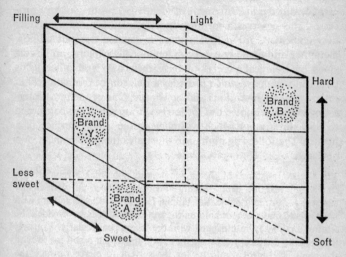

Figure 35. Multi-dimensional model relating attributes and brands

is, where 'value for money', for example, may be 'size' or 'protein value' or 'class' for different groups in relation to different types of products. Finding gaps by this method can both test new product ideas and produce new product ideas in areas of unfulfilled needs.

The systematic creation of new ideas

'Brainstorming' has been a traditional way of describing any management process of generating ideas by group discussion. It may appear strange to suggest that the social scientist can help in this area. However, it is possible that, as more comes to be known about the relationship between changing consumer needs and the evolution of new products, so the social scientist will be called in more often to analyse this relationship. At the moment this contribution is very much in its infancy, but there have been developments in the United States of a method of systematic discussion called 'synectics', which is in fact the development of creative capacity. Since many social scientists are becoming more concerned with the measurement of creativity and the creative processes, this deserves a mention here in relation to new product development. Gordon (1961) gives a detailed account of how metaphor and analogy can be systematically explored in discussions by technical experts of both their own and other fields (especially biology, which provides a rich source of analogies) in order to create inventions and new ideas. One of the most interesting examples quoted by Gordon is a group which was concerned to 'develop a paint which will cling to the chalky surface of a house'. The following quotation illustrates the development of a new idea.

The chalky resistance of the previous paint jobs makes repainting a tough job ... I'm a drop of paint and I've just been put on a chalky surface. ... I'm in a panic. I'm falling, falling. ... I'm scratching with my claws to find a decent hold on the sub-surface! (Claws provided the fruitful analogy.) I'm intrigued with the 'claws' particularly. You see, if the chalky surface was brushed ... you might put a solvent in with the paint. The ideal would be for the solvent to pierce through the chalky surface like a cat's claws, and for the paint to follow the solvent through to the undersurface! The 'claws' analogy thus leads to a new solution.

There is a considerable similarity between this use of analogy and metaphor and the development of consumer products. In fact, in the communication of many consumer products, systematic use is made of analogies and metaphor, for example MILK – CADBURYS, GOODNESS – GUINNESS, SUNSHINE – KELLOGGS, FILM STARS – LUX, SWORDS – WILKINSON. Moreover, as we have already noticed, new products tend to develop out of existing products by a continuous process of evolution. It is, therefore, possible to explore metaphors, analogies, and similes in the development of new-product ideas. The following illustration shows how Babycham might have been developed, based on desired product attributes, desired characteristics of the drinker, and free associations with each of these categories.

BRIEF – To produce a new alcoholic drink for women to drink in pubs

Desired Product Attributes	Free Associations	Desired Characteristic of the Drinker	Free Associations
SWEET	– LIKE A SUGAR CHILD	SAFE	– MOTHER, CHILD, BABY
DRY	– SOPHISTI-CATED	GENTLE	– SOFT, ANIMAL, FURRY
PURE	– NATURAL FRUIT	CHARMING	– PRINCE CHARM-ING, SNOW-WHITE, DISNEY
LIGHT	– AIRY	FUN	– PLAYFUL, KITTEN
SPARKLING	– CHAMPAGNE	NICE	– INNOCENT, VIRTUOUS
BUBBLING	– GIGGLING	NAUGHTY	– NICE
CLEAR	– PURE, UN-TOUCHED	PLAYFUL	– AMUSING
		DECEITFUL	– TRICKSY, PRETEND
		LOVED	– TOUCHED, DESIRED

Taking as starting points, 'sparkling', 'safe', 'gentle', and 'charming', we obtain:

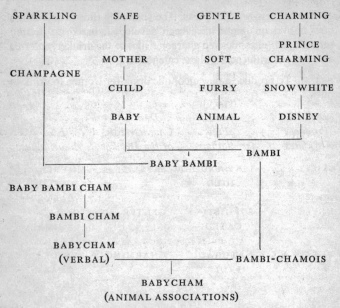

This is of course apocryphal, but there is no reason why it should not represent a systematic exploration of associations and it is clearly subject to 'synectic' treatment. This symbolic treatment is clearly relevant not only to product ideas, but also to the physical design of new products, packs, labels, advertisements, etc. It can, therefore, represent the link between the social scientist, the 'creative man', and the research and development department of the manufacturer within a management control system. It is likely that the social scientist will have an increasingly important part to play in the area of creativity in the next decade.

(2) SCREENING AND EVALUATING IDEAS

Following the origination of product ideas, either by systematic investigation of the consumer's needs or systematic exploration of ideas, there emerges usually a range of product 'concepts' – possibly as many as 30 for any product. These can be reduced to a smaller number (4–10) largely by judgement, based on considerations of economy, production, product engineering, or marketing knowledge. It is at the screening stage that management most often needs the skills of the social scientist to bridge the gap between the many possible and one or two practicable ideas.

The main technique which has been developed has been labelled 'concept testing'. A typical example might be as follows:

The 'concepts'   – usually descriptions of the product and its benefits either in verbal or visual form are listed. Take for instance the toothpaste field:

BRAND A   A toothpaste that automatically cleans the whole mouth,

BRAND B   A toothpaste which penetrates the gums and medicates the teeth,

BRAND C   A toothpaste which, if used three times a day, prevents 90 per cent of decay,

and so on.

The next stage is to administer attitude questions in order to discover reactions to these 'concepts', thereby measuring comprehension, desirability, credibility, etc. For instance, in the above example, Concept C might be the most believable, whilst Concept B might be the most desirable or Concept A might be the most understandable. It is, of course, possible to make this technique much more sophisticated than the above example. For example, the 'concept' can be produced in the form of a television advertisement – and even in pack form containing the product.

Most social scientists working on new-product development appear to be more or less dissatisfied with this method of investigation as a predictive tool. It clearly leaves much to be desired. The main weakness is that it presupposes that the verbal responses to a statement, a TV advertisement, or, indeed, a pack can be used as a means of predicting behaviour in a purchasing situation. Even if non-verbal responses (like eye-blink measurements) are used, it has still to be explained how valid these are as predictions. It is, in fact, a method of research which is almost impossible to validate (which is perhaps part of its appeal). So far as is known to the author, no study has been made of products which were then assessed in a behavioural test involving purchasing; and even if this had been done, it would only demonstrate the relationship in that particular experiment. Without inordinate expense, it could not be shown how far the product, pack, advertising, and marketing strategy had each contributed to the final result. The essential virtue of this technique is largely one relating to management decision-making. It is a technique, for example, used 'successfully' by one of the largest American food companies who, periodically, have to reduce a large number of possible new concepts to a viable number. Such a screening process has obvious advantages in helping management to make decisions. But there is no evidence that these are the right decisions and that a valuable product has not been lost because it came low in such a concept test. Psychological certainty should not be confused with accuracy – even if it does increase management confidence and the fluency of decision-making.

In the light of so little evidence as to how verbal responses relate to other forms of responses (for example purchasing), there are three main possible methods of operation:

(1) To use concept testing only as a means of management decision-making. This can be an important management function if it is clearly understood.

(2) To carry out systematic follow-up studies in a sufficiently large number of concept tests, so as to establish statistical relationships between initial verbal responses and subsequent purchases. This is possible in theory but likely to be highly expensive.

(3) To develop 'concepts' to a stage which includes more of the physical communication of pack and product and, therefore, enables purchasing responses to be measured. Although more expensive than (1) above, this is likely to be less expensive and certainly more accurate than (2).

(3) TESTING THE PHYSICAL PRODUCTS

There are many methods of testing products prior to national or test marketing. Most of these consist of placing the product either 'blind' (without identification), with or without its main competitor, or in a labelled pack together with brief instructions for use. The interviewer leaves the product (sometimes two or three units) with a sample of consumers who, according to previous 'segmentation' research, have been nominated as the 'potential' market. A week or so later the interviewer calls back and obtains behavioural and attitude information so as to determine the pattern of response to the products. The most valid use of this method of research is to assess the negative responses in order to determine whether the product should be modified in any way prior to a market test. Because of the difficulties (already discussed) of using verbal responses as predictions of behaviour, most manufacturers put very little trust in praise or enthusiasm for the product, both because of the initial halo effects, and also because of the fatigue that might well set in after more continuous usage.

It is equally difficult in many markets to make predictions from 'blind' product tests which involve pairing the test product with a 'blind' sample of the main competitor. In many markets, particularly for example in Great Britain, where there is a considerable number of traditional and well-established products, it is possible, and often likely, that a new test product will be preferred to an established product in a 'blind' test, but that the older product will be purchased in preference in the market place. For example, a recent finding by a large American food company attempting to break into the English market showed the following pattern.

	U.K. established brand	U.S. new brand
Blind test preference	30	70
Purchase preference	80	20

This perhaps demonstrates how the standing of the traditional brand (including brand name, childhood associations, advertising, etc.) can play a much more important role in the acceptability of the brand as a purchase than its physical qualities alone. This kind of apparent discrepancy illustrates once more the necessity, wherever possible, to obtain behavioural (purchasing) responses to an object which is the nearest practicable simulation to the product in its ultimate surroundings, that is in final pack and presentation form. A technique which comes quite near to simulating purchasing conditions is that of gift-choice. Here the respondent has a chance of being given either the product or cash. This may be related to a raffle in which the product is given to the winner or winners, or it may be incorporated into a standard placement test, as in the following example.

A women's toiletry product has been devised in direct competition to a main brand already commanding a sizeable section of the market. Three hundred 'potential' purchasers were given a sample of the new product for a fortnight, at the end of which the interviewers returned to inquire whether the informant wanted a further supply of either the product itself, or its main competitor, or cash (the amount of cash being carefully adjusted so as to be sufficiently lower than the value of the item). After carrying out similar calls on four more occasions at fortnightly intervals, it was possible to assess the comparative appeal of the test product in relation to its competitor. It was also possible to obtain a measure of fatigue and to refine the definition of the user, frequent user, and non-user. Using this technique, it is possible to predict how far a modified version of an established brand would compete with or add to the sales of the existing brand. The gift-choice technique appears to be effective at simulating and predicting the extent of competitiveness in the market.

A further example of an attempt to predict in product testing is given by Market, Advertising and Product Studies Ltd. A study was undertaken to estimate the characteristics of users of a product which was likely to have a relatively small market share. It was thought that if a research technique could be designed to predict these characteristics, it would be highly economical as compared with any form of market test with follow-up research, in view of the likelihood that the product would have only a minority appeal. The first step was to place the product with a pilot sample of consumers in the product field. After using supplies of the product for a fortnight, respondents were invited to undergo a highly intensive and detailed interview carried out by a social psychologist. During this interview not only were reactions to the product assessed but also a whole range of responses associated with the product and its use – but not directly concerning the product. From these 'indirect' responses, a series of hypotheses was developed and these were then expressed in the form of nine simple attitude scales.

The sample was then divided into five behavioural groups as follows:

(1) Those who had not been prepared to try the product at all when they knew what it was.

(2) Those who said they would try but had some reason for not having tried.

(3) Those who tried it but did not like it.

(4) Those who tried it and liked it, but when given the option of more product or cash, took cash.

(5) Those who preferred the product to cash.

The behavioural groups above were found to be very closely linked with scores on the nine attitude scales. As we have seen, these scales did not relate to the product directly but, in fact, to personality factors, enjoyment of certain types of social occasion, experimentalism, etc. The nine scales were then administered to a further sample who also received the product and the results predicted the behavioural groupings of this second sample in relation to the product with only a 2 per cent error. This appeared, therefore, to be a method of predicting responses to the product in a market test.

Although such a test has not yet been carried out, this appears to be a promising approach for the development of attitudinal predictors of behaviour.

*

We have outlined the use of the social sciences in new product development in five main ways.

(1) In assessing gaps in existing markets for which new products can be designed. Analysis of behaviour and measurements of attitude are useful here.

(2) In providing the systematic exploration of ideas by generating metaphor and analogy.

(3) In helping management decision-making in the screening of new product 'concepts'.

(4) In measuring *negative* reactions to products.

(5) In developing ways of predicting competitiveness, user characteristics, and market size by the use of behavioural measures stemming from gift-choice.

Further Reading

THE books listed here enlarge upon the topics covered in the text. In many cases they might well have been listed under more than one of the sections. Books which the layman will find well within his comprehension are marked with an asterisk.

INTRODUCTORY TEXTS

Miller, D. C., and Form, W. H. (1964), *Industrial Sociology* (2nd edition), Harper, New York.

Tiffin, J., and McCormick, E. J. (1965), *Industrial Psychology* (5th edition), Allen & Unwin, London.

MANPOWER UTILIZATION AND INDUSTRIAL RELATIONS

Flanders, A. (1964), *The Fawley Productivity Agreements*, Faber & Faber, London.

*Fox, A. (1965), *The Milton Plan*, Institute of Personnel Management, London.

*Jones, K., and Golding, J. (1966), *Productivity Bargaining*, Fabian Research Series, 257.

Kahn, Hilda (1964), *Repercussions of Redundancy*, Allen & Unwin, London.

Lupton, T. (1963), *On the Shop Floor*, Pergamon, London.

Marcson, S. (1961)., *The Scientist in American Industry*, Harper, New York.

O.E.C.D. (1965), *Acceptance and Resistance*, O.E.C.D., Paris.

Roberts, B. C., and Smith, J. A. (eds.) (1966), *Manpower Policy and Employment Trends*, London School of Economics and Bell, London.

Touraine, A., and Associates (1965), *Workers' Attitudes to Technical Change*, O.E.C.D., Paris.

Wedderburn, D. (1965), *Redundancy and the Railwaymen*, Cambridge University Press, Cambridge.

Wedderburn, D. (1968), *Enterprise Planning for Change – Coordination of Manpower and Technical Planning*, O.E.C.D., Paris.

Weinstein, P. A. (ed.) (1965), *Featherbedding and Technological Change*, D. C. Heath, Boston.

TRAINING FOR SKILL

*Belbin, E. (1964), 'Training the Adult Worker', *Problems of Progress in Industry*, *15*, H.M.S.O., London.

Belbin, R. M. (1965), *Employment of Older Workers: Methods of Training*, O.E.C.D., Paris.

Coulson, J. E. (1962), *Programmed Learning and Computer Based Instruction*, Wiley, New York.

Glazer, R. (1962), *Training, Research and Education*, Pittsburgh University Press, Pittsburgh.

Holding, D. H. (1965), *Principles of Training*, Pergamon, Oxford.

*King, D. (1964), *Training within the Organisation*, Tavistock, London.

Seymour, W. D. (1966), *Industrial Skill*, Pitman, London.

ERGONOMICS

*A series of twelve free booklets, 'Ergonomics for Industry', published by the Ministry of Technology, Millbank Tower, Millbank, London SW1.

Broadbent, D. E. (1961), *Perception and Communication*, Scientific Book Guild, London.

Chapanis, A. (1965), *Man–Machine Engineering*, Tavistock, London.

McCormick, E. (1957), *Human Engineering*, McGraw-Hill, New York.

Murrell, K. F. H. (1965), *Ergonomics*, Chapman & Hall, London.

*Welford, A. T. (1960), 'Ergonomics of Automation', *Problems of Progress in Industry*, *8*, H.M.S.O., London.

ORGANIZATION BEHAVIOUR

Some general introductory texts:

Blau, P. M., and Scott, W. (1966), *Formal Organisations*, Kegan Paul, London.

*Etzioni, A. (1964), *Modern Organisations*, Prentice-Hall, Englewood Cliffs, New Jersey.

*Pugh, D. S., Hickson, D. J., and Hinings, C. R. (1964), *Writers on Organisations*, Hutchinson, London.

*Schein, E. H. (1965), *Organisation Psychology*, Prentice-Hall, Englewood Cliffs, New Jersey.

*Tannenbaum, A. S. (1966), *Social Psychology of the Work Organisation*, Tavistock, London.

The following represent particular approaches to the study of organization behaviour:

INDIVIDUAL THEORISTS

Argyris, C. (1964), *Integrating the Individual and the Organisation*, Wiley, New York.

Simon, H. A. (1965), *Administrative Behavior*, Free Press, New York.

GROUP THEORISTS

Kahn, R. L. *et al.* (1964), *Organisational Stress: Studies in Role Conflict and Ambiguity*, Wiley, New York.

Likert, R. (1961), *New Patterns of Management*, McGraw-Hill, New York.

STRUCTURAL THEORISTS

Burns, T., and Stalker, G. M. (1966), *The Management of Innovation*, Tavistock, London.

Gouldner, A. W. (1965), *Industrial Bureaucracy*, Free Press, New York.

TECHNOLOGY THEORISTS

Trist, E. L. *et al.* (1963), *Organisational Choice*, Tavistock, London.

Woodward, J. (1965), *Industrial Organisation*, Oxford University Press, Oxford.

MANAGEMENT THEORISTS

*Brown, W. (1960), *Exploration in Management*, Heinemann, London.

Koontz, H. (ed.) (1964), *Towards a Unified Theory of Management*, McGraw-Hill, New York.

Some additional books on topics not listed above:

LEADERSHIP

Dubin, R., Homans, G. C., and Mann, F. C. (1965), *Leadership and Productivity*, Chandler Publishing Co., San Francisco.

*McGregor, D. (1966), *Leadership and Motivation*, M.I.T. Press, Cambridge, Mass.

TRAINING

*Argyle, M., and Smith, T. (1962), *Training Managers*, Acton Society Trust, London.

Fairhead, J., Pugh, D. S., and Williams, W. J. (1965), *Exercise in Business Decisions*, English University Press, London.

Schein, E. H., and Bennis, W. G. (1965), *Personal and Organisational Change Through Group Methods*, Wiley, London.

MOTIVATION AND INCENTIVES

*Gellerman, S. (1963), *Motivation and Productivity*, American Management Association.

*Lupton, T. (1961), 'Money for Effort', *Problems of Progress in Industry*, *11*, H.M.S.O., London.

Marriott, R. (1957), *Incentive Payment Systems – A Review of Research and Opinion*, Staples, London.

Vroom, V. (1964), *Work and Motivation*, Wiley, New York.

MARKET RESEARCH AND RESEARCH TECHNIQUES

MARKET RESEARCH

*Adler, M. K. (1959), *Modern Market Research*, Crosby, Lockwood & Sons, London.

Boyd, H. W. (1964), *Marketing Research*, Irwin, Homewood, Illinois.

Britt, S. H. (ed.) (1967), *Consumer Behaviour and the Behavioral Sciences*, Wiley, New York.

RESEARCH TECHNIQUES

Edwards, A. L. (1957), *Techniques of Attitude Scale Construction*, Appleton-Century-Crofts, New York.

Jahoda, M., and Warren, N. (eds.) (1966), *Attitudes*, Penguin Books, Harmondsworth.

Moser, C. A. (1958), *Survey Methods in Social Investigation*, Heinemann, London.

Oppenheim, A. N. (1966), *Questionnaire Design and Attitude Measurement*, Heinemann, London.

Payne, S. L. (1951), *The Art of Asking Questions*, Princeton University Press, Princeton.

Selltiz, C., *et al.* (eds.) (1959), *Research Methods in Social Relations*, Holt, New York.

STATISTICS

Guilford, J. P. (1954), *Psychometric Methods*, McGraw-Hill, New York.

McNemar, Q. (1955), *Psychological Statistics*, Wiley, New York.

Siegel, S. (1955), *Nonparametric Statistics*, McGraw-Hill, New York.

References

Acton Society Trust (1956), *Management Succession*, London.

Alford, L. P., and Beatty, H. R. (1951), *Principals of Industrial Management*, Ronald Press, London.

Allen, W. W. (1966), 'Britain in Blinkers', *Sunday Times*, 12 June.

Annett, J. (1959), 'Learning a Pressure under Conditions of Immediate and Delayed Knowledge of Results', *Quarterly Journal of Experimental Psychology*, 11, 3–15.

Anshen, M. (1965), 'Managerial Decisions', in Dunlop, J. T. (ed.), *Automation and Technological Change*, Prentice Hall, New Jersey.

Argyris, C. (1964), *Integrating the Individual and the Organisation*, Wiley, New York.

Aubert, V. (1959), 'Chance in Social Affairs', *Inquiry*, 2, 1–24.

Bakke, E. W. (1950), *Bonds of Organization*, Harper, New York.

Bedford, T. (1936), 'The Warmth Factor in Comfort at Work', *I.H.R.B. Report*, 76, H.M.S.O., London.

Beer, S. (1965), 'The Electronic Firm', in Malik, R. (ed.), *Penguin Survey of Business and Industry*, Penguin Books, Harmondsworth.

Belbin, R. M. (1965), *Training Methods*, O.E.C.D., Paris.

Ben-David, J. (1962), 'Scientific Productivity and Academic Organisation in 19th-Century Medicine', *American Sociological Review*, 25, 828–43.

Berg, I. A., and Kuhn, J. (1965), 'The Assumptions of Featherbedding', in Weinstein, P. A. (ed.), *Featherbedding and Technological Change*, D. C. Heath, Boston.

Birren, J. E. (ed.) (1959), *Handbook of Ageing and the Individual*, University of Chicago Press, Chicago.

Blake, R., and Mouton, S. (1964), *The Managerial Grid*, Gulf Publishing Co., Houston, Texas.

Blauner, R. (1964), *Alienation and Freedom*, Chicago University Press, Chicago.

Bromley, D. B. (1958), 'Some Effects of Age on Short-Term Learning and Remembering', *Journal of Gerontology*, 13, 398–406.

Bromley, D. B. (1966), *The Psychology of Human Ageing*, Penguin Books, Harmondsworth.

Brookman, E. (1963), 'Research and Development – Why?', *Imperial Chemical Industries Magazine*, 41, 111–15.

Brown, W. (1960), *Exploration in Management*, Heinemann, London.

Brown, W. (1962), *Piecework Abandoned*, Heinemann, London.

Bunker, D. R. (1965), 'Individual Applications of Laboratory Training', *Journal of Applied Behavioural Science*, 1, 131–48.

Burns, T. (1962), 'The Sociology of Industry', in Welford, A. T. *et al.* (eds.), *Society: Problems and Methods of Study*, Routledge & Kegan Paul, London.

Burns, T., and Stalker, G. M. (1961), *The Management of Innovation*, Tavistock, London.

Cardwell, D. S. L. (1962), 'The Development of Scientific Research in Modern Universities: A Comparative Study of Motives and Opportunities,' in Crombie, A. C. (ed.), *Scientific Change: Symposium on the History of Science*, Heinemann, London.

Carter, C. F., and Williams, B. R. (1959), 'Science in Industry', *Policies for Progress Series*, 3, Oxford University Press, London.

Castle, P. F. C. (1952), 'The Evaluation of Human Relations Training for Supervisors', *Occupational Psychology*, 26, 191–205.

Clark, D. G. (1966), *The Industrial Manager*, Business Publications Ltd, London.

Clegg, H. (1964), 'Restrictive Practices', *Socialist Commentary*, 9–11 December.

Clements, R. V. (1958), *Managers: A Study of Their Careers in Industry*, Allen & Unwin, London.

Cohen, J. (1964), *Behaviour in Uncertainty*, Allen & Unwin, London.

Colquhoun, W. P. (1966), 'Training for Vigilance: A Comparison of Techniques', *Human Factor*, 8, 7–12.

Committee on Manpower Resources for Science and Technology (1966), *Report on the 1965 Triennial Manpower Survey of Engineers, Technologists, Scientists and Technical Supporting Staff*, Cmnd Paper 3103, H.M.S.O., London.

Committee on Manpower Resources for Science and Technology (1966), *Interim Report of the Working Group on Manpower Parameters for Scientific Growth*, Cmnd Paper 3102, H.M.S.O., London.

Cooley, W. W., and Lohnes, P. R. (1962), *Multivariate Procedures for the Behavioral Sciences*, Wiley, New York.

Copeman, G. M. (1955), *Leaders of British Industry*, Gee & Co., London.

Cronbach, L. J. (1960), *Essentials of Psychological Testing*, Harper, New York.

Crossman, E. R. F. W. (1956), 'Perception Study – A Complement to Motion Study', *The Manager*, 24, 141–5.

Crossman, E. R. F. W. (1960), 'Automation and Skill', *Problems of Progress in Industry*, 9, H.M.S.O., London.

Currie, R. M. (1964), *Financial Incentives Based on Work Measurement*, B.I.M., London.

Devlin, Rt Hon. Lord (1965), *Final Report of the Committee of Inquiry . . . into Certain Matters Concerning the Port Transport Industry*, Cmnd Paper 2734, H.M.S.O., London.

Diebold, H. (1958), 'Automation: A Break with the Past', *Times Review of Industry*, Times, London.

Diebold, J. (1965), 'Looking Bravely Back to 1948 or So', in Malik, R. (ed.), *Penguin Survey of Business and Industry*, Penguin Books, Harmondsworth.

Easterfield, T. E. (1964), 'Optimum Variety', *Operational Research Quarterly*, 15, 71–85.

Eilon, S. (1966), 'A Classification of Administrative Control Systems', *Journal of Management Studies*, 3, 36–48.

Elliott, A. G. P. (1958), *An Experiment in Group Dynamics*, mimeographed, Simon-Carves Ltd.

Entwisle, D. B. (1959), 'Ageing: The Effects of Previous Skill on Training', *Occupational Psychology*, 33, 238–43.

Fairhead, J. (1965), 'The Validation of Business Exercises', *Bulletin of the Association of Teachers of Management*, 19, 1–16.

Fairhead, J., Pugh, D. S., and Williams, W. J., *Exercises in Business Decisions*, E.V.P., London.

Fayol, H. (1916), 'Administration industrielle et générale – prévoyance, organisation, commandement, coordination, contrôle', *Bulletin de la Société de l'Industrie Minérale*.

Fayol, H. (1949), *General and Industrial Management*, Pitman, London.

Flanders, A. (1964), *The Fawley Productivity Agreements*, Faber & Faber, London.

Flanders, A. (forthcoming), *Collective Bargaining: Prescription for Change*, Faber & Faber, London.

Fleishman, E. A. (1953), 'Leadership Climate, Human Relations Training and Supervisory Behaviour', *Personnel Psychology*, 6, 205–22.

Follett, M. P. (1941), *Dynamic Administration*, Collected papers edited by Metcalfe, H., and Urwick, L., Pitman, London.

Fox, A. (1965), *The Milton Plan*, Institute of Personnel Management, London.

Fox, A. (1966), 'Managerial Ideology and Labour Relations', *British Journal of Industrial Relations*, 4, 366–78.

Fromm, E. (1960), *Fear of Freedom*, Routledge & Kegan Paul, London.

Fruchter, B. J. (1954), *Introduction to Factor Analysis*, Van Nostrand, Princeton, New Jersey.

Gagné, R. M. (ed.) (1962), *Psychological Principles in System Development*, Holt, Rinehart and Winston, New York.

Gagné, R. (1965), 'The Analysis of Instructional Objectives for the Design of Instruction', in Glaser (ed.), *Teaching Machines and Programmed Learning II*, National Educational Association, Washington, D.C.

Gatty, R. (1954), 'Multivariate Analysis for Marketing Research: An Evaluation', *Applied Statistics*, 15, 157–72.

Gilbert, T. F. (1962), 'Mathetics: The Technology of Education', *Journal of Mathetics*, 1.

Goldsmith, M. (1963), *Careers in Technology*, Penguin Books, Harmondsworth.

Goodman, G. (1962), 'Redundancy in the Affluent Society', Fabian Tract 340, London.

Gordon, W. J. J. (1961), *Synectics – The Development of Creative Capacity*, Harper & Row, London.

Green, B. F. (1954), 'Attitude Measurement', in Lindsey, G. (ed.), *Handbook of Social Psychology*, Addison-Wesley Publishing, Cambridge, Mass.

Guest, R. (1962), *Organizational Change: The Effects of Successful Leadership*, Tavistock, London.

Habbakuk, H. J. (1962), *American and British Technology in the Nineteenth Century*, Cambridge University Press, Cambridge.

Hamilton, Sir Ian (1921), *The Soul and Body of an Army*, Edward Arnold, London.

Harris, C. M. (1957), *Hand Book of Noise Control*, McGraw-Hill, New York.

Heller, R. (1967), 'British Top Directors', *Management Today*, March, 62–5.

Herzberg, F. (1966), *Work and the Nature of Man*, World Publishing Co., New York.

Hickson, D. J., and Pugh, D. S. (1965), 'The Facts about "Bureaucracy"', *The Manager*, 33, 37–8.

Hickson, D. J. (1966), 'A Convergence in Organization Theory', *Administrative Science Quarterly*, 11, 224–37.

Hilton, J., et al. (1935), *Are Trade Unions Obstructive?*, Gollancz, London.

Hinings, C. R., Pugh, D. S., Hickson, D. J., Turner, C. (1967), 'An Approach to the Study of Bureaucracy', *Sociology*, 1, 61–72.

Holding, D. H. (1959), 'Guidance in Pursuit Tracking', *Journal of Experimental Psychology*, 57, 362–86.

Holmes, R. (1965), 'Freud, Piaget and Democratic Leadership', *British Journal of Sociology*, 16, 123–39.

Holmes, R. (1965), 'Freud and Social Class', *British Journal of Sociology*, 16, 48–67.

Hopkinson, R. G. (1963), *Architectural Physics – Lighting*, H.M.S.O., London.

Hopkinson, R. G. (1963), 'The Effect of Illumination on Performance', *Architectural Physics*, H.M.S.O., London.

Hutton, G. (1966), *Source-Book on Restrictive Practice in Britain*, Institute of Economic Affairs, London.

Inns of Court Conservative and Unionist Society (1958), *A Giant's Strength*, London.

Jahoda, M., and Warren, N. W. (eds.) (1966), *Attitudes*, Penguin Books, Harmondsworth.

Jaques, E. (1951), *The Changing Culture of a Factory*, Tavistock, London.

Jaques, E. (1961), *Equitable Payment*, Heinemann, London.

Jones, S. (1964), 'Why Can't Leaflets be Logical?', *New Society*, 14 January.

Joyce, T., and Channon, C. (1966), 'Classifying Market Survey Respondents', *Applied Statistics*, vol. xv, 3, November.

Kahn, R. L. (1956), 'The Prediction of Productivity', *Journal of Social Issues*, 12, 41–9.

Kahn, R. L., *et al.* (1964), *Organizational Stress*, John Wiley, New York.

Kann, H. R. (1964), *Repercussions of Redundancy*, Allen & Unwin, London.

Katz, D., *et al.* (1950), *Productivity, Supervision and Morale in an Office Situation*, Institute for Social Research, Ann Arbor, Michigan.

Kay, H. (1951), 'Learning of a Serial Task by Different Age Groups', *Quarterly Journal of Experimental Psychology*, 3, 166–83.

Kelly, G. A. (1955), *The Psychology of Personal Constructs*, W. W. Norton, New York.

Koontz, H. (1951), *Toward a Unified Theory of Management*, McGraw-Hill, New York.

Koontz, H., and O'Donnell, C. (1959), *Principles of Management*, McGraw-Hill, New York.

Kossoris, M. D., and Kohler, R. F. (1947), 'Hours of Work and Output', *U.S. Bureau of Labor Statistics Bulletin*, 917.

Leicester, C. (1963), 'The Composition of Manpower Requirements', *Report of the B.A.C.I.E. Spring Conference*, British Association for Commercial and Industrial Education, London.

Lesieur, F. G. (ed.) (1958), *The Scanlon Plan*, Wiley, New York.

Lewin, K. (1952), *Field Theory in Social Science*, ed. Cartwright, D., Tavistock, London.

Lewis, B. N., and Pask, G. (1965), 'The Theory and Practice of Adaptive Teaching Systems', in Glaser, R. (ed.), *Teaching Machines and Programmed Learning II*, National Educational Association, Washington, D.C.

Likert, R. (1961), *New Patterns of Management*, McGraw-Hill, New York.

Littler, T. S. (1958), 'Noise Measurement, Analysis and Evaluation of Harmful Effects', *Annual Occupational Hygiene*, 1, 11–27.

The Londoner (1961) (ed.), London Associated Rediffusion.

Lunn, J. A. (1966), 'Psychological Classification', *Commentary*, 8, 161–73.

Lupton, T. (1963), *On the Shop Floor*, Pergamon, London.

Lupton, T. (1964), 'Methods of Wage Payment and Motivation', *Work Study and Management Services*, 8, 543–9.

McCormick, E. J. (1964), *Human Factors Engineering*, McGraw-Hill, New York.

McGregor, D. (1960), *The Human Side of Enterprise*, McGraw-Hill, New York.

McGregor, D. (1966), *Leadership and Motivation*, M.I.T., Cambridge, Mass.

McIntosh, A. W. (1966), 'Does the Research Industry Meet Marketing's Needs?', *Commentary*, 8, 151–60.

McLuhan, M. (1964), *Understanding Media*, Routledge & Kegan Paul, London.

Macrae, A. W., and Holding, D. H. (1966), 'Transfer of Training after Guidance or Practice', *Quarterly Journal of Experimental Psychology*, 18, 327–33.

Mager, R. (1962), *Preparing Objectives for Programmed Instruction*, Fearon, San Francisco.

Management News (1951), American Management Association, July 1951.

Martin, A. (1965), 'The Assessment of Instructors', *Occupational Psychology*, 39, 45–55.

Maslow, A. H. (1962), *Towards a Psychology of Being*, Van Nostrand, New York.

Merton, R. K. (1940), 'Bureaucratic Structure and Personality', *Social Forces*, 18, 560–68.

Miall, S. (1931), *A History of the British Chemical Industry*, Ernest Benn, London.

Ministry of Labour (1965), 'Computers in Offices', *Ministry of Labour Gazette*, 73, 526.

Ministry of Labour (1966), 'Characteristics of the Unemployed', *Ministry of Labour Gazette*, 74, 156.

Ministry of Labour (1966), 'Mobility between Industries and Jobs', *Ministry of Labour Gazette*, 74, 380.

Morgan, C. T., Cook, J. S., Chapanis, A., and Lund, M. W. (eds.) (1963), *Human Engineering Guide to Equipment Design*, McGraw-Hill, New York.

Morse, N. C., and Reimer, E. (1956), 'The Experimental Change of a Major Organisational Variable', *Journal of Abnormal and Social Psychology*, 52, 120–29.

Murrell, K. F. H. (1965), *Ergonomics*, Chapman & Hall, London.

National Board for Prices and Incomes (1966), *Pay and Productivity during the Period of Severe Restraint*, H.M.S.O., London.

National Economic Development Council (1965), *Management Recruitment and Development*, H.M.S.O., London.

N.I.C.B. (1946), 'Organization Standards and Practices', *Conference Board Reports – Studies in Business Policy*, 18, The Conference Board.

Nicosia, F. M. (1967), *Consumer Decision Processes*, Prentice Hall, New Jersey.

O.E.C.D. (1965), *Wages and Labour Mobility*, O.E.C.D., Paris.

O.E.C.D. (1967), *The Concurrent Planning of Manpower and Technological Change at the Enterprise Level*, O.E.C.D., Paris.

Oppenheim, A. N. (1966), *Questionnaire Design and Attitude Measurement*, Heinemann, London.

Orth, C. E. (1963), *The First Year at the Harvard Business School*, Harvard University Press, Cambridge, Mass.

Osgood, C. E., *et al.* (1957), *The Measurement of Meaning*, University of Illinois Press, Urbana, Ill.

Pelz, D. C., *et al.* (1953), *Human Relations in a Research Organisation*, Ann Arbor, University of Michigan, Institute for Social Research, Michigan.

Pelz, D. C. (1957), 'Motivation of the Engineering and Research Specialist', *General Management Series*, 186, American Management Association, New York.

Pelz, E. B. (1959), *Some Factors in Group Decision*, Maccoby, E. E., Newcomb, T. M., and Hartley, E. C. (eds.), *Readings in Social Psychology*, Methuen, London.

Pratt, E. A. (1904), *Trade Unionism and British Industry*, Methuen, London.

Processes in Administrative Organization, Second Edition, Free Press, New York.

Pugh, D. S., Hickson, D. J., Hinings, C. R., Macdonald, K. M., Turner, C., and Lupton, T. (1963), 'A Conceptual Scheme for Organizational Analysis', *Administrative Science Quarterly*, 8, 389–415.

Pugh, D. S. (1966), 'Modern Organization Theory: A Psychological and Sociological Study', *Psychological Bulletin*, 66, 235–51.

Pym, D. (1964), 'A Manpower Study. The Chemist in Research and Development', *Occupational Psychology*, 38, 1–35.

Pym, D. (1965), 'Exploring Characteristics of the Versatile Worker', *Occupational Psychology*, 39, 271–8.

Pym, D. (1966), 'Technology, Effectiveness and Predispositions Towards Work Changes amongst Mechanical Engineers', *Journal of Management Studies*, 3, 304–11.

Rice, A. K. (1963), *The Enterprise and Its Environment*, Tavistock, London.

Rodger, A. (1962), 'Industrial Psychology', in *Chambers's Encyclopedia*.

Roethlisberger, F., and Dixon, W. J. (1964), *Management and the Worker*, Wiley, New York.

Rosenblith, W. A., *et al.* (1953), *Handbook of Acoustic Noise Control*, Office of Technical Services, Washington.

Ross, N. S., *et al.* (1958), *Productivity and Economic Incentives*, Allen & Unwin, London.

Rowe, K. H. (1964), 'An Appraisal of Appraisals', *Journal of Management Studies*, 1, 1–25.

Roy, D. (1954), 'Efficiency and the Fix', *American Journal of Sociology*, 60, 255–66.

Sadler, P. J. (1966), *Leadership Style, Confidence in Management and Job Satisfaction*, Ashridge Management College.

Sayles, L. (1958), *Behaviour of Industrial Work Group*, Wiley, New York.

Selznick, P. (1957), *Leadership in Administration*, Row Peterson, Evanston, Illinois.

Shepard, H. A. (1957), 'Superiors and Subordinates of Research Establishments', Paper 12, *The Symposium on the Direction of Research Establishments*, National Physical Laboratory, H.M.S.O., London.

Shriver, E. L. (1960), 'Determining Training Requirements for Electronic Systems Maintenance: Development and Test of a New Method of Skill and Knowledge Analysis', *Human Resources*

Research Office Technical Report 63, Alexandria, Va., U.S.A.

Shultz, G. P., and Weber, A. R. (1966), *Strategies for the Displaced Worker*, Harper & Row, London.

Simon, H. A. (1965), *Administrative Behaviour: A Study of Decision-Making*, Collier & Macmillan, London.

Simon, H. A. (1965), *The Shape of Automation – for Men and Management*, Harper Row, New York.

Singleton, W. T. (1966), 'Current Trends Towards Systems Design', *Ergonomics for Industry*, 12, H.M.S.O., London.

Singleton, W. T., Easterby, R. S., and Whitfield, D. (eds.) (1967), *Proceedings of Conference on the Human Operator in Complex Systems*, Taylor & Francis, London.

Skelly, F., and Nelson, E. (1965), Market Segmentation and New Product Development', *Scientific Business*.

Smith, K. U., and Smith, M. F. (1966), *Cybernetic Principles of Learning and Educational Design*, Holt, Rinehart & Winston, New York.

Smith-Gavine, S. A. N. (1963), 'A Percentage Measure of Standardization', *Productivity Measurement Review*, Special Number, December.

Sobel, I., and Wilcock, R. C. (1966), *Placement Techniques*, O.E.C.D., Paris.

Sofer, C., and Hutton, G. (1958), *New Ways in Management Training*, Tavistock, London.

Stewart, R. (1964), 'Reactions to Appraisal Interviews', *Journal of Management Studies*, 2, 83–99.

Tannenbaum, R., and Schmidt, W. H. (1958), 'How to Choose a Leadership Pattern', *Harvard Business Review*, 36, 95–101.

Taylor, F. W. (1911), *Principles of Scientific Management*, Harper & Row, London.

Thompson, J. W. (1965), 'New Lamps for Old', *J.W.T. Market Report*, 19.

Touraine, A., *et al.* (1965), *Workers' Attitudes to Technical Change*, O.E.C.D., Paris.

Treasure, J. A. P. (1966), 'A Second Survey of Market Research in Great Britain', *Commentary*, 8, 135–50.

Trist, E. L., *et al.* (1963), *Organizational Choice*, Tavistock, London.

Veblen, T. (1904), *The Theory of Business Enterprise*, B. W. Huelisch, London.

Vernon, H. M. (1920), 'The Speed of Adaptation to Altered Hours of Work', *Industrial Fatigue Research Board Report*, 6, H.M.S.O., London.

Vernon, P. E. (1965), *Personality Assessment: A Critical Survey*, Methuen, London.

Viteles, M. S. (1932), *Industrial Psychology*, Norton, New York.

Viteles, M. S. (1954), *Motivation and Morale in Industry*, Staples Press, London.

Walker, C. R., and Guest, R. H. (1952), *The Man on the Assembly Line*, Harvard University Press, Cambridge, Mass.

Weber, M. (1947), *The Theory of Social and Economic Organization*, The Free Press, Glencoe, Illinois.

Wedderburn, D. (1964), *White-Collar Redundancy*, Cambridge University Press, Cambridge.

Wedderburn, D. (1965), *Redundancy and the Railwaymen*, Cambridge University Press, Cambridge.

Wedderburn, D. (1968), *Enterprise Planning for Change – Coordination of Manpower and Technical Planning*, O.E.C.D., Paris.

Weiner, N. (1950), *The Human Use of Human Beings*, Eyre & Spottiswoode, London.

Weinstein, P. A., ed. (1965), *Featherbedding and Technological Change*, D. C. Heath, Boston; chapter by Williams Gomberg.

Welford, A. T. (1958), *Ageing and Human Skill*, Oxford University Press, London.

Welford, A. T. (1960), 'Ergonomics of Automation', *Problems of Progress in Industry*, 8, H.M.S.O., London.

White, R., and Lippitt, R. (1959), 'Leader Behaviour and Member Reaction in Three Social Climates', in Cartwright, D., and Zander, A. (eds.), *Group Dynamics, Research and Theory*, Tavistock, London.

Woodward, J. (1958), 'Management and Technology', *Problems of Progress in Industry*, 3, H.M.S.O., London.

Woodward, J. (1965), *Industrial Organization: Theory and Practice*, Oxford University Press, London.

Ziller, R. C., *et al.* (1962), 'Group Creativity under Conditions of Success or Failure and Variations in Group Stability', *Journal of Applied Psychology*, 66, 43–9.

Zweig, F. (1951), *Productivity and the Trade Unions*, Blackwell, Oxford.

Notes on Contributors

JOHN BEISHON, B.SC., D.PHIL., A.I.M., is a lecturer in psychology at Bristol University. He first qualified in metallurgy and worked for a number of years in the non-ferrous metals industry. He then took a degree in psychology at Birkbeck College, London, and subsequently joined Dr E. R. F. W. Crossman at Oxford University to work on a project concerned with automation and skill. He took up his present appointment in 1964 and has been working principally on the analysis of mental skills and the measurement of mental load. He is currently interested in managerial skills and the analysis of complex decision making. Dr Beishon is married and has four children.

EUNICE BELBIN, M.A., PH.D., and MEREDITH BELBIN, M.A., PH.D., are a husband and wife partnership in the Unit for Research into Problems of Industrial Retraining (University College, London), the former as Director of Research and the latter as Consultant (part-time). They graduated together in psychology at Cambridge in 1948, married in 1949, took their Ph.D.s in Cambridge – Eunice writing her thesis on propaganda effectiveness and Meredith on the problems of older workers. Eunice Belbin spent the next years producing two children and writing scientific papers on learning and training. R. M. Belbin's career took him and his family to the College of Aeronautics which he left to spend the next ten years as an independent industrial consultant. Currently, he is organizing demonstration projects on older worker training in U.S.A., Austria, and Sweden. Surprisingly for two psychologists, they are still married.

D. G. CLARK is a lecturer in the Department of Sociology, Government and Administration at the University of Salford. He spent some three years working in the textile industry in Lancashire and a brief period in the U.S.A. as a management trainee. Prior to his present post he lectured in a technical college mainly to industrial apprentices. He has travelled extensively in both Europe and the U.S.A. and was leader of an exchange study tour in the U.S.S.R. He is author of *The Industrial Manager*.

ALAN FOX was born in 1920. He worked as wage-earner in factories, an office and on the land before going to Ruskin College, Oxford, at the age of 27. Then, after taking a degree in politics, philosophy, and economics at Oxford University, he returned to Ruskin for six years as lecturer and tutor in industrial relations and economic organization. He was later elected to a Research Fellowship at Nuffield College, Oxford, where he published a *History of the National Union of Boot and Shoe Operatives*, and collaborated with H. A. Clegg and A. F. Thompson in *A History of British Trade*

Unions, 1889–1910. Since 1963 Alan Fox has been Oxford University lecturer in industrial sociology at the Department of Social and Administrative Studies, where he has published *The Milton Plan: An Exercise in Manpower Planning and the Transfer of Production*; *The Time-Span of Discretion Theory: An Appraisal*; *Industrial Sociology and Industrial Relations* (Research Paper No. 3 for the Royal Commission on Trade Unions and Employers' Associations), and *Managerial Ideology and Labour Relations*, in the *British Journal of Industrial Relations*, November 1966.

COLIN GOLBY graduated in 'Greats' from Worcester College, Oxford, in 1951. He worked for I.C.I. for a year and then returned to Oxford to read psychology, after which he joined a research team working for the Medical Research Council. In 1956 he went to the London advertising agency which is now Masius Wynne-Williams, where he supervised consumer attitude research. In 1962 he was appointed Managing Director of an American-based research company, specializing in advertising research – a post which he relinquished at the end of 1965. He is now a consultant carrying out psychological research for commercial and non-commercial concerns, specializing in problems involving consumer and social change.

DAVID J. HICKSON was born in Birmingham in 1931. He qualified as a Chartered Secretary in 1953, and took a diploma in personnel management at Manchester College of Science and Technology in 1958. From 1958 to 1960 he was engaged upon a study of worker output norms at the University of Manchester, and was then appointed Research Fellow in the Industrial Administration Research Unit at Birmingham College of Advanced Technology until 1963. In 1963 he was appointed lecturer in industrial sociology in the Industrial Administration Research Unit at the University of Aston in Birmingham. He was joint author of *Writers on Organization* (1964), and has been author and joint author of papers in *Administrative Science Quarterly*, *Occupational Psychology*, and other journals. At the moment he is engaged on the Research Unit's programme of research on organizations, and groups and individuals within them.

D. H. HOLDING was born in December 1925 in London, where he lived until joining the Fleet Air Arm in 1943. After flying training in Canada he spent most of the time until 1946 as an instructor. He then went to Edinburgh University and, after graduating as an M.A. in philosophy in 1951, took up studies in psychology. In 1953 he was appointed Scientific Officer (later, under protest, in the psychologist grade) at what was then the Clothing and Equipment Physiological Research Establishment at Farnborough, where he advised and experimented on ergonomic problems in the design of radar, fighting vehicles, and defence coordination systems. In 1955 he accepted a post as research psychologist in the Nuffield Department of Industrial Health, Newcastle upon Tyne, carrying out experiments on behalf of the Flying Personnel Research Committee. He was awarded his Ph.D. in 1961 for work on 'transfer of training'. In 1960 he was appointed as a lecturer in the University of Leeds, and later wrote *Principles of Train-*

ing. He is now a Research Associate in the University of Exeter, investigating problems of immediate memory.

ROGER HOLMES was born in 1924 and took his first degree in History at Exeter. After some years teaching for the British Council, he graduated in 1954 in psychology at University College, London. He then took the Diploma in Occupational Psychology, and as his first job as a psychologist taught in the department of management studies at the Regent Street Polytechnic, before moving to his present lectureship in social and industrial psychology at the London School of Economics. He teaches psychology, amongst other subjects, to students of personnel management and operational research. He is interested in organization theory and the application of psycho-analytic and sociological ideas to management psychology. He views the present state of his subject, a vacuum, with enthusiasm.

B. A. LACY served in the R.A.F. for seven years as a pilot, and then joined J. Lyons & Co. Ltd, where he received a training in business organization and work study. He first worked on the planning aspects of Lyons' manufacturing and catering divisions, then became Research and Development Manager of Lyons' Central Work Study Department. He has studied ergonomics and industrial training, and undertook the one-year postgraduate course in ergonomics and cybernetics at Loughborough. He prepared a thesis on the application of ergonomics in a manufacturing industry for which he received an M.Sc. degree from Loughborough University. In 1965 he was elected to the Council of the Ergonomics Research Society. In his present position, he is manager of a group applying ergonomics, work-study, and operational research to the production and distribution functions.

J. A. LUNN was born in 1936. He took a B.A. in psychology and philosophy at St John's College, Oxford, and an M.A. in occupational psychology at Birkbeck College, London. After four years with the Attwood Group of Companies, he joined Research Bureau Ltd as a technical manager. His present position involves organizing a series of basic research projects designed both to evolve a model of the consumer process, and to develop social research techniques, particularly in the area of attitude measurement; he also advises and lectures on the application of these techniques to practical social research problems. He is a member of the Technical Committee of the Market Research Society, and Chairman of the Society's Working Party set up to investigate methods of assessing social class. He has published and broadcast on various aspects of the place of social science in consumer research.

TOM LUPTON, M.A., PH.D., is professor of industrial sociology at the Manchester Business School. He was born in 1918 and left school at 14 to serve an apprenticeship in marine engineering. He then spent seven years in the forces. In 1946 he won a scholarship to Ruskin College and, two years later another to Oriel College. From Oxford, Professor Lupton moved to the Social Science Department at the University of Liverpool, and was subsequently appointed senior lecturer at the University of Manchester. Prior to his present appointment he was Head of the Department of Industrial Administration at the then College of Advanced Technology, Birmingham (1960–64), and Montague Burton Professor of Industrial Relations at the University of Leeds (1964–6). He has written numerous articles and seven books, among them *On the Shop Floor* and *Elements of Industrial Sociology* (to be published by Longmans). Tom Lupton is a founder member and first chairman of the Association of Teachers of Management.

DEREK S. PUGH was born in 1930 in London. He studied at Edinburgh University, receiving an M.A. in psychology, and then an M.Sc. degree for a study of human aspects of inspection in industry. From 1953 to 1956 he was research assistant at the Social Sciences Research Centre at the University of Edinburgh, and in 1956–7 Assistant Lecturer in the Department of Social Medicine. He then left Edinburgh to take up a post as lecturer in human relations and industrial psychology at Birmingham College of Advanced Technology (now the University of Aston), until 1960. In 1961 he became Senior Research Fellow at the Industrial Administration Research Unit at the University of Aston in Birmingham. Derek Pugh is a Fellow of the Royal Statistical Society and an Associate of the British Psychological Society. He was joint author of *Writers on Organizations* in 1964 and *Exercises in Business Decisions* in 1965. He was editor of the *Bulletin* of the Association of Teachers of Management from 1961 to 1966, and general editor of the Penguin Library of Management in 1967. He is currently leading an inter-disciplinary research team on organizational studies.

DENIS PYM was born in 1936 and brought up in Perth and Melbourne, Australia. He has a B.A. in social science and a Ph.D. in psychology from the Universities of Melbourne and London respectively. After working for a time with I.C.I. in Australia, he joined the Air Ministry, London, as a psychologist in 1960. From there he moved to a lecturing appointment in the Department of Occupational Psychology at Birkbeck College. Dr Pym spends a good deal of his time researching in industry, and is interested in the study of organizations and the social impact of technical change. In 1968 he returned to Australia to take up a research appointment in the new University of La Trobe.

GEOFFREY RACKHAM was born in 1934. After reading law at Cambridge, he obtained the Diploma in Social Science at Barnett House, Oxford. He has been a probation officer and a work-study officer, and is currently working as a research assistant in industrial sociology in the Management Engineering Section at Imperial College, London.

PHILIP SADLER is Director of Research at Ashridge Management College. After graduating in sociology he worked in market research for a short time and then joined the Air Ministry to supervise a research group concerned with the study of leadership, morale, and organization in the R.A.F. In 1963 he was seconded to the National Economic Development Office and in 1964 joined the Ashridge staff, where he is currently supervising a programme of research into problems of industrial management.

PETER B. SMITH graduated in psychology at Cambridge in 1959. He remained at Cambridge to make a study of the development of social structure in groups of managers on courses, for which he obtained his doctorate in 1962. During the next four years he was at the Department of Management Studies of Leeds University, specializing in the development and evaluation of T-group methods for management training. Recently he moved to a lectureship in social psychology at Sussex University, where he plans to continue studies of individual and organizational change through group methods.

K. W. TILLEY was born in 1926 and educated at Northampton Grammar School. After reading engineering at Cambridge for a year he joined the R.A.F. before going to Manchester University to take a degree in psychology. In 1951 he went to work with the Ministry of Defence (Air) and eight years afterwards was appointed Chief Research Officer, H.Q. Technical Training Command. He recently spent a year with the Scientific Affairs Division NATO exploring ways in which NATO could assist in the development of social science research.

MRS DOROTHY WEDDERBURN is 41. After taking a degree in economics at Cambridge she worked for four years in the Board of Trade. She then went to the Department of Applied Economics, Cambridge University, doing research and teaching in economics and sociology. At that time her main interest was the development of social policy, particularly in the field of ageing. She wrote *The Economic Circumstance of Old People* (with J. E. G. Utting) and *The Aged in the Welfare State* (with Peter Townsend). She is now lecturer in industrial sociology at the Imperial College of Science and Technology, London University, where she is doing research on industrial relations in the Post Office and on the differences in the terms and conditions of employment of manual and non-manual workers.

DAVID WHITFIELD was born in 1938, and has degrees in experimental and occupational psychology. His first job, in the ergonomics department of an electronics company, helped to broaden his technological training. Since then he has held two academic research posts. The present one at Aston, a new technological university, is directly concerned with industrial applications of ergonomics. His other main interests are research into human skill and the development of research techniques in ergonomics. He is co-author of a booklet in the Ministry of Technology series *Ergonomics for Industry*, and, with Professor W. T. Singleton and R. S. Easterby, edited the proceedings of a recent international conference *The Human Operator in Complex Systems*.